Feminisms in the Academy

Women and Culture Series

The Women and Culture Series is dedicated to books that illuminate the lives, roles, achievements, and status of women, past or present.

Fran Leeper Buss
Dignity: Lower Income Women Tell of Their Lives and Struggles
Forged under the Sun / Forjada bajo el sol: The Life of Maria Elena Lucas
La Partera: Story of a Midwife

Valerie Kossew Pichanick
Harriet Martineau: The Woman and Her Work, 1802–76

Sandra Baxter and Marjorie Lansing
Women and Politics: The Visible Majority

Estelle B. Freedman
Their Sisters' Keepers: Women's Prison Reform in America, 1830–1930

Susan C. Bourque and Kay Barbara Warren
Women of the Andes: Patriarchy and Social Change in Two Peruvian Towns

Marion S. Goldman
Gold Diggers and Silver Miners: Prostitution and Social Life on the Comstock Lode

Page duBois
Centaurs and Amazons: Women and the Pre-History of the Great Chain of Being

Mary Kinnear
Daughters of Time: Women in the Western Tradition

Lynda K. Bundtzen
Plath's Incarnations: Women and the Creative Process

Violet B. Haas and Carolyn C. Perrucci, editors
Women in Scientific and Engineering Professions

Sally Price
Co-wives and Calabashes

Diane Wood Middlebrook and Marilyn Yalom, editors
Coming to Light: American Women Poets in the Twentieth Century

Joanne S. Frye
Living Stories, Telling Lives: Women and the Novel in Contemporary Experience

E. Frances White
Sierra Leone's Settler Women Traders: Women on the Afro-European Frontier

Barbara Drygulski Wright, editor
Women, Work, and Technology: Transformations

Lynda Hart, editor
Making a Spectacle: Feminist Essays on Contemporary Women's Theatre

Verena Martinez-Alier
Marriage, Class and Colour in Nineteenth-Century Cuba: A Study of Racial Attitudes and Sexual Values in a Slave Society

Kathryn Strother Ratcliff et al., editors
Healing Technology: Feminist Perspectives

Mary S. Gossy
The Untold Story: Women and Theory in Golden Age Texts

Jocelyn Linnekin
Sacred Queens and Women of Consequence: Rank, Gender, and Colonialism in the Hawaiian Islands

Glenda McLeod
Virtue and Venom: Catalogs of Women from Antiquity to the Renaissance

Lynne Huffer
Another Colette: The Question of Gendered Writing

Jill Kerr Conway and Susan C. Bourque, editors
The Politics of Women's Education: Perspectives from Asia, Africa, and Latin America

Lynn Keller and Cristanne Miller, editors
Feminist Measures: Soundings in Poetry and Theory

Domna C. Stanton and Abigail J. Stewart, editors
Feminisms in the Academy

Feminisms in the Academy

Domna C. Stanton and
Abigail J. Stewart, Editors

Ann Arbor

THE UNIVERSITY OF MICHIGAN PRESS

Copyright © by the University of Michigan 1995
All rights reserved
Published in the United States of America by
The University of Michigan Press
Manufactured in the United States of America
⊗ Printed on acid-free paper

1998   1997   1996   1995   4   3   2   1

A CIP catalogue record for this book is available from the British
Library.

Library of Congress Cataloging-in-Publication Data

Feminisms in the academy / Domna C. Stanton and Abigail J. Stewart,
    editors.
        p.   cm. — (Women and culture series)
    ISBN 0-472-09566-8 (hardcover : alk. paper). —
    ISBN 0-472-06566-1 (pbk. : alk. paper)
    1. Women's studies.   2. Feminist theory.   I. Stanton, Domna C.
    II. Stewart, Abigail J.   III. Series.
    HQ1180.F44   1995
    305.42—dc20   95-13472
                                                                        CIP

Contents

Introduction

Remodeling Relations: Women's Studies and the Disciplines

Domna C. Stanton and Abigail J. Stewart

"What are these ceremonies, and why should we take part in them? What are these professions, and why should we make money out of them?" The questions that Virginia Woolf raised in 1938 about "the procession of the sons of educated men" and the professions that make their practitioners "possessive, jealous of any infringement of their rights, and highly combative if anyone dares dispute them" (1966, 63, 66) still speak to the relations between feminists and the academy in 1995, but only partially.[1] A quarter of a century after the first women's studies courses were taught in North American colleges and universities, Woolf's remarks capture the questioning of the disciplines,[2] indeed, the critical analysis of the production of knowledge that the academic arm of the women's movement continues to generate. And yet, just as the nature and extent of the oppositionality of women's studies needs to be self-consciously examined today, we, the editors of this volume, recognize that the model embedded in Woolf's comments is no longer accurate—undoubtedly, that it never was. For Woolf presupposes a unified "we" situated "outside" of disciplinary ceremonies,[3] which are cast as exclusionary, militaristic, masculinist postures hostile to intrusion of any kind[4]—a model that upholds the existence of an autonomous we able to choose to accept or reject those ceremonies.

Woolf's remarks evoke a stage in the relations between women's studies and the disciplines—a stage that still exists in particular institutional contexts—when a nascent field battles for academic legitimacy and views the traditional fields as resistant to any change.[5] In that phase women's studies sees itself as challenging the disciplines and their boundaries, by engaging in a process that Catharine R. Stimpson called "the deconstruction of error," before taking on the "reconstruction of theory" (qtd. in Schuster and Van Dyne 1985, 25). In so doing, women's studies may well exacerbate the refusal to entertain change in disciplines determined to stave off a loss of certainty and thus, in their view, of prestige. As Marilyn Schuster and Susan Van Dyne observed in 1985, faculty outside of women's studies have often felt that both "their own credentials are in doubt, [as are] the worth and integrity of their academic disciplines" (25).

A modified version of this conflictual model, which implies a one-way effort to "inject" women's studies into resistant disciplines, represents feminists as "boring from within" (see Farnham 1987). This model has the virtue of recognizing that women's studies scholars were always/already trained in, and thus never "outside of," the disciplines, but it emphasizes the need to gain the trust of disciplinary gatekeepers and to work for change from within what are still viewed as bounded and unchanging fields. This modified version does not, then, challenge disciplinary privilege or the concept of disciplinarity. On the contrary, it sacralizes the disciplinary department as the site of the production of scholarship. In this scheme women's studies is not the intellectual base for generating new knowledge and for demonstrating the weaknesses of various disciplinary paradigms; it constitutes an ancillary system for ensuring better disciplinary knowledge.

This model of reform from within aims to assimilate or integrate feminist scholarship into the existing disciplines and thereby to change them (Boxer 1982). At bottom its goals do not differ from those of "mainstreaming," the dominant metaphor for the desired development in the relations between women's studies and the disciplines in the 1980s. This aquatic rhetoric suggested a small, marginal/minority tributary spilling into and presumably changing—contaminating?—the existing disciplinary rivers. Less articulated by its proponents, however, were the consequences for the feminist tributary: Would it be contaminated, in turn, by disciplinary materials backing up, lose its autonomy, or be absorbed and disappear entirely as a field of study? Not surprisingly, then, some feminist scholars sounded the alarm against integration (Makosky and Paludi 1990, 26–28) and assimilation (Schuster and Van Dyne 1985, 7), in favor of transformation.

Yet the routes leading to this transformation—which we take to represent the more radical end of the continuum for change and thus for restructuring the academy—are not charted on any map. Indeed, for women's studies the transformation of the disciplines is fraught with tensions and contradictions. For, if women's studies is located "within" the disciplines, then how do its practitioners maintain the powerful impetus to reform the paradigms on which it depends for its lines of inquiry? To paraphrase Audre Lorde, where will feminist scholars get "other" tools even to reshape the master's house? (1984, 110–12). For some feminist scholars then, success in the battle for academic legitimacy has cost us the war. In this view women's studies is now ever more influenced by the disciplinary traditions against which it initially struggled (Kelly and Korsmeyer 1991, 294); thus, it has failed to restructure the academy (Langland and Gove 1981, 2, 6) and is on the verge of losing its "revolutionary thrust" (Paludi and Steuernagel 1990, xvi). On the other hand, marginality, which meant—and in some institutional settings still means—powerlessness,[6] cannot effectively transform the academy. Still, marginality represents a less conflicted—in some quarters, romanticized—location that allows for a less compromised critical posture. As Schuster and Van Dyne phrase the problem: "Few of us would want to reify our marginality, but we should not lose the vitality of the critical stance it provides" (1985, 7). How to be and not to be marginal at one and the same time is, of course, the proverbial rub.

It could be argued that women's studies is, and should be, both within and not within the disciplines, as it tends predominantly to be institutionally situated both within and separate from any particular disciplinary department. If the field, like its practitioners, came out of the disciplines, and came out through critiques of those disciplines, it did so by virtue of a perspective gained or a method borrowed from a practice outside of any single field or even of the academy. These include the civil rights movement, leftist politics, and the women's movement, which these oppositional practices helped to shape, as well as Marxist analysis and critical thinking at the academy's borders (Hartman 1981). Furthermore, from the beginning feminist scholars gained other scholarly perspectives by crossing boundaries, importing materials and methods from one discipline to look critically at another. The interdisciplinary circulation of disciplinary methods and materials and, more broadly, the development of various types of discipline-crossing activities, notably borrowing, has had a significant impact on the field: they helped feminist scholars pose new questions and arrive at new interpretations of accepted knowledge (Klein 1990, 93–94). The metaphoric transportation that occurred among feminist scholars, both as practitioners of different disciplines and representatives of different divisions (the humanities and the social sciences, but also, more recently, historians of science and medicine), created exchanges of knowledge that "defamiliarized" any single disciplinary paradigm or approach. In these various ways the disciplinary knowledge and the conceptual divisions that longevity had enshrined lost their aura of unassailability and inevitability.[7]

Still, these efforts tended to produce a pluridisciplinary landscape, rather than the ideal (and idealized) interdisciplinarity to which women's studies has always aspired. Of course, the idea of "interdisciplinarity" has gained great currency in the academy since the days when Comparative Literature and American Culture were the only academic units to strive for transdisciplinary perspectives. Beyond the proliferation of area studies and humanities institutes—of cultural, film, and media studies—African-American, Latino/a, Gay and Lesbian ("Queer"), and other oppositional studies now dot college and university campuses.[8] And yet these new programmatic units have not fundamentally changed practices in the academy or undermined the power of the disciplines/ departments to tenure and thus to evaluate negatively those who are engaged in interdisciplinary work.[9] As Susan Hardy Aiken et al. (1987) have observed:

A major problem with any interdisciplinary study in an academy divided along disciplinary boundary lines is that those who venture outside their own areas of specialization will often be regarded with suspicion: at best as neophytes—stereotypical tourists who cannot speak the language of the field they presume to visit and who overlook nuances and complexities apparent to the natives; and at worst as dangerous trespassers, or colonizers seeking to expropriate territory not their own. (261)

That interdisciplinarity is difficult to achieve in a powerfully disciplinary academy does not mean that its goals should be abandoned. On the contrary, it should be supported and furthered wherever possible, including through collaborative teaching.[10] It does mean, however, that the reality of multidisciplinarity within women's studies—the cumulative juxtaposition of several disciplines—should be recognized and that the paths leading from an enriching additiveness to a matrix of interactions should be conceptualized. At present women's studies might be described most accurately as metadisciplinary, after Bakhtin's definition of "metalinguistics," a practice that is actively engaged in dialogic interaction with the disciplines but that "exceeds the limits of [the disciplines] and has its own independent subject matter and tasks" (1984, 183; see also 181).[11]

Now images of border crossing and of circulation arguably still assume a model of binary opposition between the disciplines and a metadisciplinary women's studies that does not properly represent the fluidity, mutability, and heterogeneity of the disciplines. Notwithstanding their hegemony in the institution, academic disciplines (especially in the humanities and the social sciences) rarely enjoy consensus on a few, much less one, paradigms. Psychology or political science, English, art history, or Romance languages have so many constituent and often competing subfields and sections with different methodologies that the disciplines function at best as loose federations. Moreover, each of those disciplines has been and continues to be subject to internal and external pressures for change that are both independent of and, in the last two decades, related to challenges from women's studies (and other "oppositional studies"). Indeed, since the 1970s most fields in the humanities and the social sciences have been grappling with a crisis of faith in their epistemological presuppositions, knowledge, and methods. This crisis derives in part from the impact of postmodernism and what Lyotard has called the post-Enlightenment delegitimation of master narratives; thus, it also stems in part from the oppositional studies that saw in postmodernism possibilities for deconstructing the structures of power/knowledge.[12] Locally, the crises took different symptomatic forms: the linguistic turn in history, the problematics of (imperial) subjectivity in anthropology, and the generalized putting into question of positivistic truth and objectivity in the social sciences. Likewise, the humanities, which "perpetrated" postmodernism on the academy, have questioned the ideological biases of "the humanistic," struggled to define the meaning (and relevance) of "literature" in an age of developing hypertextuality and dominant popular culture, dispensed with traditional notions of good art or the possibility of a neutral "gaze," and thus displayed no fewer signs than the social sciences of a crisis in certainty. The fact that these crises have occurred is proof itself of the permeability of the disciplines and their capacity for change.

The history of an emerging women's studies over the past twenty-five years can be read as a hyperbolic instance of the shifts, conflicts, and self-critical transformations in the disciplines of the humanities and the social sciences. Thus, the shift from woman/sex to gender as a relational construct through which cultures produce differences between men and women was contested on the grounds of deflecting attention from woman as the fundamental category of (radical) feminist analysis. Even more catalytic, however, were repeated demonstrations, predominantly from feminist scholars of color, that the emphasis on the commonalities of women's oppression, subordination, and objectification— which aimed to establish the universality of "patriarchy" and thus to create a paradigm for the emerging field—denied ethnic, racial, and class differences among women (hooks 1984; Lorde 1984). Hazel Carby (1982) and Maria Lugones and Elizabeth Spelman (1983), among many other scholars, showed conclusively that the notion of "woman" in women's studies was color, class, and nation specific and that this particularity undermined the validity of its basic ("universal") theories and concepts.[13] By 1985 the critical interrogation of scholars of color had produced a paradigm shift in women's studies and promoted a radical identity politics based not only on gender, race, and class but also, by extension, on sexual orientation (which lesbian and, more recently, queer theorists have retheorized) and other geopolitical constructs ("Third World," postcolonial, subaltern). These identities and their intersections now defined the location of subjects and the place from which, and for which, they alone could speak.[14]

The rejection of universal identity in favor of particularity and heterogeneity has appeared to create, or to exacerbate, conflicts within women's studies that were sometimes papered over by the requirements of sameness.[15] Indeed, because there is often a disturbing conflation of sameness and commonality,[16] these conflicts have generated expressions of alarm in some quarters. Marianne Hirsch and Evelyn Fox Keller (1990), for example, who strive to expose "Conflicts in Feminism" and in feminist theory and to enhance the dynamism of the debates,[17] emphasize the need to learn the practice of constructive conflict in order to combat the destructive effects of enduring disagreements on political and intellectual goals (370). While they favor the recognition of differences,

Hirsch and Keller believe that feminism (and feminist theory) must have a coherent voice, "a common voice," to articulate demands on behalf of women (379–80). This definition of commonality seems nostalgic to us,[18] just as Hirsch and Keller's tendency to equate conflict with a lack of forward momentum, indeed with stasis, implies the rejection of an ongoing dialectical or dialogical process in women's studies (384–85).

In the eyes of some scholars serious conflicts also threaten the "integrity" of the field, though we might ask whether women's studies ever possessed that wholeness. For, if "woman" has multiple, fragmented, and, in Elizabeth Spelman's terms, "inessential" meanings, which are determined by the location of a specific speaking subject at a specific moment; if this category is as fundamentally elusive as "feminist" (Delmar 1986), how can a necessarily undefinable "women's studies" be said to exist as an intellectual entity? Although some scholars, such as Teresa de Lauretis and Gayatri Spivak, have in turn embraced a new (and limited) essentialism in the name of the "difference" of feminism or the greater exigency of political strategy, we, the editors of this volume, along with Delmar, favor the productiveness of uncertainty at this juncture and would endorse more local and partial (nontotalizing) efforts at forging commonality that are based on provisional affiliations, coalitions, and collaborations around specific projects or goals (Delmar 1986, 13).[19]

This crisis of uncertainty and of commonality problematizes any discussion of the relation of women's studies to the disciplines, for it predicates the idea that both terms of that relation are under constant transformation and that some fields are no longer demarcated by distinct disciplinary boundaries. Can relations between two moving, unintegral entities be meaningfully established? And, even if an Archimedean should resolve this problem, is it clear that these disciplines-in-crisis should be the primary institutional and intellectual focus of women's studies? It could be argued that the future of the field does not lie with the disciplines but, rather, with the affiliations and collaborations that can be forged with African-American, Latino/a, Postcolonial, Queer, Cultural, and other oppositional studies. In a word, does the emphasis on relations with the disciplines that structures this volume and informs individual essays resacralize, or at least reaffirm, the very disciplines whose walls, borders, and even foundations are productively loosening?

Despite that self-defeating possibility, it is a fact that the disciplines still overwhelmingly train feminist scholars and determine the structure and thus, in part, the meaning of academic knowledge. Analyses of these relations across the disciplines can shed light on past and present practices and help to construct a post-Woolfian model of relations that is properly dialogic. This model would not simply feature conversations that engage with another's discourse, it would highlight, with Bakhtin, various kinds of intersections, including confirmation, supplementation, and contradiction, which he terms the "collision of voices" (1984, 184).[20] Such a model would recognize that both the disciplines and women's studies have multiple and contradictory voices that have changed over time and may be changed as a result of their interactions or affiliations. The interactions between women's studies and any single discipline are thus also marked by differences. As Ellen Carol Dubois et al. (1985) observe, differences among disciplines exist not only over the meaning and implications of the phrase "about women" but also what can be learned "about women," which derives from different traditions of learning and, through particular research tools, different ways and kinds of knowing (196–97). As a result, women's studies has different tasks or goals in different disciplines—the critique and revision of existing research; the development of underused or unused categories, such as gender, and the applied demonstration of their value in disciplinary research traditions; and, last, the critique and re(de)finition of categories, methodologies, and paradigms (201).

Not surprisingly, some disciplines have been more "deeply transformed" by feminist studies than others for what appear to be epistemological reasons. Writing in 1985, Judith Stacey and Barrie Thorne suggested that fields such as anthropology, literature, and history have been more willing to reconsider core theoretical assumptions because they are interpretive, value theory, and are more reflexive about the ways in which knowledge is developed. Far less profound, they argued, was the impact of women's studies on sociology, psychology, political science, and economics, which are more positivistic and aspire to objectivity, abstract knowledge, and universal truths. And yet, as Stacey and Thorne recognized, the differences between the two sets of fields are mitigated by the finding that receptiveness to women's studies in anthropology, literature, and history did not necessarily mean an impact on mainstream work.[21] In fact, the status of the relations between women's studies and the disciplines becomes even more complex when differences within each field are taken into account; within Romance languages, for instance, why have French scholars been at the forefront of feminist theory in North America, in contrast to Spanish or Italian scholars?[22] In listening to the dialogues within different fields, which the essays in this volume pursue, each reader can thus discover similarities and differences among disciplinary problems, processes, and approaches, find gaps and contradictions within one's own field(s) and in women's studies, and, in so doing, engage in the kind of self-conscious pluridisciplinary and cross-disciplinary activities that may be a precondition for interdisciplinarity.

The dialogues with and about women's studies that make up *Feminisms in the Academy*[23] should be viewed as emblematic of the ways in which marginal/minority discourses struggle for space in the academy and of the tensions surrounding the production and legitimation of knowledge. We do not consider these dialogues on the interrelations between women's studies and a set of disciplines unique—indeed, we encourage others to initiate similar dialogues with other oppositional studies. Moreover, that gender is a dominant category in most of these dialogues does not mean that other categories are overlooked or denied. For gender interlocks in different ways with race and class in several essays, notably in those of Claire Kramsch and Linda von Hoene, Natalie Kampen, Asunción Lavrin, Nellie McKay, Sarah Pomeroy, Mary Poovey, and Mary Romero. Gender is a key here—not the first, best, or only key—for exposing differences and hierarchies concealed by universalizing intellectual frameworks. Like many of our colleagues in this volume, we believe that the analysis of race, class, or sexual orientation, for instance, can reveal the workings of other hierarchies of differences.

The first part of *Feminisms in the Academy,* "Outsiders Within: Challenging the Disciplines," focuses on the interrogation of unexamined assumptions in four emblematic disciplines and, in a self-reflexive turn, in women's studies as well. Helen Longino explores the ways in which feminist arguments undermine and complicate philosophical categories central to Western analytic philosophy, including the separation of mind and body and the disjunction between autonomy and attachment. Natalie Kampen's essay investigates how feminist analytic tools can be used to revise the traditional claim that the friezes on the Column of Trajan merely convey information about Roman military campaigns. While contemporary art historians have recognized the possibility of analyzing the Column's ideology, Kampen's reading of its representation of a few, strange women sheds light on ideologies of masculinity and empire. Like Kampen and Longino, Jeanne Marecek foregrounds the uneasy position of feminist scholars in disciplinary discourses, but she reveals a similar problem within women's studies as well. Her essay delineates how feminist psychologists are marginalized both as postmodern social constructionists in a positivist social science and as empirical social scientists in a women's studies increasingly suspicious of positivism—a situation that provides no easy answers to epistemological disjunctions or to methodological intolerance. Analogously, for narratives by women of color, Nellie McKay questions the adequacy of approaches to the autonomy of the self in both contemporary "mainstream" and feminist autobiographical criticism. She argues that "the black female narrative self makes of black female identity an exploration of differences from—and limits of loyalty to—black men and all others." Beginning with the challenge of feminist scholarship to the disciplines, these four essays discuss the new questions and dilemmas that this challenge has generated in the disciplines and in women's studies.

The essays in the second section, "The Differences That Gender Makes," investigate the ways in which gender, as an analytic tool, transforms disciplinary perceptions and knowledge. In rereading Dickens's *Our Mutual Friend,* Mary

Poovey demonstrates that gender illuminates previously unseen aspects of the text and provides insight into unrecognized aspects of difference—in this case, race. In contrast to Poovey's study of a canonical text, Mary Romero uses the life history of a Latina to examine the ambiguous and ambivalent social situation of female domestic workers—working-class women of color in the privileged class locations of their white employers—a position that gives them particular knowledge of class, gender, and race relations and that sometimes promotes special modes of resistance. In an ironic chronological juxtaposition, Sarah Pomeroy highlights the economic importance of domestic work—conducted by female slaves and "respectable women" (wives)—in the strictly sex-segregated culture of ancient Greece. She shows that Xenophon's *Oeconomicus* recognizes the economic value of female slave and free labor, whereas nineteenth- and twentieth-century scholars assumed that economic transactions only take place in the public sphere. In all three essays, as in those of Kampen and McKay, gender analysis reveals the workings of other categories of difference, such as class, race, and ethnicity.

The essays in part 3 address "Feminism and the Politics of Intellectual Inquiry." Margaret Conkey and Ruth Tringham explore the problems that scholars face when popular representations of their research (in this case, the "goddess movement") become important symbols in a political project. Through their critique Conkey and Tringham provide the outlines for a feminist archaeology, but they also confirm, along with Longino and Kampen, Poovey and Pomeroy, the contributions of women's studies to the production of more compelling work in the disciplines. By contrast, Asunción Lavrin emphasizes the close links in Latin America, over the past twenty years, between the emergence of feminist scholarship and of women's movements that are overtly resistant to the idea of North American feminism and that promote the ideal of "action research." More controversially, Elaine Marks examines the different degrees and kinds of political analysis in feminist criticism within French studies in the United States over the past twenty years and concludes in favor of a renewed emphasis on the traditional center of literary studies—the poetical. Indeed, of all the essays in this volume Marks speaks most clearly about the importance of disciplinary paradigms for "feminist inquiry." These texts thus highlight the problematic ways in which the politics of intellectual inquiry affect feminist scholarship—nourishing its development, creating new demands, posing difficult choices, and perhaps at times limiting or constraining its purview.

The final group of essays, "Dialogues: Feminist Scholarship and/in the Disciplines," investigates the future possibilities for the mutual transformation of women's studies scholarship and the disciplines, over and beyond the powerful tensions that exist between them. As Marecek did in her dialogue with psychology, Virginia Sapiro depicts the strains between women's studies and political science. She too insists, however, that dialogue could be enhanced if women's studies elaborated more complex analyses of power and if political science ceased to view the political world as male—developments that would work to the decided benefit of both fields. Using a more autobiographical approach, Judith Stacey explains how being "disloyal to the disciplines" in her intellectual trajectory (from socialist-feminist historical sociology to feminist and "postsocialist" ethnographic sociology) has allowed her to remain open to new trends in feminist theory that challenge mainstream sociology. Finally, through their own dialogue Claire Kramsch and Linda von Hoene exemplify the transformative value of dialogism between women's studies and the disciplines for the development of theory and practice, not only of second language acquisition but also of a pedagogy we would broadly identify as feminist. This closing dialogue, like the coauthored essay of Conkey and Tringham and this coauthored introduction by a feminist literary historian and a feminist psychologist, underscores the importance of collaborations. And, if these essays reveal persistent, unresolved tensions between women's studies and particular disciplines, or, in Lavrin's case, particular women's movements, they also confirm that conflict has been and continues to be productive.

Although they now represent a twenty-five year tradition, the various types of relations to the disciplines that the essays in this volume illustrate or invoke cannot, of course, predict the models of the future nor the cast of institutional players who will be featured in the dialogues. Still, that the essays of McKay and Romero about women of color ignore or "exceed" the disciplines (Bakhtin 1984) and that Stacey's act of personal criticism is consciously "un-disciplined" may be symptomatic of future trends. To be sure, the disciplinary imperative for women's studies will be determined not only by broad institutional pressures but also by the specific affiliations and collaborations that the field forges with other "studies." Will women's studies become one among a varying number of programs housed institutionally as oppositional studies? Or will such studies in turn forge alliances with subfields in existing disciplines and be subsumed under "cultural studies," broadly defined?[24] Or, then, will women's studies remain a programmatic field/unit, with subsections that feature (through joint appointments, curriculum, and research projects) African-American, Postcolonial (subaltern), or Queer studies? Or, finally, will there be a growing trend for women's studies to become a discipline/department in its own right? The answer, we suspect, is all of the above, and that the particular shape of programs will be a product of structures—and struggles—in specific institutional contexts with their own histories. No less important a determinant, however, will be the political climate at the national level and developments in a number of contested issues, such as the culture wars, abortion, AIDS, sexual harassment, and comparable worth.

The absence of boundaries between the academy and the larger media-saturated, superelectronic society makes it all the more imperative that feminist scholars engage in dialogues with applied researchers in technology, notably computer specialists, and with faculty in professional schools.[25] Law, education, social work, nursing, medicine, and public health number among the fields with which women's studies should develop alliances on specific issues and collaborations on particular research projects. At this juncture affiliations with applied fields may be the best way for women's studies to do cross-disciplinary work in the sciences, in which the least amount of research in feminist scholarship has been produced, despite important critiques of the history and sociology of science and some work in primatology.[26] These alliances, which need to be fashioned individually with each field, can serve to reconnect or to heighten the links between feminist scholarship and "the community," fusing theory and praxis into what scholars in Latin America, among others, call "action research" (see Lavrin in this vol.). Indeed, the real (or perceived) loss of connection to the community in the 1980s seems to go hand in hand with a reduction of interest, since the late 1970s, in international feminist scholarship,[27] an area that has been reconceptualized and reinvigorated by postcolonial and subaltern, Latin American and Middle Eastern (or Islamic) studies, for example. International work in women's studies clearly assumes a new urgency in a "global village" that transmits instant information about rape in Bosnia, virginity tests in Turkey, clitoridectomy in Egypt, and female infanticide in China. This is not to suggest that pressing issues and problems at home be ignored in favor of those abroad but, rather, that the dichotomy between "at home" and "abroad" has little meaning in a world in which, as Irigaray would say, "one does not stir without the other."

The recognition of lacunae represents only one form of self-criticism, which has marked and should continue to mark women's studies and, for that matter, any dynamic practice or field. Yet gaps and lacks are not the most painful form of self-criticism, which invariably involves the realization of blindspots, denials, and/or bad faith. Their exposure creates the kinds of conflicts we have described as existing both within women's studies and between women's studies and the disciplines—dialogic conflicts that may be painful but, more important, that are productive. Indeed, writing in 1938 to the "sons of educated men," Virginia Woolf emphasized that the daughters of those men could best help to prevent global conflict "not by repeating your words and following your methods," but "by finding new words and creating new methods." Woolf also understood, in the closing pages of her essay, that the idea of "a unity that rubs out divisions as if they were chalk marks only" is the stuff of poetic dreams (143). Daughters and sons may long for that unity at one level, but "we" also know that intellectual and political divisions are the preconditions for creating new associations through which we can transform the places in which we are located.

NOTES

1. In this text the term *academy* refers to North American academic institutions of higher learning.

2. The identification of feminism in the academy with women's studies is problematic here, in part because feminism, however it is defined, can and does "go beyond" women's studies in the academy. Moreover, many women's studies programs include cross-listed courses whose content or approach is not subject to review, much less to any litmus test about its feminism, contrary to what neoconservatives would have the media believe. Nevertheless, for purposes of convenience we use *feminist studies* and *women's studies* synonymously in the pages that follow.

3. See, for example, Woolf's Outsiders' Society (1966, 106ff.).

4. On the militaristic rhetoric of disciplinarity, see Klein 1990, 77–78.

5. On the notion of disciplinary resistance to women's studies, see, for example, Bloom and Boroviak, McIntosh, Schmitz, Schuster and Van Dyne, and Spanier and Spender, which were published in the period 1981–85. See also Thibault and, most especially, Aiken et al., whose title features "the problem of resistance"; both were published in 1987. Of course, this image of a first stage replete with disciplinary resistances cannot be separated from the contextual impact of Reaganism and its powerful backlash against women (see Faludi 1991).

6. Such powerlessness can include the inability to ensure the survival of an "undisciplined" women's studies program in times of shrinking economic resources.

7. On the complexity of the term *interdisciplinarity*, as well as its practice, see Klein 1990.

8. On the contribution that various "studies" have made in working for perspectives broader than the department/discipline for synthesis, and for a more self-reflexive scholarship, see Klein 1990, 95–103.

9. By and large, colleges and universities have not devised procedures for evaluating interdisciplinary work fairly in the discipline-based tenure process.

10. In this connection we note that social scientists and scientists engage in collaborative research as a norm, a practice that humanists should strive to emulate, for it is now exceptional (eccentric?) in the reigning ideology of humanistic individuality.

11. In this sense metadisciplinarity can be reconciled with transdisciplinarity, which, as Klein explains, citing Raymond Miller, breaks "through disciplinary barriers, and [disobeys] the rules of disciplinary etiquette" in the interest of a larger framework, issue, problem or holistic scheme (1990, 66).

12. This is not to deny the resistance that feminist studies, African-American studies, and, more recently, gay and lesbian and postcolonial studies have occasionally also manifested toward poststructuralism and postmodernism as elitist theory that denies the "experience" of oppressed groups and threatens their emerging political identity.

13. Of course, "woman" as a unitary category was not only questioned by women of color but also by postmodern skeptics of essential identity.

14. In the past five years identity politics have also been put into question for the notable reason, among others, that the concept presumes a single, fixed identity, as opposed to plural identities whose number and relative importance wax and wane over time; see, e.g., Phelan 1993; and Sandoval 1991.

15. We say "sometimes," because conflicts have always/already existed in feminism and feminist studies; see Delmar 1986; and Echols 1989.

16. The effort to define commonalities without assuming or imposing sameness, but with, in, and through differences, represents a primary political and intellectual task for women's studies in the 1990s.

17. Hirsch and Keller's anthology (1990) discusses some of these conflicts, including the so-called essentialist/constructionist debates. One not cited is the "sex wars." They exploded at the Barnard College conference on "The Politics of Sexuality"—the proceedings were late published as *Pleasure and Danger* (Vance 1984)—and divided feminists over the goals and methods of Women against Pornography, which anticensorship feminists opposed, as well as over sadomasochistic practices. The debate thus raised the broader question of "Politically Correct? Politically Incorrect?" sexuality, as Muriel Dimen ironically entitled her essay in *Pleasure and Danger* (138ff.).

18. Admittedly, there are subtle differences between Hirsch and Keller (1990), as their two-columned coda to the volume suggests; here Hirsch seems more positive about conflicts than Keller (385).

19. Or then, as McKay suggests, we need unity in diversity—that is, a unity based on diversity (1993, 280).

20. In this volume the closing essay by Kramsch and von Hoene most clearly enlists Bakhtinian dialogics.

21. The problem seems to be confirmed by Conkey and Tringham's essay in this volume. The essays of Marecek, Sapiro, and Stacey underscore the progress (and the problems) of feminist scholarship in those "positivist" social sciences. It is no accident that this volume lacks an essay on economics, which has only recently begun to have a dialogue with women's studies. Although there is no dialogue with history as a discipline in this volume, most of the essays record the history of those disciplines and of their relation to women's studies. Of course, Lavrin's essay features Latin American political and social history.

22. It is impossible to say for certain why one discipline is more conducive/receptive to feminist theory and scholarship than another; nevertheless, the visibility and valorization of women in the field—in literature, both as writers and critics, in the past and in the present—surely plays a role.

23. These exchanges first took place in several departments at the University of Michigan. Sponsored by the Women's Studies Program, the series was designed to make feminist scholarship relevant and accessible to nonpractitioners and to encourage them to use its findings and approaches in their own teaching and writing. Our thanks to the dean of the College of Literature, Science and the Arts, Edie Goldenberg; the dean of the Graduate School, John D'Arms; and then associate vice president for Academic Affairs, Mary

Ann Swain, for subsidizing this project, which occurred over an eighteen-month period in nine disciplinary departments as well as in women's studies.

24. Among the lacunae in this volume is the conspicuous absence of discussions about cultural studies—indeed, about culture. For a study of the close parallels between feminist and cultural studies, see Franklin, Lury, and Stacey (1991). It is possible, of course, that the focus on the disciplines in this volume contributed to minimizing, even to excluding, consideration of interdisciplinary fields such as cultural studies. Could this predominant focus also account in part for the lack of reference to work in lesbian studies—indeed, to sexuality and the body—which has figured prominently in feminist scholarship since the 1980s? Stanton 1992 has argued that women's studies has largely shaped the new studies of sexuality.

25. The most forceful feminist voice for engaging with late-twentieth-century technologies has been Donna Haraway in her influential "Cyborg Manifesto: Science, Technology and Socialist-Feminism in the Late Twentieth Century," and other essays in *Simians, Cyborgs and Women* (1991); see also Kramarae 1988.

26. For a good review of feminist critiques of science, see Longino and Hammonds 1990.

27. Is it symptomatic, then, that in this volume only Lavrin's essay deals with societies other than those of the First World, and/or is this a product of our emphasis on North American academic disciplines and scholarship?

WORKS CITED

Aiken, Susan Hardy, Karen Anderson, Myra Dinnerstein, Judy Lensink, and Patricia MacCorquodale. 1987. "Trying Transformations: Curriculum Integration and the Problem of Resistance." *SIGNS: Journal of Women in Culture and Society* 12, no. 2: 255–75.

Bakhtin, Mikhail. 1984. *Problems of Dostoevsky's Poetics.* Minneapolis: University of Minnesota Press.

Boxer, M. J. 1982. "For and about Women: The Theory and Practice of Women's Studies in the U.S." *SIGNS: Journal of Women in Culture and Society* 7:661–95.

Carby, Hazel. 1982. "White Women Listen! Black Feminism and the Boundaries of Sisterhood." In *The Empire Strikes Back: Race and Racism in 70s Britain,* ed. Centre for Contemporary Cultural Studies, 212–36. London: Hutchinson.

De Lauretis, Teresa. 1990. "Upping the Anti [*sic*] in Feminist Theory." *Conflicts in Feminism,* ed. Marianne Hirsch and Evelyn Fox Keller, 255–70. New York: Routledge.

Delmar, R. 1986. "What Is Feminism?" In *What Is Feminism,* ed. Juliet Mitchell and Ann Oakley, 8–33. New York: Pantheon.

Dubois, Ellen Carol, Gail Paradise Kelly, Elizabeth Lapovsky Kennedy, Carolyn W. Korsmeyer, and Lillian S. Robinson. 1985. *Feminist Scholarship: Kindling the Groves of Academe.* Chicago: University of Illinois Press.

Echols, Alice. 1989. *Daring to Be Bad: Radical Feminism in America, 1967–1975.* Minneapolis: University of Minnesota Press.

Faludi, Susan. 1991. *Backlash: The Undeclared War against American Women.* New York: Crown.

Farnham, Christie. 1987. *The Impact of Feminist Research in the Academy.* Bloomington: Indiana University Press.

Franklin, Sarah, Celia Lury, and Jackie Stacey. 1991. "Feminism, Cultural Studies: Pasts, Presents, Futures." *Media, Culture and Society* 13:171–92.

Haraway, Donna. 1991. *Simians, Cyborgs, and Women: The Reinvention of Nature.* New York: Routledge.

Hartman, Heidi. 1981. "The Unhappy Marriage of Marxism and Feminism." In *Women and Revolution,* ed. Lydia Sergant, 3–41. Boston: South End Press.

Hirsch, Marianne, and Evelyn Fox Keller. 1990. "Practicing Conflict in Feminist Theory." In *Conflicts in Feminism,* ed. Hirsch and Keller, 370–85. New York: Routledge.

hooks, bell. 1984. *Feminist Theory: From Margin to Center.* Boston: South End Press.

Irigaray, Luce. 1981. "And the One Does Not Stir without the Other." Trans. Hélène Vivienne Wenzel. *SIGNS: Journal of Women in Culture and Society* 7, no. 1 (Autumn): 60–67.

Kelly, Gail P., and Carolyn Korsmeyer. 1991. "Feminist Scholarship and the American Academy." In *Women's Higher Education in Comparative Perspective,* ed. Gail P. Kelly and Sheila Slaughter, 269–82. Boston: Kluwer Academic Publishers.

Klein, Julie Thompson. 1990. *Interdisciplinarity: History, Theory and Practice.* Detroit: Wayne State University Press.

Kramarae, Cheris, ed. 1988. *Technology and Women's Voices: Keeping in Touch.* New York: Routledge.

Langland, Elizabeth, and Walter Gove. 1981. *A Feminist Perspective in the Academy: The Difference It Makes.* Chicago: University of Chicago Press.

Longino, Helen, and Evelyn Hammonds. 1990. "Conflicts and Tensions in the Feminist Study of Gender and Science." In *Conflicts in Feminism,* ed. Hirsch and Keller, 164–83. New York: Routledge.

Lorde, Audre. 1984. *Sister/Outsider.* Trumansburg, N.Y.: The Crossing Press.

Lugones, Maria, and Elizabeth V. Spelman. 1983. "Have We Got a Theory for You? Feminist Theory, Cultural Imperialism and the Demand for 'The Woman's Voice.'" *Women's Studies International Forum* 6:573–82.

Lyotard, Jean-François. 1984. *The Postmodern Condition: A Report on Knowledge.* Minneapolis: University of Minnesota Press.

Makovsky, Vivian P., and Michele A. Paludi. 1990. "Feminism and Women's Studies in the Academy." In *Foundations for a Feminist Restructuring of the Academic Disciplines,* ed. Michele A. Paludi and Gertrude A. Steuernagel, 1–37. New York: The Haworth Press.

McIntosh, Peggy. 1983. "Interactive Phases of Curricular Revision." In *Toward a Balanced Curriculum,* ed. Bonnie Spanier, Alexander Bloom, and Darlene Boroviak, 25–34. Cambridge, Mass.: Schenkman.

McKay, Nellie. 1993. "Acknowledging Differences: Can Women Find Unity through Diversity?" In *Theorizing Black Feminisms,* ed. Stanlie M. James and Abena P. A. Busia, 267–83. New York: Routledge.

Paludi, Michele A., and Gertrude A. Steuernagel. 1990. *Foundations for a Feminist Restructuring of the Academic Disciplines.* New York: The Haworth Press.

Phelan, Shane. 1993. "(Be)coming Out: Lesbian Identity and Politics. *SIGNS: Journal of Women in Culture and Society* 18, no. 4 (Summer): 765–90.

Sandoval, Chela. 1991. "U.S. Third World Feminism: The Theory and Method of Oppositional Consciousness in the Postmodern World." *Genders* 10 (Spring): 1–24.

Schmitz, Betty. 1985. *Integrating Women's Studies into the Curriculum.* Old Westbury, N.Y.: The Feminist Press.

Schuster, Marilyn, and Susan Van Dyne. 1985. *Women's Place in the Academy.* New Jersey: Rowman and Allanheld.

Spanier, Bonnie, Alexander Bloom, and Darlene Boroviak, eds. 1983. *Toward a Balanced Curriculum.* Cambridge, Mass.: Schenkman.

Spelman, Elizabeth. 1988. *Inessential Woman: Problems of Exclusion in Feminist Thought.* Boston: Beacon Press.

Spender, Dale. 1981. *Men's Studies Unmodified.* New York: Pergamon.

Spivak, Gayatri Chakravorty. 1989. "In a Word. Interview." *differences* 1, no. 2 (Summer): 124–56.

Stacey, Judith, and Barrie Thorne. 1985. "The Missing Feminist Revolution in Sociology." *Social Problems* 32, no. 4 (April): 301–16.

Stanton, Domna C. 1992. "The Subject of Sexuality." In *Discourses of Sexuality: From Aristotle to AIDS,* ed. Stanton, 1–47. Ann Arbor: University of Michigan Press.

Thibault, Gisele Marie. 1987. *The Dissenting Feminist Academy.* New York: Peter Lang.

Vance, Carol, ed. 1984. *Pleasure and Danger: Exploring Female Sexuality.* New York: Routledge and Kegan Paul.

Woolf, Virginia. [1938] 1966. *Three Guineas.* New York: Harcourt Brace.

PART 1

Outsiders Within:
Challenging the Disciplines

Chapter 1

To See Feelingly: Reason, Passion, and Dialogue in Feminist Philosophy

Helen E. Longino

PROLOGUE

My title is borrowed from lines in Shakespeare's *King Lear*. *Lear* is a play about many things—among them the disruption in the social fabric occasioned by Lear's overstepping of his kingly/fatherly prerogatives and his daughter Cordelia's refusal to obey his demand for what she believes to be an inappropriate profession of love. Cordelia's refusal sets in train a sequence of events that turns the world upside down, a familiar theme in early-seventeenth-century England and one that we relive today as feminists refuse to accept the old rules of patriarchy and the colonized reject the rule of the colonizer. Let me say why I think *Lear* provides an apt model for the intellectual revolution that taking feminist thought seriously could generate in philosophy.

In consequence of the social disruption following Cordelia's refusal, many central characters in the play come to understand their world and their place in that world very differently. For two of them this new understanding comes at the price of a severe disabling of the ordinary routes to knowledge. Lear himself is abandoned by his wits and in his madness recognizes first his betrayal by Regan and Goneril and later the broader reach of corruption in his former domain (and in human affairs generally).

> . . . Plate sin with gold
> And the strong lance of justice hurtless breaks;
> Arm it with rags, a pigmy's straw doth pierce it.
> (4.6.161–63)

Gloucester loses not his wits but his eyes—as punishment for his continued loyalty to Lear—and twice speaks lines that provide my title, first while trying to engage his son Edgar, still disguised as poor Tom, to assist his suicide. Gloucester gives a purse of money to Edgar/Tom, saying:

Let the superfluous and lust dieted man
That slaves your ordinance, that will not see
Because he doth not feel, feel your power quickly.
(4.1.67–69)

And a few scenes later Lear and Gloucester encounter each other on the road to Dover. Lear taunts Gloucester:

Lear: O, ho! are you there with me? No eyes in your head, nor no money in your purse? Your eyes are in a heavy case, your purse in a light; yet you see how this world goes.
Gloucester: I see it feelingly.

(4.6.141–45)

Wisdom in unreason, perception and knowledge through feeling. The social world is disrupted, and the very faculties of knowledge and comprehension are not merely called into question but, in fact, turned into their conventional opposites.

In the late twentieth century we who were educated in the Euro-American tradition are living through a comparable disruption, both in social relations and in the concepts and categories through which we claim to know the world, ourselves, and others.[1] The second wave of the women's movement, begun in the 1960s, has produced an extraordinary outpouring of scholarship and critical thought overturning the received wisdom in many disciplines. Feminism is not alone in challenging intellectual tradition and social structure. The civil rights and racial liberation movements in this country and "third world" postcolonialist movements elsewhere have also been developing new and more appropriate conceptual structures for the production of new and more appropriate knowledge. All these movements, in their different ways, rebuke that man "that will not see because he doth not feel." In a search for alternative conceptual and philosophical groundings, many thinkers from these movements have embraced modes of analysis that reject the dichotomization of reason and passion, of knowledge and feeling. I will focus in these pages on those developments in feminist philosophical thought.[2]

PHILOSOPHY AND FEMINIST THOUGHT

Philosophy has been slower than some disciplines, such as history or anthropology, to respond to the challenges posed by feminist thought. It is worth taking a moment to explore the reasons why this should be so. One has to do with philosophy's character as a second-order discipline. Philosophers do not directly study persons, social groups, or natural processes. Rather, we study the assumptions, principles, and conditions of understanding and valuing. Thus, while in areas such as applied ethics, feminist philosophers, and feminist sympathizers among philosophers, had a great deal to say about such issues as affirmative action, pornography, and abortion, it was less clear that feminist thought would have any relevance to areas such as theoretical ethics, epistemology, and metaphysics.

I would identify two aspects of the second-order character of philosophy as responsible for this. First, a second-order discourse (a metadiscourse) needs a first-order discourse, and feminist philosophers too have needed a new first-order discourse about and from which to elaborate alternatives to traditional philosophical analyses. Feminist philosophers have needed the development of feminist thought in history, anthropology, literary theory, psychology, sociology, and so on, to provide us with some equivalent of the centuries of culture and tradition of which Anglo-European philosophy is a part. Not surprisingly, nonnormative feminist philosophy began with analyses of concepts such as "oppression," "sexism," and "male chauvinism" (Frye 1983), concepts of currency in the women's liberation movement, and with the observation of misogyny in the work of canonical philosophers (Agonito 1979). Alison Jaggar's monumental contribution to political philosophy, *Feminist Politics and Human Nature* (1983), one of the first extended works to engage with the philosophical tradition, did not appear until the early 1980s. It has since been followed by monographs in ethics and theory of knowledge as well as books engaged in a sustained encounter with the history of philosophy. (These include in the immediately ensuing years books by Sandra Harding [1986], Genevieve Lloyd [1984], Jane Martin [1987], and Sarah Ruddick [1989].)

Second, as a second-order discourse, philosophy is concerned with ideas in their most abstract form, whereas feminist thought is grounded in the particular experiences of particular individuals. Furthermore, however much Western philosophy has changed during its history, certain concerns recur as its subject matter: truth, knowledge, justice, the good, beauty. The generality and universality of these concerns leads some to think that philosophy is independent of its social and political context—that, while the language used in analyzing these notions might change in successive historical periods, the analyses themselves have a validity that transcends their particular contexts. (This attitude is reflected in the teaching of history of philosophy not as intellectual history but as the entry into a conversation with the likes of Plato, Aristotle, Descartes, Hume, and Kant.) Feminist thought, by contrast, is the intellectual expression of a historically situated movement of social and political transformation—and, what's worse, a movement of just one segment of society. It's not even about Mankind, it's just about women.[3]

In addition to the metadiscursive character of philosophy, both philosophical methodology and philosophy's self-understanding offer resistance to feminist concerns. Methodologically, feminist thought and philosophical thought diverge in several ways: Janice Moulton (1983) drew attention to the adversarial method of contemporary philosophical discourse, with its metaphors of defense and attack. Feminist philosophers have attempted to find a more cooperative style of discussion, reflecting feminism's concern for a usable theory. (The change in tone at philosophy meetings over the last twenty years may reflect a modest effect of feminist philosophers on the profession.) And, as Susan Sherwin points out in her essay "Philosophical Methodology and Feminist Methodology" (1989), philosophy and feminist thought seem also to be responsive to different criteria of adequacy. Philosophy attends to the logic of an argument, to its internal coherence and consistency, and to the preemptive defeat of counterexamples—no matter how implausible to common sense the conclusion of an argument might be. Feminist thought employs logic (how could it not?), but, because it has political as well as intellectual aims, theoretical claims are also assessed for their coherence with feminist values. (Neither feminist thought nor feminist values constitute a single homogeneous entity or set. Perhaps a more precise way to put this point is that coherence with some subset of a set of values, recognized as feminist by a community engaged in feminist activism, serves as a constraint for members of that community.) The demand for such coherence does not replace such values as logical consistency but serves as an additional constraint on theorizing.

Finally, the very concepts upon which philosophy constructs itself rely upon and reinforce a distinction between the domain of reason, the world of philosophy, and the domain of feeling and passion, the domain of political movements such as feminism. Far from being a neutral distinction, however, the distinction between reason and feeling is itself a highly politicized one and cannot in its most common forms withstand feminist scrutiny. It is most fruitfully examined along with two other closely related distinctions, which have also been central to Western philosophy: the distinction between mind and body and that between autonomy and attachment. These distinctions have been the subject of philosophical thought *and* have provided conceptual background for philosophical discussions of other topics. However they have been articulated, they have played a central role in Western understandings of personhood. The first two of these have attracted so much feminist philosophical attention that they are obvious candidates for a study of this type. The third distinction, that between autonomy and attachment, may not seem as salient as the other two. This is partly because it is in some respects even more complexly embedded in our thinking than they are. It is implicated in these first two as well as in distinctions between freedom and determination, between public and private, between transcendence and immanence.

Feminist analyses of these distinctions are revealing a normative substructure constituted partly by their traditional use in characterizing gender difference and partly by the use of gender metaphors in characterizing the distinctions. Exploration of this mutually constitutive relationship can show us the role of concepts and metaphors in the legitimation of social structures. It can also reveal the ways in which philosophy participates in this legitimation. Philosophy is generally understood to be a critical discipline and, like any critical discipline, reinforces what it shields from criticism. The concepts whereby a philosophical perspective articulates its critical analyses are those that are, of necessity, shielded from criticism. But, if those concepts are the very ones employed in the construction of hierarchical privilege, then those hierarchies will be to that extent immune to the criticism philosophy makes possible. Their role in philosophical thought confers a privileged status on concepts whose use and significance extend far beyond the domain of technical philosophy.[4]

I wish in what follows to explore the gendered substructure of the dichotomies mentioned and then to look at some of the other philosophical issues in which these dichotomies are deployed. I shall discuss feminist work in these areas that casts doubt on whether the dichotomies can continue in their present form. In particular I shall investigate the role of the distinction between mind and body in structuring the analysis of subjectivity, the role of the distinction between reason and feeling in constituting the ideal of impartiality in ethics, and the role of the distinction between autonomy and attachment in ideals of objective knowledge. I can only scratch the surface of these subjects in such an essay but hope, even so, to indicate the potential impact that feminist thought can have on philosophical thinking. To set the stage for this discussion I wish briefly to examine the concept of gender.

GENDER AND ITS DICHOTOMIES

Gender as Socially Constructed

One of the accomplishments of feminist scholarship of the past twenty years is its demonstration of the constructed character of gender. While feminist theorists may disagree about just what gender then is, most theorists agree in rejecting the view that gendered traits are essential aspects of being a biological male or a biological female and treat gender difference as a socially constructed mode of organizing society and culture. This mode includes the sexual division of labor and what I call the sexual division of virtue. Masculinity is taken to consist in aggressiveness, independence a.k.a. dominance, emotional control or lack of affect, insensitivity to the feelings of others, self-confidence, taciturnity. Femininity is taken to consist in submissiveness and dependence, gentleness and nurturance, sensitivity to others, lack of emotional control, lack of self-confidence, excessive chattiness (Broverman et al. 1970). Individuals may in some respects mirror this cultural idealization, but the ways in which they deviate will be masked or treated as deviance. This constructivist conception of gender contrasts sharply with that, still characteristic of our culture, which specifies that there are two basic types of human being, male and female, and that certain traits, behaviors, and occupations are appropriate for each type: masculine and feminine are natural kinds.

Feminist work contesting the traditional understanding of gender has been of several kinds: one sort examines the conceptual and empirical underpinnings of gender thinking in Western cultures; another sort engages in cross-cultural study. One of the first internal challenges to the Western construal of gender was provided by the Broverman study, which showed that the bipolar specification of human nature also involves an asymmetric valuation of the two types. Broverman and her associates investigated stereotypes of the "healthy man," the "healthy woman," and the "healthy adult" among mental health practitioners in the United States. The researchers found that the traits of the healthy man and the healthy adult were almost identical, while those of the healthy woman and the healthy adult were almost diametrically opposed.

The Broverman study revealed the misogyny inherent in the very concepts of masculinity and femininity. Since then feminist researchers have developed several types of argument to invalidate the supposition that gender is a set of correlated natural kinds and to support the notion of the constructed character of gender. One kind of argument examines the evidence for certain kinds of gender difference, for example, differences in cognitive ability or in behavioral dispositions. Eleanor Maccoby and Carol Jacklin (1974) surveyed a very large number of proposed psychological differences between the sexes and showed that empirical research offered no foundation for almost all of them (they claimed an exception for aggressivity, concurring with studies that claim it to be more strongly represented among boys). If the concepts of masculinity and femininity are not realized in actual persons, their power must rest on other grounds—for example, their role as prescriptive ideals. Another kind of argument focusing on the construction of gender within Western culture looks at the research that attempts to show that gender difference does indeed have a biological foundation. These attempts range from Aristotle's theories of reproduction to the craniometry of the late nineteenth century to the human sociobiology and behavioral neuroendocrinology of our day. Analysis of the argumentative structure of these research programs reveals that they already assume elements of the conclusions about gender that they purport to be supporting. Not only do the conclusions about the biological determination of gender not follow from the data invoked but the research itself is shaped by the gender ideology (assumptions about gender) of the social and cultural context in which it is carried out (Sterling 1985).

Cross-cultural arguments to the constructed character of gender reveal the cultural variation in gender ideologies and in "gender-role behavior." One of the most startling demonstrations of this variation remains Margaret Mead's pioneering *Sex and Temperament in Three Primitive Societies* (1935). Each of the societies deviated in significant ways from the Euro-American norms with which Mead's readers were acquainted. Among the Arapesh men and women were expected to be, and for the most part were, gentle, nurturing, cooperative, and willing to be subordinate to others. Among the Mundugamore men and women were hostile and aggressive. Among the Tchambuli men exhibited what in a Euro-American context are feminine traits and women what in a Euro-American context are masculine traits.

Subsequently, feminist anthropologists have followed Mead's lead in documenting the cultural specificity of gender ideology and gender-role behavior (Rosaldo and Lamphere 1974; MacCormack and Strathern 1980). Women in almost every culture are subordinated to men and are responsible for domestic life. The actual tasks vary considerably, especially depending on the general form of economic organization in any given society, and the characteristics alleged to qualify women and men for their respective roles also vary. The anthropologist Sharon Traweek studies the culture of high-energy physicists and has compared two national physics communities (1989). In one of them aggressiveness and competitiveness are thought to characterize those men who are capable of achieving in the field, while the more passive and nurturing/cooperative nature of women disqualifies them from achievement. In the other, supportiveness and teamwork are thought to characterize those men who will make important contributions to high-energy physics, and women, who are deemed individualistic and competitive, are held to be unsuited to productive research in the field. In addition to their cross-cultural variation, the attributes of gender are specified differently for the different racial groups and social classes constituting societies stratified along those lines, and the gender ideology for subordinated groups differs depending on whether it is articulated by members of the dominant group or members of the subordinate group (Hull, Scott, and Smith 1982). The stereotypes of the black mammy, the Black Sapphire, and the black stud are the property of white supremacist culture, not of African-American culture.

The facts of intercultural and intracultural variation are hidden by the dominant gender ideology in Europe and North America, which is drawn from white middle-class assumptions about relations and differences between the sexes. To treat gender as construction, as ideology, is to say that it must be understood not as a real attribute of individuals but, rather, as a (socially enforced) ideal animating and regulating the behavior of individuals. The representations of masculinity as active, independent, dominant, in control of emotions, and of femininity as passive, submissive, nurturant, controlled by emotion, interact with a number of distinctions of interest and importance to philosophers, in particular the distinctions previously mentioned between mind and body, reason and feeling, and autonomy and attachment. I will now turn to exploring the gendered aspects of these distinctions and then reflect on the consequences of their gendering, as made visible by current feminist scholarship.

The Philosophical Distinctions and Their Gendered Aspects

Mind and Body

Perhaps one of the most vexed questions in modern philosophy has been how to specify the relation between mind and body. (Many nonphilosophers with whom I speak express amazement that philosophers managed to detach them in the first place, but this separation has a venerable history.) This distinction has taken many forms over the centuries, but several elements remain constant. Body is inert, extended, and unthinking, and mind is the seat of intellection and will. As the seat of the will, it is (unlike body) the origin of activity. Body is spatial, characterized by shape and size. Our human bodies are particular, historically and socially located, mortal. Mind is, by contrast, nonmaterial stuff, not subject to the limitations of bodily stuff. It has neither spatial extension nor spatial location; it is immortal. Bodies are the source of temptation (lust, gluttony, and sloth), which mind or spirit overcomes. Body is malleable, mind what gives form. (It should not be surprising that Elizabeth Spelman [1989] has diagnosed Western philosophy as having a bad case of somatophobia.) More recently the contrast is drawn not between kinds of substance but between kinds of event, mental and physical, or kinds of state or attribute, mental and physical. The difficulty of reconciliation persists (cf. McGinn 1981; Strawson 1983; Nagel 1986).

The gendered character of the philosophical distinction between mind and body has a venerable history, especially through the gender associations of activity and passivity, which play a role in distinguishing mind from matter. Philo of Alexandria spelled it out: "[J]ust as the man shows himself in activity and the woman in passivity, so the province of the mind is activity, and that of the perceptive sense [identified by Philo with flesh] passivity, as in woman" (qtd. in Lloyd 1984). In the Greek view of reproduction, articulated by Aristotle within the framework of his distinction between form and matter, male semen was the source of the (form of the) new biological individual, while the female uterus provided only the nutrient material needed for the organism's growth. In spite of what has been learned about biological reproduction in the ensuing years, the identification of masculinity with activity and of femininity with passivity has continued. Biologists until recently, for example, identified unicellular organisms as male or female on the basis of their degree of motility during reproduction (Gender and Biology Study Group 1989). Freud claimed that the sexual development of females, especially the rejection of clitoral for vaginal sexuality characteristic of a "mature femininity," rendered them passive and incapable of contributing to the life of their societies (Freud 1965).

In anthropology the mind-body distinction has its parallel in the nature-culture distinction, which is often used to construct gender: the association of the male with creativity, discovery, analysis, and construction (of buildings, cities, nations), that is, with culture; and the association of the female with her role in biological reproduction, birth and lactation, hence with nature. Nature is understood as static (or at most cyclic), while culture is innovative, changing and improving upon nature (Ortner 1974). Critics of sex stereotypes in evolutionary theory have noted the treatment of the male as the locus of the variation enabling evolutionary change, while the female is treated as constant and undifferentiated (Hubbard 1979). Females are given the characteristics of body, while males are given the characteristics of mind.

While mind is characterized by its masculine qualities when its sovereignty over matter is claimed within a dualistic metaphysics, gender is differently inscribed under different philosophical regimes. Materialism, which denies the existence of a distinct realm of the mental, invests matter with masculine qualities such as hardness and impenetrability (respects in which paradigmatically male bodies differ from paradigmatically female bodies). In a kaleidoscopic shift certain phenomena—for example, emotions—associated with the body and the feminine in the dualist view become epiphenomenal manifestations causally explicable by reference to "real" material events, while phenomena associated with mind are reconceived in ways that preserve their masculinity, for example, as reasoning is reconceived as computation. The philosophical point of view is also endowed with "masculine" qualities, the tough-mindedness and intellectual courage it takes to renounce a more comforting but ultimately confused and superstitious (read "feminine") metaphysical view.[5]

Reason and Feeling

Perhaps the locus classicus for the distinction between reason and feeling is Plato's tripartite division of the soul in *The Republic* (1961). Reason and desire are represented as in conflict—desire uncontrolled by reason leading us to suffering and/or indignity. In the just soul reason, assisted by "spirit," rules feeling and desire. Not only is reason independent of and ideally master of feeling, but only reason can know the good. In other versions of the distinction reason is and produces order, while feelings are inchoate and undependable. Reason is constituted of immutable principles and generates universal truths; feelings are inconstant and occupied with the particular. Plato identified justice in the individual with justice in the state—rulers, commercial and productive workers, and soldiers playing the roles of reason, feeling, and spirit, respectively. While Plato may have favored the class to the gender metaphor in *The Republic,* the subsequent literature of the Western philosophical tradition is studded with what seem from one point of view irrelevant asides, comments associating reason, however it has been analyzed by the author, with masculinity and nonreason with femininity. Philo of Alexandria again spells it out:

> The male is more complete, more dominant than the female, closer akin to causal activity, for the female is incomplete and in subjection and belongs to the category of the passive rather than the active. So too with the two ingredients which constitute our life principle, the rational and the irrational: the rational which belongs to mind and reason is of the masculine gender, the irrational, the province of sense, is of the feminine. Mind belongs to a genus wholly superior to sense as man is to woman. (Qtd. in Lloyd 1984)

Women themselves are declared either to have deficient forms of reason (Aristotle 1984) or to be so ruled by our feelings that we are incapable of the quality of reason required for moral decision making (Kant 1960).

As Genevieve Lloyd has remarked in her study of the association of reason and masculinity in the development of the modern philosophical tradition, reason came to be thought of as "a highly abstract mode of thought, separable in principle from the emotional complexities and practical demands of ordinary life" (1984, 19). As Lloyd goes on to demonstrate, this separation of reason and feeling is implicitly and often explicitly linked with a division between the realm of public action, which is the site of development of a full, rational, autonomous self-consciousness, and a realm of domesticity identified with the feminine. Reason defines itself as being not—whatever is identified as feminine.

Autonomy and Attachment

The distinction between autonomy and attachment is discussed most directly as the opposition between freedom and determinism. Are we self-determining agents, or are our actions determined by causal laws of the same sort that govern the natural world? While the concept of autonomy plays an important role in philosophical theorizing, attachment has received much less attention; when treated at all, it appears as coercion or craven dependence. Autonomy is central to the notion of rational decision.[6]

The ideal of rational decision making, whether epistemic, moral, or pragmatic, is the ideal of the independent agent uninfluenced by prejudice, bias, or contingent social attachments. The rational agent is self-legislating. A Kantian moral agent chooses that action that duty requires because it is required by duty, that is, because that agent wills to do that which is required by duty. The agent understands through the exercise of reason that morality in general consists in doing what duty requires and can then deduce what is morally required in particular situations. A utilitarian moral agent is also self-legislating, choosing that act that promotes the greatest good of the greatest number (or, if a rule utilitarian, choosing to act according to rules that, if generally followed, would have the result of promoting the greatest good). According to the stereotypes previously outlined, it is men who can be moral agents, as they are independent and impervious to the feelings of others and capable of controlling their own. Women, as more emotional beings, sensitive to others, and incapable of independent judgment, are at best faulty moral agents (as Kant himself told us).

Again there are scientific variants of this distinction. Herbert Spencer, in the nineteenth century, articulated a description of sexual difference just like the stereotypes reported in the Broverman study and treated those differences as adaptive. Women, according to Spencer (1873), had evolved not only to be dependent on powerful men but also to take pleasure in being so dependent. During one phase of more recent human evolution studies, "Man the Hunter" was the prevailing model of the behavioral innovations providing selection pressures. Early man went off to the hunt, while early woman remained tied to supposed home sites, whether caves or shelters in the bush, caring for the children and dependent on early man to bring back the meat. Feminist anthropologists have pointed out the striking similarities of this image to more contemporary social arrangements and have developed alternative accounts of the respective roles of the sexes in evolution, which foreground the activity of female hominids.

A philosophical version of this distinction, which makes evident its association with the mind-body distinction, was discussed by Simone de Beauvoir (1953). The human task in existentialist philosophy is transcendence, the assertion and exercise of freedom over the constraints of the material world. Beauvoir points out that this task is really assigned to the male and that the role, or presumed nature, of the female precludes her seeking, let alone attaining, transcendence. Females, providing emotional nurturance to their men and material nurturance to their children, are not capable of pursuing their own projects of transcendence but remain mired, instead, in immanence. In less existentialist terms, women are defined by their attachments, men by their achievements.[7] As Elizabeth Spelman (1989) reminds us, although Beauvoir saw the gender association, she endorsed the existentialist project of transcendence and the consequent asymmetrical valuation of gender and gender roles.

Interim Reflections

These three dichotomies, as my presentation of them makes clear, are not simply interlinked distinctions between forms of life but represent a system of value that privileges masculine experience and establishes the male as the human norm. I am not arguing that these distinctions can be reduced without remainder to that between masculinity and femininity and are hence as socially constructed as gender is. The relations among these concept pairs is a much more complex one. The distinctions reflect real differences in human experience and human practice: differences between thinking and eating, or between knowing that something is the case and wishing it were so, between independence and the comforts and constraints of community, between freedom of movement and physical constraint, between desire and physical (in)capacity. There is, thus, some experiential basis for these distinctions. I am arguing, however, that the three conceptual distinctions I have discussed, which systematize, codify, and imbue with metaphysical significance these more familiar experiential contrasts, are made even sharper through their gendered connotations. The distinction between masculine and feminine is one of their constitutive elements as, over time, they have been elaborated philosophically out of the elements of daily life. Their employment, in turn, in the construction of gender difference out of anatomical difference and reproductive role cements a semantic interdependence among all four of the distinctions.[8] Because of the valuations built into the distinctions, misogyny is interwoven into the basic tools of philosophical analysis.

The point of the argument to this stage is not to claim that the philosophical distinctions are baseless but, rather, to ask what remains of them if gender is removed. Gender is used to emphasize the depth of the differences and to invest them with opposing values. Feminist analysis, however, is increasingly showing our practices and experiences may not support the burden of metaphysical and ontological dichotomization presupposed by the axiological.

The feminist analysis of gender uncovers its construction via a series of dichotomies that are deeply embedded in the Western philosophical tradition. One strategy in response to this analysis is to reclaim the conventionally devalued side of these dichotomies—to celebrate body, emotion, and attachment—and to accompany that celebration with a derogation of their correlates. As a number of feminist philosophers have noted, this leaves the dichotomies themselves unexamined. The alternative strategy, which I have just employed, is to notice that, just as gender is constructed by the dichotomies, so the dichotomies are partly constructed by gender and that our particular concepts of reason, mind, and autonomy are shaped by ideals of masculinity and femininity as much as by any other aspect of the conceptual system of which they are a part. The animation of these constitutive features of Western personhood by gender may, in fact, contribute to misconstruing the very phenomena they are intended to illuminate. Feminist philosophy on this view is not simply a reevaluation of the elements constituting the dichotomies but also a rethinking of the dichotomies themselves, a rethinking that takes into account current scholarship about the conditions of women's lives and the role of gender in the construction of knowledge. I'd like to advance this view by showing how feminist thought challenges philosophical work grounded in the dichotomies that I have described. The gendering of mind and body, reason and feeling, and autonomy and attachment has rigidified these distinctions in such a way as to undermine their applicability.

THE GENDERED DICHOTOMIES AT WORK

Mind, Body, and Subjectivity

As noted earlier, the mind is the seat of awareness and consciousness, that is, of subjectivity. Knowledge, understanding, and awareness are attributes of the mental dimension of humans, while the body is brute matter, incapable of knowledge and perception. The mind is unconditioned subject, the knower; the body is object, the known, and is conditioned by its particular spatial and temporal circumstances. But, contrary to this traditional conception, feminist analysis shows that our bodies, the kinds of bodies we are and the kinds of experiences we have as a consequence, inform our subjectivity. The lens through which we perceive, organize our perceptions of, and understand ourselves and the world is not a transparent one. The traditional analysis of subjectivity is deeply flawed, and its failings can be attributed to the mind-body distinction that underlies it.

In the traditional version of the mind-body distinction, the body, via the senses, is a problematic source of information about the world external to the subject. It is the task of the mind to analyze and correct sensory information. This presupposes a transparent subjectivity, a subjectivity transparent to itself whose principles are independent of embodied experience. For Descartes (1955) the subject is an unconditioned, simple entity. And, while Kant denied the unconditioned subjectivity posited by Descartes, nevertheless, *The Critique of Pure Reason* (Kant 1968) argues for conditions of subjectivity that hold universally, conditions that are logically prior to experience, which give our experience the form it has through their role in what Kant calls the synthesis of apperception. Details of the body and its experience are irrelevant to the structure of the conditioned Kantian subject, just as they are irrelevant to the structure of the unconditioned Cartesian subject.[9] Lorraine Code (1991) remarks on an explicit expression of this view of subjectivity in Richard Foley's *The Theory of Epistemic Rationality* (1987), in which Foley confidently invokes a standard subject, "just like us." Only those with outlandish, bizarre beliefs will be bereft of epistemic foundations, which, for the subjective foundationalist, is just as it should be. But this must presuppose that variation in body type will make no difference to the structure of subjectivity.

But *I* live and have lived since childhood with the awareness that my body is regarded as an object upon which men feel permission to play out their desire—whether for sexual gratification, for power, or for selfhood. One of women's particular forms of subjugation is through sexual possession. Our bodies mark us for this social position, whether or not we are ever personally victims of rape, incest, or sexual molestation. Every woman living in a male-dominant culture lives with the awareness that, merely by virtue of being a woman, she risks sexual victimization. We learn this through direct experience of sexual abuse as children, through the warnings we receive about talking to strangers, through our experience of sexual harassment and assault as adults, through pornography, through mass media, through observing the treatment of other women who seek redress for their harm. We may have greater or lesser degrees of this awareness, it is modified by class and racial structures that specify what sort of man may with impunity so possess what sort of woman, we may be more or less successful in repressing or fleeing it. Whether repressed or available to consciousness, however, we experience our worlds through a lens shaped by asymmetric vulnerability. Women's subjectivity is conditioned by, among other things, the vulnerability of our bodies, a vulnerability identified by our culture with who we are. Sandra Bartky (1991) has written eloquently of the effects of this culturally imposed bodily vulnerability on female consciousness. The distinction between mind and body makes no sense from the perspective of one whose subjectivity can be denied through possession of her body.

Now, one might at first (perhaps under the influence of years of analytic philosophy) think that what such reflection on the subjectivity of the subjugated shows is that the subjugated (whether women of the class and race of their subjugators; whether women of a subordinated class or race or men of a subordinated class or race) have a deprived form of subjectivity, that this is one of the harmful effects of social inequality, and that ending social inequality will enable those previously deprived to experience the world as complete subjects, just as those not subjugated already and always have. This is the dream of early forms of liberal feminism, which took over in relatively unmodified fashion the assumptions of classic liberalism: that individuals are ontologically prior to the social groups in which they find themselves, that rationality resides in individuals, and that the basis of the value of individual human beings, what qualifies them for membership in the moral and political community, is their rationality (as distinct from their biological descent). Liberal feminists such as Mary Wollstonecraft (1975), Harriet Taylor, and John Stuart Mill (1970), and many contemporary feminists, argued that women were just as capable of ratiocination as men and, as such, were equally qualified to participate in the intellectual and political life of their communities. (Well, as qualified as the men of their race and class were considered to be.) This liberal approach sees men as the norm, as experiencing a full humanity, a subjectivity unconditioned by subordination, which, because of social inequality, women are prevented from experiencing.

But, while years of exposure to the substantive assumptions made by most analytic philosophers might well encourage or facilitate such a conclusion, a slightly more sustained analysis recognizes that, just as the position of subjugated would disappear under conditions of genuine social equality, so would the social position of subjugating. The phenomenon of subjugation is a condition of correlated social positions: one does not exist without the other. If this is so, we have no reason to think that the forms of subjectivity arising in the position of subjugator are any less conditioned by that position than are the subjectivities arising in the position of the subjugated. To revert to the particular form of subjugation already discussed, it is the particular kinds of bodies that men have that enable them to enact sexual possession. Whether or not any individual man ever rapes or sexually assaults a woman, men (again, in a class- and race-stratified context, of the dominant class and race) occupy the social position of those who possess and who are not themselves possessed.

So, the correct conclusion, upon reflection on the effects of subjugation on subjectivity, is not that women have an inferior subjectivity but that, just as the subjectivity of the subjugated is conditioned by occupying the social position of subjugation, so the subjectivity of the subjugator is conditioned by occupation of the social position of subjugating. We all see feelingly. Lear toppled sees the corruption of justice by gold; Lear in power saw a world of order. Women in male-dominant society see a world possessed by others, which they not only cannot possess but also of which they are an equally possessible part. Men, as long as they are white and middle-class, see a world theirs for the taking.[10] Neither of these subjective positions can withstand examination. Women are really not for the taking, nor is the natural world. As long as the understanding of subjectivity is bound up with the seeming self-evidence of the mind-body distinction, the notion of a pure subjectivity will remain a tempting ideal. Taking the feminist challenge to unconditioned subjectivity seriously could lead us to abandon the distinction, working instead toward a unified conception of material and mental phenomena that does not reduce one to the other or privilege one at the expense of the other.

Reason, Feeling, and Moral Decision

Morality and moral decision making have, with a few notable exceptions, been entrusted to the rational faculty. Feelings are fickle and partial and, so, inadequate guides of what constitutes right action in any given situation. What reason enables the moral agent to do is to articulate and apply universal principles of justice impartially and dispassionately.

This characterization of the ideal moral agent has been called into question by Carol Gilligan's research on women's moral development (1982, 1989). Gilligan, of course, was criticizing the paradigmatic approach to moral development associated with Lawrence Kohlberg, which treats moral development as unfolding in stages. In the final stage of development, in this view, the agent finally breaks away from contingent motivators such as fear of punishment or personal loyalty and is capable of formulating and acting on judgments characterized by "impersonality, ideality, universalizability and preemptiveness." Gilligan noticed that Kohlberg had had to eliminate responses from female subjects in order to work out the particular pattern of development he describes and took upon herself the task of analyzing those rejected responses to see whether they might offer a different picture of moral reasoning—a different voice. The voice she found is one characterized by caring and responsibility, a voice situated in a particular context responsive to particular others. Her subsequent research has elaborated what she sees as a distinction between an ethics of care and responsibility and an ethics of justice and rights.

This work has stimulated a great deal of controversy, both within and without feminist scholarly circles and also within and without psychological circles. One point of controversy is Gilligan's use of a Piagetian developmental model involving fixed and hierarchically ordered stages. Another focuses on the interpretation of her work as offering an account of a distinctive women's morality. Among feminists some commentators have celebrated and developed this notion further, while others have accused Gilligan of gender essentialism. And, indeed, the attribution of different moral frameworks to women and men does seem like naturalizing the distinctions of gender that feminists have so strenuously argued are socially constructed. However much controversy Gilligan's work has occasioned, it has also been one of the main intellectual stimulants to feminist philosophers dissatisfied with traditional approaches to ethics.[11] These philosophers draw disparate and conflicting lessons from Gilligan's work. They share, however, an emphasis on the inadequacy of reason, as traditionally conceived, as a guide to moral decision making. Several features of the traditional approach are criticized using perspectives generated from Gilligan's work. One is the conception of what moral agents are (both the agents who decide and those with respect to whom they decide and act). As Eva Kittay and Diana Meyers put it in the introduction to their collection, *Women and Moral Theory* (1987):

> A morality of rights and abstract reasons begins with a moral agent who is separate from others, and who independently elects moral principles to obey. In contrast, a morality of responsibility and care begins with a self who is enmeshed in a network of relations to others, and whose moral deliberation aims to maintain those relations. (10)

The contrast is between ideas of moral worth in two very different situations: one is that of the isolated individual seeking to maximize her or his self-interest; the other is that of an individual who sees her or his self-interest as inseparable from the good of others. The rights-based approach requires that we strip the individualizing aspects away from agents and focus on their "objective" claims on us. In the care-based approach the claims on us made by others arise from their very particular identities and our relations to them (see also Benhabib 1987).

The other feature relevant to philosophical analyses is the conception of the form and content of moral decision making. Philosophers focus on various aspects of the conception associated with the rights-based approach and show that, as they are understood, they are at best incomplete as guides to moral action.

Lawrence Blum (1988) reads Gilligan's work as revealing the inadequacy of traditional accounts of moral decision as reconstructions of moral decision making. He uses as an example, for purposes of argument, the principle "Protect one's children from harm," a specification of parental duty. Suppose one's child is attacked by a bully. What does this principle require? Blum argues that whether or not intervention is required depends on knowledge possible only through a kind of caring attentiveness to that particular child. It may require protecting the child from the physical harm threatened by the bully; it may require protecting the child from the psychological harm threatened by one's own intervention—continued dependence on parents for protection or failure to learn about one's own capacities of self-defense.

In general, Blum claims, knowing what action is required in any given situation involving other persons requires knowing those others in a way that is possible only through caring for them. Reason divorced from feeling is a caricature of our actual reasoning processes and of what those processes must be in order to be adequate to the task of articulating appropriate moral judgments.

Michael Stocker (1987) argues that categories involved in rights-based theories are incompletely analyzed if understood as totally distinct from categories in care-based theories. Focusing on the categories of duty and friendship, he argues that each can only be fully understood in relation to the other. For example, as grounds in moral deliberation each can, under certain circumstances, override the other. Whereas Gilligan emphasizes the distinction between rights and care, Stocker urges us to investigate the possibility that, as duty and friendship are, so more generally rights and care or rights and responsibility are, internally connected. Stocker, that is, sees Gilligan's work as a step toward a synthesis of perspectives that on their own are incomplete.

Marilyn Friedman (1987) argues that special relationships generate morally relevant considerations that may outweigh considerations of justice. She recounts the story of Abraham and Isaac as Abraham's dilemma of "having to choose to uphold the right of life [Isaac's], thereby sacrificing relationship with a Supreme Being, or, rather, choosing relationship with a Supreme Being, thereby sacrificing considerations of rights" (196). We cannot make sense of this story without recognizing the justificatory role of special relationships in moral decision making. Friedman also draws from Gilligan's attention to context the lesson that highly abbreviated descriptions of situations of moral choice, while showing how a given principle might be relevant to a situation, falsify the complexity of actual situations in which many factors may be morally relevant and in different respects. Our standard principles, it turns out, are too narrow for direct application, and moral judgment requires selecting, ordering, and choosing principles.

While I do not have the space to sort out the differences among these philosophers and between their views and Gilligan's, I believe they all point to the inadequacy of rendering moral phenomena for judgment by a dispassionate computational reason. While they share an emphasis on returning the particularity and feelings of special relationships to the moral domain, they are not arguing for the dominance of feeling over reason. This work points to the problems of treating reason and feeling as polarized entities, one of which must be subordinated to the other. Our feelings are not ignorant, nor reason blind, because neither function in isolation. If we persist in treating reason as the antithesis of and ideally dominant over feeling, we will be unable to account for the important and legitimate role of our affections in moral deliberation, we will fail as well to appreciate the role of abstract moral principles in our affections, and we will be unable to do justice to the rich complexity of our moral lives.[12]

Autonomy, Attachment, and the Ideals of Knowledge

Feminist work on the construction of the self in a network of relations with others not only challenges our concept of reason but contrasts sharply with the ideal of autonomy in moral decision making. The dichotomy between autonomy and attachment also shapes our understanding of epistemological problems. In Western philosophy knowledge has traditionally been conceived as some sort of verisimilitude of representation, backed by reason and/or sense perception. While this conception has provided problems aplenty for philosophers to worry about, the ideal itself has not received as much scrutiny as it might have. Feminist thought again provides some new perspectives.

The paradigm knower in Western epistemology is an individual—an individual who, in several classic instances, has struggled to free her- or himself from the distortions in understanding and perception that result from attachment. For Plato, for example, knowledge of the good is possible only for those whose reason is capable of controlling their appetites and passions, some of which have their source in bodily needs and pleasures, others of which have their source in our relations with others. The struggle for epistemic autonomy is even starker for Descartes, who suspends belief in all but his own existence, in order to recreate a body of knowledge cleansed of faults, impurities, and uncertainties. For Descartes only those grounds available to a single, unattached, disembodied mind are acceptable principles for the construction of a system of beliefs. Most subsequent epistemology has granted Descartes's conditions and disputed what those grounds are and whether any proposed grounds are sufficient grounds for knowledge. Descartes's creation of the radically and, in principle, isolated individual as the ideal epistemic agent has for the most part gone unnoticed and unchallenged.[13]

A second epistemological expression of the dichotomy is to be found in the ideal of value-free knowing, an ideal of which we have taken the natural sciences to be paradigm exemplars. The natural sciences, in this view, are characterized by a methodology that purifies scientific knowledge of distortions produced by scientists' social and personal allegiances. The essential features of this methodology—explored in great detail by philosophers of science—are observation and logic. Much philosophy of science in the last twenty-five years has been preoccupied with two potential challenges to this picture of scientific methodology: the claim of philosopher-historians Norwood Hanson (1958), Thomas Kuhn (1962), and Paul Feyerabend (1962) that observation is theory laden, and the claim of physicist and philosopher Pierre Duhem (1954) that theories are underdetermined by data. One claim challenges the stability of observations themselves, the other the stability of evidential relations.

Both accounts have seemed to permit the unrestrained expression of scientists' subjective preferences in the content of science. In the first case, observation itself is conditioned by the scientist's theoretical commitments, including social theoretic commitments; in the second, the evidential relevance of observations is determined by assumptions. Neither the theoretical commitments nor the assumptions, it seems, are subject to independent constraints. As long as the scientific knower is conceived of as an individual, knowing best when freed from external influences and attachment—that is, when detached or free from her or his context—philosophical accounts of methodology remain in the grip of the gendered dichotomy of autonomy and attachment. The scientist, the real person, is autonomous, independent of her or his context, and detached from the object of study. As long as the intended contrast to autonomy is attachment perceived as dependence, as the inability to think for oneself, the puzzles introduced by the theory ladenness of observation and the dependence of evidential relations on background assumptions will remain unsolved.[14]

Evelyn Fox Keller (1984) has understood the ideal of scientific objectivity as an ideal of detachment of the scientist from the object of study. Epistemic and affective ideals are, she argues, intermingled, and, from the psychoanalytic perspective she adopts, distorted affective development has produced a distorted epistemic ideal. She has therefore proposed an alternative conceptualization of autonomy, contrasting static autonomy with what she calls dynamic autonomy, an ability to move in and out of intimate connection with the world. Dynamic autonomy provides the emotional substructure for an alternative conception of objectivity, dynamic objectivity:

> Dynamic objectivity aims at a form of knowledge that grants to the world around us its independent integrity but does so in a way that remains cognizant of, indeed relies on, our connectivity with that world. In this, dynamic objectivity is not unlike empathy, a form of knowledge of other persons that draws explicitly on the commonality of feelings and experience in order to enrich one's understanding of another in his or her own right. (Keller 1984, 117)

Keller argues that the model of scientific knowledge influential since the seventeenth century has been inextricably intertwined with a need to dominate nature. Drawing on Keller's analysis and other studies of women scientists, philosopher Jane Martin (1988) has suggested that we understand a loving attitude toward the material one studies as a mode of epistemic access to that material. Neither Keller nor Martin sees herself as arguing for the injection of emotions where there were none but, rather, for the substitution of emotions associated with exaggerated and rigid autonomy by those associated with an autonomy that also acknowledges and permits attachment.

I, too, have been interested in the concept of objectivity and its association with autonomy. Responding to conceptions of objectivity that locate it in the individual scientist's reliance on method, I have suggested that scientific knowledge is constructed not by individuals applying a method but, instead, by individuals in interaction with one another in ways that modify their observations, theories and hypotheses, and patterns of reasoning (Longino 1990). Only through such interactions are the values that permeate scientific reasoning through the medium of background assumptions made visible and accessible to scrutiny. Objectivity requires connection. An example familiar to feminists is the critique of the Man the Hunter model of human evolution. Without the criticism of physical anthropologists (women and feminists) attending to the role of females in evolution, the androcentrism of the mainstream Man the Hunter model would have gone unnoticed. That criticism has, however, made possible the revision of interpretations, the reorganization of data, and the development of new accounts of human evolution (Haraway 1991; Longino 1990). Scientific knowledge, in this view, is a consequence of the critical dialogue individuals and groups holding different points of view engage in with one another. It is constructed not by individuals but by an interactive dialogic community.[15]

Autonomy and attachment are reconceived in this view. Autonomy is not a radical isolation from the influence of others, and attachment is not a slavish dependence on it. Interaction involves mutuality and requires both independence *and* a context of relationship. If we persist in treating these as polar opposites, and in requiring a rigid autonomy as the condition of objective knowledge, we will fail to develop an account of scientific knowledge that reconciles the role of values in shaping our knowledge of the world with our need for models and theories that are not simply a projection of our fears and desires.

CONCLUSION

I wish to return to the general relation between philosophy and feminism. By reflecting on the discourse of gender produced by feminist scholars in other disciplines, feminist philosophers are beginning to identify the ways in which gender has structured the very terms within which philosophy (Western philosophy) is constructed. Philosophers often invent fantastic examples in order to get at our intuitions about certain matters. One that has received attention in recent philosophy is part of the discussion of the nature of persons and is designed to elicit our intuitions concerning the relation of self-identity to bodily identity. Suppose I (a male speaker) were, by some unknown mechanism, to assume the body of Greta Garbo. Would I or would I not be the same person as before? Annette Baier, in a recent Presidential Address to the American Philosophical Association, wondered jokingly whether the attention paid to this example did not represent a collective repudiation by male philosophers of the Y-chromosome (Baier 1991). I do not think there is such a collective repudiation. Indeed, I think the example itself presupposes one of the dichotomies structured by gender that I suggest is called into question by recent feminist work. Only if we think the mind can exist independently from the body can we entertain this conundrum. Second, philosophy, far from fleeing the Y-chromosome, as we have seen, has been characterized by a derogation of those qualities identified as female—if anything, a repudiation of the X-chromosome. Feminist philosophers have had to identify and disempower the means of that repudiation as a prolegomenon to more constructive analysis. The next stage in feminist philosophy and philosophy generally will, I predict, consist in reconstruing the phenomena described by the dichotomies and then in doing philosophy in the context of those reconstructed understandings—not arguing for but, rather, presupposing embodied knowers, impassioned reason, agents in relations of interdependence.

Finally, a note of reconciliation. To the extent that philosophy really is a critical discipline, it should welcome the perspective on its own critical apparatus that feminist analysis makes available. I have noted disparities between philosophy as sometimes conceived and feminist thought as well as the challenges to traditional philosophical distinctions being raised by feminists. In spite of these differences, philosophers and feminists are more deeply related than divided, sharing in particular a skepticism toward authority and the claims of authority. Indeed, the promise of being able to unmask the pretensions of authority is one of its aspects that attracts feminists to philosophy. This shared commitment should form the basis for a dialogue about and across those differences, a dialogue that could result in mutual transformation and mutual benefit. In my reading of *Lear* the king and father does not, in the end, fully absorb the lessons available to him. Philosophy, as a collective pursuit of species self-understanding, stands a better chance.[16]

NOTES

1. Feminism is not limited to a Euro-American context, but its specific challenges vary according to culturally specific gender relations. I limit myself here to speaking of the challenges generated by feminists in relation to Euro-American culture.

2. Even more limiting, I will focus primarily on feminist philosophical work done in North America, which is predominantly, though not exclusively in the Anglo-American or analytic tradition. Feminists are not the only contemporary thinkers to draw attention to dichotomous structures in Western philosophy. Deconstructionist thinkers, especially Jacques Derrida (1976, 1982), have done so, as have philosophers drawing on traditional African thought (Wright 1984).

3. This is, of course, an exaggeration. The growth of women's studies in the university has encouraged the development of gender studies and of men's studies.

4. One reader of this essay remarked on the similarity of the analytic strategy I employ to poststructuralist and deconstructionist techniques. While I am happy at such a coincidence, I took myself to be proceeding (with the assistance of feminist antennae) in standard Anglo-American analytic fashion. In fact, mainstream analytic philosophers such as Gilbert Ryle and John Austin have taken on some of the very dichotomies I do. Their critiques have been limited, however, by their failure to comprehend the relation of these distinctions to gender distinctions and through those to power relations.

5. I am grateful to Elizabeth Anderson for bringing this transformation to my attention. The work of materialists David Armstrong and J. J. C. Smart offers good examples of such affect-laden expression of the materialist point of view (Armstrong 1968; Smart 1959).

6. Thomas Hill's (1987) exploration of several senses of the expression *autonomy* makes this connection clear. Thomas Nagel's discussion (1986, 110–20) explores the threat to "internal" concepts of agency by the "external" perspective on human action that treats it as an item in the world's causal flux.

7. As with the mind-body distinction, when determinism has the philosophical upper hand in the freedom-determination debate, gender associations are reworked. Causality is understood mechanistically as single events determining other single events, rather than as a complex network of interdependent factors. And the philosophical stance is likewise invested with hardheadedness. This is recognized in, for example, P. F. Strawson's (1983) characterization of philosophical naturalisms as "hard" and "soft."

8. For a general theory of meaning that can support this claim of conceptual interdependence, see Kittay 1987. The explicit gendering described in this section is rarer in twentieth century philosophy and is conveyed, instead, through the metaphoric cognates of gender dichotomy: active-passive, hard-soft, etc.

9. I refer to both Kant and Descartes here just because they are so different in many respects that their similarity on this issue underscores how pervasive this conception of subjectivity is.

10. Obviously, many other factors play a role in structuring individual subjectivity. I am not claiming that all white men share an identical subjectivity but, rather, that there is a common element in their subjectivity that is a consequence of their position in the power gradient of gender, a position they occupy because of their bodies. This aspect of "normal" (i.e., culturally validated) masculinity trickles down to men who are in less powerful positions racially or economically, but not in any simple or linear way.

11. Two collections of philosophical essays in moral philosophy (Kittay and Meyers 1987; Cole and Coultrap-McQuin 1992) and an issue of the journal *Ethics* have been

devoted to issues raised by Gilligan's work or have cited it as a touchstone. Many of the authors in these collections draw explicit connections between Kohlberg's ideas and the work of John Rawls, perhaps the most influential American moral theorist of the last twenty-five years. Rawls's analytic devices, the original position and the veil of ignorance, are designed to effect a separation between the reasoning required for discernment and support of moral principles and the interfering passions of particular relationships and circumstances.

12. I have focused here on problems in accounting for moral judgment. For a discussion of the role of feeling in knowing, see Jaggar 1989. Other philosophers have also been addressing the distinction through the cognitive theory of emotions (Solomon 1976; de Sousa 1987).

13. Naomi Scheman (1983) has drawn on the late work of Wittgenstein to develop a feminist critique of individualism in the philosophy of mind. A nonfeminist critique is developed by Tyler Burge (1986).

14. In an interesting twist of gendering, Kuhn himself charges that philosophers' simplifications of situations of theory choice, which make the situations amenable to algorithmic solution, "emasculate by making choice entirely unproblematic" (Kuhn 1977, 328).

15. In an interesting convergence of epistemological with ethical philosophy, Alison Jaggar (1992) is arguing for a dialogic approach in feminist ethics.

16. I wish to thank Elizabeth Anderson, Jack Meiland, Domna Stanton, and Abigail Stewart for their comments on an earlier draft of this essay. I am obviously indebted to my many colleagues in philosophy for the development of these ideas. I have tried to recognize my specific indebtednesses but have surely in places unknowingly trod ground tilled by others and elsewhere drawn on what has become, through many conversations, common wisdom.

WORKS CITED

Agonito, Rosemary. 1979. *History of Ideas on Women*. New York: Putnam's.
Aristotle. 1984. *On the Soul*. Trans. J. A. C. Smith. *The Complete Works of Aristotle*. Princeton, N.J.: Princeton University Press.
Armstrong, D. M. 1968. *A Materialist Theory of Mind*. London: Routledge.
Baier, Annette. 1991. "A Naturalist View of Persons." *Proceedings and Addresses of the American Philosophical Association* 65, no. 3:5–17.
Bartky, Sandra. 1991. *Feminity and Domination*. New York: Routledge.
de Beauvoir, Simone. 1953. *The Second Sex*. New York: Knopf.
Benhabib, Seyla. 1987. "The Generalized and the Concrete Other: The Kohlberg-Gilligan Controversy and Moral Theory." In *Women and Moral Theory*, ed. Eva Kittay and Diana Meyers. Savage, Md.: Rowman and Littlefield.
Blum, Lawrence. 1988. "Gilligan and Kohlberg: Implications for Moral Theory." *Ethics* 98:472–91.

Broverman, Inge, et al. 1970. "Sex-Role Stereotypes and Clinical Judgments of Mental Health." *Journal of Consulting and Clinical Psychology* 34:1–7.

Burge, Tyler. 1986. "Individualism and Psychology." *Philosophical Review* 95:3–45.

Code, Lorraine. 1991. *What Can She Know? Feminist Theory and the Construction of Knowledge.* Ithaca, N.Y.: Cornell University Press.

Cole, Eve Browning, and Susan Coultrap-McQuin, eds. 1992. *Explorations in Feminist Ethics.* Bloomington: Indiana University Press.

Derrida, Jacques. 1976. *Of Grammatology.* Trans. Gayatri Spivak. Baltimore, Md.: Johns Hopkins University Press.

————. 1982. *Margins of Philosophy.* Trans. Alan Bass. Chicago: University of Chicago Press.

Descartes, Réné. 1955. *Meditations on First Philosophy. The Philosophical Works of Descartes.* Trans. Elizabeth Haldane and G. R. T. Ross. New York: Dover.

Duhem, Pierre. 1954. *The Aim and Structure of Physical Theory.* Trans. Philip Weiner. Princeton, N.J.: Princeton University Press.

Feyerabend, Paul K. 1962. "Explanation, Reduction and Empiricism." *Minnesota Studies in the Philosophy of Science,* ed. Herbert Feigl and Grover Maxwell. Minneapolis: University of Minnesota Press.

Foley, Richard. 1987. *The Theory of Epistemic Rationality.* Cambridge, Mass.: Harvard University Press.

Freud, Sigmund. 1965. "Femininity." *New Introductory Lectures in Psychoanalysis, vol. 22.* Trans. James Strachey. New York: Norton.

Friedman, Marilyn. 1987. "Care and Context in Moral Reasoning." In *Women And Moral Theory,* ed. Eva Kittay and Diana Meyers. Savage, Md.: Rowman and Littlefield.

Frye, Marilyn. 1983. *The Politics of Reality.* Ithaca, N.Y.: Crossing Press.

Gender and Biology Study Group. 1988. "The Importance of Feminist Critique for Contemporary Cell Biology." *Hypatia* 3, no. 1.

Gilligan, Carol. 1984. *In a Different Voice.* Cambridge, Mass.: Harvard University Press.

————. 1989. *Mapping the Moral Domain.* Cambridge, Mass.: Harvard University Press.

Hanson, Norwood Russell. 1958. *Patterns of Discovery.* New York: Cambridge University Press.

Haraway, Donna. 1991. *Simians, Cyborgs, and Women.* New York: Routledge.

Harding, Sandra. 1986. *The Science Question in Feminism.* Ithaca, N.Y.: Cornell University Press.

Hill, Thomas. 1987. "The Importance of Autonomy." In *Women and Moral Theory,* ed. Eva Kittay and Diana Meyers. Savage, Md.: Rowman and Littlefield.

Hubbard, Ruth. 1979. "Have Only Men Evolved?" In *Women Look at Biology Looking at Women,* ed. Ruth Hubbard, Mary Sue Henifin, and Barbara Fried. Cambridge, Mass.: Schenkman.

Hull, Gloria, Patricia Bell Scott, and Barbara Smith, eds. 1982. *All the Women Are White, All the Blacks Are Men, but Some of Us Are Brave.* Old Westbury, N.Y.: The Feminist Press.

Jaggar, Alison. 1983. *Feminist Politics and Human Nature*. Totowa, N.J.: Rowman and Allanheld.

———. 1989. "Love and Knowledge: Emotion in Feminist Epistemology." In *Gender/Being/Knowing: Feminist Reconstructions of Being and Knowing*, ed. Alison Jaggar and Susan Bordo. New Brunswick, N.J.: Rutgers University Press.

———. 1992. "Toward a Feminist Conception of Practical Reason." The Simon Lectures. University of Toronto.

Kant, Immanuel. 1960. *Observations on the Feeling of the Beautiful and the Sublime*. Trans. John Goldthwaite. Berkeley: University of California Press.

———. 1968. *The Critique of Pure Reason*. Trans. Norman Kemp Smith. New York: St. Martin's.

Keller, Evelyn Fox. 1984. *Reflections on Gender and Science*. New Haven, Conn.: Yale University Press.

Kittay, Eva Feder. 1987. *Metaphor: Its Cognitive Force and Linguistic Structure*. New York: Oxford University Press.

Kittay, Eva Feder, and Diana Meyers, eds. 1987. *Women and Moral Theory*. Savage, Md.: Rowman and Littlefield.

Kuhn, Thomas. 1962. *The Structure of the Scientific Revolution*. Chicago: University of Chicago Press.

———. 1977. *The Essential Tension*. Chicago: University of Chicago Press.

Lloyd, Genevieve. 1984. *The Man of Reason*. Minneapolis: University of Minnesota Press.

Longino, Helen E. 1990. *Science as Social Knowledge*. Princeton, N.J.: Princeton University Press.

Maccoby, Eleanor, and Carol N. Jacklin. 1974. *The Psychology of Sex Differences*. Stanford, Calif.: Stanford University Press.

MacCormack, Carol, and Marilyn Strathern, eds. 1980. *Nature, Culture, and Gender*. New York: Cambridge University Press.

McGinn, Colin. 1982. *The Character of Mind*. Oxford: Oxford University Press.

Martin, Jane Roland. 1985. *Reclaiming A Conversation*. New Haven, Conn.: Yale University Press.

Mead, Margaret. 1935. *Sex and Temperament in Three Primitive Societies*. New York: William Morrow.

Mill, John Stuart, and Harriet Taylor Mill. 1970. *Essay on Sex Equality*. Ed. Alice Rossi. Chicago: University of Chicago Press.

Moulton, Janice. 1983. "A Paradigm of Philosophy: The Adversary Method." In *Discovering Reality*, ed. Sandra Harding and Merrill Hintikka. Dordrecht, Neth.: D. Reidel.

Nagel, Thomas. 1986. *The View from Nowhere*. New York: Oxford University Press.

Ortner, Sherry. 1974. "Is Female to Male as Nature Is to Culture?" In *Woman, Culture and Society*, ed. Michelle Rosaldo and Louise Lamphere. Stanford, Calif.: Stanford University Press.

Plato. 1961. *The Republic*. Trans. Paul Shorey. In *The Collected Dialogues of Plato*, ed. Edith Hamilton and Huntington Cairns. Princeton, N.J.: Princeton University Press.

Rawls, John. 1971. *A Theory of Justice*. Cambridge, Mass.: Harvard University Press.

Rosaldo, Michelle, and Louise Lamphere, eds. 1974. *Woman, Culture, and Society*. Stanford, Calif.: Stanford University Press.

Ruddick, Sara. 1989. *Maternal Thinking: Toward a Politics of Peace*. Boston, Mass.: Beacon Press.

Scheman, Naomi. 1983. "Individualism and the Objects of Psychology." In *Discovering Reality*, ed. Sandra Harding and Merrill Hintikka. Dordrecht, Neth.: D. Reidel.

Shakespeare, William. 1946. *King Lear*. Ed. Tucker Brooke. New Haven, Conn.: Yale University Press.

Sherwin, Susan. 1989. "Philosophical Methodology and Feminist Methodology." In *Feminist Perspectives: Philosophical Perspectives on Method and Morals*, ed. Lorraine Code, Sheila Mullett, and Christine Overall. Toronto: University of Toronto Press.

Smart, J. J. C. 1959. "Sensations and Brain Processes." *Philosophical Review* 68:141–56.

Solomon, Robert. 1976. *The Passions*. New York: Anchor Press.

de Sousa, Ronald. 1987. *The Rationality of Emotion*. Cambridge, Mass.: MIT Press.

Spelman, Elizabeth. 1989. *Inessential Woman*. Boston, Mass.: Beacon Press.

Spencer, Herbert. 1873. "Psychology of the Sexes." *Popular Science Monthly* 4:30–38. Reprinted in *Men's Ideas/Women's Realities: Popular Science, 1870–1915*, ed. Louise Newman. New York: Pergamon Press, 1985.

Sterling, Anne Fausto. 1985. *Myths of Gender*. New York: Basic Books.

Stocker, Michael. 1987. "Duty and Friendship: Toward a Synthesis of Gilligan's Contrastive Moral Concepts." In *Women and Moral Theory*, ed. Eva Feder Kittay and Diana Meyers. Savage, Md.: Rowman and Littlefield.

Strawson, Peter F. 1985. *Skepticism and Naturalism: Some Varieties*. New York: Columbia University Press.

Traweek, Sharon. 1989. *Beamtimes and Lifetimes*. Cambridge, Mass.: Harvard University Press.

Wollstonecraft, Mary. 1975. *A Vindication of the Rights of Women*. Ed. M. Kramnick. Harmondsworth, U.K.: Penguin.

Wright, Richard. 1984. *African Philosophy: An Introduction*. Washington, D.C.: University Press of America.

Chapter 2

Looking at Gender: The Column of Trajan and Roman Historical Relief

Natalie Boymel Kampen

For the past several years I've been working on a group of Roman historical reliefs, sculptures whose subject matter focuses on official events and personages.[1] These reliefs were usually made for public rather than private consumption and often had the patronage of the government or state officials. I began the project in order to catalogue the reliefs of the Roman provinces, not as a feminist endeavor, but, inevitably, a set of questions about the role of gender ideologies and representations in the political life of the Roman Empire began to intrude. I became more and more aware of the lack of scholarly concern with the mechanics of Roman visual representation of gender and with ways in which the idea of masculinity, so often at the heart of Roman notions of power and politics, takes shape and meaning in Roman state art.[2] An exploration of the representation of gender in historical relief is the goal of an ongoing set of essays, of which this one, on the Column of Trajan (fig. 1), is a part (Kampen 1988, 1991).

The Column of Trajan, that grand phallic monument to the emperor's conquest of the Dacian people in the first decade of the second century C.E.[3] uses a notion of ideal "manliness," embodied by the emperor and interwoven with Romanness as well as with rank, to explain why victory for the Romans is right and inevitable. Like other Roman monuments and texts, it posits the need for continual struggle to maintain victory, and it depicts manliness in large measure as the willingness to engage in that struggle while conforming to certain (often unspoken) codes of decorum—codes that distinguish Roman from barbarian, noble from lowly, man from woman. And yet this military imagery, like Roman statecraft in general, proposed ideal manliness as a goal for Roman and conquered men alike. Women stand in an ambiguous relation to that ideal, not least because it functions as a representation of gendered citizenship—active, public, office-holding, all the things that the writings of elite Roman men reserve for themselves. The images on Trajan's Column tend to subordinate women and to restrict them to certain boundary-making roles whose function, ultimately, is to speak of men and manliness.

Fig. 1. Column of Trajan, Rome, c. 113 C.E., as seen in the Forum of Trajan. All photographs courtesy the Deutsches Archäologisches Institut, Rome. DAI Inst.neg. 79.1046.

In this essay I argue that formal devices and visual relationships on the Column of Trajan construct and support conceptual relationships that represent the emperor at the top of a hierarchy in which gender, rank, and ethnicity are interwoven. Frontier, provincial, and enemy men and women and Roman soldiers appearing around the emperor reveal the nature of the Roman ideal of manliness by similarity and contrast and by the way they interact with Trajan. Visual analysis helps to demonstrate concepts for which clear textual evidence is either lacking or not yet studied. Visual language can be as important, especially in societies in which the majority of people are illiterate, as written texts (Harris 1990).

The essay begins by considering the historiography of the Column and the problem of writing about Roman art from a feminist point of view.[4] It then discusses the Column as a monument in an architectural and political context. It goes on to an examination of the strange image (fig. 2), unlike any other on the Column, of women, clearly not Roman, attacking naked bound men, not so clearly not Roman. Looking at poses and gestures of figures as well as the composition of individual scenes, I discuss this peculiar image in relation to those that flank it and to those above and below (fig. 3). This group of scenes forms a block that could be seen by a viewer standing in one spot on the ground and looking up.[5] I chose it as my focus because it reveals the ways in which manliness is defined by what it is not. Although I discuss the construction of normative gender and ethnicity, I want to concentrate here on women as signifiers, paradoxically, of both community and the foreign or liminal.

GENDER AND THE HISTORY OF PREMODERN ART

Historians of "premodern" European art have produced far less gender scholarship than those who work in eighteenth-, nineteenth-, and twentieth-century art history and have often been less receptive to the ideas of feminist theoreticians in other disciplines.[6] The archaeological traditions of the field, which are still, to a large degree, deeply positivist and invested in "scientific" methods, and the predominance of methodologically conservative scholarship dating back to the gentlemanly nineteenth-century traditions of art history and classics, have meant that Roman art history is just beginning to produce work on gender.[7] The situation is exacerbated by the lack of the kind of visual and textual documentation available to scholars of the modern West; the problem gets more acute the further back in time one goes. During the Roman Empire art and text were made by men; the voices of women that remain today are mainly limited to formulaic inscriptions and to a few love poems by Sulpicia, who wrote in the first century C.E. and whose gender is still occasionally debated by scholars. We have no secure evidence of female painters or sculptors of the imperial period, although there are a few inscriptions about glass workers and other craftswomen; there are no traces of the autobiography that Agrippina the Elder is said to have written; and no woman's views on history remain except as presented by male writers (Pomeroy 1975; Fantham et al. 1994).

The problem of doing feminist work in this area is compounded by inade-

Fig. 2. Scene 44 and 45: *at left,* Trajan's largesse to the troops; *at right,* women attacking bound captives. Column of Trajan, Rome, c. 113 C.E. DAI Inst.neg. 31.312.

quate documentation for whole episodes and periods in Roman history. For the Column of Trajan, for example, no firsthand accounts of the wars remain unless the Column represents the work of an eyewitness, as some scholars have suggested, and there are only the faintest traces of the narrative that the emperor is supposed to have written about the wars.[8] The accounts of the wars against the

Fig. 3. Scene 39: flight to the Roman camp, building at the camp, Trajan's negotiations. Trajan's Column, Rome, 113 C.E. DAI Inst.neg. 41.1308.

Dacians all come from later periods and all are, of course, written by the conquerors; neither the women nor the men of the "other side" speak for themselves.

Basic work on how Roman art and literature conceptualized the social condition of being a woman or a man is only now beginning. The Roman literature on masculinity is just coming under consideration by scholars, and studies of rhetorical, medical, and physiognomic texts, as well as literary imagery and philosophical and religious thinking, have not yet had a major impact on art historical scholarship.[9] One still needs to ask what terms were used, if any, to evoke the modern English-language concepts of masculinity, femininity, manliness, womanliness; I use these English terms with a keen sense of their being *my* terms. Roman writers and others, such as coin moneyers, preferred to describe proper manliness by the deeds and virtues of "the real man"; the abstraction "manliness" remains buried under its examples and characterizations. Contrasts with what women do also function to define manliness through opposition, and the recent work on *cinaedi,* the men who behave like women, openly or in hidden ways (Gleason 1990), shows that a concept of manliness existed through expressions that stressed either action or appearance.

To my knowledge no scholarship has yet focused explicitly on gender in the Column of Trajan. The existing work has followed three main paths: the Column as historical document, as work of art, and as ideological construction. The earliest and most enduring tendency has been for historians (especially military historians) and archaeologists (especially those interested in Dacia) to interrogate the Column for the information—presumably factual and narrative—that it can convey about the course of the Dacian campaigns of 101–2 and 105–6 (e.g., Cichorius 1896–1900; Rossi 1971; Lepper and Frere 1988). But many individual elements of the Column refuse to cooperate in such an interpretation. The torture scene is one example. No existing literary evidence explains it; the clothing and lack of it are generic and do not reveal the ethnicity or loyalties of the parties involved; and the geographical location of the scene is unclear. Further, there are no extant scenes in Roman or earlier Greek art that resemble it. The closest images are really not very close: Amazons fighting Greeks in combat positions, the maddened female followers of Dionysus tearing apart Pentheus. And yet neither these nor the now lost statues of the Danaids, who killed their husbands on their wedding night, resemble compositionally or conceptually the Column's women, with their huddled naked victims (Lehmann-Hartleben 1926, 89; Gauer 1977, 28; among others).[10] Here and elsewhere, the expectation of "documentary" scholarship—that accuracy and clarity can always be found in the Column's reliefs—has its limits.

Work on the Column as "art" has modified the documentary position in a salutary way. Early twentieth-century scholars (and recent ones as well) explored the way the Column's images relate to one another vertically as well as horizontally to generate clusters of visually related areas and studied the repetition, reversal, and modification of individual elements that unify the frieze and the sense of narrative flow created by the composition (Lehmann-Hartleben 1926; Gauer 1977; Farinella 1981; Settis 1988). These compositional concerns demonstrated that documentation was not the only, perhaps not the central, governing principle in the Column's creation; the artists used modular elements both for efficiency and for holding this enormously complex and long helical relief together visually. Those elements were combined with traditional models, drawn from earlier Greek and Roman art, for individual figures and compositional groups. Rather than assuming, then, that the whole relief was based on eyewitness reconstruction of events, these art historians demonstrated the complexity of the creative process, and this led to far greater sophistication in the analysis of the Column's possible meanings, including current readings based on semiotic and communications theory (Scheiper 1982; Hölscher 1984; Settis 1988). Challenging the positivism of the documentary views by seeing the reliefs as independent text and participant in an intertextual system of communication provided the possibility for analyzing the Column's ideological assumptions, political context, and constructions. Embedded in the political and artistic program of the Forum of Trajan, where it stands, in the iconography of the city of Rome, the state, and the emperor, the Column becomes a monument whose narrative and documentary character uses an often illusory "realism" to demonstrate ideological positions.

This historiographic review is designed not only to explain how various scholars believe the Column's reliefs work; it shows that there is an intellectual foundation on which gender studies can build. The work on Roman art as socially embedded and ideologically motivated prepares the ground for gender analyses. I use this foundation to explore gender on Trajan's Column, combining it with feminist assumptions about the problematic nature of "manhood," which is always being made, remade, protected, and argued about and is always entangled with political structure, ideology, and representation. Always treated in relation to other social categories, such as age, rank, or ethnicity, and to what it is not, womanhood, *manliness* is a constant term in debates about power—who can have it and how it can be used.

MASCULINITY AND THE MUTING OF WOMEN

Erected around 113 c.e., the Column of Trajan stands in the Forum of Trajan in the center of Rome (Zanker 1970; Amici 1982; Fehr 1985–86). The Forum contains a great landscaped plaza in which an equestrian statue of the emperor once stood, a law court with hemicyclic ends, a court flanked by buildings that functioned as libraries, in the center of which stood the Column, and a temple to the divinized emperor and his wife, Plotina, completed during the reign of his successor, Hadrian. Beside one of the hemicycles and built up the hill that surrounded it was a multistoried shop area and a covered market. The Column of Trajan thus belonged to an extensive architectural and decorative program in which military, intellectual, commercial, legal, and religious elements were integrated into a complex set of spaces.

Trajan's Column, the only military part of the program to survive in place, had a hollow base and contained the emperor's tomb. It was undoubtedly accompanied not just by the equestrian statue of the emperor and by reliefs with military subjects in other parts of the complex[11] but also by a variety of ritual and ceremonial epiphanies by the emperor and his officers.[12] It was thus a visible marker for the Forum and its axial orientation, a military monument with images to remind the populace of Roman victories, a tomb or cenotaph for the emperor, and perhaps an unconscious reminder of the phallic power and fertility of the emperor and the state.

The imagery of the Column clarifies the gendered nature of the Forum's program and the conceptual universe it creates. The military world was man's territory, like the world of official government, public intellectual performance (rhetoric and public declamation especially), and much of state religion and state involvement in commerce. Women were officially excluded from holding military and civil office. Those who lived in Rome moved about in a relatively unrestricted way; they entered virtually all public spaces (even, at times, the Senate chambers), but they controlled few. Elite women exercised influence and used wealth, bloodlines, and marital alliances behind the scenes but without the permanence that comes from structural and ideological bases for power. That they owned, inherited, and controlled private property, including great estates and fortunes, is clear from legal and historical texts. Roman writers indicate that such elite women often intervened in political and legal affairs outside of, as well as within, the family, and the authors frequently criticize them as too autonomous for society's good (Pliny *Letters*, e.g., 7.24; Tacitus *Annals* 3.33–34; Marshall 1975a and b).

The Forum of Trajan makes no explicit acknowledgment of the public presence and activity of women, except for the later dedication of the temple to Plotina as well as Trajan. The space concentrates on emperor, soldiers, magistrates, and scholars and takes their masculinity for granted. The visual dominance of men in Roman historical relief participates in the construction of a world of public power that belongs to men. In these images men battle over and use power or have it used on them without the presence or intervention of women, except in very limited ways and for the very specific purpose of clarifying and enhancing male power (Kampen 1991). This absence of women dominates historical relief, as it does Roman military and administrative life.

Like the spaces and program of the Forum as a whole, the imagery of the Column of Trajan makes a comparable equation between masculinity and power. To render that equation convincing, it uses certain visual strategies, such as the rich detail and the great length of the frieze, to suggest that what one is seeing is "documentary reality" in which specific knowable and unique events are taking place. The documentary illusion is furthered partly by the repression of images of women; on the Column only 8 of the 155 scenes contain women, whereas the rest are filled with men. The absence of women is to be seen by Roman viewers as natural, since war is "men's business," and so the "natural" social order remains undisturbed.

THE ANOMALOUS WOMEN: THE COLUMN'S TORTURE SCENE

Although detail functions to convince viewers of the "truthfulness" of both messages and medium throughout the monument, in the strange torture scene (fig. 2) the structure of this truthfulness breaks down. Figures cluster in a hilly space marked only by a little stone building. Some women are beating three naked, bound men and burning them with torches. The facial features and hair of the captives are puzzling because the one in the center looks like a young and beardless Roman soldier or officer (as in the group to the left attending Trajan), whereas the other two, bearded but with short hair, resemble the men who do the rowing, the lifting, and the building under the direction of the officers (fig. 3). With their long thick bowl-like haircuts and their shaggy beards, they do not look like the majority of the Dacians (fig. 4); however, they do resemble somewhat those frontier folk who come seeking the protection of the Roman camp (scene 39, left [fig. 3]) or the German allies of the Romans. Without clothing to identify them, they lack clear signs of ethnicity or rank. Without external knowledge about the "story" behind the scene, there seems no way to identify them with any certainty.

Roman viewers lacking prior knowledge or the aid of someone to act as a guide (and it is unclear what proportion of the audience fell into this category) would probably have understood that the captives ought not to be considered Roman legionary troops. The kind of unheroic and "déclassé" nakedness and evidence of pain would immediately have reminded most Romans of the hundreds of images of barbarian prisoners on state monuments, coins, and statues they saw daily both in Rome and in the provinces. By sheer repetition these figures denied any possibility of Roman defeat; they insisted on inevitable and eternal Roman victory. The sight of a naked, bound, tortured Roman legionary was simply out of the question.

In contrast to the writhing captives, the women are upright and fully clothed in garments similar to those worn by women fleeing or being driven from their villages. Their clothing consists of a long-sleeved undergarment, a sleeveless girt jumper, and a wrapped mantle and distinguishes them from the women standing with husbands and children at the edge of a town where Trajan makes a sacrifice (fig. 5). The women here, their overgarments with short sleeves and their mantles knotted below the breasts, wear a head covering that drapes full in the back, unlike the women in the torture scene, whose tied scarves wrap their heads and the hair at the nape of the neck in separate sections. The women at the front are distinguished by context and costume from those in pacified areas, even when the latter are made to watch the emperor's ceremony at a distance, among trees that signify the edge of town and thus, apparently, a minimal amount of contact with "civilization." Since the women involved in the war

Fig. 4. Scene 75: Trajan (*seated at left*) and Decebalus (*standing at right*) at Sarmizegethusa Regia. Trajan's Column, Rome, 113 C.E. DAI Inst.neg. 83.464.

Fig. 5. Scene 91: Trajan sacrifices at a frontier town; detail of frontier families watching (*right half*). Trajan's Column, Rome, 113 C.E. DAI Inst.neg. 31.375.

itself are not distinguished by costume from one another, one cannot tell their ethnicity or where their loyalties rest.

Are the captives of the torture scene Dacians, Roman auxiliaries (perhaps Germans), people from a neighboring territory (such as Moesia, overrun by the Dacians), or Romans? Are the women Dacians or some other frontier women, perhaps Moesians? And does the scene represent Dacian women with Roman prisoners, Moesian women taking vengeance on Dacians, or one or the other punishing collaborators, as others have suggested?[13] The internal evidence cannot provide an "explanation," in a single documentary truth, but, in my view, it does not need to. What matters most is to use the scene and its anomalous content and form to analyze Roman gender ideals.

GENDER AND COMPOSITION

The Column of Trajan uses visual relationships established through multiscene compositions to locate the emperor in a network of gender, rank, and ethnicity. His manliness is inextricably interwoven with his Romanness and his imperial rank, all three of which become descriptors for his ideal status and for his right to lead. In a sense he guarantees victory because he embodies Roman virtue as well as Roman power.[14] The compositional relationships among scenes serve to demonstrate this nexus of power and virtue.

At first the composition of the torture scene seems centripedal and self-contained in relation to the horizontal frieze in which it appears (figs. 2 and 6). Above or behind the small building two of the bound prisoners are dragged about by their captors. The topmost captive faces to the right, his hair pulled by a woman with her back to the viewer.[15] A second woman standing behind the bound man touches a flaming torch to his shoulder. The group is closed and makes no reference to the figures of Roman soldiers in the scenes to the right and left of this one (of which more shortly). Below this first group of figures there is a second with a similar composition. The captive's twisted body moves to the left, and his head turns back toward the woman, who seems to strike him with a rod or torch. Meanwhile, the woman to the left grasps the prisoner by the shoulder as she raises her right fist. This group, like a two-level triptych, seems compositionally closed, especially in comparison with the woman to the left of the building at the bottom of the frieze. She faces left above her bound, seated victim, who is writhing as the woman plunges her torch to his left shoulder. Woman and captive almost blend into the group of soldiers who stand next to them but belong to the preceding scene on the left.

In compositional terms the upper part of the torture scene seems closed and separate from the scenes flanking it. And yet, looking at the Column from

Fig. 6. Scene 46: Trajan's departure. Trajan's Column, Rome, 113 c.e. DAI Inst.neg. 41.1339.

below, the eye is carried easily across the upper part of the register by a succession of horizontal bands and repeating rhythms. The horizontal organization connects the upper part of the torture scene to its neighbor on the left (fig. 2: Trajan sits surrounded by his soldiers) and to the figures moving onto Trajan's ship on the right (fig. 6). For example, the ground line under Trajan's stool helps lead the eye to the building in the torture scene and then to the top of the wheel house on the boat to the right. The sense of separateness among the upper parts of the three scenes depends on a set of enframing elements whose power is undercut by the visual links that create a clear horizontal rhythm.

The lower group of woman and prisoner functions in a slightly different way. The two figures, woman and captive, turn the viewer's eye back to the left and, in so doing, reinforce his or her association with the awestruck soldiers who stare up at the emperor. At the same time, the two-figure group joins visually with the small building beside it and with the unpopulated area at the lower right of the departure scene, in which the ship and water appear to form a visual halt in the rhythm of the frieze. A new section begins, marked as well by the powerful vertical of the soldier standing on the boat; larger than the women, strongly undercut and in higher relief than they are, he and the structure to his right also define the beginning of a new scene. Two things are crucial here: the combination of visual strategies for unifying, while also separating, the parts of the frieze, and the encasing of the torture scene between two scenes whose focus on Trajan turns them away from this horror both visually and conceptually.

Directing the viewer's eye back to the scene at the left of the torture (assumed by many to show Trajan giving bonus money to his victorious troops), the woman and her captive in the lower part of the scene insist on their inversion of the "normal" order of social relationships, even in war. At the top of the image, to the left, Trajan sits in profile, facing left, his hand taken by the deeply bowing soldier (fig. 2: left). The emperor appears on a rise, indicated by rocky ground beneath him, and he forms both the center of a three-dimensional space and the focus of attention for all the figures. Below, his soldiers stare up at him, gesture toward him, and embrace one another in celebration of victory; he is the still and serene core of the image, larger than the other figures and enframed by them through their poses, gestures, and glances in the same centripedal way as the captives in the torture scene.

To the right of the torture, beginning a new sequence of geographical movement, Trajan again anchors the scene and is revealed by its composition as the most important figure (fig. 6). His departure on a ship on the Danube places him, standing frontally and with his right hand extended in a gesture of clemency, among his soldiers, as they bring to him and his officers two Dacian men, whose bent poses and outstretched imploring hands indicate their petition for mercy (Brilliant 1963). Unifying the scene, the architectural background of a fortified area also draws the viewer's eye toward Trajan, the only figure seen completely, and again the largest figure. Here, as everywhere on the Column, his pose is quiet and controlled, his facial expression serious but composed. The focus of poses, the gestures and glances, his size and serenity, mark him as leader without visual fanfare or the imposition of rigid centrality (Lehmann-Hartleben 1926).

The three scenes form a conceptual group through compositional links and boundaries. The end of a campaign marked by the emperor's kindness to the troops, the torture, and the departure marked by Trajan's clemency cohere within a frame of imperial virtue, inside which is a terrible demonstration of all that emperor and troops, Romanness and manliness, oppose. Whether or not the group was consciously constructed by the artist(s) or patrons (the emperor and his advisors), the effect on viewers, standing at a distance and looking up at this section of the frieze (about a third of the way up the Column), depends on the compositional devices that calculatedly unify the images.

These visual unifiers make conceptual links that clarify imperial virtue. Trajan's deeds and his placement and relation to those around him testify to his moderation (*moderatio* is a favorite term in Pliny's *Panegyric*), his paternal nature (he had been acclaimed *pater patriae* fifteen years earlier), and his *humanitas* (in the sense of humaneness) (fig. 7).[16] The ruler's bravery is attested by his interventions in time of need as well as by his presence at the battle front near, though not in, the action.[17] Perhaps his value is too great for him to be endangered, but the result is to place him above violence, apart from it, and thus to underscore his serenity.

The emperor's remove from violence runs throughout the Column and is typical of state art through the first century as well. In almost all of the scenes that show fighting, Trajan is at least one compositional unit away from the actual bloodshed (e.g., scenes 36–38 or 40–42). In the few images that place him directly at a battle, the artist uses reverses and blocking structures to separate him from the violence. The best example of this strategy occurs when Trajan approaches a roaring battle (scene 114 [fig. 7]). Coming to the battle site on foot and surrounded by his soldiers, he moves from right to left against the dominant direction of the entire Column.[18] A patterned sweep of wall separates him from the battle itself. His troops follow, and then a tree acts as the boundary to the right of his entourage; beyond it the battle breaks out again. In this splendidly transparent way the emperor is in the midst of the battle yet totally separated from it, both physically, by the wall, and visually, by the reversal of direction.[19] Removed from violence, his role is to guide and control, to negotiate and judge, to show piety to gods and men, to exhort and reward.[20] He is the *exemplum virtutis,* the model for his troops and for all men.

Comparing Trajan to the conquered Dacian men reveals the nature of his ideal Roman manliness. The artists used group direction, pose and gesture, and facial expression to make Dacian defeat clear and convincing. Whereas the Romans march and fight facing to the right most of the time (when they are in or around a fort they sometimes move to the left toward the fort), the Dacians move to the left to fight (unless they are in relation to a fort or are surrounded or being chased) (fig. 8). To negotiate (fig. 3) and to submit (fig. 4), they face left, but in more than half the cases they flee to the right. Since the movement of the Column's spiral is up and to the right, defeat is signified by opposition to this dominant direction. Further, their poses and gestures underscore the preordained nature of their defeat. They are the ones who fall, lie dead or dying (fig. 8), collapse on one knee, fling up their hands in terror or misery, and hold hands out, palms up (fig. 4), as they grovel for mercy before the emperor (Gleason 1991). No Roman is seen in these poses; in battle the aggressive bodies

Fig. 7. Scenes 113–15: *to the left of center,* Trajan approaches the battle field from which he is separated by a winding wall. Trajan's Column, Rome, 113 C.E. DAI Inst.neg. 73.2398.

Fig. 8. Scene 40–43: *from left*, captives being bound as Roman soldiers tend one another's wounds; the emperor watches a battle; the enemy dying and in flight. Trajan's Column, Rome, 113 C.E. DAI Inst.neg. 73.2396.

of the Roman soldiers (both legionaries and auxiliaries) lunge or rear back, their weapons raised or thrust forward. Their bodies remain controlled—as prescribed by Roman and Greek physiognomists, philosophers, and rhetoricians—to demonstrate the appropriate manliness of high status and Roman or Greek birth. They neither fall nor die, and even their faces reveal stoic calm (Brown 1991; Gleason 1991). Dacian brows wrinkle, mouths gape, eyes stare upward, but Roman faces remain smooth and serene, as if to follow the model of the emperor himself.

An important exception to the pattern of emotionality and submissiveness for the defeated Dacians appears in the figure of Decebalus, their leader. The Column represents the ruler of the Dacians as both parallel and in contrast to Trajan. Seen several times on the Column's upper part, Decebalus is larger than the rest of the Dacians, physically more controlled than they, often separated from the chaos of battle by enframing architecture or trees, and, at the end, permitted a degree of nobility in his suicide. In the most significant representation of the Dacian leader, he and his people appear before Trajan at Sarmizegethusa Regia, their capital (fig. 4). Facing the seated emperor across the massed submissive figures of his men, Decebalus stands on a rise, his head higher than all the others around him, framed by a hill behind him. He looks to the left toward Trajan and extends his right hand, but, unlike the other Dacians whose outstretched arms signal submission, Decebalus stands straight and solemn. His elbows close to his body, his pose indicates self-control and noble reserve. Self-consciously wrought to dignify the war and its heroic character, the play between Roman and Dacian leaders here merges the idea that high rank confers nobility of demeanor with notions of ideal manliness. Rank can overcome the ethnicity of the loser, although it supports that of the winner.

The suicide of Decebalus, however, complicates the connection of high rank and male gender. The problem is not that Decebalus kills himself, since that was a perfectly respectable way to die with honor for an elite Roman; it is, rather, his defeat that problematizes manliness. The pose of Decebalus, frontal and down on one knee before the Roman soldiers, evokes associations with dying niobids, amazons, and giants on mythological friezes and paintings. The deaths of those children, of primitive monsters killed by the gods, and of the wild women whom gods and heroes always defeat serve to reassert the "proper" relations of gender and status. With one hand, then, the artists give Decebalus nobility; with the other, they take it away to project the complex image of relations among gender, rank, and ethnicity that are necessary to maintain the ideology of victory.

In the horizontal and vertical relationships among the scenes that circulate around the torture scene, women and captives invert what Trajan's ideal character stands for. Like the barbarians, the female figures do things that the Roman men cannot or would not do, and so they provide the edges against which

Roman manliness can be defined. Looking at the scenes above and below the torture, as well as those on either side of it, allows the viewer to make a series of connections fostered by content as well as composition; the women, marked as they are by their rarity on the Column, draw the eye to places and relationships of significance. Thus, for example, the images around the torture scene use women as signifiers both of community and of liminality. They indicate the inside of their own world and define its entirety by their association with their men, children, and the landscapes and buildings of their world. Yet they also stand at the borders or edges of scenes and meanings to indicate the boundaries of normative conduct and geography. Seeing the women with their children at the edge of the Roman camp, at the edge of a frontier town, at the edge of the fortress of Sarmizegethusa Regia, always just outside or just between, the viewer can grasp the paradoxical message: women represent community yet signify marginality, borders, edges.

The other scenes, even the liminal ones above and below the torture, all stress "normal" Roman military relationships—emperor to men, emperor to the enemy, emperor to those in need, soldiers to the enemy and to one another (fig. 8), and even, perhaps, Dacians to one another (as in the family groups, the mourning scenes, and the rank distinctions). The torture scene refuses to fit, however, and continues to raise questions. Roman sternness, tenderness, and *moderatio* disappear when the women turn weapons the Romans use for destroying towns onto their bound and naked captives. What men would fall so low as to be tortured by women? And what manner of women are these whose conduct is so unlike that of all the other women on the Column? Those other women flee or stand by passively with their children, watching from the edges. Only the women in the torture scene appear without children and stand outside the system of representation in which women should be passive and signify family and community.

VIOLENT WOMEN AND THE IDEOLOGY OF *ROMANITAS*

Despite its anomalous character, the torture scene on the Column does fit into a pattern of representing women as liminal through composition and content.[21] Even more important, it fits a pattern of stories and images that associates the violent acts and emotions of women with foreignness. Thus, Tacitus describes the women of Mona in Britain like Furies, dressed in black, their hair disheveled, waiving torches and shrieking at the Roman troops as they come ashore (*Annals* 14.30; Königer 1966, 55–62). Stories and images of Medea killing her children (Simon 1954) merged foreignness with violence, as did the myth of the Egyptian Danaids who slew their husbands on their wedding night (Ovid,

Tristia 3.1.62; Zanker 1983; Keuls 1986) and the ubiquitous representations of the Amazons (Devambez 1981). Even the illiterate of the empire who listened to storytellers or watched the performances in the arena would have had such associations. Male gladiators fought in amphitheaters in every corner of the empire and used combat styles and weapons called by the names of barbarous peoples such as Gauls and Thracians (Maurin 1984, 104). There, too, wild animals imported from far away were hunted, and condemned prisoners acted out sexual burlesques that ended in death (Apuleius, *Transformations of Lucius* 10.34). Female gladiators could be seen decked out as Amazons, as on a stele from Halikarnassos whose inscription tells us that the gladiators are *Amazones* fighting for their freedom (Smith 1900, 2:143, no. 1117; also Suetonius, *Domitian* 4). The arena made clear to Romans of every rank and condition the relationship between violence and the "other." At the same time, it mixed gender with ethnicity and rank in a hierarchy that the performances made visible to all (Maurin 1984). By opposition these associations help the Column's images to establish the desirable features of those who belong: Romanness, manliness, high rank or status. The women in the torture scene thus participate in the construction of a social hierarchy for men, a hierarchy with Trajan— symbol of Roman virtue, victory, and power—at the top.

By contrast to the women in the torture scene, the Dacian women, who are liminal figures, markers of the edge of civilization as they flee or go into exile, nonetheless also serve as signifiers for community and family on the Column. They clarify the implications of Roman conquest for a whole population because their appearance with children comes to mean "everyone," symbols of the community's future and its fate. Paradoxically, they signify "entirety" by virtue of their rarity. Unlike the men, who can be understood as soldiers, elders, negotiators, or prisoners, women can only be mothers and wives, signifiers of the family and the group.

As they appear in the context of images of provincial and frontier towns, women reveal the ways in which individuals and groups could rise in the hierarchy established by the Column: they could draw nearer to Rome through loyalty. The comparison of the Dacian women (e.g., fig. 3) with the "frontier" women watching Trajan's sacrifice beneath the trees (fig. 5) reveals the way both groups stand visually at borders, but borders with vastly different stakes. The Dacian women stand between battle and safety, war and exile, the presence and the departure of the emperor. The frontier women, however, stand between town and country, at the border between old ways and new, and thus on the edge of Romanization itself. This becomes clearer when the frontier women are juxtaposed to the hellenized and urban women who appear in another, nearby cycle in which Trajan is again welcomed to a provincial city to make a sacrifice on his way to the front (fig. 9). The wealth of classical architecture and sculpture

Fig. 9. Scene 86: Trajan sacrifices at a hellenized city with local families watching. Trajan's Column, Rome, 113 C.E. DAI Inst.neg. 41.1521.

reveals the prosperity of the community, and their Greek clothing makes their civilization obvious. Both scenes describe the benefits of peace that come from the emperor and the gods, properly honored, and both suggest a movement from urban to rural, from civilization to frontier. The images convey the possibility of movement upward, toward Trajan and the ideal of Romanness.

Romanness, high rank, and manliness all come together in the person of Trajan, who stands as the guarantor of victory and the physical embodiment of the relationship of virtue and power. The connection of the Roman army, provincial peoples, and auxiliary troops—such as the bare-chested German auxiliaries and the Mauritanian horsemen, with their corkscrew curls—to this ideal depends on the degree of connection with Rome. At the same time, the hierarchy formed by conceptual proximity to the emperor contains a degree of fluidity; the empire absorbs the conquered. The few women on the Column have positions in the hierarchy and also the possibility of movement for their communities within it. However, the women in the torture scene also illustrate the reversal of the proper order of things. Everything that Rome stands for, everything exemplified by Trajan, is inverted by the anomalous content and form of the relief in which the women attack their naked captives. By the presence of that inversion, the ideals of self-control, clemency, piety, and the correct relationships among people become that much more visible as *the* crucial messages in the Column's program.

The rich details of clothing, architecture, and machinery and the great length of the frieze add to the illusion of evidence to support the Column's ideological messages, as does the anomalous scene of the torturing women, so different from the traditional images of historical relief. The ideological messages are supported as well by the compositional relationships and by the artists' use of associations and models drawn from myth and public performance for the compositional units and figures (e.g., the fallen or dying amazon or niobid as prototype for the dying Decebalus). The coalescence of the documentary, the mythological, and the ideological creates a political program that is constructed as Truth—temporally and geographically specific but also inevitable and timeless.

Notes

1. The problematic nature of the term *historical relief,* with its failure to acknowledge the debates over what constitutes history, has received little discussion in the field of Roman art, in part because the concept of history dominant in the imagery resembles the one articulated by elite Roman male historians and also because contemporary criticism, feminist and otherwise, has not penetrated Roman studies until very recently. The main work on historical relief in the last few years shows minimal interest in challenging the notion of history as male, public, and official (Koeppel 1982; Torelli 1982; Hölscher 1984); this is especially striking in light of work by historians such as Brown (1988), Nicolet (1991), and Shaw (1992). But see, more recently, Hölscher (1988) on the relation of historical memory and culture.

2. The work of early scholars of Roman art and history such as Rodenwaldt (1935) and Alföldi (1952, 1953) laid the foundations for such inquiry into manliness by considering the way in which elite men, emperors in particular, were represented in art and text; it failed, however, to make gender an explicit category of inquiry. Today studies of sexuality, in which *manliness* is a central term, are in their infancy. Foucault (1986), Brown (1988), Rousselle (1988), Gleason (1990), and Winkler (1990), among others, explore these issues, as does the anthology on ancient pornography edited by Richlin

(1991). The analysis of elite historians and poets and of state and mythological works of art has also just begun; see, e.g., D'Ambra (1992) and Edwards (1993).

3. The Dacians lived along the Danube in what is currently Romania.

4. Of the enormous bibliography on the Column and its form and content, see especially Cichorius 1900; Lehmann-Hartleben 1926; Gauer 1977; Scheiper 1982; and Settis 1988; for a good current bibliography, see also Coulston 1990.

5. The conventions of discussion of visual objects include *the viewer* or *viewers,* terms that do not necessarily parallel the problematic use of *the reader* or unspecified readers in literary criticism. When the process of viewing is the same for ancient or modern, male or female, Roman or Dacian viewers—for instance, in the physical location of looking or of angles of vision—I assume the appropriateness of *viewer.* Of course, I recognize that interpretation of what is seen is conditioned by the social location of the individual doing the seeing.

6. For discussion of current feminist work in art history, see Gouma-Petersen and Mathews 1987. A review of work dealing with questions of gender and issues of masculinity and of sexuality continues to be needed, although the extremely useful bibliography by Simons (1988) can serve as a model for categories to be included. There is increasingly interesting work in these areas, as the essays in Broude and Garrard 1992 show.

7. Art historical work on gender in Roman art includes articles by, for example, Kleiner (1978, 1987), Bammer (1982), Wood (1988), and D'Ambra (1989). See also S. Brown (1993) on the way archaeologists have (not) dealt with gender.

8. The only narrative of the Dacian War is a brief sketch, found in tenth- and eleventh-century epitomes (précis written by monastic scholars) of a missing section of the early-third-century Roman history by Dio Cassius (Lepper and Frere 1988, 211–26). That Trajan wrote his own account is suggested only by a comment in the work of the sixth-century writer Priscian (Lepper and Frere 1988, 226–29).

9. See, for example, Gleason 1990; as well as other essays in the same anthology and those in Richlin 1991.

10. A story in Pausanias about worshipers of Demeter in Laconia (4.17.1) has been useful to my work on this scene. Probably taken from the hellenistic authors Callisthenes and Rhianus and reiterated in the middle of the second century c.e. by Polyaenus, the story occurs at a sanctuary to Demeter in Laconia and concerns Aristomenes, the Messinian hero of the archaic period.

> Aristomenes and his men knew that the women were holding a festival there: but by some power from the goddess the women were inspired to defend themselves and most of the Messenians were wounded, either with knives the women had been using to slaughter victims or with spits they used for spitting the meat to roast it; Aristomenes was beaten with burning torches and taken alive, but the same night he escaped to Messinia. (*Pausanias: Guide to Greece,* trans. P. Levi [New York, 1971], 2:142)

The passage suggests that the rods with which the Column's barbarian women attack their nude captives are related to spits or skewers. Moreover, it seems that the motif functions in a framework of conflated images and ideas about women and violence. For an important discussion of the image see Detienne (1979).

11. It is unclear whether the Great Trajanic Frieze, with its representation of the emperor in battle and at a sacrifice that now stands on the Arch of Constantine, originally came from the Forum, but it seems likely to most scholars (Leander Touati 1987, 88–91).

12. On the relationship of ritual and ceremony to public spaces and their creation of ideology, see Price 1984; as well as Zanker 1988.

13. Others who have interpreted this scene as Dacian women torturing Roman soldiers include Cichorius (1896–1900, 2:217–18); Lehmann (1926, 119); and Blancken-hagen (1957, 80). For Moesian women taking revenge on Dacian and Sarmatian invaders, see Gauer 1977: "die erbitterten Frauen der eingesessenen Bevölkerung" (28).

14. A reading of the Panegyric for Trajan, delivered in 100 C.E. by Pliny the Younger, provides a full list of imperial virtues and the interesting revelation that manliness is taken for granted and never receives comment with a direct term, such as *virilitas*. The noble virtues of the ruler, as expressed here and in the shield of Augustus—which listed justice, clemency, virtus (usually meaning military bravery but also righteousness) and piety—appear in two forms in Pliny's time: in abstract personifications or emblemmata (as on coins or the Great Frieze); and in narrative form, as deeds that demonstrate virtue (as on the Column or, perhaps, the Arch at Benevento). Military and governmental deeds, leisure pursuits such as hunting, rather than poetry or music, and other actions that were considered inappropriate to women were listed and testify to manliness without the need for further comment or for abstract nouns.

15. Figures whose hair is being pulled are always barbarian enemies and prisoners, women and men alike. See, for example, the bottom register of the Gemma Augustea in Vienna or the reliefs of the Column of Marcus Aurelius in Rome.

16. The amount of space given to actual fighting is about 20 percent of the whole relief frieze, not including preparations and marches; on the lower half about 16 percent and on the upper half about 23 percent of the relief area contains fighting. The rest is travel, building, negotiation, and mopping up.

17. As in scenes 96 and 113. Scene numbers refer to Cichorius' arrangement; the photographs with this numbering can be found also in Lepper and Frere 1988; and Settis 1988.

18. See, for example, scenes 24 and 73, in which Trajan is shown the severed heads of Dacians; scene 36, in which he rides to a tree beyond which Roman soldiers approach from the right; scenes 40 and 68, in which a Roman soldier pushes a prisoner toward the emperor from the right; and scene 66, in which a Dacian in three-fourths left pose kisses Trajan's hand.

19. The other major scene with a comparable reversed direction shows the emperor again separated by a wall from a battle he approaches from the right.

20. Other reasons why Trajan's military bravery requires no representation here might include the idea that, having fought before becoming emperor, he has no further need to demonstrate his *virtus*. Possibly—but this is both the most problematic reason and the one most in need of research—the narrative setting of the Column was seen as *too* realistic. The vision of Trajan killing on a narrative relief might have been considered too

violent and insufficiently clearly contained as virtue. Certainly, the distinction between Trajan and his troops—he is above the fighting; they are in the midst of it—serves to clarify the hierarchy of rank on the Column, but the motives for the removal of the ruler from the active engagement with the enemy in battle remain in need of further examination.

21. The gendered nature of anomaly needs further study, as do the perils of working in fields in which virtually every image of women is anomalous.

WORKS CITED

Alföldi, A. 1952–53. "Die Geburt der kaiserlichen Bildsymbolik, 3: Parens Patriae." *Museum Helveticum* 9:191–215 and 10:103–24.

Amici, C. M. 1982. *Il Foro di Traiano: Basilica Ulpia e biblioteche.* Rome: X Ripartizione antichita belle arti e problemi di cultura.

Bammer, A. 1982. "Die Angst der Männer vor den Frauen: oder Asthetisierung als Entmachung." *Hephaistos* 4:67–77.

Blanckenhagen, P. H. 1957. "Narration in Hellenistic and Roman Art." *American Journal of Archaeology* 61, no. 1 (Jan.): 78–83.

Brilliant, R. 1963. *Gesture and Rank in Roman Art.* New Haven: The Academy.

Broude, N., and M. Garrard, eds. 1992. *The Expanding Discourse: Feminism and Art History.* New York: Harper and Row.

Brown, P. 1988. *The Body and Society: Men, Women, and Sexual Renunciation in Early Christianity.* New York: Columbia University Press.

Brown, S. 1993. "Feminist Research in Archaeology: What Does It Mean? Why Is It Taking So Long?" In *Feminist Theory and the Classics,* edited by N. S. Rabinowitz and A. Richlin, 238–71. New York and London: Routledge.

Carettoni, G. 1988. "Die Bauten des Augustus auf dem Palatin." *Kaiser Augustus und die verlorene Republik,* 263–67. Mainz: von Zabern.

Church, A. J., and W. J. Brodribb, trans. 1942. *The Complete Works of Tacitus.* New York: The Modern Library.

Cichorius, C. 1896–1900. *Die Reliefs der Traianssäule.* Berlin: G. Reimer.

Coulston, J. C. N. 1990. "Three New Books on Trajan's Column." *Journal of Roman Archaeology* 3:290–309.

D'Ambra, E. 1989. "The Cult of Virtues and the Funerary Relief of Ulpia Epigone." *Latomus* 48:392–400.

———. 1993. *Private Lives, Imperial Virtues: The Frieze of the Forum Transitorium in Rome.* Princeton, N.J.: Princeton University Press.

Dauge, Y.-A. 1981. *Le Barbare (Collection Latomus* 176) Brussels: Latomus.

Detienne, M. 1979. "Violentes eugénies," in M. Detienne and J. P. Verrant, 183–214, *La Cuisine du sacrifice en pays giec.* Paris: Gallimard.

Devambez, P., and A. Kauffman-Samaras. 1981. "Amazones." *Lexicon Iconographicum Mythologiae Classicae* (Zurich and Munich). 1, no. 1:622–35.

Edwards, C. 1993. *The Politics of Immorality in Ancient Rome.* Cambridge: Cambridge University Press.

Fantham, E., H. P. Foley, N. B. Kampen, S. B. Pomeroy, and H. A. Shapiro. 1994. *Women in the Classical World: Image and Text.* New York: Oxford University Press.

Farinella, V. 1981. "La Colonna Traiana: un esempio di lettura verticale." *Prospettiva* 26:2–9.

Fehr, B. 1985–86. "Das Militär als Leitbild: Politische Funktion und Gruppenspezifische Wahrnehmung des Traiansforums und der Traianssäule." *Hephaistos* 7–8:39–60.

Florescu, F. Bobu. 1966. *Die Traianssäule.* Rudolf Habelt Verlag: Bucharest and Bonn.

Foucault, M. 1986. *History of Sexuality,* vol. 3: *The Care of the Self.* Trans. R. Hurley. New York: Vintage Books.

Gauer, W. 1977. *Untersuchungen zur Trajansäule I: Darstellungsprogramm und künstlerischer Entwurf. (Monumenta Artis Romanae 13).* Berlin: Mann.

Gleason, M. 1990. "The Semiotics of Gender: Physiognomy and Self-Fashioning in the Second Century A.D." In *Before Sexuality,* edited by D. Halperin, J. Winkler, and F. Zeitlin, 389–415. Princeton, N.J.: Princeton University Press.

Gouma-Peterson, T., and P. Mathews. 1987. "The Feminist Critique of Art History," *Art Bulletin* 69, no. 3 (Sept.): 326–57.

Graves, R., trans. 1951. *Apuleius: Transformations of Lucius.* New York: Farrar, Straus and Giroux.

Hamberg, Per Gustav. 1945. *Studies in Roman Imperial Art.* Almqvist: Uppsala.

Harris, W. 1989. *Ancient Literacy.* Cambridge, Mass.: Harvard University Press.

Hölscher, T. 1984. *Staatsdenkmal und Publikum (Xenia 9).* Konstanz.

———. 1988. *Kultur und Gedächtnis.* Frankfurt am Main: Universitätsverlag.

Hölscher, T., L. Baumer, and L. Winkler. 1991. "Narrative systematik und politisches Koncept in den Reliefs der Traianssäule. Drei Fallstudien." *Jahrbuch des Deutschen Archäologischen Instituts* 106:261–66, 287–95.

Kampen, N. B. 1988. "The Muted Other." *Art Journal* 47, no. 1 (Spring): 15–19.

———. 1991. "Between Public and Private: Women as Historical Subjects in Roman Art." In *Women's History and Ancient History,* edited by S. B. Pomeroy, 218–48. Chapel Hill: University of North Carolina Press.

Keuls, Eva. 1986. "Danaides." *Lexicon Iconographicum Mythologiae Classicae* (Zurich and Munich). 3, no. 1:337–41

Kleiner, D. E. E. 1978. "The Great Friezes of the Ara Pacis Augustae." *Mélanges de l'École française à Rome* 90, no. 2:753–85.

———. 1987. "Women and Family Life on Roman Imperial Altars." *Latomus* 46:545–54.

Königer, Hans. 1966. "Gestalt und Welt der Frau bei Tacitus." Ph.D. diss., Erlangen-Nürnberg.

Koeppel, Gerhard. 1982. "The Grand Pictorial Tradition of Roman Historical Representation during the Early Empire." *Aufstieg und Niedergang der römischen Welt,* edited by H. Temporini and W. Haase, pt. 2, vol. 12, no. 1, 507–35. Berlin and New York: De Gruyter.

Leander Touati, A.-M. 1987. *The Great Trajanic Frieze.* Stockholm: Svenska Institutet i Rom.

Lehmann-Hartleben, Karl. 1926. *Die Traianssäule: ein römisches Kunstwerk zu Beginn der Spätantike.* Berlin and Leipzig.

Lepper, F., and S. Frere. 1988. *Trajan's Column: A New Edition of the Cichorius Plates.* Gloucester: Alan Sutton.

Levi, P., trans. 1971. *Pausanias: Guide to Greece.* New York.

Marshall, A. J. 1975. "Roman Women and the Provinces." *Ancient Society* 6:110–19.

Maurin, J. 1984. "Les barbares aux arènes." *Ktema* 9:103–11.

Nicolet, C. 1991. *Space, Geography, and Politics in the Early Roman Empire.* Ann Arbor: University of Michigan Press.

Radice, B. 1975. *Pliny, the Younger: Letters and Panegyricus.* Cambridge, Mass.: Harvard University Press.

Pomeroy, S. B. 1975. *Goddesses, Whores, Wives, and Slaves: Women in Classical Antiquity.* New York: Schocken Books.

Price, S. R. F. 1984. *Rituals and Power: The Roman Imperial Cult in Asia Minor.* Cambridge: Cambridge University Press.

Richlin, A., ed. 1991. *Pornography and Representation in Greece and Rome.* New York: Oxford University Press.

Rodenwaldt, G. 1935. "Ueber den Stilwandel in der antoninischen Kunst." *Abhandlungen der deutschen Akademie der Wissenschaft zu Berlin* 3:1–27.

Rolfe, J. C. 1970. *Suetonius: Lives of the Caesars.* Cambridge, Mass., and London: Harvard University Press.

Rossi, L. 1971. *Trajan's Column and the Dacian Wars.* Ithaca, N.Y.: Cornell University Press.

Rousselle, A. 1988. *Porneia: On Desire and the Body in Antiquity.* Trans. F. Pheasant. New York and Oxford: Basil Blackwell.

Scheiper, R. 1982. *Bildpropaganda des römischen Kaiserzeit: unter besonderer Berücksichtigung der Trajanssäule in Rom und korrespondierender Münzen.* Bonn: R. Habelt.

Settis, Salvatore. 1985. "La Colonne Trajane: Invention, Composition, Disposition." *Annales ESC* 40, no. 5 (Oct.): 1151–94.

———. 1988. *La Colonna Traiana.* Torino: G. Einandi.

Shaw, B. 1992. "The Cultural Meaning of Death: Age and Gender in the Roman Empire." In *The Family in Italy from Antiquity to the Present,* ed. D. I. Kertzer and R. P. Saller. New Haven, Conn.: Yale University Press.

Simon, Erika. 1954. "Die Typen der Medeadarstellung in der antiken Kunst." *Gymnasium* 61:203–27.

Simons, P. 1988. *Gender and Sexuality in Renaissance and Baroque Italy.* Sydney: Pomer Institute of Fine Arts Publications.

Smith, A. H. 1900. *A Catalogue of Sculpture in the Department of Greek and Roman Antiquities, British Museum.* London: British Museum.

Torelli, M. 1982. *Typology and Structure of Roman Historical Reliefs.* Ann Arbor: University of Michigan Press.

Wheeler, A. L. 1975. *Ovid: Tristia and Ex Ponto.* Cambridge, Mass., and London: Harvard University Press.

Winkler, J. 1990. "*Phallos Politikos:* Representing the Body Politic in Athens." *differences* 2, no. 1:29–45.

Wood, S. 1988. "*Memoriae Agrippinae:* Agrippina the Elder in Julio-Claudian Art and Propaganda." *American Journal of Archaeology* 92, no. 3 (July): 409–26.

Zanker, Paul. 1970. "Das Trajansforum in Rom." *Archäologischer Anzeiger,* 499–544.

———. 1983. "Der Apollontempel auf dem Palatin." In *Città e Architettura nella Roma Imperiale (Analecta Romana* suppl. 10), 21–40. Rome.

———. 1988. *The Power of Images in the Age of Augustus.* Trans. A. Shapiro. Ann Arbor: University of Michigan Press.

Chapter 3

The Narrative Self: Race, Politics, and Culture in Black American Women's Autobiography

Nellie Y. McKay

From their earliest writings in the West, autobiography was sufficiently central to the welfare of African Americans to make it the genre of preference in the development of black literary culture. As early as the eighteenth and nineteenth centuries, displaced Africans realized how critical it was for them to gain the language of the dominant group in order to enter the white debates on the humanity of Africans and to challenge western European discourses on freedom and race. Through a mastery of the literacy and the language of the enslaver group, they anticipated proving to their oppressors and to sympathetic white readers that people with black skins were as intelligent and human as other groups.[1] Since then the life story (or portions of it) has been the most effective forum for defining black selfhood in a racially oppressive world.

For race (which also implied class) was the crucial ground on which relations of power developed between black and white people in eighteenth- and nineteenth-century America, making blackness and U.S. citizenship virtually antithetical to each other and the power relations in race and politics together central to both secular and religious black autobiographical narrative. Challenging white hegemony, black autobiographers used narrative to fight their battle against chattel slavery and to engage in the search for political and psychological freedom for all black people. For the black writer did not and could not participate in an ideology of self that separated the self from the black community and the roots of its culture. Consequently, the personal narrative became a historical site on which aesthetics, self-confirmation of humanity, citizenship, and the significance of racial politics shaped African-American literary expression.

In a world that denies black humanity, black autobiographers almost always focus on the racial authentication of self. Their narratives begin from a stated (sometimes disguised) position that establishes and asserts the reality of self through experience. Critic Craig Werner believes that the internal pressure for self-authentication in the black narrative originates in the African American's awareness of a contingent "self": an ever shifting social construct that makes it impossible for powerless people to take the self for granted (Werner 209). "I write my experiences and thus establish my reality" was the subtext of "Written by Him/Herself" on the title page of a number of early black self-narratives, as was the phrase, "I was born," with which numerous such stories began. As signifying metaphors, in black words printed on white pages from a black perspective, these stories announced authentic selves secure in their sense of individual worth, group pride, and the humanity of black people. The texts were linguistic achievements affirming a rejection of white-imposed denigration of the black self and, in the best of American traditions, making proud assertions of a new identity. Early black autobiographers appropriated the master's tools to write themselves into being and their community into freedom (Werner 204). Using the white oppressor's language and black cultural tropes (like masking), they transformed the racially inferior, abstract African self of the master's text into the narrative of the ultimately triumphant black experiential self. These selves, inhabitants of the slave and spiritual self-stories, were the legacy of twentieth-century autobiographers as different as W. E. B. Du Bois, Richard Wright, and Maya Angelou. For the autonomous black self in the United States is the achievement of a racial and/or sexual self that is the product of mediation through peculiar experiences of oppression and survival (Andrews 1–31). But, while the struggle for agency on these terms is central to the black self in narrative, that is not its end: for there is no monolithic representation of black identity, and the richness of the autobiographical tradition includes its multiplicity and complexity of narrative strategies and its various forms of self-representations that delineate differences among and between black women and men.

This study assumes gender as a force in black women's stories interrogating the narratives of black male sexism, white female racism, and white patriarchal authority. For, in spite of the racial and class oppressions black women share with black men and the gender oppressions they share with white women, they see themselves differently from black men and white women. On one hand, white people drove black slave women, punished them as severely as men, and valued them like men for their productive labor. In addition, the women's worth as property included their reproductive value and sexual availability to white men, activities that forced them to be victims of unrelenting sexual abuses, many even bearing children for white and black men at the same time. On the other hand, nineteenth-century ideologies of white womanhood enabled white women, from their own subordinate position, to negotiate a relationship with patriarchy that joined their class interests with those of white men and actively discouraged them from forging alliances with black women (Carby 17–18). Thus, in the struggle against oppressive sexual and racial authority, the black female self stands at once alongside and apart from white women and black men, joined to the struggles of each but separated from both in a system that still privileges whiteness and maleness. From this complex angle of vision the black female narrative self makes of black female identity an exploration of differences from—and limits of loyalty to—black men and all others.

Differences in how black women and men see themselves, want to be perceived, and exploit the circumstances and opportunities available to them to assert autonomy in the world were apparent from the earliest autobiographical texts from which black female and male selves emerged. For instance, most slave autobiographers identify a dramatic moment when the slave in the self and the self in the slave confront each other and the self overcomes the slave. For example, the transformation from "slave" to "man" occurred, Frederick Douglass tells us, in a public moment of high drama, when he uses physical force to refuse to be further brutalized by his temporary master, Edward Covey (Douglass 89–105). Douglass declares that from that time, though he was still technically a slave, his relationship to white power changed. It was only a matter of time before he engineered his own freedom from the hateful and hated institution. Douglass expressed the triumph of self in gendered terms, recognizing himself as a man in his victory over Covey.

Conversely, Linda Brent, the persona of female slave Harriet Jacobs's *Incidents in the Life of a Slave Girl,* metamorphosizes from helpless slave girl to woman with some control over her life (also a gendered transformation) with her secret determination to resist the sexual harassment of her owner, Dr. Flint. In both texts these events are alike in their focus on concrete experiences that link the selves in the texts to the writers of the texts. They also parallel each other in that it is their status as slaves (race and class) that generates their oppressions. However, gender makes the difference among these characters in their development from passive slaves to conscious human agents. For his moment of self-recognition the virile Douglass selects a public confrontation with his master, contesting relations of force. The imminent danger in his situation (Covey might have killed him for resisting the whipping and for striking a white man) increases his male heroic stature in a struggle of wills turned into one over manhood.

In a reversal of this situation, in the cross-racial sexual relationship between the nubile young female slave and her master, the fifteen-year-old Brent chooses to challenge her oppressor in private. For one thing, she knew her success depended on leaving his public image as master intact. In addition, any revelation of her dilemma, even to those closest to her, would have compromised her standing in the community, increasing her sexual vulnerability. Her subsequent concealment in the crawl space of her grandmother's house and her life in seclusion as a fugitive after she escaped the South are extensions of links between privacy and female survival that intimately connect to experiential differences between black women and men in search of dignity and selfhood. Brent's presentation of her life during and after her enslavement includes a portrait of the constricted physical and psychological spaces allotted to black women and contrasts sharply with Douglass's audacious statement of "walking away from slavery," followed by his meteoric rise to abolitionist spokesman par excellence. For most of her story Brent remained within the domestic sphere, while Douglass had considerable mobility, even as a slave.[2] But in the outcome of her efforts to forge her own freedom Brent's strategies deserve great applause. Her political insights, her ingenuity in thwarting her master, and her ultimate success in depriving him of power over her life make her text extremely significant in the larger struggle for black freedom. It is also noteworthy that as a seemingly helpless orphaned teenage girl, Brent believed that she was not completely a victim (no doubt from observing her grandmother's life) and that it was in her power to manipulate her erstwhile abused womanhood in the struggle against white male power. Such comparison of the narrative selves in Douglass's and Brent's texts reveals some of the differences in black male and female psychological developments toward agency as slaves unshackled themselves from a system designed to rob them of selfhood. For men agency was the power of self in the public image of manhood; for women it was a self-recognition of their ability to manipulate the power in the self even when they were in otherwise powerless situations.

This is not to suggest that some slave women did not frontally attack the slave system. But, with some notable exceptions, many were constrained by confinement to their owners's households as workers and nurturers of their own children and those of others, including those of their masters, and by a deep sense of loyalty to family and community. As a consequence, fewer engaged in "macho" tactics that would have put them and others at greater risk than came with day-to-day life. One exception to this pattern was the fair-skinned Ellen Craft, who, accompanied by her dark-skinned husband disguised as her slave, daringly escaped by passing herself off as a white southern gentleman traveling for reasons of ill health. Harriet Tubman, well-known for her bold missions of rescue, was another. After her escape North, Tubman returned to the South several times and led dozens of slaves to freedom. The courage of women like Craft and Tubman indicate that female slaves did not fear to challenge the system boldly, but the oppressiveness they experienced of sex and gender roles influenced them to engage in more cautious modes of resistance.

In spiritual narratives black women also constructed their identities differently from men.[3] In their move for independence a number of free nineteenth-century black women rejoiced in their transformation from uneducated menial laborers to professionals when they became itinerant preachers and/or missionaries. Unlike men, however, ideological conflicts over women's roles in the black church hierarchy restricted their access to the clergy. But this did not deter them. They confronted, contested, and engaged black male perceptions of entitlement to exclusive power in the religious life, challenged black male gender oppression, and created a new place for themselves in their communities. Their faith grounded in spiritual beliefs and biblical doctrine, they fought battles for selfhood and independent black womanhood on the religious frontier and discovered new and affirming identities in claims to self-authority. They, too, used autobiography to express and record the history of black women's liberation (Foster 128–29; McKay 141–52).

Other kinds of texts also shed light on the conduct of free nineteenth-century black women and their assertions of self as women in a restrictive world. For example, A Narrative of the Life and Travels of Mrs. Nancy Prince (1850), the work of a free-born Massachusetts black woman (1799), focuses on Prince's travels in Russia, Europe, and Jamaica. The common center in these varied women's narrative constructions (slave, spiritual, and travel narratives) of their lives revolves around their survival in the face of racial and sexual oppression, pride in their achievements, and in their celebrations of self in male and female communities of support and affection. Drawing on resources inside of themselves and their communities, the selves in these narratives asserted control over how they saw and presented themselves to the world outside.[4] They were conscious of strength in spite of great adversity and used those insights against the difficulties they faced.

Early black male autobiographers also celebrated liberated selves in their texts but, in contrast to women, almost always in public stories of individual masculine heroism explicitly enacted to recuperate the manhood they lost to white patriarchy as slaves. For African enslavement in the West and European colonialization of Africa cost black men—holders of economic and political power over women, children, and weaker men in their homelands—the power to exercise dominance over others. Thus, white patriarchy rendered African men powerless (like women), psychologically emasculating them and effecting a symbolic relational change in their sexual status to the systems of power. Since Reconstruction institutionalized racism, as a force in the social fabric of American life, has reinforced the subordinate status of black men.[5] In reaction to this perception of loss, black male concepts of manhood, since slavery, developed in conformity to the western European paradigm (almost universally accepted by men) with domination ("power over" others) as its most important component: power over women, over less powerful men, economic and political power. Consequently, the long history of violent confrontation between black male powerlessness and white male power, from slavery to the present, has deep roots in the black male quest to recover a black manhood that, unfortunately, is predicated on the exercise of power and control outside of the self.[6] No comparable aspect of a search for womanhood exists in black women's stories, although black women in slavery lost control over their productive and reproductive labor and, since Reconstruction, have suffered the racial and sexual oppressions of institutionalized racism, sexism, and classism. Their losses appear not to have destroyed them psychologically as women.

The identity construction of black women in autobiography thus comes out of a separate tradition from black men's. For twentieth-century black women identity is grounded in models of nineteenth-century black women who passed on to their generations the most vital lesson of their experiences: black womanhood was not static or a single ideal. The selves in the stories of the early foremothers reveal black female identity as a process of ongoing reinvention of self under the pressures of race, class, and gender oppressions. While one cannot overestimate the damaging effects of black and white, male and female dominance on black women's agency, the group turned away from absolute victim status by rejecting other-determined and unachievable (for them) models of womanhood to shape its identity out of its own self-definition. For example, slave or free-born nineteenth-century black women, as members of a white-designated inferior racial group, knew that the conditions of their lives denied them access to the construct of white womanhood. As a result, they set about the task of reconstructing selves out of the only reality they could claim: their experiences and the need to survive.[7] Sojourner Truth's well-known declaration that in spite of the brutalization she suffered in slavery she was still a woman (Akron, Ohio, 1851) remains one of the most militant assertions of self-assuredness of black womanhood and black women's rejection of the model of white womanhood. And, instead of lamenting their inability to be like white women, or the other patriarchal efforts to defeminize them such as with stereotypes of the mammy and the whore, Truth and other women like her focused attention on how to survive and how to enable others (black men and children) to do likewise. For that it was necessary to maintain flexibility in determining their survival strategies but also to define "true black womanhood" through race-centered analyses that promoted "uplift" for the entire black group. The black female narrative tradition thus evolved from the process of reinventing the self out of the specificities of each black woman's experiences. The narratives of Brent and others of her time illustrate that black survival (their own and that of others), not the quest to recuperate lost selves, motivated these women's active subversion of black victimization. They turned to their own resources and discovered a power within their powerlessness that enabled them to resist the devastating impact of white power over the black self.[8]

Twentieth-century daughters and granddaughters of earlier "scribbling" black women continue to write themselves through issues of individual and

collective survival in a world that still denigrates blackness and privileges maleness over femaleness. Among the writings of this group there is a visible trend
that extends the implications of nineteenth-century self-assuredness of black
womanhood into a complex recognition of different levels of power in the self,
even under the racist and sexist conditions of modern American life. The single
most pronounced aspect of these narratives is in their narrators's rejection of
black victim status in favor of a self-empowered black female self at the center
of their identity. To examine this trend, this study focuses on the autobiographies of Zora Neale Hurston, Marian Anderson, and Lorene Carey. These three
women came of age at different times in this century, their experiential narrative
selves are strikingly different from one another, but through the strategies of
identity construction they create narrative selves who assume a measure of
ownership of their lives. The narratives in this study, published during periods
when major black male writers had race-representative black selves exploding
against their victimization by white racism, present female narrators that are
less psychologically embattled and more in control of their lives than male
narrators. These women make of the black self-story a mechanism that adds
their own revolutionary dimension to a now long and culturally significant
tradition. This tradition rejects some accepted black cultural conventions and
sees autobiography as a weapon in the continuing search for black freedom,
thus reinforcing the centrality of the tradition. Each writer presents a self that,
to quote Tony Morrison, is "solitary and representative" (339), both individual
and a member of the "tribe." Above all, each writer rejects the discourse of
racist and/or sexist definitions of the black self and seeks to empower black
people to take control of their lives.

Hurston's view of herself and her world (black and white) were affected by
forces outside of the experiences of most black people born in the South at
the end of the nineteenth century. Her early years in Eatonville, Florida, the
first black incorporated town in the country, not only saved her from the harshness of grinding poverty and white violence that large numbers of southern
blacks in that era experienced but also fueled her antipathy to an identity
embedded in racial and sexual victimization. Although some of her works have
enjoyed literary eminence since the 1970s, her refusal to subscribe to a race-
representative identity based on group oppression made her singularly unpopu-
lar with many of her cohorts, the black writers of the Harlem Renaissance.[9]

Hurston's autobiography, *Dust Tracks on a Road,* was published in 1942.
The book sold well, winning the *Saturday Review's* $1000-prize for its con-
tributions to "the field of race relations." But for black critics then, and
many black and white critics now, it is a problem text. No lesser a Hurston
advocate than Alice Walker, who was most responsible for recuperating that

writer from close to thirty years of literary neglect, calls it the most "unfortunate" thing Hurston ever wrote. Complaints focus on Hurston's distortion of some facts of her life, the book's lack of racial conflict, which some detractors see as a betrayal of black group interests, and perceptions of its obsequiousness to whites.

Even excluding political materials that Hurston's biographer Robert Hemenway discovered were editorially excised from the original manuscript of *Dust Tracks*,[10] this book, viewed from another angle, is a fascinating construction of a black female narrative self that transgresses popular expectations of black women's autobiography. In Hurston's refusal to produce a race-representative text of oppression, *Dust Tracks* breaks with certain rhetorical patterns of the slave narrative tradition in favor of a strategy that frees black autobiography from the ideological supremacy of race.[11]

In this text the narrator Hurston makes no attempt to castigate whites in general for injustices to blacks. Black people in *Dust Tracks* do not suffer from direct malevolent racism. In fact, the protagonist suffers her most personal injuries at the hands of blacks: the community, which left her mother alone on the day of her birth to attend a "hog-killing"; her mother's death, which orphaned the girl while she was still young in years; her father's desertion of his children by immediately remarrying after his wife's death; the wicked stepmother, whom she almost killed in a fight; and the marriage she left because her husband objected to her career ambitions. But these failings in black people do not overshadow her positive experiences within the black community. From her mother and other black women in Eatonville, the young narrator learned lessons of independent black female selfhood in a sexist black world. As a young woman alone, in Baltimore and Washington, D.C., black teachers and professors supported her financially and emotionally. Her first story was published in a black journal, and, even more important, the southern black folk community entrusted her with their cultural lore, from which she created for herself a place in literary history.

Many white people figure prominently in this narrative. In the story of her birth the narrator chooses to highlight the help of a white man against the absence of the black nanny who ought to have been there and to point out the man's interest in her while she was growing up. Equally important to the early stages of her development, she writes, were the white women from the North who complimented her childhood intelligence and gave her the first books she owned; the help of a white woman who enabled her to attend Barnard College; the interest of Franz Boaz, her Barnard mentor, even beyond her college years; and the patronage of a wealthy white woman who supported her research for many years. These and other positive connections with white people in Hurston's text transgressed the conventions of black autobiography, and depict a racial harmony between blacks and whites that was unprecedented in black literature of her era.

Hurston's work previous to *Dust Tracks* cast her as a rebel among the black literati of her day, and her autobiography placed her further outside of that circle.[12] But she must have known this would happen when she deliberately wrote against the grain of popular black expectations of this narrative form. For, in contrast to the level of black anger, rage, and hostility toward whites at the time, *Dust Tracks* was a black voice rejecting the call for a representative black victim self. Her text specifically responded to the explicit brutality and violence of texts such as Richard Wright's novel *Native Son* (1940) and later his autobiography, *Black Boy* (1945). More graphically than any before them, these books depicted the pain, anguish, and despair of what it meant to be black and male in white America and indicted white patriarchy for crimes against black manhood.

While still writing in the tradition of the search for freedom in black autobiography, Hurston used *Dust Tracks* to argue that the "self" in her text was not the self in Wright's. She matched the reality of his Mississippi of demoralized and alienated black people—the total despair, brutality, hunger, and death—with her Eatonville, with its luscious fruit for the picking and a segregated black culture, where the folk worked hard, loved, hated, and fought one another with great passion, separated from the worst aspects of racism. Lacking constant, direct contact with white culture, these blacks nevertheless had their full share of life's pleasures and sorrows. Hurston's narrative self identifies with them and not with the characters in Wright's texts and, in so doing, ensured that the life of the folk was equally represented in black literary culture. Besides, she did not want to deny her own positive experiences with some whites.

Hurston's racial tolerance was not in conflict with her identification with black culture. In fact, in foregrounding her identity in the richness and emotional security of the preurban nonmaterialistic black culture of her "village," she offered an alternative (positive) perspective on the black experience. In representing black people for the most part as emotionally independent of white people, with control over their lives, and in suggesting her protagonist's greater harmony with the white world than most blacks and whites were aware of, she refuted the representativeness of the black racial protest text and challenged the patriarchal text of Euro-American white discourse on black life. Faced with black group demoralization inscribed in the texts on both sides of black-white relations, Hurston used *Dust Tracks* to invent a narrative identity that rejected the primacy of slave history and the supremacy of white racism over black lives. At the same time, in her use of dazzling metaphors in the black idiom and stories of the colorful exploits of the folk, she maintained allegiance to her community, the most autonomous American blacks of her time.

Looking closely at the inner life of the community, *Dust Tracks* was the first secular autobiography by a black woman that explicitly addressed personal tensions between black women and men and highlighted the sexism of black men and their domination of women.[13] In her own home, as a child, the textual Hurston knew of conflicts between her parents and her mother's unhappiness in her marriage. She also observed the ill treatment other women received at the hands of their husbands and lovers as well as black male efforts to silence women especially by excluding their voices from ritual storytelling sessions— the community's most significant group activity. She acclaimed the folk culture but did not deny the subordinating effects of black male authority on women. Her discussions of black male sexism were most personal in her choice to end her marriage, rather than sacrifice her career on the altar of a love that required her to accept male domination.

But *Dust Tracks* is more than a revision of the racial/sexual self in black and black women's narrative. Hurston does not only break with—or expand— earlier patterns in personal narrative; she strengthens women's tradition of valorizing peer group and intergenerational bonds between black women. In her childhood Hurston's best girlfriend's ear was a safe place for her wild fantasies. Her mother listened and encouraged her stories and was the buffer between Hurston and her father, who sought to stifle her imagination with his ideas of women's place in the world.

Dust Tracks liberated black identity from the straitjacket of racial struggle and replaced this central element with black womanhood in negative and positive inter- and intraracial and sexual group relationships and encounters. Although most of her peers saw her strategy as a betrayal of the community's political agenda for black writing, Hurston's text boldly inscribed a revolutionary alternative for women's narrative into the black tradition. As autobiography, it expanded the boundaries of the slave narrative tradition and examined previously unexplored gender conflicts and tensions between black women and men. Her use of folk language and traditions reinforced connections between the educated protagonist of her text and the people of her village and lessened the gap between the city and the country in black cultural expression. *Dust Tracks* was groundbreaking, leading the way to other self-empowering creative inventions of narrative identities that enrich the black autobiographical tradition.

Singer Marian Anderson's autobiography, *My Lord, What a Morning* (1956), appeared shortly before the mass demonstrations and civil disobedience of the 1960s and in the wake of *Brown v. Board of Education* (1954).[14] It is doubtful that Anderson ever heard of Hurston or read *Dust Tracks on a Road*. But, while the circumstances of these women's lives were different, strategies of identity construction in their autobiographies make Anderson's text a direct descendant of Hurston's. For, like her predecessor, she rejected the black victim self and did not postulate race and class (the text does little with gender considerations) as obstacles that have the ultimate power to determine the destiny of black people who worked hard and willed themselves to succeed.

Born in Philadelphia into "genteel poverty," in 1902, Anderson was the eldest of three daughters.[15] Before marriage her mother taught in the state, but afterward, to help out the family's finances, she took in laundry. Her father, a laborer, died when Marian Anderson was eight years old. Left almost destitute, the mother and her daughters moved into the home of the children's paternal grandparents. Three women headed that household: a grandmother, who dominated the home and cared for children of working mothers in her home; a young mother reduced to backbreaking menial labor to contribute to the family's fiscal welfare; and an aunt, who ran the house. In turn-of-the-century Philadelphia racial and economic conditions made life especially difficult for blacks, but the Anderson women together survived the city's worst hardships with dignity. Anderson writes with pride of her mother's personal dignity even under the most difficult circumstances.

Marian Anderson made her singing debut when she was eight (she began singing in the choir at age six), in Union Baptist Church, where her family worshiped. Through her teenage years she sang in churches around the city and at events outside of the church. In high school she decided to become a classical concert performer. Successful appearances in many countries in Europe in the 1930s and 1940s set the stage for her subsequent acceptance on the white American stage. She later became the best-known and most widely acclaimed black singer in the world. The musical career of the "Lady of Philadelphia," as Anderson was by then called, reached its pinnacle in 1955, when she became the first black person to sing with the New York Metropolitan Opera.

As the narrative self of a black woman in white America, *My Lord, What a Morning* is as troublesome to some as Hurston's *Dust Tracks*. Between her birth at the turn of the century and the book's publication, just past its midpoint, Anderson lived through momentous world events that must have seriously affected her outlook on life, but that she never mentions in *My Lord*. For instance, she gives cursory attention to difficulties she faced traveling in the Jim Crow South in the 1930s and 1940s (between her European trips); she volunteers none of her reactions to the fascist rise to power in Europe in the 1930s (she was there during the unfolding of that tragedy) nor to the success of *Brown v. Board* and its implications for legal segregation in this country. Throughout the work there are numerous silences on personal and public matters. Anderson does not discuss her family's financial situation when she was growing up nor offer information on her friends and their relationship to music. Nor do readers learn if singing in church led her to the career that she chose or how, when, and who introduced her to opera. Even the Daughters of the American Revolution's (DAR) refusal to permit her to sing in Constitution Hall in 1939 and the triumph of her Easter morning concert at the Lincoln Memorial are treated without fanfare or the credit due their importance as history. The self in *My Lord, What a Morning* does not indulge in emotional feelings: neither hurt nor anger, arrogance or even pride in her achievements over the course of her extraordinary musical career.[16] Analogically, the text is a site that envelops, almost entirely, Marian Anderson's positive journey through the silken cocoon of the world of *her* music.

Following in the footsteps of Hurston, Anderson's autobiography does not protest white racism through the black victim. But there are differences between the selves created by each woman in her narrative. Unlike Hurston, whose text makes clear that there is no cultural gap between the folk culture and the educated urbanized protagonist, Anderson's single-minded focus on concert music suggests a separation between her and the concerns of her group. Even her inclusion of spirituals as standard parts of her repertoire does not dispel the impression that Anderson (although the lesser academic of the two women) loses the connection that the college-educated intellectual Hurston maintained with the roots of black culture.[17]

While it can reasonably be argued that Anderson's apparent separation from her cultural roots has links to the demands for undivided loyalty that a success-ful career in opera—the music of high culture—made on her, I believe other political motives were at work here. For, although Anderson openly supported no ideological platform and avoided overt political involvement, she was not apolitical, and, in spite of her fame and achievements, she cared deeply about the welfare of the black community.[18] The self-presentation in *My Lord* was a deliberate rhetorical strategy growing out of political intentions she had for this work.

Those intentions are most apparent in linguistic differences between Hurston's and Anderson's texts. Hurston's language and style (in spite of its folk culture qualities) are explicit in their address to an erudite audience of white and black adults, while Anderson's text, although compelling, is rendered in clear, unembellished, uncomplicated expository prose, with few metaphors. In my view she wrote *My Lord* for a young black audience. To this group the text offered an alternative black identity at a time when racial group pressures were weighted on the side of loud vocal anger and hostility toward whites for their treatment of blacks. Written to appeal to less violent internal sensibilities, like *Dust Tracks, My Lord, What a Morning* repudiates what Anderson might have seen as vulgarity in the overt protest of Wright's *Native Son* and *Black Boy*, Ann Petry's *Street* (1946) (a work it is unlikely she read), and James Baldwin's *Notes of a Native Son* (1955).[19] These writers lashed out in rage at white America through narrative selves that shocked most readers. In her focus on her art Anderson's protagonist empowered herself to achieve success in an oppressive society and at the same time to avoid painful displays of impotent anger. This was the message she wanted to give to a young black audience. But how does one achieve this level of self-empowerment?

Self-confidence, beginning at an early age, is one of the fundamental elements in the text's recipe for engendering power in the self in the white world. She was very young when she made her decision to be a classical concert singer, and she was alone in her choice, without role models to emulate. Although she had the emotional support of her family, none among them was able to counsel or advise her. That aloneness reverberates in the silences in her autobiography. Yet there is no doubt that she knew what she wanted, and she used that knowledge along with personal commitment and the determination to work hard toward her goals.

How did a black teenage girl from a poor inner-city family headed by women find the self-confidence and the other qualities that enabled her to break through the walls of a profession far removed from the lives of the most successful black people she could have known? An answer lies in nineteenth-century black women's history, in the self-stories of early- and mid-century women such as Harriet Jacobs, Jarena Lee, and dozens of others who grounded survival and achievement in a community of women supporting one another.[20] An even larger number of late-nineteenth- and early-twentieth-century black women, successful across a broad spectrum of professions, from medicine to education, built on earlier foremother examples by responding to the "cult of true womanhood" with a self-chosen life's mission of their own: to "lift as they climbed." As influential "race women" in their communities, individually and collectively (the black women's club movement), they redefined true womanhood to combine black feminist politics with intellectual goals and the practical aspects of day-to-day black life for the racial uplift of all black people. At the turn of the century, in black communities across the country, they exerted a powerful presence on those around them; they were household names filtering through churches and the civic organizations they helped to shape in their communities.[21] Anderson knew some of their names (maybe some of the women) and their successes. Her church, too, had an influence on her. But her most influential models were the remarkably strong, independent women in her household. Secure in themselves as black women who could survive against the odds, they did not indulge in self-pity or lament their hard lot in the world. They nurtured Anderson and her sisters, and they handed down lessons for survival in a difficult world: responsibility, the value of work, tolerance, understanding, and respect for themselves and all others.

Self-confidence and a Victorian concept of human dignity are linked in Anderson's text. In its stylistic presentation, its language, content, and silences, dignity is the signature of *My Lord*. Dignity embodies, among other qualities, the self-control to refrain from publicly expressing rancorous anger and to endure great hardships without complaint. The textual mother—whom the textual daughter reports never complained and never expressed anger—has the same kind of personal dignity that the narrative self in this book espouses. In her instructions to young black people coming of age in the 1950s, the narrator strives to convey the value of that dignity through her own success.

Making of silence a companion to dignity enabled Anderson's protagonist to focus almost entirely on the high artistic life. On one hand, her ideal must have disappointed black readers, who expected militant political narrators in black autobiography, while, on the other, it confounded white racists, who believed in barbaric emotionalism among African Americans. As author of her text, Anderson declares to both groups that there is no single black self. To protect further the image of dignity and self-control she crafts for herself, the protagonist of *My Lord* does not associate herself with black protest movements, although her agenda is similar to many of theirs. Such deliberate strategical actions make this autobiography as political a document as Wright's or any in the school of more overt protest literature. Written against the white text of black people's inability to achieve through hard work, patience, and dignity and against the black text of the dehumanized black brute of Richard Wright's *Native Son* and the angry young man of James Baldwin's *Notes of a Native Son*, *My Lord, What a Morning* joins *Dust Tracks on a Road* to rewrite the narrative of the victimized racial self and to produce a self-empowered survivor of race, politics, and gender oppression.

In the United States, where people of color continue to face humiliating race problems each day, Marian Anderson wanted young black readers to see the possibilities in themselves to excel. Her success, as her narrator accounts for it, combined talent and dedication with the goal of transcending the external limitations of race and class. *My Lord, What a Morning,* perhaps the single most inspiring of black self-narratives, has roots in the mythology of the quintessential "American" character of three hundred years ago who firmly believed that hard work and the will to succeed determine destiny. The story also embodies strong echoes of Booker T. Washington's gospel of passive nonconfrontation with white society. More subtle are its Du Boisian ideals of resistance, which claim power in the self to change some things in the world. Like Du Bois (the archetypal black Victorian of his generation), Anderson used dignity and decorum to a radical end: to undermine a hostile privileged system and to raise herself and her race to a "new sphere." For, like the man who noted in the year following her birth that he walked and conversed on terms of equality with Shakespeare and other (white) historical luminaries and who refused second-class citizenship in America, Anderson's survival included her right of claim to the pinnacle of her profession, where no black person before her had been. Like Du Bois, she refused to accept a white-prescribed place in the world, and she wanted others to do the same. Her long psychological journey from her birth in a South Philadelphia rented room to the Metropolitan Opera Company in New York City had no resemblance to the geographical distance between those cities and was as difficult as any made by other Afro-American survivors. In the best sense of the phrase, she was one of Du Bois's admirable Philadelphia Negroes.[22]

Zora Neale Hurston and Marian Anderson were born in the same decade but grew up in separate worlds and with different goals and ambitions. For all black people in the first half of this century, legalized racism and segregation made upward social and economic mobility extremely difficult to achieve. With few opportunities for decent employment, the productive labor of most black women was cruelly exploited in domestic or farm work. Hurston, during the earlier part of her adulthood, and Anderson, for all of her career, were more fortunate than most. With skill, determination, and the help and encouragement of black and white people, Hurston, for a part of her life, and Anderson, for all of hers, avoided the dead end of menial work. Through no fault of her own, Hurston's career declined by mid-century, while Anderson's reached its high-water mark at that time. Given their interests and lifestyles, it is unlikely these women met each other or that Anderson even heard of her contemporary. Hurston, however, would have heard of Anderson's 1939 Lincoln Memorial Easter morning concert, had she not been aware of her before, and, in rural Florida, where she spent her last years, perhaps even of the triumph of the black woman who was the first of her race to sing with the Metropolitan Opera Company. For all the differences between them, these women were successful pioneers who early in their lives did not perceive race or gender as insurmountable barriers to how they chose to live in the world. It does not surprise, then, that both wrote narratives rejecting the impotence of black group victim status for the possibilities of individual agency. While Hurston later discovered limits to her ability to control her destiny, her narrative is a monument to the ideal of autonomy and success achieved by a few, like Anderson, and a sign—a promise by the side of the road for younger women such as Lorene Carey.[23]

Born in Marian Anderson's home city in 1957, more than half a century after the "First Lady," Lorene Carey is a member of the first black post–civil rights generation in America. Her autobiography, *Black Ice* (1991), appeared almost fifty years after the publication of *Dust Tracks on a Road* and thirty-five years after *My Lord, What a Morning*. She may not have read Anderson's autobiography, but she was familiar with the accomplishments of the black woman whom large numbers of white people across the world and almost all other black people knew by name and whom, more than all others, middle-class Philadelphians held in enormous esteem.

When Carey entered college (in Philadelphia) just past the mid-1970s, many social changes in the country, begun in the 1950s, had altered the America that Hurston and Anderson knew in their times. Hurston's literary significance, thanks to writer Alice Walker and white and black feminist critics, was then in its contemporary ascendancy. In college Carey would have heard of—and most likely read at least one work (probably not the autobiography) by—the rambunctious black woman who refused to conform to white or black expectations during and after the Harlem Renaissance and who wrote the first novel with a black female protagonist who consciously sought and gained personal autonomy.[24] She would have learned of Hurston's involuntary disappearance from the literary world for almost three decades; of her subsequent indigence; of Alice Walker's pilgrimage to find her; and of the likelihood that Hurston's body lies buried in an unmarked Florida grave.[25] When Lorene Carey walked through the doors of her university, there were some black men and a few black women professors in her school, and some of them had not attended black colleges; there were courses in black studies and black literature, and in some selected courses in American literature students read black women writers.[26] By a long stretch, the world she entered was not perfect, but black women were achieving and competing in places in which earlier writers of that group could not have imagined themselves. And, while racism and sexism were still rampant, Carey did not have to begin where black women of earlier generations had.

In addition to the social and institutional changes of the 1960s and 1970s, Carey's black middle-class background offered her many advantages that were foreclosed to Hurston and Anderson in their young years. On her father's side she was a descendant of "old, genteel black Philadelphia" and was born into a family with sufficient past successes to permit her claims of entitlement to advantages larger than those of her parents. Her father, a graduate of Lincoln University in Pennsylvania and a high school teacher, was the son of a mother who inherited a real estate business from her father, the profits of which helped to provide scholarships for black college students. His father, a corporate salesman, had once played semiprofessional baseball in the Negro Leagues. The family valued education highly and was in a financial position to assist the children in their search for goals higher than their elders had achieved. Carey's protagonist often reminds herself that she was "raised" for those advantages:

> Why else had my mother personally petitioned the principal of Lea School so that I could attend the integrated showcase public grade school at the edge of the University of Pennsylvania? . . . Why else would she have dragged me across the street on my knees when I balked on the morning before the big

I.Q. test, the one that could get me into the top first-grade class, the class on which free instrument and French lessons, advanced Saturday-morning classes, and a special, individualized reading series were bestowed? . . . Why else had I learned to hold myself [at such an early age] to standards just beyond my reach? . . . the thriftshop Dickens volumes . . . *Weekly Readers,* and Spanish flashcards? (32)

Black Ice covers a very small period of time in comparison to the narratives of Hurston and Anderson, who wrote their stories much later in their lives than Carey. In place of the broad sweep of experience in the earlier works, this text recalls only two years, the time in the mid-1970s that Carey spent in New England, at the exclusive St. Paul's School, in Concord, New Hampshire, and her exploration seventeen years later of their memory. Unlike the self-assured mature views of self in Anderson and Hurston, this book focuses on the late-teen protagonist's recall of her feelings of displacement from her customary community of support and her engagement in a personal struggle for emotional maturity and space for herself in a world larger than that in her former life. Unlike Hurston's and Anderson's life stories, however, which are structured around deliberate silences, Carey's style (in contrast to the memoir) suggests youthful openness as a goal: the writer's search for self-knowledge through writing. The book, a self-reflective presentation of the protagonist's search for an understanding of who she was at St. Paul's School, explores the silences surrounding the "pain and shame and cowardice and fear . . . kept secret" (193) in the stories of most black women. The textual Carey writes, she says, to "audit the layers of reminiscences, to check one against the other" (127), taking into account that she cannot completely trust what she thinks she remembers. For "memory is a card shark, reshuffling the deck to hide what [she] fears to know, unable to keep from fingering the ace at the bottom of the deck even when [she's] doing nothing more than playing Fish in the daylight with children" (127).

In her story Carey's narrator observes that, by the time she was accepted at St. Paul's School, she and her family were ready for and receptive to new educational opportunities and emotional experiences for her and her sister. Although she thought she knew that St. Paul's School would change her when she entered it, the "foreign" territory of the New Hampshire prep school taught her how thoroughly unprepared she was for her two years there. The feelings of isolation and alienation experienced by the narrator and her black cohorts at St. Paul's were not unrelated to changes occurring in the school at the time; among them, the institution, recently turned coed and multiracial, was struggling to define its new identity. But, vastly outnumbered and far removed from their communities of support, this generation of African-American pioneers were burdened by a sense of multiple expectations of them—from families and friends, the black community in general, St. Paul's School, and, worst of all, their expectations of themselves. Why were they in such a strange place, separated from families, friends, and the culture of blackness? In the tradition of black intellectuals before them, they surmised they were preparing for careers as "race" women and men. But such a high calling offered no comfort in the daily events of their lives, and Carey's protagonist admits to often feeling "self-loathing, made worse by a poised bravado . . . duty and obligation to . . . family, to the memory of dead relatives, to [black] people" (5). There were confusion and unanswerable questions as well: "Was it true that these [white] teachers expected less of [blacks] than of [their] white peers? Or had [they] mistaken kindness for condescension? Were [the] black kids a social experiment?" (5). Living constantly with these anxieties took a toll on their lives.

The time at St. Paul's School for the textual Lorene Carey was brief but intensely emotional. Toward the end of her second year, shortly before graduation, Vernon Jordan, then president of the National Urban League, visited the school and left the black students even more convinced of the seriousness of their social responsibilities. He told them: "The most important thing . . . is to get everything you can here. You kids are getting a view of white America that we never even got close to. . . . We couldn't even dream of it" (202). Already full of their own idealism, the words reinforced for these students the obligations of the educated black elite to the masses, including the less fortunate of their group; it was a restatement of the early-twentieth-century black dictum: racial uplift and the call to "the Talented Tenth."[27] Carey and her friends "wolfed down" Jordan's visit among the experiences of the school, holding them to "digest" later.

In *Black Ice* Carey's protagonist attempts to recapture her youthful feelings of St. Paul's School from a distance of seventeen years and to recreate the self that survived those experiences. Her return to the school after fifteen years (as teacher and later as a member of the Board of Trustees) and her need to write this book were part of her effort to reclaim the girl she left behind for a long time in New Hampshire, hoping to forget her. To go back was to accept the meaning of "old rage and fear, ambition, self-consciousness, love, curiosity, energy, hate, envy, compulsion, [and] fatigue"; to end her denial of these feelings while there (4). Unlike Hurston and Anderson, she admits to the unreliability of memory and the uncertainty of "truth" in her reconstruction of self. And, because of differences between her time and theirs, Carey's protagonist seeks to reconcile the racial self with the American self without denying one for the other: to claim her American identity in its entirety, a unity denied black people in the United States for generations.[28]

But, while Carey's construction and her complex interrogation of the racial self in the white world and tensions in intrafamilial relationships signal new advances in the development of black autobiography, she remains reticent to probe the issue of violence between black women and men like most of her female predecessors. Most notably, her neglect to explore her ambivalence surrounding the rape she suffers at the hands of a visiting black male student to the school (even though she includes the incident in the text) is an unfortunate silence in an otherwise open story.

Through generations of black women writing-the-self in the United States, the center of their life stories remains black survival. Lorene Carey's book is no exception. Amid the pain of the St. Paul's school experiences, one of the elements this protagonist credits for her survival was the "narratives," including those of her great grandfather, which, with those of other people in her life, spoke to her "honestly about growing up black in America" (6). Of them she writes: "[The narratives] burst into my silence, and in my head, they shouted and chattered and whispered and sang together. I am writing this book to become part of that unruly conversation . . ."(6); and "Without the stories and the songs, I am mute" (237).

Like Hurston and Anderson, Lorene Carey tells her story so that her narrative will also be a part of the stories that speak to growing up black in America and surviving beyond the victimization of whiteness. But *Black Ice* differs from Hurston's *Dust Tracks,* in which the black-white conjunction is cast mainly in positive terms, and from Anderson's *My Lord,* in which, aside from the musical connections, that conjunction is muffled. Instead, Carey foregrounds race in her text without embracing the tenets of the popular protest literature of the 1940s and 1950s or the silences in Hurston's and Anderson's texts. Rather, Carey's story confronts head-on the hurt and the pain that is the price blacks pay for claiming their racial selves in their American lives. As a new-generation black woman survivor, the self in the text refuses to deny or keep secret the trauma of becoming that self without compromising her dignity. In this respect *Black Ice* also breaks new ground and is a "story not to pass on,"[29] for it is painful and healing as it brings together the complex, inseparable strands of the American/African-American self: "I began writing about St. Paul's School when I stopped thinking of my prep-school experience as an aberration from the common run of black life in America" (6). *Black Ice,* a new story in a venerable tradition of resistance, sings its own song of black liberation, which, like Hurston's and Anderson's texts, among others, embraces the challenge to survive by transforming the would-be victim of race and sex into a self-empowered free self.

Hurston, Anderson, Carey, and generations of black women writers use multiple strategies to tell their stories in fiction, autobiography, poetry, drama, and the personal essay. These stories shape black female identity in a way that the self, whatever the nature of invention, is a witness against the racism, sexism, and classism of the master text and not its absolute victim. Do black women writers who participate in this self-affirmation compromise their racial and/or gender integrity by rejecting a tradition that isolates and centralizes the worst effects of racism on black people in narrative? This is clearly not so. For whatever their strategies of self-construction, active resistance to oppressions of all kinds has been at the center of the history of black women's lives in this country from slavery to the present time, and narratives like these are as politically significant as those that foreground more overt modes of protest. The many varieties of black women's stories need to be heard and accorded their rightful place in the tradition.

For too long in the West, dominant patriarchy excluded the voices of other groups from the general discourse. The 1960s were the beginning years of the serious challenge to that authority. Then black studies and women's studies began to thrust themselves into the intellectual arena and the practical life of the nation. Even then, the stories of black women, for all of their contributions to the liberation movements, continued to be ignored and excluded. Black men, preoccupied with the recovery of lost manhood, were hostile to having "their" women be other than subservient to them, wanted them to walk behind them in the struggle for black rights, bear black babies for the revolution, remain economically dependent, and permit themselves to be abused by men to help them feel like "real" men. White middle-class women, leaders of the women's movement, also preoccupied with the frustrations of the nineteenth-century pedestal on which they were long confined, gave no thought to race or class. By the mid-1970s "All the Women Are White, All the Blacks Are Men"[30] defined the tensions between black men and white women, on one side, and black women, poor women, and other groups of color, on the other.

Thanks to the strenuous efforts of pioneering black women and their supporters, over the past two decades the voices of black women have prominently entered the intellectual and political arenas of American life.[31] And yet the history is clear that, although black women's voices were silenced for a long time, they were never silent. From Phillis Wheatley's eighteenth-century metaphysical poetry to the fiery essays of early- and late-nineteenth-century women such as Maria Stewart and Anna Julia Cooper and the award-winning writings of late-twentieth-century women, black women in the United States have always raised their voices, even when no one else listened. In an interview Toni Morrison once remarked that she would write even if there were no one to buy her books.[32]

By no measure representative of all black women's strategies for writing the self, the black women's texts explored in this essay examine a particular trend that is observable in some twentieth-century writers, a trend that also illustrates the significance of varieties of black women's writings for study in the academy. Issues of identity construction are vital in understanding one's relationship to—and behavior in—the world, and black women's identities have been shaped by forces other than those that shaped black men's and white women's. Black studies and women's studies programs fail in their mission to revise the patriarchal exclusionary system of education when they do not give full recognition to the lives and experiences of black and other women of color. On the larger educational canvas U.S. education will continue to fail the future of the nation until all young people have access to materials that will teach them to respect the lives and experiences of all peoples, including black women.

All of our students need to have access to black women's stories for classroom discussions if we are to provide them with a sound education, which involves a political education as well. Additionally, the act of writing, especially by groups historically marginalized in Western culture, is political, and black writing in the United States has been and continues to be a political act. With its explicit aim to break down barriers of prejudice and injustice against an entire group, the act of writing the black female self in the West is the most political of all. And, while all autobiography is a struggle for literary control over an individual life, for Afro-American women an assertive self—expressed in Western terms within the constraints of race, class, and gender—is a political and discursive achievement. The history of the struggle and courage of antebellum slave women (and men) to gain literacy and the zeal that makes black women's autobiographies—from *Incidents in the Life of a Slave Girl* to *Black Ice*—contributors to a tradition that interrogates the race, class, and gender ideologies of the master narrative speak volumes about the successful negotiation that occurs at the intersection of self-empowerment, self-representation, aesthetics, and politics in African-American culture.

NOTES

1. The relationship between the acquisition of literacy and the black challenge to racial oppression in the eighteenth and nineteenth centuries significantly contributed to the development of African-American written traditions and the making of the Afro-American self in America at that time. Somewhat mistakenly, many slaves even believed that literacy, forcibly denied them by their masters and the law in some regions, would lead to—or actually was—freedom. The seriousness with which they held these beliefs can be readily understood by looking at their determination to acquire the rudiments of reading and writing, even at the risk of life and limb. Their awareness that the Western debate over the humanity of Africans included the issue of their intellectual capability to

learn to read and write, even as that instruction was withheld from them, made the stakes in achieving literacy more than an intellectual activity. Thus, when former slaves made "Written by Him/Herself" a part of their texts, the words were a declaration of immense personal and group pride in physical and psychological survival.

2. This does not suggest that all male slaves enjoyed the kind of sanctioned mobility that Douglass did. In fact, Douglass was permitted more mobility than the majority of male slaves, including those who rose to prominence after their escape from bondage.

3. During the antebellum period spiritual narratives were written by free blacks, some of whom were former slaves.

4. One of the remarkable attributes of American slaves was how little each of them appeared to have internalized a lack of her or his self-worth. The sense of value in the self kept alive their hopes for release from undeserved bondage and fueled the fires of their efforts to struggle against slavery. For slave women their realization of the interlocking nature of race and gender oppression forced them to greater self-dependency in order to survive. Central to the will to survive was the knowledge that others, especially children, could not survive unless they did. This sense of responsibility for the future of the race, handed down from one generation of women to the next, together with the support that emanated from within the women's community, were among the most important of internal resources on which slave women drew to sustain themselves and help those who depended on them.

5. The horrendous racial oppression of black men is a fact. A number of good studies focus on the effects of institutionalized racism on the status of the group in America since the end of the Civil War. Although slavery was brutal before that time, racial violence and white supremacy after the war combined to intimidate all black people in an even more bloody way than before. In the late nineteenth and first third of the twentieth century the lynching of black men was the most potent weapon that white men used to reinforce their racial supremacy. See, for instance, Hall 1979; Finkelman 1992; McGovern 1982; and Tolnay and Massey 1992.

6. I am grateful to Kimberly Benston (following the May 1991 conference on politics and culture at Harvard University at which this essay was first presented) for suggesting the need to discuss differences between male and female identity formation; and to Stanlie James, Florencia Mallon, Nell Irvin Painter, Judylyn Ryan, and Craig Werner, who were my sounding boards as I worked through the concept of lost black manhood in comparison to the greater security black women have in their black womanhood and the relationship between black women's identity and their strategies for survival. I also thank Nanci Calamari, student and friend, for her useful and perceptive reading of the first draft of the final version of this essay.

7. Although reality, like experience, is mediated by the subjectivity of one's perceptions of day-to-day life and the circumstances of that life, for nineteenth-century black people in America, experience filtered through memory, as unreliable as that is, in addition to a strong faith in ultimate justice and a sense of their own human value, offered the only ground on which they could develop a theory of who they were as human beings.

8. My argument is that, although black women share race and class with black men, issues of sex and sexual exploitation make identity construction between the two groups

different. At the same time, conditions of slavery and discriminations of race, sex, and class made it impossible for nineteenth-century black women to have access to the identity of the "cult of true womanhood." The survival of all black people required of them an all-inclusive theory of "true black womanhood." Poet Nikki Giovanni believes that black women are the only "group that derives its identity from itself" (Giovanni 1971, 144). Conversely, I argue, the degree to which black male narrators focus on racial oppression against them by white men reinforces the notion that black men perceive black freedom as the struggle for power vested in Western images of manhood.

9. In comparison to most southern blacks, Hurston, born in Eatonville, Florida, in the 1890s, had the benefit of an emotionally and economically stable childhood until her mother's death when she was twelve years old (she says). Subsequent disagreements with her family caused her to leave home at age fourteen, and in 1925, following stops in Baltimore and Washington, D.C., she arrived in New York, where she became one of the writers involved in the activities of the Harlem Renaissance. But Hurston's insistence on writing about the black folk culture and portraying black people outside of the ever-constant debilitating effects of white racism led many of her associates to think she was using her talents to betray the best interests of black people. Black critics were especially severe on her because of this issue.

10. See appendix to Hurston [1942] 1984, 332–44.

11. In the slave narrative tradition the life moves from a period of innocence of her or his condition to awareness of the horrors of slave reality. This is followed by the decision to free the self from this condition and the eventual release that depends largely on the protagonist's initiative. The narratives include recitations of the degradation of slave life and call for well-thinking white northerners to seek actively the abolition of slavery. Hurston turns away from that model and depicts southern black life with positive and negative effects on individuals in the black community, which she views as a place for black renewal, since it was the source of her creativity. Yet this deviation did not interfere with the narrative's representing the black search for freedom in a racially and sexually restrictive country.

12. Most notably, Hurston's novel *Their Eyes Were Watching God*, perhaps her best work, was not well received by the most influential black writers and critics of her day. See note 9 for further elaboration on the disagreement other black writers and critics had with Hurston.

13. In nineteenth-century spiritual narratives tensions between black women and men occur largely over the women's right to preach. In other kinds of autobiography black women, until Hurston, foregrounded race in their autobiographies to present to the world a racially solid front with black men. Hurston shows, however, that even in Edenic Eatonville black women were not treated as equals by black men, and she does not hesitate to condemn sexism by black men in her own and other women's lives.

14. A substantial part of the discussion on Marian Anderson in this essay also appears in the introduction to the reprint edition of the autobiography. See the introduction by Nellie Y. McKay in Anderson [1956] 1993.

15. *Genteel poverty* is a term Gwendolyn Brooks uses in her autobiography, *Report from Part One*, to indicate the condition of poor people who are not demoralized by their

poverty and who do not internalize the situation as irremediable. In the case of both Brooks and Anderson the stress their parents put on education and the permission the families gave each of these young girls to see herself as poet and concert artist, although those seemed like unrealistic goals, illustrate aspects of gentility in spite of poverty. Both Brooks and Anderson had poor parents who expected their children to hold a higher social position in the world than they did. They grew up in surroundings permeated by the politics of racial uplift.

16. Black women's autobiographies are well-known for silences regarding their private lives, from silences about sexuality to ones concerning feelings on social subjects. In this way Anderson's narrative is not singular. What makes her stand out, however, is her reticence even in how she expresses her sense of joy over her successes. Far from appearing to be the superstar she really was, she tells her story with an understatement that makes it seem that others with her ambition can succeed as easily as she did. This posture is what partly led me to conclude that she saw her audience for the book as one not sufficiently worldly-wise to be overwhelmed by her accomplishments and for whom she could be a good role model.

17. I am grateful to Paul Lauter for pointing out to me that even Anderson's musical renditions of the spirituals have much in common with her operatic productions.

18. There are anecdotal accounts of how Anderson, as a celebrity traveling through the South, took time to talk to the black people she met, even to children, about their lives and hers. A close friend of mine, while still in high school in the South, once interviewed Anderson and continues to speak of her warmth, generosity, and genuine concern for the lives of black people.

19. Both *Street* (a novel) and *Notes of a Native Son* (autobiographical essays) are very angry books. Petry explores the racial and sexual oppression of black women through the plot of an ambitious single mother living in grinding poverty who eventually murders the black man intending to rape her before passing her on to his white "boss." Writing a decade after that novel, Baldwin is superbly eloquent in his condemnation of U.S. racism. In her autobiography Anderson employs very different narrative strategies.

20. Jarena Lee was a very successful itinerant preacher who did battle with the hierarchy of the black male church for the right to preach. Without male approval she traveled widely in the North and the border states and ministered to large numbers of black and white converts. At least on two occasions she petitioned her bishop for ordination and was refused. At her own expense she published her narrative, *The Life and Religious Experience of Jarena Lee, a Coloured Lady*, first in 1836 (a thousand copies), then in 1839 (a second thousand copies), and a final expanded version in 1849.

21. I wish to thank my friends at Simmons College, who listened and offered criticism on this essay before its completion. Special thanks goes to David Gullette, for his insightful comments on the influence that black women associated with the ideology of "racial uplift" would have had on Marian Anderson. For further discussion on the work of "race" women and the philosophy of "lifting as they climb," see Mosselle [1894] 1988; and Giddings 1984.

22. For all of the hardships of their lives early-twentieth-century blacks in Philadelphia exhibited a pride of self identified with themselves in their city. That claim became one of

the most potent of Afro-American signifiers: "the Philadelphia Negro," a term adopted from Du Bois's book by that name, published in 1899. This group of people found in that self-designation the implications of communal success, capable leadership, and personal dignity and heroism in the face of the oppressive forces of racism. Du Bois's study was not uncritical of some in the black community, but he had high praise for those who subscribed to a politics of the future uplift of their race grounded in educational achievements, the accumulation of property, adherence to Victorian moral standards, and meaningful social engagement. Unquestionably, Marian Anderson and the members of her family, from humble origins, were representative of those whom Du Bois would have identified with the highest accolades he gave to the group.

23. Hurston's literary fortunes began to fall in the late 1940s and continued to do so in the following decade. She continued to write but was unable to find publishers for her works. Ill health also plagued her in the 1950s, and in 1959, without resources and suffering from a stroke, she entered a welfare nursing home in Florida, where she died in 1960. She was buried in an unmarked grave. In the early 1970s writer Alice Walker, following the discovery of Hurston's most outstanding novel, *Their Eyes Were Watching God* (1937), went on a pilgrimage to "find Zora." In the place where she might be buried Walker left a plaque inscribed to the woman whom she called "a genius of the South." Hurston's literary fame is now worldwide, and she is often referred to as the foremother of late-twentieth-century black women writers.

24. In *Their Eyes Were Watching God* Janie, the heroine, actively seeks personal fulfillment in her own right. She is generally conceded to be the first black feminist fictional heroine. Earlier, Nella Larsen's Helga Crane (*Quicksand* [1928]) tried to engineer her independence as a single black woman but did not succeed.

25. Although Alice Walker left a marker that bears Hurston's name and other data about her in the graveyard in which she is buried, Walker was not sure she had found the actual site because of the poor condition of the graves.

26. Even today the majority of black college graduates attend historical black colleges. Before the 1960s and the pressure for school integration at the higher education level, only a handful of blacks attended white colleges and universities. By the late 1960s, however, the numbers of those in these previously all-white schools had risen significantly. At the same time, during the era when few blacks attended white colleges and universities, the number of black professors in these institutions was negligible. When radical black college students demanded changes in that system, they called for the establishment of black studies programs, the employment of black faculty, and the recruitment of black students to these campuses. In general those efforts have yielded a different (if still not altogether satisfactory) U.S. profile on today's northern college campus.

27. The idea of racial uplift and the Talented Tenth were signifiers for black middle-class responsibilities to the black masses from the later years of the nineteenth century through the early years of the twentieth. The latter was the name that familiarly identified the 10 percent of the black population who were college educated and/or seen as intellectuals.

28. In 1903, in his classic work, *The Souls of Black Folk*, W. E. B. Du Bois first wrote of the "double-consciousness" of African Americans. The American black, he said, was

allowed no "true self-consciousness" and always felt her or his "twoness,"—"an American, a Negro; two souls, two thoughts, two unreconciled strivings; two warring ideals in one dark body" (45). Furthermore, he noted, "the history of the American Negro is the history of this strife,—this longing to attain self-conscious manhood [*sic*], to merge his double self into a better and truer self" (45). Carey attempts to find what Du Bois would have called the black American true self-consciousness. Interestingly, some contemporary theories in black literature argue for double consciousness as a positive aspect of the black experience.

29. Toni Morrison uses this phrase toward the conclusion of her Pulitzer Prize–winning novel *Beloved* (1987): "It is not a story to pass on." The syntax suggests the fiction is not to be retold and perhaps is best forgotten, but in reality Morrison intends the exact opposite: it is one to be remembered, one not to be passed over.

30. This pioneering volume declared the existence of a "Black Women's Studies."

31. It is necessary to acknowledge that over the past twenty-five years black women have found many invaluable supporters of their cause among white women and black and white men, who decry the injustices of the multiple oppression of this group.

32. Toni Morrison, in conversation with Nellie McKay, in her office at Random House, New York, in the fall of 1982.

WORKS CITED

Anderson, Marian. [1956] 1993. *My Lord, What a Morning.* Intro. Nellie Y. McKay. Madison: University of Wisconsin Press.

Andrews, William L. 1986. *To Tell a Free Story: The First Century of Afro-American Autobiography, 1760–1865.* Urbana: University of Illinois Press.

Baldwin, James. 1955. *Notes of a Native Son.* New York: Beacon Press.

Carby, Hazel. 1987. *Reconstructing Womanhood: The Emergence of the Afro-American Woman Novelist.* New York: Oxford University Press.

Carey, Lorene. 1991. *Black Ice.* New York: Knopf.

Douglass, Frederick. [1845] 1960. *Narrative of the Life of Frederick Douglass, An American Slave, Written by Himself.* Ed. Benjamin Quarles. Cambridge: Harvard University Press.

Du Bois, W. E. B. [1903] 1969. *The Souls of Black Folk.* Intro. Nathan Hare and Alvin Poussaint. New York: New American Library.

———. 1899. *The Philadelphia Negro.* Philadelphia: University of Pennsylvania Press.

Finkelman, Paul, ed. 1992. *Lynching, Racial Violence, and Law.* New York: Garland.

Foster, Frances. 1984. "Neither Auction Block nor Pedestal: 'The Life and Religious Experience of Jarena Lee, A Colored Lady.'" In *The Female Autograph,* ed. Domna Stanton, 126–51. Chicago: University of Chicago Press.

Giddings, Paula. 1984. *When and Where I Enter: The Impact of Black Women on Race and Sex in America.* New York: William Morrow.

Giovanni, Nikki. 1971. *Gemini: An Extended Autobiographical Statement on My First Twenty-Five Years of Being a Black Poet.* New York: Viking Press.

Hall, Jacqueline Doud. 1979. *Revolt Against Chivalry: Jesse Daniel Ames and the Women's Campaign Against Lynching.* New York: Columbia University Press.

Hurston, Zora Neale. [1942] 1984. *Dust Tracks on a Road.* 2d ed. Ed. and intro. Robert Hemenway. Urbana: University of Illinois Press.

———. [1937] 1990. *Their Eyes Were Watching God.* Foreword by Mary Helen Washington. New York: Harper and Row.

Jacobs, Harriet A. [1861] 1987. *Incidents in the Life of a Slave Girl, Written by Herself.* Ed. Jean Fagan Yellin. Cambridge: Harvard University Press.

Larsen, Nella. 1928. *Quicksand.* New York: Knopf.

McGovern, James R. 1982. *Anatomy of a Lynching: The Killing of Claude Neal.* Baton Rouge: Louisiana State University Press.

McKay, Nellie Y. 1989. "Nineteenth-Century Black Women's Spiritual Autobiographies: Religious Faith and Self-Empowerment." In *Interpreting Women's Lives,* ed. the Personal Narratives Group, 139–54. Bloomington: University of Indiana Press.

———. 1983. "An Interview with Toni Morrison." *Contemporary Literature* 24 (Winter): 413–29.

Morrison, Toni. 1987. *Beloved.* New York: Knopf.

Mosselle, Mrs. N. F. [1894] 1988. *The Work of the Afro-American Woman.* Intro. Joanne Braxton. New York: Oxford University Press.

Prince, Nancy Gardener. 1855. *A Narrative of the Life and Travels of Mrs. Nancy Prince.* Boston: by the author.

Tonay, Stewart, and James Massey. 1992. "Legal Execution of Blacks as Social Control in the Cotton South, 1890–1929." In *Social Security Quarterly* (September): 627–44.

Walker, Alice. 1983. "Looking for Zora." *In Search of Our Mothers' Gardens,* 93–116. New York: Harcourt Brace Jovanovich.

Wright, Richard. 1945. *Black Boy.* New York: Harper and Row.

———. 1940. *Native Son.* New York: Harper and Row.

Chapter 4

Psychology and Feminism: Can This Relationship Be Saved?

Jeanne Marecek

Since its early days the field of psychology has issued pronouncements about women and set out prescriptions for their mental health and proper conduct. Women in the discipline often dissented from the pronouncements and prescriptions of mainstream psychology, but for much of psychology's one hundred–year history women's voices were few and far between. The past quarter of a century has witnessed a dramatic increase in the overall number of women in psychology. Moreover, many women, committed to feminism in their personal lives, have been committed to feminist ideals in their work as researchers, therapists, and teachers as well. Two organizations, one within the main professional association (the Division of the Psychology of Women of the American Psychological Association, established in 1973) and one outside (the Association for Women in Psychology, established in 1969), exist, providing a locus of collegiality and institutional support for feminist scholarship and activism (Mednick and Urbanski 1991; Tiefer 1991).

This essay concerns scholarship produced by feminist psychologists during the past twenty-five years.[1] The array of scholarship is impressive in its quantity, scope, and diversity. Yet developments have been uneven, with theory building lagging behind fact finding. In consequence, as the trees grow thicker, the contours of the forest seem harder, not easier, to discern. At the same time, the transformation of the mainstream discipline that feminist psychologists had predicted early on has not come. Instead, there has been only a "slow leak of feminist scholarship into the mainstream, [with] little change over historic time" (Fine and Gordon 1989). Thus, the record of the past is simultaneously one of positive accomplishment and of unfinished business. Critical reflection on that record is crucial to deliberating the character of future endeavors. This essay is one of many possible ways of viewing developments in feminist psychology to date. It should not be read as a definitive appraisal of the field; rather, I hope it will serve as a stimulus for a variegated set of reflections and reconstructions.

In the early 1970s many of us in feminist psychology were happy to locate ourselves at the intersection of psychology and women's studies. As time has gone on, however, that position has become awkward for some. From the perspective of mainstream psychology, the subfield of psychology of women remains marginal to the field, a "special interest" that many regard as having a dubious and "unscientific" character. Note, for instance, that a recent survey showed that members of the American Psychological Association (APA) rated the Division of the Psychology of Women in the bottom third of divisions of the association in terms of interest and in the bottom quarter in terms of importance (Harari and Peters 1987).

Some feminist psychologists have come to feel undervalued and marginalized within women's studies as well. What many feminist scholars who are not psychologists identify as psychology of women lies at (or beyond) the periphery of the field as it is defined by most of those on the inside. Referring to the "different-voice" theory of Carol Gilligan, Zella Luria has said, "If this is the whole of the psychology that our feminist sisters in other disciplines adopt, then feminists in psychology will have failed their responsibilities" (1991, 486). Luria was pointing to the thousands of quantitative studies, published in *Psychology of Women Quarterly, Sex Roles,* and other disciplinary journals, that are largely unknown outside the discipline.

The epistemological turn in feminist theory—with its critiques of objectivism, empiricism, quantification, experimentalism, and positivism—has added to some psychologists' sense of estrangement from women's studies. These tenets have been and remain the dominant foundational assumptions of most of psychology and of most of feminist psychology in the United States. Nonetheless, it would be inaccurate to portray feminist psychologists as universally estranged from women's studies or as univocally committed to the traditional assumptions and methods of psychology. A small but growing number of feminist psychologists have embraced the epistemological debates in feminist theory and, indeed, have argued that the foundational assumptions of psychology, as well as its conventional practices and procedures, operate to contain, silence, and sanitize feminism (Bohan 1993; Fine 1985; Hare-Mustin and Marecek 1994; Kahn and Yoder 1989; Marecek 1989; Marecek and Hare-Mustin 1991; Morawski 1990; Parlee 1990).

I will set the stage for examining present-day feminist psychology by pointing to a few recurring themes in mainstream psychology's efforts to answer the "woman question." There are, of course, many ways in which ideas about gender weave through psychological knowledge, and there is much more to the history of the discipline than I can mention here. Next, I will take up some of the many strategies that scholars, both early and present day, have used to forge a union of the intellectual, philosophical, and ethical commitments they have as feminists and as psychologists. Much has been accomplished, but these very accomplishments expose problems and contradictions that were hitherto hidden. In the latter part of the essay I consider possible new directions for feminist psychology, new directions that build on work in other women's studies disciplines. One such direction re-envisions gender as performative rather than constitutive, focusing inquiry on the practices by which gender is accomplished as a social fact. Another employs the developments in feminist theory and elsewhere to interrogate the discipline of psychology, its metatheory and epistemology.

THE WOMAN QUESTION IN PSYCHOLOGY

Women have been subjected to the gaze of psychologists since the earliest days of the discipline, one hundred years ago. At moments when women stepped out of "their place" or an eruption of feminism threatened the social order, male intellectuals and social critics of the day felt impelled to decide the question of "women's nature." The very form of the question "What is women's nature?" contains intimations of its answer. Women's nature was taken to be separate from human nature (i.e., men's nature), implying that, whatever they were, women were not fully human. Orthodox psychology has not hesitated to render its judgment of women's nature. In the late nineteenth century questions of women's nature were addressed in terms of mental capacities. Efforts to assess these capacities were carried out with reference not to skills and abilities but, rather, to various lobes, areas, and physical dimensions of women's brains (Shields 1975). It was even argued at one point that the brain itself was a secondary sex characteristic.

One of the most persistent ideas about women characterizes their psychology in relation to their reproductive physiology and function. This strategy has been a rich source of invention, but it is one that perforce focuses on the ways that men and women are different or even, as some would have it, "opposite." For Freud (1925) a little girl's realization that she is without a penis sets in motion a sequence of intrapsychic events that culminate in a normal feminine personality that is morally, socially, sexually, and emotionally deficient. Erik Erikson shifted the emphasis from external genitalia to women's awareness of their "inner space," the "somatic design" that "harbors . . . a biological, psychological, and ethical commitment to take care of human infancy" (1964, 586). Thus, for Erikson it is only within (heterosexual, monogamous) marriage and motherhood that women can find their identity and fully develop. In contrast, men's somatic design (their "outer space") gives rise to (pun intended) intrusiveness, excitement, mobility, achievement, domination, and adventure seeking. A similar line of reasoning was advanced (albeit with less stylistic grace) by Iago Galdston (1958), an eminent American psychiatrist, who proclaimed woman to be "a uterus surrounded by a supporting organism and a directing personality."

Other theorists tied women's cognitive and perceptual abilities to their reproductive physiology:

> Known sex differences in cognitive abilities reflect sex related differences in physiology. . . . Females surpass males on simple, overlearned, perceptual-motor tasks; males excel on more complex tasks requiring an inhibition of immediate responses . . . in favor of responses to less obvious stimulus attributes. (Broverman, Klaiber, Kobayashi, and Vogel 1968, 23)

The words of Helen Thompson Woolley, penned in 1910, seem apt at this point. Describing the literature on sex differences even back then as a "motley mass," she offered the following assessment:

> There is perhaps no field aspiring to be scientific where flagrant personal bias, logic martyred in the cause of supporting a prejudice, unfounded assertions, and even sentimental rot and drivel, have run riot to such an extent as here. (1910, 340)

Helen Thompson Woolley's work, like that of Mary Whiton Calkins and Leta S. Hollingworth, exemplifies one way to marry feminism and psychology. These women set about empirical research that was self-consciously aimed at debunking sexist assertions about women. Using the accepted research procedures of the day, they hoped to provide corrective scholarship that would counter unfounded assertions and call into question prevailing "rot and drivel" about women. Their strategy was akin to what Sandra Harding (1986) has called feminist empiricism. They were, to paraphrase Audre Lorde, using the master's tools to dismantle the master's house.

CORRECTIVE SCHOLARSHIP

Feminist empiricism—wedding the sensibilities of feminism to positivist epistemology and empirical research methods—still flourishes today. Indeed, it remains the predominant strategy for producing knowledge in feminist psychology. Moreover, the question of sex differences has remained an important subject of inquiry.

Sex Differences

Like Woolley, Calkins, and Hollingworth, contemporary feminist psychologists took up research on sex differences with the intention of debunking psychology's shibboleths about female deficiencies. *The Psychology of Sex Differences* by Eleanor Maccoby and Carol Jacklin (1974) stands as a classic feminist inquiry into sex differences. Maccoby and Jacklin collated and summarized fourteen hundred psychological studies comparing boys and girls on a large number of cognitive abilities and personality traits. Of these traits and abilities, only four showed consistent evidence of a male-female difference. Maccoby and Jacklin drew several conclusions from their analyses. They pointed out recurring methodological weaknesses in the corpus of research: flawed measuring instruments, faulty research designs, and ill-chosen comparison groups. They also warned against uncritical biologizing, noting that there are many possible mechanisms through which male-female differences could come into being. Finally, they pointed out that beliefs about sex differences far outstripped reality.

Today research on sex differences is carried forward by the use of a statistical technique called meta-analysis. Like the conventional narrative review of the literature, meta-analysis aims to collate the results of many previous studies into a single integrated summary. In meta-analysis, however, the form of the summary is quantitative (i.e., numerical) rather than verbal. Advocates of meta-analysis believe that it is more precise and less open to error and misjudgment than narrative summaries. More important, meta-analysis incorporates information not only about whether or not a statistically significant difference occurred but also about the size and practical import of that difference. Of course, meta-analysis has shortcomings as well. It relies on extant studies, and thus it cannot be other than retrospective. Moreover, meta-analysis cannot reach beyond (or behind) published research. If publication biases exist such that only certain types of findings merit publication, these biases will infect the results of the meta-analysis. Feminist researchers have carried out meta-analyses of sex differences in a number of traits and capacities, including mathematical abilities, verbal abilities, certain personality traits, and sexual behavior (e.g., Eagley and Crowley 1986; Eagley and Steffen 1986; Hyde and Linn 1986).

What has the first century of research on psychological sex differences yielded? Under the lens of empirical scrutiny, sex differences have taken on a "now you see 'em, now you don't" quality, a quality evident in the tremendous inconsistencies that Maccoby and Jacklin found. Perhaps more troubling is that sex differences also have taken on a "you see 'em, I don't" quality. That is, most feminist psychologists have tended to read the empirical record as showing fewer or smaller sex differences than have their nonfeminist colleagues. Some claim that feminists are ideologically predisposed to minimize differences in order to favor women (Eagley 1987; Stanley 1989). Most feminist psychologists see ideological bias on the other side, believing that feminist researchers have substituted better (i.e., gender neutral or nonsexist) methods of analysis for conventional sex-biased ones.

Feminist contentions of sex bias in conventional research have been backed up by an impressive set of arguments. The opening volley was fired by Naomi Weisstein (1968), in an article entitled "Kinder, Küche, Kirche as Scientific Law: Psychology Constructs the Female." Carolyn W. Sherif's piece "Bias in Psychology" (1979) followed suit with a deeply thoughtful critique of epistemology and method in psychology, a critique that unfortunately remains just as pertinent today as when she wrote it. Maureen McHugh and her colleagues presented an exhaustive description of the myriad points in the process of designing, executing, interpreting, and reporting psychological experiments at which sex bias can enter (McHugh, Koeske, and Frieze 1986). Kathy Grady (1981) and Carol Jacklin (1981) pointed to yet other ways that bias was rooted in the conceptual schemas and interpretive modes of conventional psychological research. At the same time, other critics have noted heterosexism and racial/ethnic bias in research (e.g., Herek, Kimmel, Amaro, and Melton 1991; Landrine, Klonoff, and Brown-Collins 1992).

My own reading of such critiques is two-pronged. On the one hand, I applaud the sharp insights and critical acumen of the authors. On the other, the cumulative effect of their work is a sinking feeling and a strong sense of pessimism. I am reminded of Aylmer, the scientist of Nathaniel Hawthorne's story "The Birthmark" (1893). Obsessed with the birthmark that blemishes the skin of his otherwise perfect bride, Aylmer struggles to devise a potion strong enough to remove the blemish. When he succeeds, the dose turns out to be deadly. What had appeared to be a superficial blemish reached deep to the heart. Like the bride's birthmark, biases in psychology may be inextricably connected to the heart of the discipline.

I will develop this point in detail later. For now let us turn back to the subject of sex differences. As is often true of feminist empiricism, the questions guiding sex difference research are questions received from mainstream psychology, echoing mainstream culture. The feminist response is an effort to contest accepted wisdom and to disrupt the production of invidious stereotypes about women. Important though this work is, it inevitably has drawbacks. Contesting sexist claims paradoxically serves to dignify them as worthy of attention and continuing debate. Moreover, when feminist scholars assume a reactive stance, they relinquish control of the agenda. Keeping the focus on the "data" of sex differences serves to contain feminists' energies and imaginations (Hare-Mustin and Marecek 1988).

Lurking behind the question of male-female difference is the question of hierarchy: Which is better? The question is not "How are men and women different?" but, rather, "How do women differ from men?" In other words, how do women measure up to the norm, or typical case? Are women as good as men? The form of the question thus begs the answer and puts feminist researchers in a no-win situation: if we conclude that sex differences exist, we admit women's deficiency. If we conclude that no differences exist, we are asserting only that women are "as good as" men, implicitly acceding to the premise that the male is the standard or referent against which women should be judged.

Many feminist psychologists have carried out studies of sex differences in the hope of setting the record straight on matters that would lead to fairer treatment of women, a goal that fits squarely with psychology's self-proclaimed interest in promoting human welfare. But feminists should be wary of trusting that a dispassionate assessment of "the facts" can serve as the basis for redistributing power, privilege, and resources. Whose version of the facts will be heard, published, and advanced and whose muffled or silenced? The history of psychology is, regrettably, replete with instances in which dubious facts were marshaled to reaffirm the social hierarchies already in place.

Research on male-female differences has perhaps been most useful to feminists as a springboard to other questions. A sex difference (or a lack of difference) is never an explanation, only a description. Thus, the results of sex difference research do not provide an answer; they only prompt a further question: "Why?" In the mid-1970s scholars in women's studies began to use the term *gender* to open up new conceptual space for theorizing that question. That is, they appropriated a term previously used mainly by grammarians and linguists to make reference to the social quality of distinctions between maleness and femaleness (Scott 1985). Perhaps it was no coincidence that the term *gender* was borrowed from the study of language. Language is the medium by which social realities such as gender are constructed and legitimated.

Gender Roles and Socialization

A sex difference (or similarity) prompts the question "What is it about the social experiences of women and men that explains why they might think/feel/behave this way?" Feminist psychologists' efforts to answer this question have produced empirical studies numbering in the thousands. Much of this work can be encompassed by the rubric of gender (or sex) roles and its companion concept, gender-role (or sex-role) socialization. The term *gender role* lacks a precise definition, but it has been used to refer to the normative expectations for men and women. Gender-role socialization refers to the processes by which individuals (usually children) acquire knowledge of gender-role norms and come to accept them. The fuzziness of the concept of gender role leads ultimately to conceptual impasses, which I will describe later. Nonetheless, the construct has served as a useful lens for examining societal expectations imposed on women, as the abundance of published studies indicates.

Psychological Androgyny

One of the most popular ways for feminist psychologists to interrogate the consequences of gender roles was the construct of psychological androgyny. For nearly a decade, beginning in the mid-1970s, androgyny was a pivotal construct in feminist empirical psychology and feminist clinical practice. Psychological androgyny was advocated by some as a requisite for optimal mental health as well as a prime goal of feminist therapy (Bem 1978; Kaplan 1979; Marecek 1979). Sandra Bem (1976), whose work introduced and operationalized the concept of androgyny in psychology, defined it as follows:

> An androgynous sex role thus represents the equal endorsement of both masculine and feminine personality characteristics, a balance, as it were, between masculinity and femininity. . . . Both masculinity and femininity must each [sic] be tempered by the other, and the two integrated into a . . . more fully human, a truly androgynous personality.

Research on androgyny used a measuring instrument devised by Bem (1974), known as the *Bem Sex-Role Inventory (BSRI)*. To complete the *BSRI* individuals were asked to consider a list of sixty psychological characteristics and to indicate the extent to which each described them. From this, scores were calculated that purported to index masculinity and femininity; individuals were then categorized according to what Bem called their "sex-role orientation." An avalanche of studies quickly followed the publication of this simple measuring device. Sex-role orientation was correlated with such diverse attributes and behaviors as women's depression, male feminism, preferred coital positions, and diagnostic practices of therapists. By the mid-1980s, however, the *BSRI*, along with the concept of psychological androgyny, succumbed to the weight of various conceptual and methodological critiques and reformulations (Bem 1984; Locksley and Colten 1979; Morawski 1985, 1987; Spence 1984). The *BSRI* industry crumbled, leaving little imprint on the field.

Conceptual difficulties with the idea of androgyny have been articulated by many scholars across women's studies disciplines, and I will not repeat them here. Instead, I focus on aspects of the development and deployment of the concept of androgyny that are peculiar to psychology. In doing so, I hope to illustrate some of the tensions that psychology engenders for feminists, and vice versa.

The construct of androgyny as a sex-role orientation tacitly shifted the domain of gender roles from the social interpersonal world to the mental, intraindividual one. Despite its title, the Bem Sex-Role Inventory is not an inventory of "sex roles," as that term is conventionally defined. That is, it does not address the roles of men and women (e.g., daughter, husband, worker, mother). Rather, the *BSRI* measures individuals' self-assessments of the extent to which they possess particular attributes or traits (e.g., compassion, leadership abilities). Thus, Bem's conception of androgyny shifted ground from *social* roles to *mental* self-conceptions.[2] This slide from the social and interpersonal to the mental could occur without notice because it is a move that takes place over and over in psychological theorizing. Yet focusing on self-concept as the locus of gender ignores the way in which gender (along with other socially demarcated categories, such as ethnicity, class, and sexual orientation) is a structuring principle of ongoing social relations in nearly every setting and institution in our society.

Like much of contemporary psychology, psychologists' ideas about gender roles and androgyny are often framed by the antimony of individual versus society. Bem (1976), for instance, saw androgyny as a liberation from society's "restricting prison" of "artificial constraints" on the freedom to express "one's own unique blend of temperament and behavior." Rather than taking the distinction between individual and society as a provisional one, androgyny theory took it as real. As psychology characteristically does, it posited a preexisting "true self" independent of the matrix of social institutions and ongoing relationships in which human beings are embedded. In this view the self exists in opposition to society: freedom from society allows people to be more truly themselves. Social life is seen as a constriction of human possibility, rather than the locus of all possibilities. Such ways of construing self and society echo themes in late-nineteenth-century romanticism, liberal individualism, and humanism, and they have come under scathing attack by a variety of contemporary critical thinkers (Marecek and Hare-Mustin 1990; Sass 1988).

The constructs of gender roles, gender-role socialization, and androgyny deserve further critical analysis. Like many of mainstream psychology's variables, they are mechanistic and simplistic abstractions, compressing the flux and flow of human life into a few static constructs. The construct of gender-role socialization too often has implied a unitary norm of behavior (a "gender role"), imparted early in life and enacted robotlike for the duration of the life span. It makes invisible the ways that culture, language, and relationships continually construct individuals as gendered beings, and it obscures the complexity, multiplicity, and contradiction in the meanings of gender. Mechanistic notions of gender-role socialization also leave little room to explain women's acts of resistance—their outright rebellions, silent refusals and subterfuges, ironic exaggerations. How could socialization theory explain Madonna? Or, for that matter, feminists themselves?

Psychologists' theories of gender roles and gender-role socialization often have skirted the issues of power, dominance, and subordination (see Stacey and Thorne 1985). Androgyny theory, like sex difference research, took gender to be merely an aspect of personal identity, a set of qualities resident within the person. This diverted attention from more politically charged meanings of gender. Indeed, masculinity and femininity were sometimes said to be parallel and complementary and even regarded as if they were equivalent in the degree to which they created unhappiness and blocked personal development. Nonetheless, many feminist psychologists practiced what they did not seem to preach. Therapists who adopted androgyny as a goal of therapy seemed to work exclusively with female clients. The goal of "resocialization" entailed helping women acquire "masculine" skills and attributes in order to enhance their success and life satisfaction. Little attention was paid to the idea that men's lives would be enhanced by acquiring attributes of femininity, nor was there indication of a male clientele interested in pursuing such ends. In the domain of research as well the focus was on women's roles, perhaps because few men experienced the normative prescriptions for masculinity as problematic or debilitating.

The vicissitudes of sex differences, gender roles, and androgyny point up some of the strains of lodging feminist psychology within the conceptual and methodological framework of mainstream psychology. As a discipline, psychology has insistently set its sights on the individual and the mental. It has characteristically set the individual apart from (and at odds with) society and then trained its gaze on the individual. In theorizing gender roles, feminist psychologists too have tended to take the societal for granted, to merely wave in the direction of "societal forces" or "cultural expectations," as if those constructs had a single, self-evident, agreed-upon referent and needed no unpacking.

Historically, psychology has been committed to the discovery of presumed universals in human experience—"laws of human behavior" that transcend history, culture, class, caste, and material circumstances. Thus, the valued means of producing knowledge has been the experiment, in which behavior is extracted from its usual social context. Moreover, the study of specific groups of people has been viewed as "applied" research that is peripheral to and of lesser value than the "basic" mission of the discipline. Psychology is the study of "human behavior," but the psychology of women is only the study of a "special population." Similarly, psychology has "regard[ed] whites as 'people' and all other ethnic groups as 'subcultures' or nonpeople" (Landrine, Klonoff, and Brown-Collins 1992, 147). The folly of this orientation has been noted by critics, but practices within the discipline have not shifted appreciably. For example, a recent survey of the psychology research literature noted that studies of African Americans have actually declined in number over the past two decades (Graham 1992).

Over the past ten years or so, calls for a more inclusive feminist psychology have become increasingly insistent. Ethnic, cultural, sexual, and other forms of diversity are better represented in feminist psychology than they are in the discipline as a whole. Yet, to date, women who are not white, not middle-class, and not heterosexual are underrepresented in the research literature. More important, in producing knowledge about women's lives, feminist psychology (especially experimentation) has often elided the role of material resources, institutional biases, historical contingencies, and cultural differences.

TOWARD FULLER ACCOUNTS OF WOMEN'S LIVES

Another way of joining psychology and feminism has been to eschew male-centered notions of what is important to study and, instead, to center the inquiry on women's lives. This approach has produced a rich tapestry of women's activities and experiences, at once diverse, complex, bewildering, and compelling. One women-centered strategy has been to focus attention on uniquely female life events, such as menarche, menstruation, pregnancy, childbirth, breastfeeding, the transition to motherhood, and menopause. Much of this work broke new ground by bringing unexamined issues to light and by reexamining old issues in new ways. By making women the center of inquiry, negative value judgments and invidious interpretations could be challenged and replaced. Much of the research refuted long-standing cultural biases, calling into question the notion of women's "raging" cyclical hormones, the sentimentalization of motherhood, hormonal explanations of the "new-baby blues," and associations between menopause and depression.

Much of this work has challenged the idea that biology shapes women's psychological destiny. But, paradoxically, the corpus of work as a whole stands as an unintended reaffirmation of a pervasive cultural assumption about women: that women, but not men, are defined by their bodies; and that women's psychology is connected to their physiology (Ortner 1974). Or, as one of psychology's founding fathers put it: "All that is distinctly human is man; all that is truly woman is merely reproductive" (Allen 1889). Thus, feminist work detailing the sociocultural meanings of reproductive events is only a first step. The next step is to question whether such events do (and should) define women's lives.

The transformative potential of this work is limited in more serious ways as well. Much of it takes its agenda to be disentangling the biological from the sociocultural. Behind this agenda is a set of ideas about biology and culture that demands critical scrutiny. In psychological theorizing, biology is traditionally accorded primacy as the "bedrock" of human experience. Biological explanations of human behavior are habitually privileged in the psychological literature, as they are in the popular media. Even Freud, whose psychology relies heavily on symbol systems and mentalistic constructs, held that the discipline of psychology was just a stopgap, a waystation to pass the time until the science of neurology produced the ultimate cures for mental disorders. As Robert Connell (1987) says, the assumption that biology is the root cause of human experience is so powerful in U.S. intellectual life that biologism repeatedly co-opts intellectual currents initially unsympathetic to it.

Women's studies scholars in many disciplines have sharply challenged the presumed divide between the biological and the social as well as the notion of a core biological essence unmediated by language and social experience. Their work examines the ways in which the meanings of the body and bodily processes are situated within a given historical, cultural, and social framework. Key to this work is an analysis of language and the systems of metaphors deployed in talk about the body in health and illness. Emily Martin (1987), for example, has investigated the metaphors that women from different social class backgrounds use to talk about menstruation. Leonore Tiefer (1992) has interrogated the masculinist and heterosexist assumptions that frame diagnoses of sexual dysfunctions as well as the concept of the "human sexual response cycle." John D'Emilio and Estelle Freedman (1988) have described how the meanings of sexuality and its regulation in U.S. society have shifted from colonial times to the present. In the aftermath of the confirmation hearings of Supreme Court Justice Clarence Thomas, a number of scholars have turned attention to the myths of the hypersexuality of African-American men and women (Chrisman and Allen 1992; Morrison 1992). Other scholars have explored the "epidemic of signification" (in Paula Treichler's phrase [1987]) that HIV infection has unleashed. In short, the meaning and experience of bodily phenomena depend on interpretation and values and on the language available to talk about them. Rather than being separable and in opposition, biology and culture are interrelated and interdependent. Culture, through the apparatus of language, creates the reality of biology and the body as we know it.

There is another way that culture creates biological realities. The social practices, material resources, and cultural values of any particular historical and societal context create what appear to be biological "givens." Take, for example, the monthly menstrual cycle. In many societies, especially those in which subsistence agriculture is practiced, women's menstrual cycles are neither monthly nor cyclical (e.g. Winslow 1980). Women reach puberty at a late age, marry shortly thereafter (if not before), conceive as quickly as possible, breastfeed for long periods, have several pregnancies spaced closely together, and die at a relatively young age. Thus, in their lifetimes they may experience relatively few menstrual periods, and there may be only limited spans of time when a regular monthly cycle is established. In our own time and place practices such as rigorous dieting, strenuous exercise, and the use of hormone-based contraceptives can interrupt monthly hormonal cycles. And, as medical advances extend the life span, the proportion of a lifetime during which women menstruate is diminishing and is presently only about 50 percent. Age at menarche is also influenced by social practice, and here too there is wide variation across history and across different social groups. In the United States the age at menarche has dropped dramatically during this century. At present it is not uncommon for a girl to reach menarche as young as the age of ten. In other locales menarche may occur as late as the age of seventeen. Social practices—among them, nutrition, dietary preferences, and activity levels—effectively dictate biology. The metaphor of biology as bedrock is inapt on two counts: biology is neither solid and unchanging nor at the bottom of human existence.

Breaking the Silence: Women and Violence

Though marriage and motherhood are often taken to be the emblems of womanhood, intimate violence and sexual victimization are perhaps more ubiquitous. Male violence is a threat to women of all social groups, and the threat is sustained throughout the life span. Victimization often takes place in the context of relationships of love and trust and thus is especially hurtful. Like other cultural institutions, orthodox psychology heeded the long-standing taboo against acknowledging violence against women. Even clinicians who worked with distressed women or with couples in marital conflict often overlooked or minimized the possibility of intimate violence in their clients' lives.

It was feminists who broke the silence within the discipline of psychology. Feminist activism and scholarship on issues of victimization stand as a sustained and successful example of claims making, transforming a set of conditions that, as Gloria Steinem once quipped, had been "just called life" into an urgent social problem. Thus, one accomplishment was interpretive change: violence against women became a public issue rather than a private problem. Feminist scholarship also challenged the conventional wisdom that minimized violence against women. Violence against women in all its forms—rape, child sexual abuse, wife beating, sexual harassment—was shown to be far more prevalent than had been imagined (Koss 1990) and to have more damaging effects on women's mental health and well-being (cf. Browne and Finklehor 1986; Herman 1981). At the same time, feminists pointed out that fear of violence affects women every day, causing them to worry and to take preventive measures that are restrictive, expensive, and time consuming (Gardner 1989; Gordon and Riger 1991). Feminist therapists and counselors have also contributed to knowledge about treatment for women (and men) with violence or sexual abuse in their past (e.g., Courtois 1988; Goldner, Penn, Sheinberg, and Walker 1990).

Feminist work on violence against women also has theorized the origins of violence and sexual victimization of women. The analyses have insisted upon a connection between the victimization of women and quotidian male-female power dynamics (Burt 1980; Hollway 1984; Malamuth 1981; Walker 1989). Thus, some researchers have examined cultural assumptions about women, about heterosexuality, about male entitlement to women's sexual services, and about male-female antagonism. Others have explored how exposure to images of violence and violent sexuality affects rape-related attitudes. A key feature of these analyses is that violent and abusive acts are not the acts of deviant, disordered individuals but, rather, extreme manifestations of culturally accepted patterns of dominant-subordinate gender relations.

Women's Problems

Another strategy for producing women-centered knowledge has been focusing upon the difficulties women encounter as a result of the cultural imperatives of femininity. An early instance was Matina Horner's (1970) work on "fear of success." Horner identified what she characterized as a deep-seated feminine motive to avoid success, stemming from fear of negative interpersonal consequences. Over the years a succession of other attributes have been imputed to women to explain their (supposed) reluctance to undertake certain "masculine" endeavors, their (supposed) lack of success, or their unhappiness: math anxiety, the "impostor phenomenon," the "Cinderella Complex," lack of assertiveness, "secrets your mother never taught you," and lack of self-esteem. In the realm of psychopathology feminist clinicians, pointing to the parallels between stereotypic feminine attributes and the symptoms of certain psychiatric disorders, argued that conventional femininity placed women at psychiatric risk (e.g., Rothblum and Franks 1983; Widom 1984).

Although such efforts were often inspired by a feminist impulse to help women improve their lives, their common assumptive framework—which Mary Crawford and I (1989) called "Woman as Problem"—has had some unforeseen and unfortunate implications. Declaring that a problem is a "woman's problem" implies that it is universal among women and even an essential aspect of female psychology. This has rarely proven true; upon close scrutiny most "women's problems" have turned out to affect only some women and to affect men as well. In addition, when women's behavior is identified as the problem, the behavior associated with men is often taken to be correct or mentally healthy. For example, the truism that women have problems expressing anger implies that men's ways of expressing anger are unproblematic and to be emulated. But, of course, men, like women, express anger in many different ways, and not all of them are constructive or socially appropriate. Moreover, psychological analyses of women's problems abstract the problem from its context, locating it within women themselves. The proposed solutions—remedial education, counseling and psychotherapy, "pop psych" self-help books—are all directed toward helping individual women remedy their deficiencies. In effect, they exhort women to make private changes in order to adapt better to social conditions.

In the Woman-as-Problem approach, as in other lines of endeavor, the relentless individualism that is part of psychology's heritage channeled the inquiry along a particular path. When attention is fixed on the self in isolation, women's difficulties appear as personality traits, motives, or deeply rooted personal attributes. The slide into essentialism is all too easy. When the focus is broadened to locate the phenomena in their social context, other formulations about their origins, continuation, and meaning emerge. An alternative interpretation of fear of success, for example, connects it not to gender but, rather, to relations of subordination. When success involves going "above one's station," people, whatever their gender, may fear that they will incur social penalties and thus may appear to "fear success." Perhaps math anxiety, lack of assertiveness, and "impostor feelings" too can be reinterpreted as ways of managing social relationships. They might serve as strategies for negotiating from a position of low status or as self-presentations simultaneously necessitated and enabled by conventional gender definitions (Hare-Mustin and Marecek 1986).

Revaluing Women

The Woman-as-Problem approach takes women's difference as a problem to be remedied and thus tacitly accepts the premise of male superiority. Other psychologists working within the woman-centered framework have rejected the conflation of difference with deficiency and, instead, have asserted the value, if not the superiority, of women's ways of being. Carol Gilligan's (1977) "different voice" is perhaps the most popular example of this approach. Gilligan's formulation was intended to counter work claiming that women evinced a less-developed moral sensibility than men. Gilligan argued that women formulated their moral judgments within a different framework of moral assumptions, a framework that privileged care over principles of abstract justice. In subsequent work Gilligan has expanded her original claim to assert a uniquely female sense of self and a unique path of adolescent development for girls. In moves that closely parallel Gilligan's, other psychologists have asserted that there exist uniquely female ways of knowing, modes of connectedness, and so on (e.g., Belenky, Clinchy, Goldberger, and Tarule 1986; Jordan, Kaplan, Miller, Stiver, and Surrey 1991).

By and large, these projects have received a cool reception from academic feminist psychologists. One persisting line of criticism has focused on technical inadequacies in the work, with critics noting departures from the logical and methodological standards customary in psychological research. Another line of criticism takes exception to the universalizing of women (cf. Broughton 1988; Crawford 1989). Essentialist accounts of women's psychology, no matter how flattering, conceal important differences among women and ignore the ways that the meaning of gender is intertwined with ethnicity, social class, and other categories of difference (Hare-Mustin and Marecek 1990; Spelman, 1988). Moreover, although these accounts intend to place women at the center of inquiry, to break out of gender comparisons, this intention seems to misfire. Claims of a woman's "voice," ways of knowing, and connectedness all seem to draw implicit comparisons to men, just as do claims of problems and syndromes unique to women. Even when the researchers demur, saying that they are *not* intending such comparisons, it is difficult to read their formulations without reading gender distinctions into them. Indeed, it seems logically impossible to speak about what is unique to women without implying difference from men.

Focus on Overlooked Groups of Women

With its avowed goal of discerning universal laws of human behavior, the field of psychology has historically been uninterested either in ethnic diversity or in history and culture. Researchers set their sights on college sophomores, a group that was at hand and could be pressed into service as research subjects at little or no cost. Feminist psychology, born during the women's movement of the 1970s, shared the concern of the women's movement with women's oppression in their everyday lives. Despite this concern, early research efforts focused primarily on white, young, middle-class, heterosexual women and produced knowledge about "generic" women.

Feminist psychology is now squarely confronted with the need to be more inclusive. Indeed, political developments on campuses, in the nation, and in the world at large are urgent indicators of just how little universality of experience there is and how fragile supposed commonalities among "us"—whether *us* refers to women, Americans, or even feminists—are (Rosaldo 1989). The moral and political commitment to the goals of diversity and inclusion is strong, but making good on this commitment will be difficult, and accomplishments are likely to be uneven. The body of work on lesbian women is growing, due in large part to the presence of many vocal and active lesbians in feminist psychology. This work has brought to light often-hidden experiences and challenged discriminatory stereotypes (e.g., Falk 1989; Rohrbaugh 1990). It has also been a source of methodological and epistemological innovation (e.g., Boston Lesbian Psychologies Collective 1987; Brown 1989). Studies of middle-aged and older women are also beginning to appear in the literature of feminist psychology. Indeed, a recent issue of the *Psychology of Women Quarterly* (14, no. 4) was devoted exclusively to this topic. As cohorts of feminist psychologists have moved through the life course, many have turned their scholarly attention to the issues that have emerged in their personal lives. As in other women's studies disciplines, personal experience is a valued source of scholarly inspiration. Relatively few women in academic psychology are nonwhite, and virtually none are from impoverished backgrounds (in terms of their present circumstances, if not that of their family of origin). Thus, the task of making feminist psychology inclusive of all women cannot be passed on to scholars who claim membership in these groups.

The commitment to study women from diverse backgrounds, ethnic groups, and ages is a tacit repudiation of psychology's goal of discovering universal laws of behavior. If a universalist psychology were possible, then studies of college sophomores would serve our purposes as readily and far more conveniently. This repudiation of psychology's traditional mission needs to be made explicit and debated openly. If the goal of a universalist psychology is untenable, then what kinds of knowledge can (and should) feminist psychology produce? Knowledge about women that is historically situated and context sensitive will be judged not important (or perhaps even not psychology) according to the traditional standards of the discipline.

"DOING GENDER"

Throughout its history feminist psychology has conceptualized gender in terms of fixed attributes resident within the individual. Against this background of essentialist thought, constructivist theories of gender have become important sources of innovation in psychology. For example, Candace West and Don Zimmerman (1987) have reimagined gender as something people *do,* rather than something people *are* or *have.* In this view the focus of study becomes the actions, conversations, and relationships through which gender is accomplished as a social fact and made to seem natural.

Two pieces of work, one by a sociologist and one by an anthropologist, may help to show what this approach can yield. Arlie Hochschild (1989) examined how family work is shared between employed wives and husbands, focusing on how partners negotiate disparate gender ideologies, emotional commitments, and gendered identities to arrive at a workable, if not always fair or amicable, distribution of family labor. What she called gender strategies, the "plan[s] of action through which a person solves problems at hand, given the cultural notions of gender at play," can be seen as ways of doing gender (1989, 15). So, for example, a husband may do the cooking and other housework but account for his behavior by explaining that he must "help out" his less-than-competent wife with "her" responsibilities. Such a gender strategy enables divergences from traditional norms without calling the norms themselves into question.

Another study of doing gender turned attention to women in public places (Gardner 1980). Gardner examined street remarks, that is, comments, gestures, and other forms of communication that pass from men to women in public places. She noted the content of the remarks, the circumstances that elicited them, and how recipients understood and responded to them. In Gardner's analysis street remarks serve as a powerful means of enacting male dominance: they assert that women are on display for male approval or disdain, claim public space as a male preserve, and may raise threats of male violence or sexual attack. At a metacommunicative level street remarks put their female targets in a double bind in which any response (including no response) is effectively a gesture of submission.

The concept of doing gender is a provocative one, but it is hard to accommodate within psychology's customary research practices. To study doing gender, researchers need to observe mundane encounters and quotidian interactions situated in the "real-life" contexts in which they customarily take place. They cannot rely on self-reports elicited via inventories, scales, and questionnaires or on behavior witnessed in contrived laboratory situations. Moreover, if, in accord with psychology's traditional dictum, researchers restrict inquiry to observable behavior, the resulting accounts will be limited. Instead, researchers need to go beyond overt behaviors to examine people's accounts of their intentions and the meanings they impute to their own and others' behavior. This will require research approaches akin to ethnography, participant observation, and even literary criticism, ways of working that are far less codified and rigid than the procedures psychology typically endorses.

Breaking free of the methodological orthodoxy imposed by mainstream psychology is not an easy step. Psychology warrants its claims to truth on the basis of its highly elaborated "scientific method" of procedure. Many psychologists are deeply distrustful of interpretive ways of working, especially because these ways of working lack procedures for verification equivalent to those claimed by psychology. Moreover, adherence to the so-called scientific method is one of the few features (perhaps the only feature) that links the disparate areas of psychology and gives psychologists a disciplinary identity.

Studies like those of Hochschild and Gardner strain the frame of psychology in another crucial way. The knowledge gained from such studies does not take a form akin to the results of psychological research. The results of research in psychology customarily are cast as cause-and-effect relationships, which in turn are cast into generalized statements concerned with the prediction of future behavior. Hochschild and Gardner, however, are more modest in both their aims and their claims. Their studies yield "thick descriptions," to use Geertz's

(1973) phrase: richly detailed, historically contingent, situation-specific descriptions of behavior.

The concept of doing gender offers an important counterpoint to the construct of gender-role socialization. It challenges the idea that people are socialized into a monolithic "gender-role orientation" in childhood, which shapes their actions for the remainder of their lives. In place of that idea it asserts that people "do [and redo] gender" in innumerable context-specific ways throughout their lives. Thus, gender is at issue in all interactions throughout the life span. Moreover, in this conception individuals become agents in creating gender. At different times and in various ways they may enact, refuse, or ironize cultural definitions of gender.

FEMINIST SKEPTICISM

Like other social technologies, psychology is a modernist invention. The field flourished and expanded in the twentieth century, and its character and aspirations reflect the spirit of those times. Its approach to knowledge is ahistorical, and functionalism has been an important theme. The discipline has placed faith in technology, in the development of knowledge by rational analysis, and in the myth of progress through change. As the modern era draws to a close, American intellectual life has entered a period of broad-ranging skepticism about these tenets and especially about conventional ideas of knowledge and truth. Key among postmodern doubts are questions about the nature of knowledge: What can we know? How do we know? Who is the subject of knowledge? How does the social position of the knower affect the production of knowledge? What is the connection between knowledge and politics? How does a discipline (such as psychology) produce and warrant knowledge? How do its formal methods of knowledge seeking, as well as its everyday practices, inform the understandings of human behavior that it produces and promulgates?

Many of these questions have a familiar ring to them. They echo, albeit in a general and more abstract form, the questions and concerns that feminists have been raising about psychology's knowledge of women. Thus, feminists are well represented among the psychologists who have criticized psychology from either a postpositivist or postmodern stance (e.g., Allen and Baber 1992; Bohan 1992; Gavey 1989; Hare-Mustin and Marecek 1988; Hollway 1989; Landrine, Klonoff, and Brown-Collins 1992; Morawski 1990). It is premature to sketch the eventual contours of a feminist psychology that fully incorporates such stances, but it is possible to indicate some of the prime areas of inquiry.

The Critique of Positivism

Positivism, the reigning epistemology for psychology since its origins, holds that only the positive data of sensory experience should count as truth. The means to gain such data is scientific observation; by following scientific procedures of knowledge seeking, knowers can be assured of objectivity.

Objections to positivist doctrines have come from many quarters of intellectual life. In psychology they have been raised by a number of theorists, among them some feminists. As mentioned previously, feminist psychologists have documented how the procedures for producing knowledge in psychology are susceptible to the values and biases of researchers. Although some believe that correctives applied to these procedures can yield "purified" methods and bias-free knowledge, others are pessimistic. Disputing the positivist premise that facts can be separated from values, they hold that all knowledge is "biased," (i.e., inclined toward the predilections of the knower) and, thus, facts and values cannot be neatly separated. In this view the very constructs we use to talk about psychic life carry implicit valuations, and thus description is always intertwined with prescription.

The positivist doctrine of objectivity requires that knowers be separate from the objects of study and that they suspend their preconceptions, values, personal inclinations, and interests, because these would contaminate their observations. Skeptics assert that it is not possible for these conditions to obtain in the production of psychological knowledge. Researchers cannot detach themselves from their social, cultural, and historical context by an act of will, nor can they put aside biography and experience. All knowledge is thus necessarily situated knowledge (Haraway 1988).

Questions about positivism raise further questions about possible alternatives. How can we go beyond objectivism to new doctrines of knowledge and truth? How should feminists warrant their claims to truth? If we set aside the positivist faith in objectivity, how can we keep from sliding into radical relativism? If we assert that knowledge is situated and that it depends on the standpoint of the knower, then how do we choose the best among the multiple views of reality that confront us? One feminist has used the image of trying to climb a greased pole while hanging on to both ends to characterize feminists' struggles with these issues. For feminist psychologists it has often seemed that, without empirical facts, there are no grounds for feminist demands for political change and social justice. Thus, challenges to objectivity seem to open the way to political paralysis (Allen and Baber 1992).

The Social Construction of Knowledge

Social constructionism, a theory of knowledge with deep roots in the Western philosophical tradition, has gained prominence lately in certain quarters of psychology. Social constructionism holds that knowledge is not a matter of a priori truths awaiting discovery but, rather, the construction of a community of knowers. That is, human knowers devise accounts of reality, and certain of these accounts come to be accepted as the true ones through processes of social negotiation (Berger and Luckmann 1966). Constructionism is, thus, in sharp opposition to positivism.

As an alternative to positivism, constructionism resonates with the unease that many feminists in psychology have felt about the discipline (Bohan 1992). Yet, as the idea that gender is a social construct has been introduced into feminist psychology, much of the force of social constructionism has been lost. Some have confused social constructionism with the unexceptional idea that behavior is a product of social forces rather than biology. Others have read social constructionism as nothing more than the study of varying explanations or attributions that individuals give for their own or others' behavior. Rather than studying the *social* processes through which knowledge is created and legitimated, the focus shifts to *individual* mental processes. Knowledge remains a subjective experience, rather than intersubjective collaboration and cocreation.

What has most often slipped out of sight as the term *social constructionism* has come into wide use in feminist psychology, though, is its epistemological force. The heart of social constructionism is its antirealist epistemology (Gergen 1985). That is, social constructionism disavows the idea of a preexisting reality outside of socially negotiated accounts of reality. Thus, like other postpositivist theories of knowledge, social constructionism presents feminists with the "greased pole" challenge to devise new doctrines of objectivity and truth.

Taking the full implication of social constructionism seriously would have far-reaching effects on feminist psychology. Constructionism opens a series of hitherto unexplored questions. For example, it asks how accounts of reality are devised and rhetorically justified. It also asks about the social processes and institutional mechanisms by which certain accounts are legitimated and others discredited. For feminist psychologists a key issue is how existing categories of psychological knowledge reflect and reaffirm the masculinist bias of society as a whole. So, for example, critiques have been launched against the construction of sexuality (Gavey 1989; Tiefer 1995) and heterosexuality (Hollway 1984). Other efforts have investigated the character of certain areas of psychological investigation, such as research on maternal employment and child care (Silverstein 1991) and attributions of blame and responsibility in childhood sexual abuse (Gavey 1990; Lamb 1986).

Language, Meaning, and Politics

A good deal of feminist critical thought has focused on the search for biases in the procedures used to carry out empirical research. This is consistent with psychology's emphasis on empiricism and scientific method. For constructivists and other postpositivists critical scrutiny of the conceptual apparatus that organizes psychological understanding of psychic life is equally important. Language is not a transparent medium through which we view reality; rather, language gives form and meaning to reality as we know it. The categories of meaning that psychology has created shape knowledge of psychic life for psychologists themselves as well as for consumers of psychology, a group that includes students, psychotherapy clients, and readers of self-help books. Consider such constructs as self-esteem, assertiveness, mother-infant attachment, and female masochism. These categories have profound effects on personal identity, on social reality, and on the character of social relations. Clinical diagnostic labels also convey strong messages about social relations, including the power relations between people with problems and the experts who claim to help them (Edelman 1974; Wakefield 1992). An important line of feminist inquiry, then, is to trace the history and sociology of psychological constructs, asking when those constructs came into use, how and with what effects they have been deployed, who has deployed them, and who has contested them. One example is Mary Parlee's (1989) elegant portrayal of the contest waged by medical specialties, feminists, and corporate interests for the "ownership" of premenstrual syndrome (PMS). Another is Leonore Tiefer's (1991) inquiry into the construct "human sexual response cycle."

Textual analysis is another means of investigating how language shapes knowledge in psychology. Sharon Lamb (1991), for example, examined articles on wife beating to show how stylistic features of the writing obscure issues of male responsibility. Another investigation traced metaphors of control and mastery in research reports on social cognition, pointing out how the language inscribed a hierarchy of domination, with the researchers positioned at the top (Morawski and Steele 1991). Others have investigated the narrative forms in which psychologists have cast their accounts of human behavior. Inquiry into linguistic practices is likely to yield new and deeper knowledge about the way that psychology constructs gender. In addition, such inquiry may also point out ways in which gender constructs psychology. We can ask how certain dichotomies (such as reason/emotion; task orientation/socio-emotional orientation; and active/passive) take their meaning and their valuation from their cultural association with maleness and femaleness.

Uncovering Work Practices and Social Relations

Formal statements of the scientific method of psychology both reveal and conceal the operations of the discipline. Day-to-day work practices and the mundane conditions of work are not part of the formal record, nor do the social relations among members of the discipline or between psychologists and their various constituencies (e.g., funders, students, university and clinic officials, patients, research participants) receive attention. Critical attention to the full array of work practices and social relations would yield fuller knowledge of the discipline and of how it operates to produce and warrant knowledge.

Ongoing efforts to uncover the history of women in the discipline reveal the obstacles women faced, the limits placed on their activities and roles, and the containment of their research agendas as well as their successes and triumphs (Scarborough and Furumoto 1987). Such histories and biographies provide knowledge that can assist scholars as they theorize how the social relations of the discipline give shape to the knowledge it produces.

Another set of work practices involves scientific communication. The *Publication Manual of the American Psychological Association* (APA 1994) provides remarkably detailed instructions governing both content and style. It dictates the narrative form for research reports, a form that is largely fictitious, insofar as it substitutes an orderly progression of discrete steps for a process that likely was nonlinear, disorderly, and far more inchoate. The manual privileges the production of data over inspiration, conceptualization, reflection, and interpretation. Thus, by and large, doing psychology is tacitly equated with nothing more than data collecting and statistical analysis. The manual further prescribes writing conventions that portray the researcher as objective, detached, and neutral; personal experience and the political or ethical stance of the researcher are not considered germane.

The *Publication Manual* effectively serves as a gatekeeper for knowledge in the discipline. Conformity to so-called APA style is required by the officially sponsored journals of the American Psychological Association as well as many other journals in the discipline, including the two primary journals of feminist psychology in the United States, *Psychology of Women Quarterly* and *Sex Roles*. Thus, prestige and wide readership—both highly desirable to scholars—come at the price of playing according to rules of writing that serve to sustain a pristine aura of science.

What is gained by disclosing one portion of psychology's work practices while keeping another invisible? Psychology's self-presentation serves to convey the image of elite experts whose knowledge places them above and apart from ordinary citizens. Uncertainty, ambiguity, and the intrusion of personal interests are all concealed from view, thus bolstering claims to authority. This serves to reaffirm the myth that psychology is outside society, with loyalties only to the abstract ideals of scientific integrity and objectivity. Researchers' dependence on government, corporate, and military sources for funding is minimized, as is the role of political, economic, social, and defense priorities in determining which research questions rise to the fore.

Power/Knowledge

Interrogating the politics of knowledge is a central project of postmodern thought. Since the Enlightenment, tradition has held that knowledge (including self-knowledge) is a means of liberation and a source of power. In the postmodern account the connection between knowledge and power is more sinister; knowledge is not a means of liberation but, instead, a technology of social control (Foucault 1980). What is promulgated as the truth serves to legitimate and perpetuate existing hierarchies of power.

At one level the idea that knowledge can be used to control women is not new to feminist psychology. From early on feminists have taken issue with received truths that pathologized women (or certain groups of women), that limited women's sphere of activity and influence, that valorized deference to men, and that excused male violence and sexual coercion. Postmodern thought takes a further step to ask what interests are served by competing ways of giving meaning to the world and by the very projects of Western thought, such as psychology itself.

Postmodern, social constructionist, and other critical theories all take a skeptical stance. A feminist psychology that takes this stance would define itself as an arena for debate about the production and justification of knowledge and a place in which the authority of mainstream psychology could be challenged. It would continually engage in efforts to problematize customary categories, concepts, and meanings and to interrupt self-serving idealizations of psychology's goals and practices (Fine 1992; Marecek 1989).

CONCLUSION

My title asks (somewhat facetiously) whether the relationship between feminism and psychology can be saved. What I have said thus far has not answered that question, only problematized it. The relationship has not been without its difficulties. Each of the strategies that feminists in psychology have employed has its own mix of problems and possibilities, pleasures and burdens.

Feminist psychologists who work within the positivist framework are in the most comfortable relationship to mainstream psychology. They can view their work as adding new and more accurate information on women to psychology's knowledge base and thus enriching the discipline. Their criticisms of bias may be received with anger or impatience by mainstream psychology, but those criticisms are offered in a spirit of confidence in psychology's self-described scientific procedures and faith in its overall self-proclaimed project of promoting human welfare. But the price of this loyalty to psychology seems to be marginalization within women's studies. Feminist psychologists who conceive of themselves as "scientists" have felt excluded, and even attacked, by the discussions about truth and knowledge under way in women's studies as well as by attacks on conventional theories of objectivity and the repudiation of the Archimedean stance of neutrality.

Skeptics within feminist psychology, on the other hand, appear to make little common cause with mainstream psychology. No dutiful daughters, their skepticism ranges broadly over the foundational assumptions of the discipline, the character of psychological constructs, psychology's methods of producing knowledge, the resulting knowledge, and the uses to which that knowledge is put. Nonetheless, even skepticism can be seen as a kind of loyal opposition: the hope is to reconstruct psychology, not annihilate it.

Waiting for the Phone to Ring?

The question "Can this relationship be saved?" begs a prior question: Does a relationship exist? Feminist psychologists themselves would answer yes. But answers from the rest of psychology would include some resounding no's and many more "Huh's?" Many, perhaps even most, psychologists remain unaware of the knowledge produced by feminist psychologists. Moreover, even though academics usually take great pains to avoid displays of ignorance, this particular form of ignorance is displayed without compunction. Indeed, in everyday conversations colleagues in the field often use language that locates the study of women and gender outside the disciplinary boundary of psychology. I have heard, for example, colleagues say that psychology is "losing" female students because they get interested in studying women and gender. For many in mainstream psychology there is no relationship to be saved and no interest in entering into one. Indeed, there is even reason to question the apparent gains that women have made as members of the discipline. As the number of women entering psychology has increased, official alarms have been sounded in the American Psychological Association; a few years ago a task force was duly constituted to study (and stem?) what was officially labeled the "feminization" of psychology.

Studies tracing the impact of feminist scholarship on the discipline at large confirm these everyday impressions. Time after time such studies have reached discouraging conclusions: the knowledge produced by feminist psychologists has had limited impact on other fields of psychology (as evidenced by the citation patterns in professional journals), and it has not found its way into mainstream textbooks, training curricula, etc. (Fine and Gordon 1989; Marecek and Hare-Mustin 1991; Peterson and Kroner 1992).

If Not a Romance, Then What?

Perhaps the metaphor of a romantic relationship is simply the wrong one for feminism and psychology. Within the academy a relationship between feminism and psychology will always be a marriage of unequals, with psychology claiming the intellectual high ground and holding control over the purse strings. When interests conflict, pressures will mount on feminist psychologists to fall in line on the side of psychology.

Is it possible that feminist psychologists have expended enough energy on getting accepted by mainstream psychology? Maybe the time has come to look elsewhere, to play the field. Loosening the bond with psychology might allow feminists to face their differences from (and with) the mainstream discipline more squarely. Liaisons with other disciplines and with emerging interdisciplinary groupings could infuse new ideas into attempts to understand women's psychic life. Methodological promiscuity would surely lead to richer and fuller understandings of women's lives. Indeed, it may even be time to set aside the hope of a romance entirely and to recast the relationship between feminism and psychology in a different system of metaphors, one that highlights feminism's disruptive potential and rebellious possibilities.

NOTES

1. I use the terms *feminist psychologist* and *feminist psychology* for reasons of personal preference and stylistic convenience. Many scholars in the field do not refer to themselves or to the field this way, preferring the more neutral *psychology of women*. The primary journal in the field is called *Psychology of Women Quarterly;* only since March 1990 has the journal's description on the inside cover used the phrase "a feminist journal."

2. Sandra Bem (1981) herself offered a reformulation of androgyny theory, in which the focal point shifted from personality attributes to cognition. Her own subsequent investigations have centered on "gender-schematic processing," that is, a generalized readiness to encode and organize information on the basis of cultural definitions of gender.

REFERENCES

Allen, Katherine, and Kristin M. Baber. 1992. "Ethical and Epistemological Tensions in Applying a Postmodern Perspective to Feminist Research." *Psychology of Women Quarterly* 16, no. 1:1–16.
American Psychological Association. (APA). 1994. *Publication Manual of the American*

Psychological Association, 3d ed. Washington, D.C.: American Psychological Association.

Bass, Ellen, and Laura Davis. 1988. *The Courage to Heal: A Guide for Women Survivors of Child Sexual Abuse*. New York: Harper and Row.

Belenky, Mary F., Blythe M. Clinchy, Nancy R. Goldberger, and Jill M. Tarule. 1986. *Women's Ways of Knowing: The Development of the Self, Voice, and Mind*. New York: Basic Books.

Bem, Sandra L. 1974. "The Measurement of Psychological Androgyny." *Journal of Consulting and Clinical Psychology* 42:155–62.

―――. 1976. "Probing the Promise of Androgyny." In *Beyond Sex-Role Stereotypes: Readings toward a Psychology of Androgyny*, edited by Alexandra G. Kaplan and Joan P. Bean. Boston: Little, Brown.

―――. 1978. "Beyond Androgyny: Some Presumptuous Prescriptions for a Liberated Sexual Identity." In *Psychology of Women: Future Directions of Research*, edited by Julia Sherman and Florence Denmark. New York: Psychological Dimensions.

―――. 1981. "Gender Schema Theory: A Cognitive Account of Sex Typing." *Psychological Review* 88:369–71.

―――. 1984. "Androgyny and Gender Schema Theory: A Conceptual and Empirical Integration." *Nebraska Symposium on Motivation* 32:179–226.

Berger, Peter L., and Thomas Luckmann. 1966. *The Social Construction of Reality: A Treatise on the Sociology of Knowledge*. Garden City, N.Y.: Doubleday.

Bohan, Janis S. 1992. *Seldom Seen, Rarely Heard: Women's Place in Psychology*. Boulder, Colo.: Westview Press.

―――. 1993. "Regarding Gender: Essentialism, Constructionism, and Feminist Psychology." *Psychology of Women Quarterly* 17:5–22.

Boston Lesbian Psychologies Collective. 1987. *Lesbian Psychologies*. Urbana: University of Illinois Press.

Broughton, John M. 1983. "Women's Rationality and Men's Virtues: A Critique of Gender Dualism in Gilligan's Theory of Moral Development." *Social Research* 50, no. 3:597–642.

Broverman, Donald M., Edward L. Klaiber, Yutaka Kobayashi, and William Vogel. 1968. "Roles of Activation and Inhibition in Sex Differences in Cognitive Abilities." *Psychological Review* 75, no. 1:23–50.

Brown, Angela, and David Finkelhor. 1986. "Impact of Child Sexual Abuse: A Review of the Literature." *Psychological Bulletin* 99, no. 1:66–77.

Brown, Laura. 1989. "New Voices, New Visions: Toward a Lesbian/Gay Paradigm for Psychology." *Psychology of Women Quarterly* 13, no. 4:445–58.

Burt, Martha. 1980. "Cultural Myths and Supports for Rape." *Journal of Personality and Social Psychology* 38:217–30.

Cherry, Frances. 1983. "Gender Roles and Sexual Violence." In *Changing Boundaries: Gender Roles and Sexual Behavior*, edited by Elizabeth R. Allgeier and Naomi B. McCormick. Palo Alto, Calif.: Mayfield.

Chrisman, Robert, and Robert L. Allen, eds. 1992. *Court of Appeal*. New York: Ballantine.

Connell, Robert T. 1987. *Gender and Power*. Stanford, Calif.: Stanford University Press.

Courtois, Christine A. 1988. *Healing the Incest Wound: Adult Survivors in Therapy*. New York: W. W. Norton.

Crawford, Mary. 1989. "Agreeing to Differ: Feminist Epistemologies and Women's Ways of Knowing." In *Gender and Thought: Psychological Perspectives*, edited by Mary Crawford and Margaret Gentry. New York: Springer-Verlag.

Crawford, Mary, and Jeanne Marecek. 1989. "Psychology Reconstructs the Female, 1968–1988." *Psychology of Women Quarterly* 13:147–65.

D'Emilio, John, and Estelle B. Freedman. 1988. *Intimate Matters: A History of Sexuality in America*. New York: Harper and Row.

Eagley, Alice H., and Maureen Crowley. 1986. "Gender and Helping Behavior: A Meta-Analytic Review of Social Psychological Literature." *Psychological Bulletin* 100, no. 3:283–308.

Eagley, Alice H., and Valerie J. Steffen. 1986. "Gender and Aggressive Behavior: A Meta-Analytic Review of the Social Psychological Literature." *Psychological Bulletin* 100, no. 3:309–30.

Edelman, Murray. 1974. "The Political Language of the Helping Professions." *Politics and Society* 4, no. 3:295–310.

Erikson, Erik H. 1964. "Inner and Outer Space: Reflections on Womanhood." *Daedelus* 93:583–606.

Falk, Patricia J. 1989. "Lesbian Mothers: Psychological Assumptions in Family Law." *American Psychologist* 44, no. 6:941–47.

Fine, Michelle. 1985. "Reflections on a Feminist Psychology of Women: Paradoxes and Prospects." *Psychology of Women Quarterly* 9:167–83.

————. 1992. *Disruptive Voices: The Possibilities of Feminist Research*. Ann Arbor: University of Michigan Press.

Fine, Michelle, and Susan Gordon. 1989. "Feminist Transformations of/despite Psychology." In *Gender and Thought: Psychological Perspectives*, edited by Mary Crawford and Margaret Gentry. New York: Springer-Verlag.

Foucault, Michel. 1980. *Power/Knowledge: Selected Interviews and Other Writings, by Michel Foucault*. Edited by Colin Gordon. New York: Pantheon.

Freud, Sigmund. 1925. "Some Psychical Consequences of the Anatomical Distinction between the Sexes." In *Freud on Women*, edited by Elizabeth Young-Bruehl. New York: W. W. Norton.

Gardner, Carol Brooks. 1988. "Passing By: Street Rights, Address Rights, and Urban Female." *Sociological Inquiry* 50, nos. 3–4:328–56.

————. 1989. "Analyzing Gender in Public Places: Rethinking Goffman's Vision of Everyday Life." *American Sociologist* 20, no. 1:42–56.

Gavey, Nicola. 1990. *Technologies and Effects of Heterosexual Subjugation*. Paper presented to the Department of Psychology, University of Auckland, Auckland.

Gavey, Nicola, Joy Florence, Sue Pezaro, and Jan Tan. 1990. "Mother-Blaming, the Perfect Alibi: Family Therapy and the Mothers of Incest Survivors." *Journal of Feminist Family Therapy* 2, no. 1:1–25.

Geertz, Clifford. 1973. *The Interpretation of Cultures*. New York: Basic Books.

Gergen, Kenneth J. 1985. "The Social Constructionist Movement in Modern Psychology." *American Psychologist* 40:266–75.

Gilligan, C. 1977. "In a Different Voice: Women's Conception of the Self and of Morality." *Harvard Educational Review* 47:481–517.

Goldner, Virginia, Peggy Penn, Marcia Sheinberg, and Gillian Walker. 1990. "Love and Violence: Gender Paradoxes in Volatile Attachments." *Family Process* 29:343–64.

Gordon, Margaret T., and Stephanie Riger. 1991. *The Female Fear: The Social Cost of Rape.* Urbana: University of Illinois Press.

Grady, Kathy. 1981. "Sex Biases in Research Design." *Psychology of Women Quarterly* 5:628–38.

Graham, Sandra. 1992. " 'Most of the Subjects Were White and Middle Class': Trends in Published Research on African Americans in Selected APA Journals, 1970–1989." *American Psychologist* 47:629–39.

Harari, Herbert, and Jean M. Peters. 1987. "The Fragmentation of Psychology: Are APA Divisions Symptomatic?" *American Psychologist* 42:822–24.

Haraway, Donna. 1988. "Situated Knowledges: The Science Question in Feminism and the Privilege of Partial Perspective." *Feminist Studies* 14:579–99.

Harding, Sandra. 1986. *The Science Question in Feminism.* Ithaca, N.Y.: Cornell University Press.

Hare-Mustin, Rachel T., and Jeanne Marecek. 1986. "Autonomy and Gender: Some Questions for Therapists." *Psychotherapy* 23:205–12.

———. 1988. "The Meaning of Difference: Gender Theory, Postmodernism, and Psychology." *American Psychologist* 43:455–64.

———. 1990. *Making a Difference: Psychology and the Construction of Gender.* New Haven, Conn.: Yale University Press.

———. 1994. "Asking the Right Questions: Feminist Psychology and Sex Differences." *Feminism and Psychology* 4, no. 4:531–37.

Hawthorne, Nathaniel. 1893. "The Birthmark." *Mosses from an Old Manse.* New York: Houghton-Mifflin.

Herek, Gregory M., Doug C. Kimmel, Hortensia Amaro, and Gary B. Melton. 1991. "Avoiding Heterosexual Biases in Psychological Research." *American Psychologist* 46:957–72.

Herman, Judith L. 1981. *Father-Daughter Incest.* Cambridge, Mass.: Harvard University Press.

Hochschild, Arlie. 1989. *The Second Shift.* New York: Viking Penguin.

Hollway, Wendy. 1984. "Gender Difference and the Production of Subjectivity." In *Changing the Subject: Psychology, Social Regulation and Subjectivity,* edited by J. Henriques, Wendy Hollway, Cathy Urwin, C. Venn, and Valerie Walkerdine. London and New York: Methuen.

———. 1989. *Subjectivity and Method in Psychology: Gender, Meaning and Science.* London: Sage.

Horner, Matina. 1970. "Femininity and Successful Achievement: A Basic Inconsistency." In *Feminine Personality and Conflict,* edited by J. Bardwick, E. Douvan, M. Horner, and D. Gutman. Belmont, Calif.: Brooks/Cole.

Hyde, Janet S., and Marsha C. Linn, eds. 1986. *The Psychology of Gender: Advances through Meta-analysis*. Baltimore: Johns Hopkins University Press.

Jacklin, Carol N. 1981. "Methodological Issues in the Study of Sex-Related Differences." *Developmental Review* 1:266–73.

Jordan, Judith, Alexandra G. Kaplan, Jean B. Miller, Irene Stiver, and Janet Surrey. 1991. *Women's Growth in Connection: Writings from the Stone Center*. New York: Guilford Press.

Kahn, Arnold S., and Janice D. Yoder. 1989. "The Psychology of Women and Conservatism: Rediscovering Social Change." *Psychology of Women Quarterly* 13:417–32.

Kaplan, Alexandra G. 1979. "Clarifying the Concept of Androgyny: Implications for Therapy." *Psychology of Women Quarterly* 3, no. 3:223–30.

Koss, Mary P. 1990. "The Women's Mental Health Research Agenda." *American Psychologist* 45:374–80.

Lamb, Sharon. 1986. "Treating Sexually Abused Children: Issues of Blame and Responsibility." *American Journal of Orthopsychiatry* 56, no. 2:303–7, 459–63.

———. 1991. "Acts without Agents: An Analysis of Linguistic Avoidance in Journal Articles on Men Who Batter Women." *American Journal of Orthopsychiatry* 61, no. 2:250–57.

Landrine, Hope, Elizabeth A. Klonoff, and Alice Brown-Collins. 1992. "Cultural Diversity and Methodology in Feminist Psychology." *Psychology of Women Quarterly* 16, no. 2:145–63.

Locksley, Anne, and Mary Ellen Colten. 1979. "Psychological Androgyny: A Case of Mistaken Identity?" *Journal of Personality and Social Psychology* 37, no. 6:1017–31.

Luria, Zella. 1991. Review of *Maternal Thinking*, by S. Ruddick. *Psychology of Women Quarterly* 15, no. 3:485–87.

Maccoby, Eleanor E., and Carol N. Jacklin. 1974. *The Psychology of Sex Differences*. Palo Alto, Calif.: Stanford University Press.

McHugh, Maureen D., Randi D. Koeske, and Irene H. Frieze. 1986. "Issues to Consider in Conducting Nonsexist Psychological Research: A Guide for Researchers." *American Psychologist* 41:879–90.

Malamuth, N. 1981. "Rape Productivity among Males." *Journal of Social Issues* 37:138–57.

Marecek, Jeanne. 1979. "Social Change, Positive Mental Health, and Psychological Androgyny." *Psychology of Women Quarterly* 3, no. 3:241–47.

———. 1989. "Introduction." *Psychology of Women Quarterly* 13:367–77.

Marecek, Jeanne, and Rachel T. Hare-Mustin. 1990. "Toward a Feminist Poststructural Psychology: The Modern Self and the Postmodern Subject." Paper presented at the American Psychological Association meeting, Boston, August.

———. 1991. "A Short History of the Future: Feminism and Clinical Psychology." *Psychology of Women Quarterly* 5:521–36.

Martin, Emily. 1987. *The Woman in the Body: A Cultural Analysis of Reproduction*. Boston: Beacon Press.

Mednick, Martha T., and Laura L. Urbanski. 1991. "The Origins and Activities of APA's Division of the Psychology of Women." *Psychology of Women Quarterly* 15, no. 4:651–63.

Morawski, Jill G. 1985. "The Measurement of Masculinity and Femininity: Engendering Categorical Realities." *Journal of Personality* 53:196–223.

———. 1987. "The Troubled Quest for Masculinity, Femininity, and Androgyny." *Review of Personality and Social Psychology* 7:44–69.

Morawski, Jill G., and Robert S. Steele. 1991. "The One and the Other: A Textual Analysis of Masculine Power and Feminist Empowerment." *Theory and Psychology* 1:107–31.

Morrison, Toni, ed. 1992. *Race-ing Justice, En-gendering Power*. New York: Pantheon.

Ortner, Sherry B. 1974. "Is Female to Male as Nature Is to Culture?" In *Women, Culture and Society*, edited by Michelle Z. Rosaldo and Louis Lamphere. Stanford, Calif.: Stanford University Press.

Parlee, Mary B. 1989. *The Science and Politics of PMS Research*. Paper presented at the meeting of the Association for Women in Psychology, Newport, R.I., March.

Parlee, Mary B. 1990. "Feminism and Psychology." In *Revolutions in Knowledge: Feminism in the Social Sciences*, edited by Sue R. Zalk and Janice Gordon-Kelter. Boulder, Colo.: Westview Press.

Peterson, Sharyl B., and Traci Kroner. 1992. "Gender Biases in Textbooks for Introductory Psychology and Human Development." *Psychology of Women Quarterly* 16:17–36.

Rohrbaugh, Joanna B. 1990. *Lesbian Parenting: Psychological Implications of Family Structure*. Paper presented at the Annual Convention of the American Psychological Association, Boston, August.

Rosaldo, Renato. 1989. *Culture and Truth: The Remaking of Social Analysis*. Boston: Beacon Press.

Rothblum, Ester, and Violet Franks, eds. 1983. *The Stereotyping of Women: Its Effects on Mental Health*. New York: Springer.

Sass, Louis A. 1988. "Humanism, Hermeneutics, and the Concept of the Human Subject." In *Hermeneutics and Psychological Theory*, edited by Stanley B. Messer, Louis A. Sass, and R. L. Woolfolk. New Brunswick, N.J.: Rutgers University Press.

Scarborough, Elizabeth, and Laurel Furumoto. 1987. *Untold Lives: The First Generation of American Women Psychologists*. New York: Columbia University Press.

Scott, Joan W. 1985. *Is Gender a Useful Category of Historical Analysis?* Paper presented at the meeting of the American Historical Association, New York, December.

Sherif, Carolyn W. 1979. "Bias in Psychology." In *The Prism of Sex*, edited by Julia A. Sherman and Evelyn T. Beck. Madison: University of Wisconsin Press.

Shields, Stephanie A. 1975. "Functionalism, Darwinism, and the Psychology of Women." *American Psychologist* 30:739–54.

Spelman, Elizabeth V. 1988. *Inessential Woman*. Boston: Beacon Press.

Spence, Janet T. 1984. "Gender Identity and Its Implications for the Concept of Masculinity and Femininity." *Nebraska Symposium on Motivation* 32:59–96.

Stacey, Judith, and Barrie Thorne. 1985. "The Missing Feminist Revolution in Sociology." *Social Problems* 32:301–16.

Stanley, Julian. 1989. "Selective Citation." *American Psychologist* 44, no. 10:1328.

Thorne, Barrie, and Zella Luria. 1986. "Sexuality and Gender in Children's Daily Worlds." *Social Problems* 33, no. 3:176–90.

Tiefer, Leonore. 1991a. "A Brief History of the Association of Women in Psychology." *Psychology of Women Quarterly* 15:635–49.

———. 1991b. "Historical, Scientific, Clinical, and Feminist Criticisms of 'The Human Sexual Response Cycle' Model." *Annual Review of Sex Research* 2:1–23.

———. 1992. "Critique of the DSM-III-R Nosology of Sexual Dysfunctions." *Psychiatric Medicine* 10, no. 2:227–45.

———. 1995. *Sex Is an Unnatural Act*. Boulder, Colo.: Westview Press.

Treichler, Paula A. 1987. "AIDS, Homophobia, and Biomedical Discourse: An Epidemic of Signification." *Cultural Studies* 1, no. 3:263–305.

Wakefield, Jerome C. 1992. "The Concept of Mental Disorder: On the Boundary between Biological Facts and Social Values." *American Psychologist* 47, no. 3:373–88.

Walker, Lenore E. A. 1989. "Psychology and Violence against Women." *American Psychologist* 44, no. 6:695–702.

Weisstein, Naomi. 1968. *Kinder, Küche, Kirche as Scientific Law: Psychology Constructs the Female*. Boston: New England Free Press.

West, Candace, and Don H. Zimmerman. 1987. "Doing Gender." *Gender and Society* 1:25–51.

Widom, Cathy S., ed. 1984. *Sex Roles and Psychopathology*. New York: Plenum.

Winslow, Deborah. 1980. "Rituals of First Menstruation in Sri Lanka." *Man* n.s. 15:603–25.

Woolley, Helen T. 1910. "Psychological Literature: A Review of Recent Literature on the Psychology of Sex." *Psychological Bulletin* 7:335–42.

PART 2

The Differences That Gender Makes

Chapter 5

The Differences of Women's Studies: The Example of Literary Criticism

Mary Poovey

When I first began to think about the history of women's studies within literary criticism in preparation for writing this essay, I thought in terms of the straight-forward narrative that has become a truism of feminist literary history. In the first phase of women's studies in the U.S. academy, scholars looked at sex; in the second, they (we) look at gender.[1] In addition to helping simplify complex and overlapping intellectual trends, this narrative also enables us to tell the story in terms of scholarly "progress." Whatever the losses associated with substitut-ing gender for sex, it implies, the gains are far greater, for gender allows femi-nists to discuss not only how women as a group have been "oppressed" by "patriarchy" but also how patriarchal institutions construct gendered identities for everyone and use gender as a principle of discrimination. Focusing on gen-der, in other words, encourages students and teachers to practice a form of resistance that "goes beyond" merely including more women writers in the canon, because it directs our attention to the processes of categorization and abjection that constitute the conditions for exclusionary practices like the canon in the first place.

I do think that the turn to gender within many women's studies courses and theoretical texts has opened new terrains to politically fruitful analysis and work, but I have now begun to think of the relationship between sex and gender within women's studies programs and literary criticism in particular in a more complex way than my first narrative allowed. This revision in my own thinking has come about partly in an attempt to account for the recent emergence of divisive strains within women's studies, especially around the significance of race, and the even more recent emergence of subspecialties within literary criti-cism that concern sex and even gender but not necessarily women. These subspecialties—and here I have in mind gay studies and the study of mas-culinity, in particular—ought to be the allies of women's studies, but some-times, given today's fiscal restraints, they actually compete with women's studies' concerns for faculty and funds. These developments have led me to conceptualize the history of women's studies not in terms of a progressive evolution or the emergence of something new but, rather, as the surfacing and disaggregation of heterogeneous elements that have *always* informed women's studies, even when it focused on women and sex. According to this model, the relationship between sex and gender as objects of analysis within women's studies would not be temporal and progressive but, instead, deconstructive or demystifying: the emergence of the latter, along with the tensions and subspecialties to which I have just alluded, would thus be seen to deconstruct the illusion of stability from which the former acquired its initial identity. The best way of describing the relationship between the two would therefore not be a narrative of successive phases but a model of mutual constitution and inter- (if sometimes rivalrous) dependence.[2]

Let me be more specific. In the two-phase Whiggish history with which I began, academic women's studies in the United States is depicted as having developed out of and alongside the women's movement, which itself developed in relation to the civil rights movement in the 1960s. The basic premise of women's studies in this first phase was that the knowledge that the academy claimed was representative and universal was actually neither because it overlooked half of the population—women. Despite the claims that the terms *man* and *mankind* were representative of all human beings, that is, early proponents of women's studies argued that the knowledge commonly assumed to describe and analyze "man" did not apply equally to women, because what counted as knowledge was actually limited to the activities generally performed by men. Thus, history usually concerned itself with wars, politics, or wage labor, not with domestic relations, philanthropy, or housework; economics dealt with macro and micro systems, not with the contributions (often nonmonetary) that women made to the family resources; and literary criticism focused on writings by men, because men had written almost all of the "great" works on "universal" themes—like war, heroism, and territorial expansion, while women writers had confined themselves to "inferior" subjects like marriage and domesticity.

These examples should make it clear that one complaint of early women's studies courses was that the claim to universality that had underwritten the academic curriculum and legitimized its authority was based on a principle of exclusion. The political work of this phase of women's studies—and, within this, feminist literary criticism—was to restore to visibility women as agents and, as part of this process, to revalue the work women had performed. One thing this entailed was teaching texts by women (and sometimes urging publishers to reprint these texts—or founding publishing ventures ourselves). Another was to focus attention on the stereotypes and attitudes formulated in writing by men that reinforced the devaluation of women's lives, such as those depicting women as angels or whores. This phase of women's studies was inaugurated by such pathbreaking books as Mary Ellmann's *Thinking about Women* (1968), Patricia Spacks's *Female Imagination* (1975), Judith Fetterly's *Resisting Reader* (1978), and Sandra Gilbert and Susan Gubar's *Madwoman in the Attic* (1979). It culminated, in one sense at least, with the publication of the *Norton Anthology of Literature by Women* (1985).[3]

What I initially wanted to call the second phase of women's studies began sometime in the 1980s, after women's studies had been institutionalized in hundreds of U.S. colleges and universities.[4] The problem with thinking of this as a second "phase," however, becomes clear as soon as I acknowledge that it had multiple "origins" and that each of these origins can be read in several ways. Marked by the publication of books such as Cherríe Moraga and Gloria Anzaldúa's *This Bridge Called My Back* (1981) and Teresa de Lauretis's *Alice Doesn't* (1985), one origin of this phase makes it seem like a logical extension of the original critique of (male) knowledge; upon closer examination, however, this shift can also be seen as an actualization of the internal divisions always implicit in this critique of knowledge. For, once an argument has been made that the claim to universality advanced by the old curriculum is based on a principle of exclusion, it becomes increasingly difficult to argue that *any* knowledge *could* be universal or complete—including the version of knowledge constructed by women. The extent to which what came to be articulated as a criticism of women's studies was constitutive of women's studies was adumbrated by the fact that some of those who voiced this position most persuasively were women who were (more or less) within women's studies. Thus, some women of color charged that women's studies was actually *white* women's studies, and some lesbians argued that a woman-centered curriculum was at least potentially as compulsorily heterosexual as the old curriculum was.

Meanwhile, during the late 1970s and throughout the 1980s, a second origin had appeared. This consisted of the gradual assimilation by U.S. literary critics of the work of (largely French) poststructuralists, which emphasized the semiotics of culture and the socially constructed nature of reality. Within this heterogeneous body of theory two strains had particular impact on U.S. women's studies. On the one hand, the "French feminisms" of writers like Luce Irigaray, Julia Kristeva, and Hélène Cixous hypothesized an alternative, potentially subversive, or "feminine," semiotics.[5] On the other, Michel Foucault's work on the history of sexuality conceptualized sex as one of many diacritically marked units within a complex semantic system that was produced and disciplined as the very nature of social reality.[6] While the effects of poststructuralism on literary criticism have been too diffuse and diverse for me to survey here, two readings of its implications deserve particular notice in the present context. The first, which has recently been formulated by Judith Butler, suggests that sex does not occupy the position of stable "other" to gender in a binary relationship. As a consequence, Butler argues, genders may well be not only multiple but also "performative"—that is, wholly responsive to and constitutive of social semantics.[7] The second, which has yet to be so rigorously theorized, implicitly interrogates the privilege previously given to women's studies within the study of gender. Once a critic argues that discrimination against women is only one code within a semiotics of culture, then the ground for focusing on women as a group over and above other sex- or gender-defined groups comes into question. The logical extension of this position would be to argue that, once a critic decides that discrimination by sex does not operate in isolation from other social codes, the justification for using sexual "identity" or even sexual behavior as a privileged principle of analysis disappears. This last move, however, has rarely been taken. Much more common, within literary studies at least, has been the extension to other genders and sexualities of the privilege previously given to women.[8]

If the history of the turn to gender is most accurately figured as a deconstructive story—as the playing out of tensions that facilitated the differentiation and articulation of women's studies in the first place—then what are the implications of this turn for the present and the future? Will some feminists—women of color, for example—be forced to choose between women's studies and black studies? Will women's studies itself splinter into countless new subspecialties? Will the acknowledgment that multiple factors determine social meanings and discriminations obliterate sex altogether as a privileged category of analysis? Obviously, I cannot answer these questions with any authority for literary studies as a whole or even for my own institution, but I can offer an example of one kind of analysis that follows from recognizing the differences within women's studies. Following more obviously from what I identified as the first origin of the turn to gender than from the second, this reading of a canonical literary text focuses on the place that gender occupies in relation to race in the 1860s. This emphasis places my analysis in the company of other recent attempts to rethink overdetermination and to map the interdependence of determinants of identity.[9] In rewriting the difference of women's studies as differences, this approach seems to me to be more promising than simply turning to another group defined by (and often discriminated against because of) its "identity," for it helps illuminate more precisely the *dynamics* of discrimination and privilege. Just as women as a group have been treated differently from men because of sex, some women have been (and are) treated differently from other women (by women as well as men) because of other determinants such as race.[10]

Let me make one more prefatory remark, this time about my choice of text. In what follows I present a reading of Charles Dickens's *Our Mutual Friend*. I have chosen a canonical text by one of the century's most popular male authors partly to demonstrate that the turn to gender enables us to see beyond "images of women" to the production of sexual stereotypes as a contribution to the creation of cultural meanings (or ideological work). Partly, my choice suggests that, in carrying out this ideological work, writers like Dickens helped formulate the terms in which identity was understood in the nineteenth century. In so doing, Dickens helped constitute the conceptual conditions that made modern, and now postmodern, subjectivity possible. This ideological work was itself a response (as well as a contributor) to material and institutional changes—in this case, the threat posed to the traditional division of waged labor by organized feminism and the volatile possibilities opened to British investors by new financial instruments. Not unlike some voices of today's "backlash" against feminism, Dickens experienced these changes as an assault on masculine subjectivity. His response was to shore up imaginatively the masculine subject by mobilizing idealized stereotypes of femininity and, as these stereotypes proved unstable, to call up the newly significant demarcation of race. Thus, we see Dickens contributing to the semiotic skein that is the historical antecedent of our own ideological configuration. In this densely textured cultural code, gender cannot be separated from race-specific meanings, just as masculinity cannot achieve coherence without femininity to mark its difference. Because they help expose (as well as compose) the system of overdetermined meanings that stand behind twentieth-century Western visions of subjectivity, novels like *Our Mutual Friend* also help create the conceptual conditions that have made the present moment of feminism possible.

My analysis of *Our Mutual Friend* depends on a certain amount of historical knowledge, because my first assumption is that articulations of identity are historically as well as textually and culturally specific. Unfortunately, given the constraints of space, I'm going to have to construct this history very briefly and as a kind of unproblematized "background" to the novel and you're just going to have to take my word that I don't think that historical narratives are either unproblematic or mere background. For the purposes of this essay it is most important to know that the period during which Dickens wrote *Our Mutual Friend*, 1863–65, was the culmination of more than a decade of legal and economic revisions in patterns of capital organization and investment. Among these revisions were the passage of a series of laws that established limited liability, the rapid expansion of banking and credit facilities, and the dramatic increase in speculative opportunities for English investors both at home and abroad.[11] These developments generated mixed effects, for, while limited liability and new forms of credit created the possibility for enormous returns, the same conditions that underwrote these financial innovations also made fraudulent enterprises and fiscal irresponsibility not only possible but almost irresistible. The mania for profit, combined with legal provisions that encouraged but did not regulate company formations or investing on margin, produced a concentration of financial abuses, which, for sheer recklessness and audacity, surpassed even the credit frauds associated with the railway mania of the 1840s.[12] Although the most egregious deceits only became public after the crash of 1866, businesses had already begun to fail in 1863 and 1864, and the bank rate had reached the unprecedented level of 7 percent.

The most extensive treatment of speculation in *Our Mutual Friend* centers on Alfred Lammle, who has created the illusion of wealth by speculating in stock market shares.[13] But Lammle's speculations do not end here; he also gambles in another market—the marriage market—by taking Sophronia Akershem as his wife on the basis of a rumor that she is rich. Lest the reader miss the link being established between the financial market and market behavior in the domestic sphere, Dickens introduces yet another version of the market—the "orphan market," in which hopeful parents speculate on the profit a child might bring. "Fluctuations of a wild and South-Sea nature were occasioned, by orphan-holders keeping back, then rushing into the market a dozen together," Dickens wryly comments. "But the uniform principle at the root of all these various operations was bargain and sale" (1971, 244).

In order to counteract the anxieties generated both by the risk associated with a market economy and by the extent to which "bargain and sale" have penetrated the home, Dickens casts the romance between John Harmon and Bella Wilfer as another version of "speculation." In this domestic speculation Dickens converts Bella's desire to marry a rich man into an appreciation for the "gold" of domestic affection. Bella's education, which Harmon oversees, thus involves learning that literal gold is only a metaphor—that is, inherently without meaning or value—while metaphorical gold is truly valuable because it stands for love. At the end of Bella's education her father makes this transvaluation clear: Bella, he says to Harmon, "brings you a good fortune when she brings you the poverty she has accepted for your sake and the honest truth's." John Harmon, who takes a job in London's financial district while further testing his wife's resolve, describes Bella as more valuable than shares, thereby proving that metaphorical stock is more trustworthy than literal shares, which are, like money and gold, inherently meaningless because metaphorical. "He cared, beyond all expression, for his wife," Dickens writes, "as a most precious and sweet commodity, that was always looking up, and that was never worth less than all the gold in the world" (1971, 750).

Dickens is able to guarantee the outcome of John Harmon's speculation because moving the market to the home enables him to mobilize two cultural assumptions about women. The first is that the "true" woman desires only what the man who (legally) represents her desires. Thus, when Harmon realizes Bella's wishes at the end of the novel, he also realizes his own.[14] The second is that women can themselves stand in for the inhumane systems that control men.

Literal women, in other words, can function like metaphors, which represent and displace something they are not. Thus, substituting a woman for stocks, as in John Harmon's depiction of his work, seems to allay the man's anxiety about a sphere he cannot control through displacement—because the domestic sphere apparently offers him an arena in which he can exercise control and, thus, an antidote to the uncertainties of the market. Actually, of course, both of these assumptions depend on another displacement: they depend on men effacing the possibility that women may have desires that do not coincide with men's.

If one accepts these two assumptions, then John Harmon's domestication of Bella can serve as a corrective substitution for the entire system of exploitation and fraud associated with speculation and debt: if one assumes that a good woman wants only to make a man happy and that women can stand in for other forces beyond men's control, the illusion can be produced that that which seems to be beyond man's control actually answers his deepest needs. While this symbolic solution is dramatized in *Our Mutual Friend,* however, it only works in what amounts to a narrative vacuum; by the end of the novel the John Harmon story is almost completely cordoned off from the other plots, and the mutually gratifying partnership that Bella and John share cannot affect even the domestic imbalance that lies closest to Bella—the travesty of her parents' marriage. In order to understand why what happens in John Harmon's home cannot lay to rest all of the anxieties associated with speculation and deceit, we have to turn to the subplot of *Our Mutual Friend,* in which money and domestic virtue seem *least* entwined—the plot that centers on Lizzie Hexam.

Lizzie Hexam, Gaffer's daughter, is apparently completely unlike Bella Wilfer. Instead of leaving her family to advance herself, Lizzie sacrifices her education for her father. Instead of wanting to marry for money, Lizzie refuses to capitalize on her love for Eugene Wrayburn or to give in to Bradley Headstone, who is at least advancing in social rank. At a deeper level, however, Lizzie's virtue can be seen to engender almost as many harmful effects as does Bella's greed. Not only is Lizzie implicitly responsible for the blame cast upon her father by Miss Abby Potterson; Lizzie also explicitly causes Eugene to feel like a criminal when he tracks Gaffer, to become a Peeping Tom when he spies on Lizzie, and to consort with Mr. Dolls when he seeks to discover where she is hiding. Unintentionally, of course, Lizzie is also the first cause of the assault upon Eugene and of the conspiracy that results in the drownings of Bradley Headstone and Rogue Riderhood. In the scene of his agonized proposal to her, Bradley Headstone insists that Lizzie exercises a dangerous power: she can cause either evil or good because she can bring out in a man his baseness or his virtue. "You draw me to you," Headstone raves. "You could draw me to fire, you could draw me to water, you could draw me to the gallows, you could draw me to any death, you could draw me to any exposure and disgrace. But if you would return a favourable answer to my offer of myself in marriage, you could draw me to any good—every good—with equal force" (Dickens 1971, 254-55).

The power Headstone attributes to Lizzie assigns her the responsibility not only for gratifying his desire but, more important, for domesticating his passion, for making him desire the right thing. Yet this power is clearly dangerous to Headstone and all the other men who come under her influence. The precise nature of the danger Lizzie poses seems to reside in the fact that she is not only powerful but also independent. Certainly, Dickens suggests that Lizzie's independence is dangerous when he repeatedly links it to sexual, economic, and physical agency. Lizzie's agency receives scant narrative elaboration, but it is critical to the plot: her willful desire for Eugene sets the Headstone/Wrayburn dynamic moving; the money she has apparently saved finances her brother's education and thus puts him in contact with Headstone; and the physical strength Lizzie has acquired as a "female waterman" enables her to pull Wrayburn's body into the boat after Headstone has assaulted him.

The combination of Lizzie's ambiguous "purity" with such stereotypically "masculine" traits as economic agency and muscular strength suggests that Lizzie's dangerous power may not so much originate in her independence from men as it expresses her assimilation to men. That is, despite the fact that Lizzie is said to have the ability to reform both Eugene and Bradley because she is different from them, she is actually, in some very basic ways, a better "man" than either of her suitors. Lizzie's "masculinity" is most obviously attributable to her class position: as a working-class woman, Lizzie lacks both the leisure and the resources to enhance her "femininity." Yet Dickens specifically downplays Lizzie's class origins: she never speaks as a working-class woman; she (correctly) imagines that Eugene will see her as his equal; she never wants for resources or protectors; and at the end of the novel Twemlow decisively declares that she is a "lady" (Dickens 1971, 891). Moreover, the fact that her suitors' competition for *her* is transformed into an obsession with one another suggests that Lizzie's class position is, in some important senses, subordinate to her role in bringing these two men into a cross-class, homosocial relationship.[15]

Lizzie's ambiguous status—as a working-class "lady" and a masculine woman—begins to explain why the Harmon marriage can provide neither the moral center nor the organizing principle for *Our Mutual Friend*, as David Copperfield's marriage to Agnes was able to do in Dickens's earlier novel. The key to this insufficiency lies in the peculiar nature of Lizzie's status: she does not become a literal lady or a literal man but demonstrates, instead, that she can metaphorically cross class and sexual barriers—that, in other words, class and sex meanings are, in some sense at least, *only* metaphorical. Despite the fact, then, that Lizzie is Bella's opposite in not wanting money, she brings into the novel the same association between woman and figuration that is thematically associated with Bella. In Lizzie, moreover, we see that the cultural association between woman and figuration posed threats as well as alleviated anxieties. If Bella's status as a metaphorical "commodity" allows John Harmon to realize a good investment, Lizzie's status as a metaphorical "lady" and a metaphorical "waterman" undermines men's ability to be certain that she is only what she seems to be. In order to understand why the link between women and figuration might have seemed problematic in the 1860s, it is necessary to turn for a moment to the history of the cultural association between these two terms.

Catherine Gallagher has recently argued that, in the late seventeenth century, the figure of "woman" was conceptually positioned in relation to a number of other critical concepts, including "politics," "virtue," "the public," and "fiction."[16] In a process I can only summarize here, during the early eighteenth century "woman" and "the feminine" were conceptually linked to the anxieties generated by the new market economy and to the symbolic solutions formulated to resolve these anxieties. Thus, for example, "femininity" was associated with the fantasies and appetites unleashed in men by new commercial opportunities at the same time that social interactions with real women were expected to enhance the refined and polite behaviors that could theoretically control these excesses.

The financial revolution of the 1690s also generated a new model of politics and, along with this, new anxieties about the nature of political discourse. This new politics was "public" in the sense both that it involved more people and that it was increasingly conducted in the newly expanded medium of the press. At the same time, however, the nature of this public political participation was shaped by the libel law, which virtually mandated anonymity, pseudonymity, and the use of allegorical or coded modes of description and analysis. The libel law, in other words, encouraged the use of fiction as a vehicle for political discourse. This use of fiction aroused the same kind of anxieties also generated by the newly expanded press, for both fiction and the press called attention to the possibility of creating a world of words that had no connection to the world outside language. As Gallagher explains, invoking the concept of feminine writing—and female practitioners of this writing like Mary Delarivier Manley—constituted a basis for discriminating among kinds of writing and, thus, for alleviating anxiety about public writing per se.[17]

By the early 1860s the links welded during the eighteenth century between "woman," "fiction," "politics," and new forms of commercial transaction like speculation had undergone significant alteration. In the first place, partly because of a general cultural shift after the French Revolution toward the moralism associated with the emergent bourgeoisie and partly because of the material role women played in helping men establish their credit worthiness, "woman" increasingly came to be associated not with "politics" or "fiction" as "scandal" but, rather, with morality and even "truth," both of which were held to be "above" or "outside of" politics. Coventry Patmore deified this cultural association in the mid-1850s in his celebration of the "angel in the house," but it is also important to recognize that Victorians believed this idealization to have a biological basis. The moralization of woman, in other words, was also a moralization of the female body—a displacement of the seventeenth-century obsession with female sexuality by an increasingly biologized focus on "maternal" instincts and the certainty of a woman's parental relation to her child. By the 1860s woman was understood by middle-class Victorians literally to embody and thus metaphorically to guarantee truth and to stand as surety against both the economic vicissitudes of the market economy and the competitive drive of one man to deceive another, even in the "tenderest" relation of all.

The second important change involved the relation between fiction and political discourse. On the one hand, the repeal of the libel law and various stamp acts had considerably loosened restrictions on public participation in politics, thus obviating the need for political discourse to disguise itself in fictions. On the other hand, of course, partly through the "feminizing" poetics of romantic realists such as Wordsworth, Scott, and Dickens, fiction had acquired a moral authority of its own, and authors could advance political positions through fictions, just as fictions were sometimes cited in Parliament to further political arguments. While the relationship between political discourse and fiction had not been severed, then, fiction, like woman, had undergone a process of moralization that helped cleanse it of connotations of excess and scandal.

Given the revaluation of "woman" and "fiction" and the naturalization of womanly virtue, why might Dickens reanimate the old anxieties once generated by the link between women and figuration? For this is exactly what Dickens's portrayal of Lizzie Hexam does: it ties what most Victorians thought of as the natural capacity of women to incarnate morality and value to a series of threats posed to the male characters. These threats, moreover, are specifically associated with the traditional connection between fiction, woman, and the capacity of financial speculation to conjure something out of nothing—the very threats that had been moralized away by the middle of the nineteenth century. I want to suggest that this set of ominous meanings was available again in the early 1860s because of the historical conjunction between the economic factors I have alluded to and the emergence of the first specific challenge to the naturalization of female virtue. This challenge was articulated in the 1850s in a self-consciously politicized feminist movement, which was itself a response to the increasing number of women entering the work force.[18] One of the first campaigns of this movement was to rectify the law that prohibited married women from being economic agents, capable of owning their own property or keeping the wages they earned. Even though the 1857 Married Women's Property Bill did not become law, the controversy it aroused interjected the issues of women's rights, property, and work into parliamentary discussion, quarterly review articles, and popular novels as well.

Dickens's representation of Lizzie Hexam and Bella Wilfer must be read in the context of emergent feminism. For the most part, Dickens's treatment of women is a conservative, even nostalgic, recuperation of the domesticated female in defiance of some feminists' claims that sexuality was not the determinate characteristic of women and, therefore, that woman's biology was not the natural ground of her character or of womanly truth. Like many of his conservative contemporaries, for example, Dickens consistently marginalizes and discredits Lizzie's waged work: either he idealizes her labor, as in his depiction of her work in the paper mill, or else he subordinates it to her domestic relationships, as he does with whatever labor generated the money that finances Charley's education. Similarly, Dickens gives Lizzie's moral influence more narrative attention than any of her waged occupations, and he grants *it*—not her money— credit for making Charley aspire beyond a waterman's life. Finally, Lizzie's moral influence over Eugene is depicted as being more restorative than her brute strength (even though it wasn't working *before* she pulled him from the water), since, presumably, had Eugene not seen the error of his ways, he would have been morally better off dead than alive.

Despite these nostalgic recuperations, however, Dickens also, perhaps inadvertently, reveals the threat implicit in the challenge posed to the naturalization of womanly virtue by women working and demanding rights. That the form this threat takes reanimates the eighteenth-century link between woman and figuration poses a particular threat to Dickens's narrative project, for he finds himself trying to use a fiction about women to quiet old fears about the link between fiction and women. This threat is alluded to in Mortimer's defense of Lizzie Hexam at the end of the novel. When asked whether Lizzie has ever been a female waterman, Mortimer answers firmly that she has not. Mortimer's answer is correct in the strictest sense, since *waterman* was a term specifically applied to ferrymen and not to all-purpose boatmen like Gaffer, but Mortimer's legalistic answer misses the import of Lizzie's having assumed a metaphorical version of this role: Eugene is alive only because Lizzie *has* been a kind of female waterman. Acknowledging the metaphorical nature of the term *waterman*, however, mobilizes the ominous nature of Lizzie's link to figuration. If Eugene's life depends on Lizzie's capacity to be like a man, yet his moral salvation depends on her being (like) a woman, then what is she, by nature? Or, phrased differently, if Lizzie can be like a man when Eugene needs to be pulled from the water and like a woman when he is ready for a wife, then is it possible that her character is *not* an expression of some underlying female nature but merely a projection of a man's needs?

The implications of this question were far-reaching in the 1860s—and not just for the moralizing project of fiction. If the virtue men assigned to female nature proved to be only a figment of men's desire, then it might be possible that the sexed body did not guarantee moral difference. And, if moral difference (or virtue) was not guaranteed by the female body, then it was possible that there was no basis for virtue at all—apart, that is, from men's desire that virtue exists. This structure of wishful projection, of course, is exactly the same principle that informs speculation and makes it so volatile and so threatening. For, if nothing but (men's) desire underwrites value, then there will be nothing outside of (men's) desire to counteract the desirer's darker impulses. The vertiginous possibilities this notion raises surface repeatedly in *Our Mutual Friend,* and nowhere more starkly than in Dickens's brief description of a world in which there are no women at all, the world of sailors.

At the dark heart of the womanless seaman's world is the scene in which John Harmon is attacked just after his return to England. Everything about this episode signals ontological chaos. The assault itself is focused not just on Harmon, who is disguised as the sailor George Radfoot, but also on the other man who resembles him, and the melee quickly spreads to every man in the room. The attack is narrated as a distorted, almost hallucinatory memory, and its disclosure marks the moment of maximum narrative dislocation in the novel— the eight-page segment in which John Harmon wonders aloud whether to re-main dead or to reclaim his life and name.[19] Here is part of Harmon's description:

> I saw a figure like myself lying dressed in my clothes on a bed. What might have been, for anything I knew, a silence of days, weeks, months, years, was broken by a violent wrestling of men all over the room. The figure like myself was assailed, and my valise was in its hands. . . . I could not have said that my name was John Harmon. . . . I cannot possibly express it to myself without using the word I. But it was not I. There was no such thing as I, within my knowledge. (Dickens 1971, 426)

In one sense, as Rogue Riderhood explains it, the confusion of identity that Harmon experiences here is nothing unusual for a sailor. "There's fifty such [sailors] ten times as long as [Radfoot]," Riderhood laughs, "through entering in different names, re-shipping when the out'ard voyage is made, and what not" (Dickens 1971, 416). In another sense, it epitomizes the proclivity for disguise men exhibit repeatedly in the novel, whether it be John Harmon miming secretary, Boffin playing miser, or Bradley Headstone pretending to be Riderhood. But the ontological instability these episodes figure is no laughing matter, as the assault and all its ramifications reveal. Such instability is both cause and effect of the violence that Harmon, Wrayburn, and Riderhood all suffer, because it is the characteristic feature of a world deprived of any reliable criterion of difference, without a ground outside of metaphor to anchor meaning and value. This instability follows from the same mental gesture by which Bella can be made to replace stocks. It follows, that is, from turning what had been the guarantor of difference into sheer metaphor, which reflects only male desire, not some nature beyond fantasy and language. As this scene and all the other masquerades in the novel suggest, the effect of this gesture is to locate difference inside of man, hence to imperil both the guarantee of virtue and the integrity of male identity itself.

The threat posed to the natural guarantor of difference by the developments of the late 1850s momentarily exposed the possibility that difference resides not between men and women but, rather, within every individual man. Like but also because of its conjuncture with the passage of the limited liability laws, this exposure generated profoundly ambiguous effects. On the one hand, both limited liability and the obliteration of natural difference catapulted men into a giddy world beyond moral restraint, in which nothing checked their ability to speculate and conceive (deceits, plots, disguises, money-making schemes). On the other hand, the two developments exposed each man to the rapacity of his brother's desire, mirror image of his own, and, in pitting one man against another for what they both desired, such developments created value out of nothing and violence from the general struggle for scarce resources. In *Our Mutual Friend* the first of these two effects is figured in the general hysteria that characterizes the scene of John Harmon's assault and in the speculations that energize Alfred Lammle and Fascination Fledgby. Even these explosions of energy have sinister effects, of course, effects that are elaborated in the scenes in which sameness generates masquerade and, finally, a fight to the death. When one man can be "taken" for another, as Radfoot is taken for John Harmon, then a man can be taken down with another like himself, as Headstone takes Rider-hood into their mutual, watery grave.

The unmasking of sex—by which I mean the adumbration, at least, of what we would call gender—proceeds intermittently in *Our Mutual Friend,* not only because conceptualizing difference as sheer artifice or fiction was potentially ruinous to Dickens's artistic project but also because another principle of differentiation had become available by the 1860s to compensate for, and complicate, the increasingly shaky demarcation of sex. This difference was the difference of race. While Dickens invokes racial difference only three times in the novel, and though he relegates it to the margins of his text, racial difference proved to be the barrier by which sex could be at least temporarily insulated from gender in the early 1860s.[20]

The first reference to a "coffee-coloured" man in *Our Mutual Friend* appears in Bella's fantasy that she is married to "an Indian Prince, who was a Something-or-Other, who wore Cashmere shawls all over himself, and diamonds and emeralds blazing in his turban" (Dickens 1971, 374). The second black man is real but even more uncanny than Bella's fantasy. Struggling to be "exact" about his assault, John Harmon isolates one detail: "There was a black man . . . wearing a linen jacket, like a steward, who put the smoking coffee on the table in a tray and never looked at me" (Dickens 1971, 425). The third black man is supposedly more real than Bella's prince but less real than Harmon's servant. Mr. Wilfer summons this black king from a book "of African travel." Such black kings, Mr. Wilfer says, are "cheap" and "nasty," they bear "whatever name the sailors might have happened to give [them]," and they tend to wear only "one good article at a time": "The king is generally dressed in a London hat only, or a Manchester pair of braces, or one epaulet, or an uniform coat with his legs in the sleeves, or something of that kind" (438).

Why do black men appear in these three passages—at the heart of Bella's materialistic fantasies, at the site of maximum stress on male identity, and in the comic figuration of Mr. Wilfer's sartorial embarrassment? The answer to this question is partially revealed by the content of the first reference. Bella's fantasy that she will marry an Indian prince is the last in a series of fantasies about her future, in which she first imaginatively brings John Harmon back to life and marries him then "consign[s Harmon] to his grave again" and marries "a merchant of immense wealth" who gradually metamorphoses into the Indian prince. Bella's fantastic marital odyssey concludes with the comment that her coffee-colored prince is "excessively devoted; though a little too jealous" (Dickens 1971, 374).

What this passage suggests is the power of language to conjure characters from sheer desire. Because of the coincidence between one of the figments of Bella's fantasy and Harmon, a character in the novel, this power refers to and comments upon Dickens's power to do the same thing, but it also links this power both to murder and to male jealousy. Bella's imaginative "murder" of Harmon repeats the murder with which the novel opens, and her reference to the prince's jealousy casts the shadow of male competition over the parade of husbands she entertains. Thus, the coffee-colored prince is linked to figuration, desire, and the knot of deceptions and acts of homosocial violence that the assault on John Harmon most problematically describes. In this sense the coffee-colored prince has something in common with women.

The second clue to the significance of the black men is provided by the relationship that the last two passages bear to each other. That is, the reference to black kings, which occurs in the chapter immediately following the narration of John Harmon's assault, is offered as an antidote to the black servant: even if a black man dispensed the deranging drug, this placement suggests, such blacks are our puppets—we (white men) give them their names, their orders, and their desires. Just as Mr. Wilfer's story about Bella's generosity ostensibly offsets the heartlessness she has just displayed to John Harmon, then, and just as Mortimer Lightwood's assertion that Lizzie has never been a female waterman supposedly neutralizes the fact that she *has* been, the story of the black kings reveals that the black servant is really a projection of a white man's needs. In all three cases, however, the retraction does not actually cancel the initial assertion but merely completes a determinate contradiction central to *Our Mutual Friend* and to the structure of wishful projection that it addresses. That is, the fact that the deranging drug is passed to John Harmon by someone *like* him (a man "like a steward," who is dressed as a white man dresses)—like the fact that Bella and Lizzie, in critical ways and at critical moments, resemble men—is as important to the ideological work of *Our Mutual Friend* as is the fact that Harmon is drugged by someone *unlike* him (a black man) or the fact that, for most of the novel, Bella and Lizzie are *not* like men.

This contradiction—the other is like me; the other is different—is essential to the economic and representational systems that *Our Mutual Friend* simultaneously participates in and resists. It is impossible to separate these two systems or to determine which had priority in the 1860s, for the social and economic developments of the mid-Victorian period brought the fantasies inherent in this system of representation home to Englishmen as never before, while the representational system of self and other gave a particular semantic cast to the activities in which the English were involved. The logic of this system is as follows: the power of English men (hence the "proof" of their natural superiority) rested upon their ability to make the world over in their own image. In the 1840s and early 1850s this quest primarily took the form of religious conversion, as missionaries set about transforming "heathens" in India, South and Central America, and Africa into Christians, with the carrot of philanthropy and the stick of brute force. Economic investment in these areas accelerated throughout this period as well, often by piggybacking on the missionary and philanthropic rhetorics that already defined relations with these countries.[21]

Events in the late 1850s and early 1860s, however, most notably the Indian Mutiny of 1857 and the Jamaica uprising of 1865, gave England's relationship to at least some of these countries a new cast. Reports about the slaughter of women and children at the Well of Cawnpore stressed the inhumanity of the dark-skinned Indians and prompted Englishmen to speculate about the "savagery" of the "brutes." The fact that these reports did not mention British atrocities at Benares and Allahabad in June of 1857, for which Cawnpore might well have been a retaliation, suggests the extent to which the likeness between the English and the dark-skinned Indians was denied or repressed. The savagery of dark-skinned peoples was proved once more—to some Englishmen, at least—by the Jamaica uprising in early October of 1865. This native rebellion and the brutal retaliation it occasioned from the British governor, Eyre, caused the leading English men-of-letters to choose sides and publicly declare their positions on race. To Dickens, who deplored what he saw as the inhumanity of "the black—or the native or the Devil—afar off," this episode merely hardened the opinion he had expressed as early as 1853 in an essay satirically entitled "the Noble Savage": "Cruel, false, thievish, murderous, addicted more or less to grease, entrails, and beastly customs, [the black man] is a wild animal with the questionable gift of boasting; a conceited, tiresome, bloodthirsty, monotonous humbug" (Dickens 1853, 337).

By the early 1860s, then, even as the proliferating examples of speculative fraud and violent rhetorical and physical retaliations exposed one kind of rapacity in Englishmen, newly intensified meanings associated with the difference of race had become available to guarantee that the likeness between the "natives" and "us," which was so crucial to establishing English superiority, had its limit. Englishmen conquered the formal and informal colonies economically by creating in natives the desire to be like the Englishman, but they contained the threat implicit in that assertion of likeness by emphasizing the natural difference of race. The native in whose country Englishmen invested was like the investor (in his desires) but unlike him (in being "nasty" because black).

Here is where the neat parallelism between women and the racial other ends. For the fact that a woman, Bella Wilfer, symbolically drives home the difference between black men and white by giving her father what even a black king cannot have—a complete new suit of clothes—suggests that Dickens was not so much shoring up or even supplementing the difference of sex by invoking a parallel difference of race as he was establishing a relationship of mutual dependence between the two. That is, the same act with which Bella proves that her father is different from (read, better than) a black king also proves her to be a good (read, virtuous) woman. Bella's femininity, in other words, is momentarily stabilized as other to masculine self-interestedness through her relation to the black man, for femininity could acquire its definition not only through virtuous behavior toward men but, more specifically, through charitable acts that also inscribe racial difference with moral meaning. The one troubling aspect to this symbolic solution, of course, remains Bella's fantasy of "killing" John Harmon and marrying the Indian prince. This trace of violence within the woman lingers as a reminder of the instability of the solution Dickens advances, for, as the site of overdetermined meanings, this fantasy concentrates the threats to difference posed by the artificiality upon which it is based: in one reading this fantasy shows a woman wanting a man who is unlike John Harmon (in being black); in another it shows a woman wanting (another) man who is like Harmon (in being jealous); in another it shows the rapacity and violence within woman; in another it shows that this violence is in everyone—the jealous black prince, the woman, and the man who imagines them both.

My turn to race at the end of this analysis is partly an articulation of what the emphasis on gender in late-twentieth-century women's studies has brought into visibility. Because the difference of sex mobilized by Dickens in the 1860s and by founders of women's studies courses in the 1960s has now been elaborated into differences, of which sex is only one, looking at sex now leads many feminists to look at other determinants of difference (not just class and race but homosocial relations, generational differences, and definitions of masculinity as well). But I want to stress again a point I made at the beginning of this essay. The relationship between sexual difference and other kinds of difference in any particular time and place is not simply additive or supplemental but is also mutually constitutive. To be more precise about the example I have just given, the process of colonial expansion that allowed for a new kind of racism after 1840 helped shape the kind of feminism that emerged in the 1850s—just as the meanings of race were shaped by feminism as it emerged. In other words, partly because racial difference was available as a bulwark to shore up binary thinking in the 1850s, the women's movement of that decade tended to deemphasize difference and to stress instead (white) women's equality with men, even in the hitherto taboo arena of paid employment. But at least partly because the image of woman mobilized *by* the new racism emphasized womanly virtue, the feminism that developed in the 1860s and that culminated in the Social Purity Movement increasingly emphasized, once more, woman's difference from man.[22]

As this example suggests, the relationship between a particular formulation of racial difference and a particular formulation of sexual difference must always be specified as part of a historical context of meanings and material practices. This historical specificity matters because, just as the oppressions generated by the intersection of such determinants of difference vary according to the exact nature of their mutual articulation, so too do the opportunities for resistance to those oppressions. Because the women's movement in the United States was able to borrow emancipatory rhetoric from the civil rights movement, women as a group were able to initiate a new set of claims for "emancipation."[23] But, by the same token and to a certain extent at least, because the women's movement gradually came to compete for social and legal attention with the civil rights movement in the 1970s and 1980s, many women of color continue to find themselves torn by allegiances that conflict, and many women's studies programs find themselves trying (again) to accommodate the racial difference from which women's studies as a social and academic enterprise took at least some of its energy.[24]

What I am suggesting for women's studies in the 1990s, then, is not just that feminists add race (and class and sexual preference and so on) to sex as part of the analysis of positionality (and therefore gender) but also that feminists continue to work on a detailed history of the mutually constitutive relationship among these determinants in particular contexts (including the present). Canonical works such as *Our Mutual Friend* provide one arena for such work, but so do legal decisions and institutional practices and scientific technologies. So, too, do our classrooms, in which the dynamics and political discussions will only become more energetic as students and teachers learn how complex every cultural self has always been.

Notes

1. That this generalization is overly simplistic has been pointed out by Culler (1982), among others. Despite the recognition by most feminists that sex is never purely a biological category, however, this interpretation remains available for use and abuse. See, for example, Paglia 1980; and Kerrigan 1991. Among the many articles on the phases of women's studies, see Schuster and Van Dyne 1985.

2. For a compatible revision of the history of women's studies from another disciplinary perspective, see Scott 1991.

3. This group of texts has now been joined by *The Feminist Companion to Literature in English: Women Writers from the Middle Ages to the Present*. The publication of this important book proves that what I initially called a "first phase" is (thankfully) not over.

4. The National Women's Studies Association Task Force reports that by the late 1980s there were 520 women's studies programs as well as 235 majors and 404 minors in women's studies.

5. A convenient anthology of French feminist writings is *New French Feminisms* (1981). See also Irigaray 1985; Kristeva 1980; and Cixous and Clément 1986.

6. Foucault 1978. See also Foucault 1985 and 1986.

7. See Butler 1990.

8. The most important figure in gay studies is Eve Kosofsky Sedgwick. See Sedgwick 1985 and 1990. Examples of the newer, and still relatively heterogeneous, "men's studies" or "studies in the history of masculinity" include Kimmel 1987; Mangan and Walvin 1987; Swindler 1989; and Roper and Tosh 1991.

9. One of the first works to make the argument that gender should be examined alongside other determinants of difference was Kaplan 1986. More recent examples of this kind of study include Riley 1988; Rose 1991; Martin 1991; and Parker, Russo, Sommer, and Yeager 1992.

10. The emphasis on differences, not unexpectedly, brings with it costs as well as

rewards. For, once difference becomes differences, it becomes impossible to stabilize any identity (even one nuanced according to sex, race, class, and so on), because differences also manifest themselves *within* every individual. This, some critics have argued, makes it difficult to muster any programmatic initiatives, whether they be academic or political, for, without something stable in relation to which to organize activities and interests, it is impossible to compete with other interests and programs. This last difficulty may well be behind what seems to me to be the current emphasis in many women's studies courses and feminist theory on the local, the particular, and the positional. For analyses of these challenges, see Alcoff 1988; and Ebert 1992.

11. The most important laws were the 1844 Registration Act, the Limited Liability Act of 1855, the Joint Stock Companies Act of 1856, and the 1862 consolidating act, the Companies Act. Helpful discussions of limited liability include Shannon 1933; Jeffreys 1954; Checkland 1964, 39, 43, 104–7, 129–30; and King 1936, 238–45. A discussion of new forms of banking and mobilizing capital can be found in Checkland 1964, 22–26, 50–51.

12. See King 1936, 238.

13. Relevant treatments of speculation in Victorian novels include Feltes 1974; Cotsell 1985. Characters specifically associated with various kinds of metaphorical and literal speculation include Silas Wegg; that "happy pair of swindlers," the Lammels; Mr. Veneering, who invests £5000 in the initials "M. P."; and Fascination Fledgby and his parents.

14. Laurie Langbauer (1989) gives this principle more ahistorical significance than I do, but her description of its dynamics is shrewd. She argues that "our forms of representation attempt to order our existence in a way that will establish for the male subject a comfortable relation to what controls him." Langbauer's thesis is that a woman is typically assigned the role of representing—so as to displace—whatever controls the male subject: "Although he cannot ignore or escape it, the system offers him this consolation: it directly reflects his desires . . . and is always there to minister to his needs" (230–31).

15. For a discussion of this dimension of *Our Mutual Friend*, see Sedgwick 1985, 161–79.

16. Catherine Gallagher (1994) makes this argument.

17. According to Gallagher,

> As the press became an increasingly important political forum, the correspondence between the words that poured out of it and their putative referents became a topic of concern. Had politics become "mere" words? . . . Was political discourse "fictional"? One strategy for answering these questions and containing their attendant anxiety was to divide political writings into the reputable and the disreputable. Foremost in the latter category were the excessively "feminine" writings of Delarivier Manley, for these were worse than mere fictions with no relation to reality; they were scandals, *dis*creditings, that bore a potentially negative relationship to the polity. (176)

18. Useful recent works on the Victorian feminist movement include Holcombe 1983; Herstein 1985; Levine 1987; and Shanley 1989.

19. In his introduction to the Penguin edition of *Our Mutual Friend* (Dickens 1971), Stephen Gill calls the Harmon plot "the albatross about Dickens's neck" and book 2, chapter 13—the scene of Harmon's deliberation—"a confession of [narrative] breakdown" (22).

20. Angus Wilson makes the following comment on Dickens's attitude toward race: "Gradually, and markedly after the Indian Mutiny in 1857, [Dickens] . . . had come to believe that the white man must dominate and order the world of the blacks and the browns" (Dickens 1987, 25).

21. Useful works on Victorian imperialism include Brantlinger 1988 (esp. chap. 7); and Davi and Huttenback 1988.

22. For an important analysis of the relationship between women's achievements in Britain and imperialism, see Mohan and Hennessee 1989.

23. Here are just two examples of the early relationship between the civil rights movement and the women's movement in the United States: sex discrimination became illegal because it was included in the jurisdiction of the Equal Employment Opportunity Commission, which was established in 1964 by the Civil Rights Act; the National Organization for Women (NOW) was founded in 1966 when the national conference of the state commissions voted not to fight sex discrimination as vigorously as race discrimination. See Scott 1992.

24. See King 1988, 42–72; and hooks 1990, 29.

WORKS CITED

Alcoff, Linda. 1988. "Cultural Feminism versus Post-Structuralism." *Signs* 13, no. 3:405–36.

Blain, Virginia, Isobel Grundy, and Patricia Clements. 1990. *The Feminist Companion to Literature in English: Women Writers from the Middle Ages to the Present.* New Haven, Conn.: Yale University Press.

Brantlinger, Patrick. 1988. *Rule of Darkness: British Literature and Imperialism, 1830–1914.* Ithaca, N.Y.: Cornell University Press.

Burke, Peter. 1991. *New Perspectives on Historical Writing.* Cambridge: Polity Press.

Butler, Judith. 1990. *Gender Trouble: Feminism and the Subversion of Identity.* New York: Routledge.

Carus-Wilson, E. M. 1954. *Essays in Economic History.* London: Edward Arnold.

Checkland, S. G. 1964. *The Rise of Industrial Society in England, 1815–1885.* London: Longmans, Green.

Cixous, Hélène and Catherine Clément. 1986. *The Newly Born Woman.* Trans. Betsy Wing. Minneapolis: University of Minnesota Press.

Cotsell, Michael. 1985. "The Book of Insolvent Facts: Financial Speculation in *Our Mutual Friend.*" *Dickens Studies Annual* 13:125–43.

Culler, Jonathan. 1982. *On Deconstruction.* Ithaca: Cornell University Press.

Davi, Lance E., and Robert A. Huttenback. 1988. *Mammon and the Pursuit of Empire: The Economics of British Imperialism.* Cambridge: Cambridge University Press.

De Lauretis, Teresa. 1985. *Alice Doesn't: Feminism, Semiotics, Cinema*. Bloomington: Indiana University Press.

Dickens, Charles. 1853. "The Noble Savage." *Household Words* 7, no. 168:337–39.

———. 1971. *Our Mutual Friend*. Ed. Stephen Gill. Harmondsworth: Penguin Books.

———. 1987. *The Mystery of Edwin Drood*. Ed. Angus Wilson. Harmondsworth: Penguin Books.

Ebert, Teresa L. 1991. "The 'Difference' of Postmodern Feminism." *College English* 53, no. 8 (December): 886–904.

Ellmann, Mary. 1968. *Thinking about Women*. New York: Harcourt, Brace, and World.

Feltes, N. N. 1974. "Community and the Limits of Limited Liability in Two Mid-Victorian Novels." *Victorian Studies* 17 (June): 362–67.

Fetterly, Judith. 1978. *The Resisting Reader: A Feminist Approach to American Literature*. Bloomington: Indiana University Press.

Foucault, Michel. 1985a. *The History of Sexuality*, vol. 1: *An Introduction*. Trans. Robert Hurley. New York: Random House.

———. 1985b. *The Use of Pleasure*. Trans. Robert Hurley. New York: Random House.

———. 1986. *The Care of the Self*. Trans. Robert Hurley. New York: Random House.

Gallagher, Catherine. 1994. *Nobody's Story: The Vanishing Acts of Women Writers and the Marketplace*. Berkeley: University of California Press.

Gilbert, Sandra M., and Susan Gubar. 1979. *The Madwoman in the Attic: The Woman Writer and the Nineteenth-Century Literary Imagination*. New Haven: Yale University Press.

———. 1986. *The Norton Anthology of Literature by Women*. New York: W. W. Norton.

Herstein, Sheila R. 1985. *A Mid-Victorian Feminist: Barbara Leigh Smith Bodichon*. New Haven, Conn.: Yale University Press.

Holcombe, Lee. 1983. *Wives and Property: Reform of the Married Women's Property Law in Nineteenth-Century England*. Toronto: University of Toronto Press.

hooks, bell. 1990. "From Scepticism to Feminism." *Women's Review of Books* 7, no. 5:29–30.

Irigaray, Luce. 1985. *Speculum of the Other Woman*. Trans. Gillian Gill. Ithaca, N.Y.: Cornell University Press.

Jeffreys, J. B. 1954. "The Denomination and Character of Shares, 1855–1885." In *Essays in Economic History*, ed. E. M. Carus-Wilson, 1:344–57. London: Edward Arnold.

Kaplan, Cora. 1986. *Sea Changes*. London: Verso.

Kerrigan, William. 1991. "The Perverse *Kulturgeschichte* of Camille Paglia." *Raritan* 10, no. 3:134–45.

Keynes, J. M., and D. H. MacGregor. 1933. *Economic History*. London: Macmillan.

Kimmel, Michael S. 1987. *Changing Men: New Directions in Research in Men and Masculinity*. London: Sage.

King, Deborah K. 1988. "Multiple Jeopardy, Multiple Consciousness: The Context of a Black Feminist Ideology." *Signs* 14, no. 1:42–72.

King, W. T. C. 1936. *History of the London Discount Market.* London: George Routledge and Sons.

Kristeva, Julia. 1980. *Desire in Language: A Semiotic Approach to Literature and Art.* Trans. Thomas Gora, Alice Jardine, and Leon S. Rondiez. New York: Columbia University Press.

Langbauer, Laurie. 1989. "Women in White, Men in Feminism." *Yale Journal of Criticism* 2, no. 2 (April): 219–43.

Levine, Philippa. 1987. *Victorian Feminism, 1850–1900.* Tallahassee: Florida State University Press.

Mangan, J. A., and James Walvin. 1987. *Manliness and Morality: Middle-Class Masculinity in Britain and America, 1800–1940.* Manchester: Manchester University Press.

Marks, Elaine, and Isabelle de Courtivron. 1981. *New French Feminisms.* New York: Schocken Books.

Martin, Biddy. 1991. *Lou Andreas Salome.* Ithaca, N.Y.: Cornell University Press.

Mohan, Raji, and Rosemary Hennessee. 1989. "The Construction of Woman in Three Popular Texts of Empire: Towards a Critique of Materialist Feminism." *Textual Practice* 3, no. 3:323–59.

Moraga, Cherríe and Gloria Anzaldúa. 1981. *This Bridge Called My Back: Writing by Radical Women of Color.* Watertown, Mass.: Persephone Press.

Paglia, Camille. 1990. *Sexual Personae: Art and Decadence from Nefertitti to Emily Dickinson.* New Haven, Conn.: Yale University Press.

Parker, Andrew, Mary Russo, Doris Sommer, and Patricia Yeager. 1992. *Nationalisms and Sexualities.* London: Routledge.

Riley, Denise. 1988. *"Am I That Name?" Feminism and the Category "Women" in History.* Minneapolis: University of Minnesota Press.

Roper, Michael, and John Tosh. 1991. *Manful Assertions: Masculinities in Britain since 1800.* London: Routledge.

Rose, Jacqueline. 1991. *The Haunting of Sylvia Plath.* London: Virago.

Schuster, Marilyn R., and Susan R. Van Dyne. 1985. "Curricular Change for the Twenty-First Century." In *Women's Place in the Academy: Transforming the Liberal Arts Curriculum,* ed. Schuster and Van Dyne, 3–12. Totowa, N.J.: Rowman and Allanheld.

Scott, Joan W. 1991. "Women's History." In *New Perspectives on Historical Writing,* ed. Peter Burke, 42–66. Cambridge: Polity Press.

Sedgwick, Eve Kosofsky. 1985. *Between Men: English Literature and Male Homosocial Desire.* New York: Columbia University Press.

———. 1990. *The Epistemology of the Closet.* Berkeley: University of California Press.

Shanley, Mary Lyndon. 1989. *Feminism, Marriage, and the Law in Victorian England, 1850–1895.* Princeton: Princeton University Press.

Shannon, H. A. 1933. "The Coming of General Limited Liability." In *Economic History,* ed. J. M. Keynes and D. H. MacGregor, 2:267–91. London: Macmillan.

Spacks, Patricia Meyer. 1975. *The Female Imagination.* New York: Knopf.

Swindler, Victor J. 1989. *Rediscovering Masculinity: Reason, Language and Sexuality.* London: Routledge.

Chapter 6

Life as the Maid's Daughter: An Exploration of the Everyday Boundaries of Race, Class, and Gender

Mary Romero

INTRODUCTION

The call for inclusion across disciplines has arrived at a time when the United States is reassessing the gains in the area of race relations, particularly in the face of continued segregation in our schools, communities, churches, and homes. Distinct boundaries dividing men and women of different racial, ethnic, and class backgrounds are exemplified in the data on salary and educational levels, housing markets, rates of unemployment and underemployment, and health care. Differences point to the existing gaps between the social, economic, and political worlds people live in and seriously challenge the assumptions that researchers and politicians have made about society based on groups depicted as "mainstream." While the realities of the persons depicted as mainstream are affirmed and enhanced by a wide range of institutional mechanisms, they are not good informants about the social structure. As members of the status quo, their knowledge is embedded in ideological systems that justify their superior social positions, and, consequently, their experiences are quite limited. Understanding the everyday realities of race, class, and gender requires uncovering the knowledge gained from individuals negotiating between social boundaries and those who are considered "outsiders." Persons of color who move from one social setting dominated by the white middle class to one dominated by an ethnic working class are aware of the different standards of behavior governing each domain. Patricia Hill Collins (1986) refers to "outsiders within" to describe the unique standpoint of persons marginalized by both their race and gender.

Numerous researchers investigating the work experiences of women of color employed as private household workers have pointed to the type of knowledge poor and working-class African American (Coley 1981; Rollins 1985; Dill

1988; Tucker 1988; Kousha 1990), West Indian (Colen 1986), Japanese-American (Glenn 1985), Chicana (Romero 1992), and Mexican immigrant (Hondagneu-Sotelo 1990) women obtain doing domestic work in white middle-class homes. Unlike the volumes of letters to the editors and journal articles over the last century that have documented employers' complaints about the "servant problem" (Martin and Segrave 1985), the recent studies of private household workers locates the experience of paid reproductive labor from the standpoint of women of color employed in a low-wage, low-status occupation. From the standpoint of the workers, knowledge of the class-based, gendered, racist social order is revealed through their struggles against denigration, humiliation, and exploitation. According to Judith Rollins (1985, 212–13), the information used by household workers consists of their "intimate knowledge of the realities of employers' lives, their understanding of the meaning of class and race in this country, and their value system, which measures an individual's worth less by material success than by the kind of person you are, by the quality of one's interpersonal relationships and by one's standing in the community."

It is not surprising that researchers have turned to the peculiar social setting of domestic service to explore issues of race, class, and gender. The relationship between employee and employer in domestic service brings several important factors to play simultaneously: same-gender relations; interracial and interclass oppression; and location with women's primary unrecognized workplace, the household (Romero 1992). Social settings rarely offer the opportunity to investigate interpersonal relationships between persons who usually do not share the same social space. The situation of domestic service, however, provides a unique setting in which women of different socioeconomic, racial, and ethnic backgrounds come together in the intimate setting of the home. Unlike their employers, household workers must learn how to move from their own social world in poor and working-class ethnic communities into the homes of white, middle-class families. Research that begins with the reality of women of color as private household workers can uncover the systems of knowledge and the meanings attached to everyday routines and practices that maintain race, class, and gender domination. Research conducted from other standpoints cannot uncover what is unrecognized or unknown to white women or men who are not in powerless positions and are not forced to evaluate the Euro-American social order or the taken-for-granted reality of white, middle-class privilege.

The limited perspective produced by ignoring issues of race and class is evident in the literature that appeared early on in the second wave of feminism. Juliet Mitchell (1971), M. Dalla Costa (1972), Ann Oakley (1974), and others argued that housework is central to women's oppression and that the burden of housework united women. Juliet Mitchell (1971), for example, suggests women's work in the home as the focal point for analyzing gender inequality. M. Dalla Costa and Selma James (1972, 19) assert:

> All women are housewives, and even those who work outside the home continue to be housewives. . . . [It] is precisely what is particular to domestic work . . . as quality of life and quality of relationships which it generates, that determines a woman's place where ever she is and to which ever class she belongs.

Nona Glazer (1980, 249) argues that domestic labor remains "central to understanding women's continued subordination in both advanced capitalist and socialist societies," regardless of whether they actually do the work themselves. Domestic labor is analyzed from the position of women's unpaid work within the family. Assumptions about the nature of housework are made on the basis of the work as unpaid labor, suggesting to some feminists that monetary value will change the plight of women. For instance, Margaret Benson (1973, 121) argues:

> In a society in which money determines value, women are a group who work outside the money economy. Their work is not worth money, is therefore valueless, is therefore not work, can hardly be expected to be worth as much as men, who work for money.

Several studies estimate the monetary value of housework by calculating the accumulated market values of each household task by listing the hourly wage of each occupation, such as cooks, teachers, nurses, and chauffeurs (Walker and Gauger 1973; Ferber and Birnbaum 1980; Berch 1982). The experiences of women of color employed as domestics, however, debunk the myth that monetary value transforms the status of housework.

Researchers interviewing women of color about paid household labor have not found evidence to suggest that their work is elevated to the status of cooks, chauffeurs, nurses, or teachers. Rather than focusing on the shared realities of female employers and female household workers, studies explore the asymmetrical interpersonal relationships between employee and employer. Several authors concentrate on the dialectical concepts of domination drawn from Hegel and Fanon to discuss the psychology of the relation between white employers and nonwhite employees. The most prominent research on the dialectic of intimacy and domination between African-American employees and their white employers is Judith Rollins's book *Between Women* (1985). Other research in the area includes Susan Tucker's book *Telling Memories* (1988) and the studies by Bonnie Thornton Dill (1988) and Shellee Colen (1986). Other studies move toward a structural analysis of the dialectics of domestic work, such as Evelyn Nakano Glenn's (1985) study of Japanese-American women in the Bay Area, Soraya Moore Coley's (1981) research on union and nonunion members of the National Committee of Household Employment (NCHE), Mahnaz Kousha's (1990) research on Black domestics and mistresses in the South, Pierrette Maria Hondagneu-Sotelo's (1990) study of Mexican immigrant women, Leslie Salzinger's (1991) ethnography of two cooperatives employing Latina immigrant women as domestics, and my own work on Chicana household workers (Romero 1992).[1]

My current research attempts to expand the sociological understanding of the dynamics of race, class, and gender in the everyday routines of family life and reproductive labor. Again I am lured to the unique setting presented by domestic service; this time, however, my focus is shifted, and I turn to the realities experienced by the children of private household workers. This focus is not entirely voluntary. While presenting my research on Chicana private household workers, I was approached repeatedly by Latina/os and African Americans who wanted to share their knowledge about domestic service—knowledge they obtained as the daughters and sons of household workers. Listening to their accounts about their mothers' employment presents another reality to understanding paid and unpaid reproductive labor and the way in which persons of color are socialized into a class-based, gendered, racist social structure. The following discussion explores issues of stratification in everyday life by analyzing the life story of a maid's daughter. This life story illustrates the potential of the standpoint of the maid's daughter for generating knowledge about race, class, and gender. It is, at the same time, exemplary of the challenge scholarship grounded in the experience of feminist women of color has posed to women's studies scholarship that has presumed to be "universal."

SOCIAL BOUNDARIES PRESENTED IN THE LIFE STORY

The first interview with Teresa,[2] the daughter of a live-in maid, eventually led to a life history project. I am intrigued by Teresa's experiences with her mother's white, upper-middle-class employers while maintaining close ties to her relatives in Juarez, Mexico, and Mexican friends in Los Angeles. While some may view Teresa's life as a freak accident, living a life of "rags to riches," and certainly not a common Chicana/o experience, her story represents a microcosm of power relationships in the larger society. Life as the maid's daughter in an upper-middle-class neighborhood exemplifies many aspects of the Chicano/*Mexicano* experience as "racial ethnics" in the United States, whereby the boundaries of inclusion and exclusion are constantly changing as we move from one social setting and one social role to another.

Teresa's narrative contains descriptive accounts of negotiating boundaries in the employers' homes and in their community. As the maid's daughter, the old adage "Just like one of the family" is a reality, and Teresa has to learn when she must act like the employer's child and when she must assume the appropriate behavior as the maid's daughter. She has to recognize all the social cues and interpret social settings correctly—when to expect the same rights and privileges as the employer's children and when to fulfill the expectations and obligations as the maid's daughter. Unlike the employers' families, Teresa and her mother rely on different ways of obtaining knowledge. The taken-for-granted reality of the employers' families do not contain conscious experiences of negotiating race and class status, particularly not in the intimate setting of the home. Teresa's status is constantly changing in response to the wide range of social settings she encounters—from employers' dinner parties with movie stars and corporate executives to Sunday dinners with Mexican garment workers in Los Angeles and factory workers in El Paso. Since Teresa remains bilingual and bicultural throughout her life, her story reflects the constant struggle and resistance to maintain her Mexican identity, claiming a reality that is neither rewarded nor acknowledged as valid.

Teresa's account of her life as the maid's daughter is symbolic of the way that racial ethnics participate in the United States; sometimes we are included and other times excluded or ignored. Teresa's story captures the reality of social stratification in the United States, that is, a racist, sexist, and class-structured society upheld by an ideology of equality. I will analyze the experiences of the maid's daughter in an upper-middle-class neighborhood in Los Angeles to investigate the ways that boundaries of race, class, and gender are maintained or diffused in everyday life. I have selected various excerpts from the transcripts that illustrate how knowledge about a class-based and gendered, racist social order is learned, the type of information that is conveyed, and how the boundaries between systems of domination impact everyday life. I begin with a brief history of Teresa and her mother, Carmen.

LEARNING SOCIAL BOUNDARIES

Background

Teresa's mother was born in Piedras Negras, a small town in Aguas Calientes in Mexico. After her father was seriously injured in a railroad accident, the family moved to a small town outside Ciudad Juarez. Teresa's mother soon became involved in a variety of activities to earn money. She sold food and trinkets at the railroad station and during train stops boarded the trains seeking customers. By the time she was fifteen she moved to Juarez and took a job as a domestic, making about eight dollars a week. She soon crossed the border and began working for Anglo families in the country club area in El Paso. Like other domestics in El Paso, Teresa's mother returned to Mexico on the weekends and helped support her mother and sisters. In her late twenties she joined several of her friends in their search for better-paying jobs in Los Angeles. The women immediately found jobs in the garment industry. Yet, after six months in the sweatshops, Teresa's mother went to an agency in search of domestic work. She was placed in a very exclusive Los Angeles neighborhood. Several years later Teresa was born. Her friends took care of the baby while Carmen continued working; child care became a burden, however, and she eventually returned to Mexico. At the age of thirty-six Teresa's mother returned to Mexico with her newborn baby. Leaving Teresa with her grandmother and aunts, her mother sought work in the country club area. Three years later Teresa and her mother returned to Los Angeles.

Over the next fifteen years Teresa lived with her mother in the employer's (Smith) home, usually the two sharing the maid's room located off the kitchen. From the age of three until Teresa started school, she accompanied her mother to work. She continued to live in the Smiths' home until she left for college. All of Teresa's live-in years were spent in one employer's household. The Smiths were unable to afford a full-time maid, however, so Teresa's mother began doing day work throughout the neighborhood. After school Teresa went to whatever house her mother was cleaning and waited until her mother finished working, around 4 or 6 P.M., and then returned to the Smiths' home with her mother. Many prominent families in the neighborhood knew Teresa as the maid's daughter and treated her accordingly. While Teresa wanted the relationship with the employers to cease when she went to college and left the neighborhood, her mother continued to work as a live-in maid with no residence other than the room in the employer's home; consequently, Teresa's social status as the maid's daughter continued.

ENTRANCE INTO THE EMPLOYERS' WORLD

Having spent her first three years in a female-dominated and monolingual, Spanish-speaking household in Juarez and in a Mexican immigrant community in Los Angeles, Teresa had a great deal to learn about the foreign environment presented by her mother's working conditions as a live-in maid. As a preschooler, Teresa began to learn that her social status reflected her mother's social position. In Mexico her mother was the primary wage earner for her grandmother and aunts. In this Mexican household dominated by women, Teresa received special attention and privileges as Carmen's daughter. Teresa recalled very vivid memories about entering the employers' world and being forced to learn an entirely new set of rules and beliefs of a Euro-American social order that consisted of a white, monolingual, male-dominated, and upper-middle-class family life. Teresa's account of her early years in the employers' homes is clearly from the perspective of the maid's daughter. She was an outsider and had to learn the appropriate behavior for each setting.

Rules were a major theme in Teresa's recollections of growing up in the employers' homes. She was very much aware of different rules operating in each home and of the need to act accordingly. In one of her mother's work sites, she was expected to play with the employer's children, in another she was allowed to play with their toys in specific areas of the house, and in other workplaces she sat quietly and was not allowed to touch the things around her. From the beginning she was socialized by the employers and their children, who emphasized conformity and change to their culture. The employers did not make any attempt to create a bicultural or multicultural environment in their homes or community. Teresa was expected to conform to their linguistic norms and acquiesce to becoming "the other"—the little Spanish-speaking Mexican girl among the English-speaking white children.

In the following excerpt Teresa describes her first encounter with the boundaries she confronted in the employers' homes. The excerpt is typical of her observances and recollections about her daily life, in which she is constantly assessing the practices and routines and reading signs in order to determine her position in each social setting and, thus, select the appropriate behavior. While the demands to conform and change were repeated throughout her experiences, Teresa did not embrace the opportunity to assimilate. Her resistance and struggle against assimilation is evident throughout her account, as indicated by her attempt to leave the employer's home and her refusal to speak English:

> I started to realize that every day I went to somebody else's house. Everybody's house had different rules. . . . My mother says that she constantly had to watch me, because she tried to get me to sit still and I'd be really depressed and I cried or I wanted to go see things, and my mother was afraid I was going to break something and she told me not to touch anything. The kids wanted to play with me. To them, I was a novelty and they wanted to play with the little Mexican girl. . . .
>
> I think I just had an attitude problem as I describe it now. I didn't want to play with them, they were different. My mother would tell me to go play with them, and in a little while later I'd come back and say: "Mama no me quieren

aguntar"—obviously it was the communication problem. We couldn't communicate. I got really mad one day at these girls, because "no me quieran aguntar," and they did not understand what I was trying to say. They couldn't, we couldn't play, so I decided that I was going to go home, and that I didn't like this anymore. So I just opened the door and I walked out. I went around the block and I was going to walk home, to the apartment where we lived. I went out of the house, and walked around and went the opposite direction around the block. The little girls came to my mom and said: Carmen your little daughter she left! So my mom dropped everything and was hysterical and one of the older daughters drove my mom around and she found me on the corner. My mom was crying and crying, upset, and she asked me where I was going and I said: "Well, I was going to go home, porque no me quieran aguntar," and I didn't want to be there anymore, and I was gonna walk home. So my mother had to really keep an eye on me.

I would go to the Jones [employers], and they had kids, and I would just mostly sit and play with their toys, but I wouldn't try to interact with them. Then they tried to teach me English. I really resented that. They had an aquarium and fishes and they would say: "Teresa, can you say Fiishh?" and I would just glare at them, just really upset. Then I would say "Fish, no, es pescado." You know, like trying to change me, and I did not want to speak their language, or play with their kids, or do anything with them. At the Smiths they tried to teach me English. There were different rules there. I couldn't touch anything. The first things I learned was "No touch, no touch," "Don't do this, don't do that."

At different houses, I starting picking up different things. I remember that my mother used to also work for a Jewish family, when I was about five, the Altman's. We had to walk to their house. Things were different at the Altman's. At the Altman's they were really nice to me. They had this little metal stove that they let me play with. I would play with that. That was like the one thing I could play with, in the house. I immediately—I'd get there and sit down in my designated area that I could be in, and I'd play there. Sometimes, Ms. Altman would take me to the park and I'd play there. She would try to talk to me. Sometimes I would talk and sometimes I would just sit there.

Teresa's account of going to work with her mother as a toddler was not a story of a child running freely and exploring the world around her; instead, her story was shaped by the need to learn the rules set by white, monolingual, English-speaking adults and children. The emphasis in her socialization within employers' homes was quite different than that given to the employers' male children; rather than advocating independence, individuality, and adventure,

Teresa was socialized to conform to female sex roles, restricting her movement and playing with gendered toys. Learning the restrictions that limit her behavior—"No touch. Don't do this"—served to educate Teresa about her social status in the employers' homes. She was clearly different from the other children, "a novelty," and was bound by rules regulating her use of social space and linguistic behavior. Teresa's resistance against changing her language points to the strong self-esteem and pride in her culture and Mexican identity that she obtained from her experience in a Mexican household. Teresa's early memories were dominated by pressure to assimilate and to restrain her movement and activity to fit into a white, male-dominated, upper-middle-class household.

The context in which Teresa learned English was very significant in acquiring knowledge about the social order. English was introduced into her life as a means of control and to restrict her movement within employers' homes. The employers' children were involved in teaching Teresa English, and they exerted pressure that she conform to the linguistic norms governing their households. Teresa was not praised or rewarded for her ability to speak Spanish, and her racial and cultural differences were only perceived positively when they served a function for the employer's family, such as a curiosity, entertainment, or a cross-cultural experience. While her mother continued to talk to Teresa in Spanish when they were alone, Carmen was not able to defend her daughter's right to decide which language to speak in the presence of the employers' families. Furthermore, Teresa observed her mother serving and waiting on the employers' families, taking orders, and being treated in a familiar manner. While Teresa referred to the employers formally, by their last names, the employers' children called Teresa's mother by her first name. The circumstances created an environment whereby all monolingual, Spanish-speaking women, including her mother, were in powerless positions. The experiences provided Teresa with knowledge about social stratification—that is, the negative value placed on the Spanish language and Mexican culture—as well as about the social status of Spanish-speaking Mexican immigrant women.

ONE OF THE FAMILY

As Teresa got older, the boundaries between insider and outsider became more complicated, as employers referred to her and Carmen as "one of the family." Entering into an employer's world as the maid's daughter, Teresa was not only subjected to the rules of an outsider but also had to recognize when the rules changed, making her momentarily an insider. While the boundaries dictating Carmen's work became blurred between the obligations of an employee and that of a friend or family member, Teresa was forced into situations in which she was expected to be just like one of the employer's children, and yet she remained the maid's daughter.

The expectations of responsibility and obligation created by the pseudofamily relationships were demonstrated in the incidents related to Mr. and Mrs. Smith's decision to pay Teresa's school tuition rather than pay her mother a salary. While the arrangement served to decommercialize the Smith's relationship with Carmen and allowed her not to pay taxes on the income, the arrangement also created the appearance that the Smiths, rather than Teresa's mother, were paying her tuition, as they did their own children. Teresa attributed the arrangement to blurring the boundaries between the employer and employee families. The employer assumed the right to act on Carmen's behalf and made decisions about Teresa's education. Teresa recalled, for instance, that the decision to take Spanish rather than French class was a decision the employer made:

> I really wanted to learn French. I was really upset that the Smiths had enrolled me in the Spanish course. I said, "How come I have to take Spanish? I already know Spanish." "No, we want you to speak perfect Spanish, we want your Spanish to be like—so you can talk to the queen of Spain." It took me a long time to get over it.

While Teresa asked her mother to support her decision to take French, Carmen submitted to the employer's decision. If Carmen had paid the tuition directly out of her salary, the employer's paternalistic relationship to the worker and her daughter and their power to make parental decisions for Carmen may have been reduced. Instead, the arrangement created a situation in which Mr. and Mrs. Smith could claim a right to make decisions about Teresa's education. Similar paternalistic actions in other employer households shaped their relationship to Teresa and her mother, blurring the boundaries between Teresa and Carmen as a family unit and as separate from the employers' families.

While boundaries between insider and outsider were frequently ignored, Teresa never lost sight of the fact that her mother was the maid and spent long hours cleaning, picking up, and caring for the employers and their families. Unlike the Smith family, Teresa was constantly drawing the distinction between the household tasks Carmen did as her mother and the tasks completed as the maid. Furthermore, she understood that the additional demands an employer's family made resulted in less time she had to spend with her mother. Teresa forcefully expressed her resentment over an employer's requests for Carmen to work overtime, including weekends and holidays. She wanted her mother to have time and energy to do things with her, as a family, such as visiting friends and relatives in the Mexican barrio. No doubt she also wanted to receive some of the caring and nurturing she observed her mother giving to the employer's children. She was also aware of the physical demands of housecleaning and was concerned about her mother's health.

Living under conditions established by the employers made Teresa and her mother's efforts to maintain a distinction between their family life and an employer's family very difficult. Analyzing incidents in which the boundaries between the worker's family and the employer's family were blurred highlights the issues that complicate the mother-daughter relationship. Teresa's account of her mother's hospitalization was the first of numerous conflicts between the two that stemmed from the live-in situation and their relationships with the employer's family. The following excerpt demonstrates the difficulty in interacting as a family unit and the degree of influence and power employers exerted over their daily lives:

When I was about ten my mother got real sick. That summer, instead of sleeping downstairs in my mother's room when my mother wasn't there, one of the kids was gone away to college, so it was just Rosalyn, David and myself that were home. The other two were gone, so I was gonna sleep upstairs in one of the rooms. I was around eight or nine, ten I guess. I lived in the back room. It was a really neat room because Rosalyn was allowed to paint it. She got her friend who was real good, painted a big tree and clouds and all this stuff on the walls. So I really loved it and I had my own room. I was with the Smiths all the time, as my parents, for about two months. My mother was in the hospital for about a month. Then when she came home, she really couldn't do anything. We would all have dinner, the Smiths were really, really supportive. I went to summer school and I took math and English and stuff like that. I was in this drama class and I did drama and I got to do the leading role. Everybody really liked me and Ms. Smith would come and see my play. So things started to change when I got a lot closer to them and I was with them alone. I would go see my mother everyday, and my cousin was there. I think that my cousin kind of resented all the time that the Smiths spent with me. I think my mother was really afraid that now that she wasn't there that they were going to steal me from her. I went to see her, but I could only stay a couple hours and it was really weird. I didn't like seeing my mother in pain and she was in a lot of pain. I remember before she came home the Smiths said that they thought it would be a really good idea if I stayed upstairs and I had my own room now that my mother was going to be sick and I couldn't sleep in the same bed 'cause I might hurt her. It was important for my mother to be alone. And how did I feel about that? I was really excited about that (having her own room)—you know. They said, "Your mom she is probably not going to like it and she might get upset about it, but I think that we can convince her that it is ok." When my mom came home, she understood that she couldn't be touched and that she had to be really careful, but she wanted it (having her own room) to be temporary. Then my mother was really upset. She got into it with them and said, "No, I don't want it that way." She would tell me, "No, I want you to be down here. Que crees que eres hija de ellos? You're gonna be with me all the time, you can't do that." So I would tell Ms. Smith. She would ask me when we would go to the market together, "How does your mom seem, what does she feel, what does she say?" She would get me to relay that. I would say, "I think that my mom is really upset about me moving upstairs. She doesn't like it and she just says no." I wouldn't tell her everything. They would talk to her and finally they convinced her, but my mom really, really resented it and was really angry about it. She was just generally afraid. All these times that my mother wasn't there, things happened and they would take me places with them, go out to dinner with them and their friends. So that was a real big change, in that I slept upstairs and had different rules. Everything changed. I was more independent. I did my own homework; they would open the back door and yell that dinner was ready—you know. Things were just real different.

The account illustrates how assuming the role of insider was an illusion because neither the worker's daughter nor the worker ever became a member of the white, middle-class family. Teresa was only allowed to move out of the maid's quarter, where she shared a bed with her mother, when two of the employer's children were leaving home, vacating two bedrooms. This was not the first time that "space" determined whether Teresa was included in the employer's family activities. Her description of Thanksgiving dinner illustrates that she did not decide when to be included but, rather, the decision was based on the available space at the table:

I never wanted to eat with them, I wanted to eat with my mom. Like Thanksgiving, it was always an awkward situation, because I never knew, up until dinner time, where I was going to sit, every single time. It depended on how many guests they had, and how much room there was at the table. Sometimes, when they invited all their friends, the Carters and the Richmans, who had kids, the adults would all eat dinner in one room and then the kids would have dinner in another room. Then I could go eat dinner with the kids or sometimes I'd eat with my mom in the kitchen. It really depended.

Since Teresa preferred to eat with her mother, the inclusion was burdensome and unwanted. In the case of moving upstairs, however, Teresa wanted to have her "own" bedroom. The conflict arising from Teresa's move upstairs points to the way in which the employer's actions threatened the bonds between mother and daughter.

Teresa and Carmen did not experience the boundaries of insider and outsider in the same way. Teresa was in a position to assume a more active family role when employers' made certain requests. Unlike her mother, she was not an employee and was not expected to clean and serve the employer. Carmen's responsibility for the housework never ceased, however, regardless of the emotional ties existing between employee and employers. She and her employers understood that, whatever family activity she might be participating in, if the situation called for someone to clean, pick up, or serve, that was Carmen's job. When the Smiths requested Teresa to sit at the dinner table with the family, they placed Teresa in a different class position than her mother, who was now expected to serve her daughter alongside her employer. Moving Teresa upstairs in a bedroom alongside the employer and their children was bound to drive a wedge between Teresa and Carmen. There is a long history of spatial deference in domestic service, including separate entrances, staircases, and eating and sleeping arrangements. Carmen's room reflected her position in the household. As the maid's quarter, the room was separated from the rest of the bedrooms and was located near the maid's central work area, the kitchen. The room was obviously not large enough for two beds because Carmen and Teresa shared a bed. Once Teresa was moved upstairs, she no longer shared the same social space in the employer's home as her mother. Weakening the bonds between the maid and her daughter permitted the employers to broaden their range of relationships and interaction with Teresa.

Carmen's feelings of betrayal and loss underline how threatening the employers' actions were. She understood that the employers were in a position to buy her child's love. They had already attempted to socialize Teresa into Euro-American ideals by planning Teresa's education and deciding what courses she would take. Guided by the importance they placed on European culture, the employers defined the Mexican Spanish spoken by Teresa and her mother as inadequate and classified Castillan Spanish as "proper" Spanish. As a Mexican immigrant woman working as a live-in maid, Carmen was able to experience certain middle-class privileges, but her only access to these privileges was through her relationship with employers. Therefore, without the employers' assistance, she did not have the necessary connections to enroll Teresa in private schools or provide her with upper-middle-class experiences to help her develop the skills needed to survive in elite schools. Carmen only gained these privileges for her daughter at a price; she relinquished many of her parental rights to her employers. To a large degree the Smiths determined Carmen's role as a parent, and the other employers restricted the time she had to attend school functions and the amount of energy left at the end of the day to mother her own child.

Carmen pointed to the myth of "being like one of the family" in her comment, "¿Que crees que eres hija de ellos? You're gonna be with me all the time, you can't do that." The statement underlines the fact that the bond between mother and daughter is for life, whereas the pseudofamily relationship with employers is temporary and conditional. Carmen wanted her daughter to understand that taking on the role of being one of the employer's family did not relinquish her from the responsibility of fulfilling her "real" family obligations. The resentment Teresa felt from her cousin who was keeping vigil at his aunt's hospital bed indicated that she had not been a dutiful daughter. The outside pressure from an employer did not remove her own family obligations and responsibilities. Teresa's relatives expected a daughter to be at her mother's side providing any assistance possible as a caretaker, even if it was limited to companionship. The employer determined Teresa's activity, however, and shaped her behavior into that of a middle-class child; consequently, she was kept away from the hospital and protected from the realities of her mother's illness. Furthermore, she was submerged into the employer's world, dining at the country club and interacting with their friends.

Her mother's accusation that Teresa wanted to be the Smiths' daughter signifies the feelings of betrayal or loss and the degree to which Carmen was threatened by the employer's power and authority. Yet Teresa also felt betrayal and loss and viewed herself in competition with the employers for her mother's time, attention, and love. In this excerpt Teresa accuses her mother of wanting to be part of employers' families and community:

> I couldn't understand it—you know—until I was about eighteen and then I said, "It is your fault. If I treat the Smiths differently, it is your fault. You chose to have me live in this situation. It was your decision to let me have two parents, and for me to balance things off, so you can't tell me that I said this. You are the one who wanted this." When I was about eighteen we got into a huge fight on Christmas. I hated the holidays because I hated spending them with the Smiths. My mother always worked. She worked on every holiday. She loved to work on the holidays! She would look forward to working. My mother just worked all the time! I think that part of it was that she wanted to have power and control over this community, and she wanted the network, and she wanted to go to different people's houses.

As employers, Mr. and Mrs. Smith were able to exert an enormous amount of power over the relationship between Teresa and her mother. Carmen was employed in an occupation in which the way to improve working conditions, pay, and benefits was through the manipulation of personal relationships with employers. Carmen obviously tried to take advantage of her relationship with the Smiths in order to provide the best for her daughter. The more intimate and interpersonal the relationship, the more likely employers were to give gifts, do favors, and provide financial assistance. Although speaking in anger and filled with hurt, Teresa accused her mother of choosing to be with employers and their families rather than with her own daughter. Underneath Teresa's accusation was the understanding that the only influence and status her mother had as a domestic was gained through her personal relationships with employers. Although her mother had limited power in rejecting the Smiths' demands, Teresa held her responsible for giving them too much control. Teresa argued that the positive relationship with the Smiths was done out of obedience to her mother and denied any familial feelings toward the employers. The web between employee and employers' families affected both mother and daughter, who were unable to separate the boundaries of work and family.

MAINTAINING CULTURAL IDENTITY

A major theme in Teresa's narrative was her struggle to retain her Mexican culture and her political commitment to social justice. Rather than internalizing meaning attached to Euro-American practices and redefining Mexican culture and bilingualism as negative social traits, Teresa learned to be a competent social actor in both white, upper-middle-class environments and in working- and middle-class Chicano and *Mexicano* environments. To survive as a stranger in so many social settings, Teresa developed an acute skill for assessing the rules governing a particular social setting and acting accordingly. Her ability to be competent in diverse social settings was only possible, however, because her life was never completely submerged in the employers' world. While living and going to school with the employer's children, Teresa and her mother maintained another life—one that was guarded and protected against any employer intrusion. Their other life was Mexican, not white, was Spanish speaking, not English speaking, was female dominated rather than male dominated, and was poor and working-class, not upper-middle-class. During the week Teresa and her mother visited the other Mexican maids in the neighborhoods, on weekends they occasionally took a bus into the Mexican barrio in Los Angeles to have dinner with friends, and every summer they spent a month in Ciudad Juarez with their family. Without the constant emergence in the *Mexicano* community, Teresa's story would simply be another version of Richard Rodriguez's *Hunger of Memory*—a story of assimilation and rejection of bilingualism and biculturalism as a way of life.

Teresa's description of evening activity with the Mexican maids in the neighborhood provides insight into her daily socialization and explains how she

172 • Feminisms in the Academy

learned to live in the employer's home without internalizing all their negative attitudes toward Mexican and working-class culture. Within the white, upper-class neighborhood in which they worked, the Mexican maids got together on a regular basis and cooked Mexican food, listened to Mexican music, and gossiped in Spanish about their employers. Treated as invisible or as confidants, the maids were frequently exposed to the intimate details of their employers' marriages and family life. The Mexican maids voiced their disapproval of the lenient child-rearing practices and parental decisions, particularly surrounding drug usage and the importance of material possessions:

> Raquel was the only one [maid] in the neighborhood who had her own room and own tv set. So everybody would go over to Raquel's. . . . This was my mother's support system. After hours, they would go to different people's [maids'] rooms depending on what their rooms had. Some of them had kitchens and they would go and cook all together, or do things like play cards and talk all the time. I remember that in those situations they would sit, and my mother would talk about the Smiths, what they were like. When they were going to negotiate for raises, when they didn't like certain things. I would listen and hear all the different discussions of what was going on in different houses. And they would talk, also, about the family relationships. The way they interacted, the kids did this and that. At the time some of the kids were smoking pot and they would talk about who was smoking marijuana. How weird it was that the parents didn't care. They would talk about what they saw as being wrong. The marriage relationship, or how weird it was that they would go off to the beauty shop and spend all this money, go shopping and do all these weird things and the effect that it had on the kids.

The interaction among the maids points to the existence of another culture operating invisibly within a Euro-American and male-dominated community. The workers' support system did not include employers and addressed their concerns as mothers, immigrants, workers, and women. They created a Mexican-dominated domain for themselves. Here they ate Mexican food, spoke Spanish, listened to the Spanish radio station, and watched novellas on TV. Here Teresa was not a cultural artifact but, instead, a member of the Mexican community.

In exchanging gossip and voicing their opinions about the employers' lifestyles, the maids rejected many of the employers' priorities in life. Sharing stories about the employers' families allowed the Mexican immigrant women to be critical of white, upper-middle-class families and to affirm and enhance their own cultural practices and beliefs. The regular evening sessions with other working-class Mexican immigrant women were essential in preserving Teresa and her mother's cultural values and were an important agency of socialization for Teresa. For instance, the maids had a much higher regard for their duties and responsibilities as mothers than as wives or lovers. In comparison to their mistresses, they were not financially dependent on men, nor did they engage in the expensive and time-consuming activity of being an ideal wife, such as dieting, exercising, and maintaining a certain standard of beauty in their dress, makeup, and hairdos. Unlike the employers' daughters, who attended cotillion and were socialized to acquire success through marriage, Teresa was constantly pushed to succeed academically in order to pursue a career. The gender identity cultivated among the maids did not include dependence on men or the learned helplessness that was enforced in the employers' homes but, rather, promoted self-sufficiency. However, both white women employers and Mexican women employees were expected to be nurturing and caring. These traits were further reinforced when employers asked Teresa to babysit for their children or to provide them with companionship during their husbands' absences.

So, while Teresa observed her mother adapting to the employers' standards in her interaction with their children, she learned that her mother did not approve of their lifestyle and understood that she had another set of expectations to adhere to. Teresa attended the same schools as the employers' children, wore similar clothes, and conducted most of her social life within the same socioeconomic class, but she remained the maid's daughter—and learned the limitations of that position. Teresa watched her mother uphold higher standards for her and apply a different set of standards to the employers' children; most of the time, however, it appeared to Teresa as if they had no rules at all.

Sharing stories about the Smiths and other employers in a female, Mexican, and worker-dominated social setting provided Teresa with a clear image of the people she lived with as employers rather than as family members. Seeing the employers through the eyes of the employees forced Teresa to question their kindness and benevolence and to recognize their use of manipulation to obtain additional physical and emotional labor from the employees. She became aware of the workers' struggles and the long list of grievances, including no annual raises, no paid vacations, no social security or health benefits, little if any privacy, and sexual harassment. Teresa was also exposed to the price that working-class immigrant women employed as live-in maids paid in maintaining white, middle-class, patriarchal communities. Employers' careers and lifestyles, particularly the everyday rituals affirming male privilege, were made possible through the labor women provided for men's physical, social, and emotional needs. Female employers depended on the maid's labor to assist in the reproduction of their gendered class status. Household labor was expanded in order to accommodate the male members of the employers' families and to preserve their privilege. Additional work was created by rearranging meals around men's work and recreation schedules and by waiting on them and serving them. Teresa's mother was frequently called upon to provide emotional labor for the wife, husband, mother, and father within an employer's family, thus freeing members to work or increase their leisure time.

DISCUSSION

Teresa's account offers insight into the ways racial ethnic women gain knowledge about the social order and use the knowledge to develop survival strategies. As the college-educated daughter of an immigrant Mexican woman employed as a live-in maid, Teresa's experiences in the employers' homes, neighborhood, and schools and her experiences in the homes of working-class *Mexicano* families and barrios provided her with the skills to cross the class and cultural boundaries separating the two worlds. The process of negotiating social boundaries involved an evaluation of Euro-American culture and its belief system in light of an intimate knowledge of white, middle-class families. Being in the position to compare and contrast behavior within different communities, Teresa debunked notions of "American family values" and resisted efforts toward assimilation. Learning to function in the employers' world was accomplished without internalizing its belief system, which defined ethnic culture as inferior. Unlike the employers' families, Teresa's was not able to assume the taken-for-granted reality of her mother's employers because her experiences provided a different kind of knowledge about the social order.

While the employers' children were surrounded by positive images of their race and class status, Teresa faced negative sanctions against her culture and powerless images of her race. Among employers' families she quickly learned that her "mother tongue" was not valued and that her culture was denied. All the Mexican adults in the neighborhood were in subordinate positions to the white adults and were responsible for caring for and nurturing white children. Most of the female employers were full-time homemakers who enjoyed the financial security provided by their husbands, whereas the Mexican immigrant women in the neighborhood all worked as maids and were financially independent; in many cases they were supporting children, husbands, and other family members. By directly observing her mother serve, pick up after, and nurture employers and their families, Teresa learned about white, middle-class privileges. Her experiences with other working-class Mexicans were dominated by women's responsibility for their children and extended families. Here the major responsibility of mothering was financial; caring and nurturing were secondary and were provided by the extended family or children did without. Confronted with a working mother who was too tired to spend time with her, Teresa learned about the racial, class, and gender parameters of parenthood, including its privileges, rights, responsibilities, and obligations. She also learned that the role of a daughter included helping her mother with everyday household tasks and, eventually, with the financial needs of the extended family. Unlike her uncles and male cousins, Teresa was not exempt from cooking and housework, regardless of her financial contributions. Within the extended family Teresa was subjected to standards of beauty strongly weighted by male definitions of women as modest beings, many times restricted in her dress and physical movements. Her social worlds became clearly marked by race, ethnic, class, and gender differences.

Successfully negotiating movement from a white, male, and middle-class setting to one dominated by working-class, immigrant, Mexican women involved a socialization process that provided Teresa with the skills to be bicultural. Since neither setting was bicultural, Teresa had to become that in order to be a competent social actor in each. Being bicultural included having the ability to assess the rules governing each setting and to understand her ethnic, class, and gender position. Her early socialization in the employers' households was not guided by principles of creativity, independence, and leadership but, rather, was based on conformity and accommodation. Teresa's experiences in two different cultural groups allowed her to separate each and to fulfill the employers' expectations without necessarily internalizing the meaning attached to the act. Therefore, she was able to learn English without internalizing the idea that English is superior to Spanish or that monolingualism is normal. The existence of a Mexican community within the employers' neighborhood provided Teresa with a collective experience of class-based racism, and the maids' support system affirmed and enhanced their own belief system and culture. As Philomena Essed (1991, 294) points out, "The problem is not only how knowledge of racism is acquired but also what kind of knowledge is being transmitted."

Teresa's life story lends itself to a complex set of analyses because the pressures to assimilate were challenged by the positive interactions she experienced within her ethnic community. Like other bilingual persons in the United States, Teresa's linguistic abilities were shaped by the linguistic practices of the social settings she had access to. Teresa learned the appropriate behavior for each social setting, each marked by different class and cultural dynamics and in which women's economic roles and relationships to men were distinct. An overview of Teresa's socialization illustrates the process of biculturalism—a process that included different sets of standards and rules governing her actions as a woman, as a Chicana, and as the maid's daughter.

While most racial ethnics do not share intimate social space with individuals of different cultural and social class background, Teresa's experiences living with her mother's employers provided insight into the ways in which a class-based, gendered, racist social order is maintained through a process of inclusion and exclusion. In Teresa's case inclusion occurred under the rubric of being like one of the family. Teresa adjusted her behavior to fit this new role, but she never actually quit being the maid's daughter, and she did not become white, middle-class, or a member of the employer's family. The employer was always in the position of power to decide when Teresa was to behave like one of the family and when she was expected to assume her position as the maid's daughter. The incidents of inclusion were symbolic and did little to change the social order, but the illusion of equality allowed white, middle-class employers to maintain images of themselves as generous, kind, and honest. By distorting the relationship between employer and employee, the Smiths were able to withhold Carmen's salary and claim they were providing Teresa with the same education their own children received. The arrangement affirmed their generosity, allowed them to claim credit for Teresa's successes, and denied Carmen her parental rights. Analysis of Teresa's experiences points to the function of maintaining the current social order through symbolic rituals of inclusion. Only through her relationship with the employers was Teresa able to enjoy certain privileges; thus, mother and daughter were locked into modes of behavior that maintained the social order.

Teresa's narrative of life as the maid's daughter challenges many traditional concepts in sociology. The socialization process of racial ethnics is not simply an either/or proposition resulting in individuals becoming assimilated. Socialization cannot be fully understood without analyzing social structure. Understanding the social order is essential in recognizing the lack of multiculturalism in our society; few, if any, social settings are governed by standards or cultural practices of groups considered to be racial ethnics. Consequently, we live in a society in which only individuals are bicultural or multicultural, not our neighborhoods, schools, communities, or families. Conceptualizing assimilation or biculturalism requires an analysis of the opportunity structure as experienced by groups outside the mainstream who have knowledge of the social order. A class-based, racist social order is maintained through social constraints establishing monolingualism and monoculturalism in social institutions. Providing incidents of inclusion creates the illusion that multiculturalism exists and suggests to conservatives that there has been a transfer of power—to women or to racial ethnics, for example—that threatens the American way of life. Without an analysis of the social order, concepts are based purely on ideology. Placing the experiences of women of color at the center of the discipline uncovers the taken-for-granted reality embedded in sociological assumptions used to develop theory.

Exploring the reproductive labor in white, middle-class households from the standpoint of the Mexican maid's daughter challenges assumptions, embedded in feminist scholarship, about women's universal experiences. When reproductive labor becomes the devalued and underpaid work of ethnic immigrant women, an analysis of housework and child care is incomplete without considering the relationship between the female employer and female employee. The experiences of household workers and child care workers cannot simply be ignored or translated into inappropriate concepts and categories used to describe white, middle-class women as mothers and wives—and we cannot rely on the old adage that "a woman's work is never done." The life story of the maid's daughter exposes the way that white female employers can use their class and race privilege to shift the burden of sexism onto women of color employed as household workers. Mothering is not always unpaid labor, and the family or household unit can be transformed into a workplace in which women sell their physical, mental, and emotional labor. Only by exploring the wide range of gender experiences in society can feminist scholarship address the complexities of sexism in a class-based, racist social order.

NOTES

This essay was originally presented as a paper at the University of Michigan, "Feminist Scholarship: Thinking through the Disciplines," 30 January 1992. I want to thank Abigail J. Stewart and Domna Stanton for their insightful comments and suggestions.

1. There are also several recent studies on private household workers generated from research on underground and undocumented immigrant labor. These studies are primarily concerned with domestic service as an entry job, and immigration issues are central to the analysis rather than issues focusing on paid reproductive labor or race relations (Warner and Henderson 1990; Solorzano-Torres 1988).

2. The names are pseudonyms.

REFERENCES

Benson, Margaret. 1973. "The Political Economy of Women's Liberation." In *Women in a Man-Made World,* edited by Nona Glazer-Malbin and Helen Youngetson Waehier, 119–28. Chicago: Rand McNally.

Berch, Bettina. 1982. *The Endless Day: The Political Economy of Women and Work.* New York: Harcourt Brace Jovanovich.

Colen, Shellee. 1989. "'Just a Little Respect': West Indian Domestic Workers in New York City." In *Muchachas No More: Household Workers in Latin America and the Caribbean,* edited by Elsa M. Chaney and Mary Garcia Castro, 171–94. Philadelphia: Temple University Press.

Coley, Soray Moore. 1981. "And Still I Rise: An Exploratory Study of Contemporary Black Private Household Workers." Ph.D. diss., Bryn Mawr College.

Collins, Patricia Hill. 1986. "Learning from the Outsider Within: The Sociological Significance of Black Feminist Thought." *Social Problems* 33:514–32.

Costa, M. Dalla, and Selma James. 1972. "Women and the Subversion of Community." *Radical America* 6:67–102.

Dill, Bonnie Thornton. 1988. "'Making Your Job Good Yourself': Domestic Service and the Construction of Personal Dignity." In *Women and the Politics of Empowerment,* edited by Ann Bookman and Sandra Morgen, 33–52. Philadelphia: Temple University Press.

Essed, Philomena. 1991. *Understanding Everyday Racism.* Newbury Park, Calif.: Sage Publications.

Ferber, M. A., and B. G. Birnbaum. 1980. "Housework: Priceless or Valueless?" *Review of Income and Wealth* 26:387–400.

Glazer, Nona. 1980. "Everyone Needs Three Hands: Doing Unpaid and Paid Work." In *Women and Household Labor,* edited by Sarah Fenstermaker Berk, 249–73. Beverly Hills, Calif.: Sage Publications.

Glenn, Evelyn Nakano. 1986. *Issei, Nisei, War Brides Three Generations of Japanese American Women in Domestic Service.* Philadelphia: Temple University Press.

Hondagneu-Sotelo, Pierrette. 1990. "Gender and the Politics of Mexican Undocumented Immigrant Settlement." Ph.D. diss., University of California, Berkeley.

Kousha, Mahnaz. 1990. "Best Friends: Power Relations among Black Domestics and White Mistresses." Ph.D. diss., University of Kentucky.

Martin, Linda, and Kerry Segrave. 1985. *The Servant Problem: Domestic Service in North America.* Jefferson, N.C.: McFarland.

Mitchell, Juliet. 1971. *Women's Estate.* Harmondsworth, Eng.: Penguin.

Oakley, Ann. 1974. *Woman's Work: The Housewife, Past and Present.* New York: Pantheon Books.

Rodriguez, Richard. 1982. *Hunger of Memory: The Education of Richard Rodriguez: An Autobiography.* Boston: Godine.

Romero, Mary. 1992. *Maid in the U.S.A.* New York: Routledge.

Rollins, Judith. 1985. *Between Women: Domestics and Their Employers.* Philadelphia: Temple University Press.

Salzinger, Leslie. 1991. "A Maid by Any Other Name: The Transformation of 'Dirty Work' by Central American Immigrants." In *Ethnography Unbound: Power and Residence in the Modern Metropolis,* edited by Michael Burawoy et al., 139–60. Berkeley: University of California Press.

Solorzano-Torres, Rosalia. 1988. "Women, Labor, and the U.S.-Mexico Border: Mexican Maids in El Paso, Texas." In *Mexicanas at Work in the United States,* edited by Margarita Melville, 75–83. Houston: Mexican American Studies. Monograph no. 5, Mexican American Studies Program, University of Houston.

Tucker, Susan. 1988. *Telling Memories among Southern Women: Domestic Workers and Their Employers in the Segregated South.* Baton Rouge: Louisiana State University Press.

Walker, Kathryn E., and William Gauger. 1973. "The Dollar Value of Household Work." Information Bulletin no. 60, Consumer Economics and Public Polity, 5, Ithaca, N.Y.: Cornell University.

Warner, Judith Ann, and Helen K. Henderson. 1990. "Latina Women Immigrant's Waged Domestic Labor: Effects of Immigration Reform on the Link between Private Households and the International Labor Force." Paper presented at the 1990 meeting of the American Sociological Association.

Chapter 7

The Contribution of Women to the Greek Domestic Economy: Rereading Xenophon's *Oeconomicus*

Sarah B. Pomeroy

Xenophon wrote the *Oeconomicus,* a "Discourse on the Skill of Estate Management" presented in the form of a Socratic dialogue, in the first third of the fourth century B.C.E. The *Oeconomicus* makes a major contribution to our understanding of the economy of ancient Greece, for it is the only extant Greek didactic work to draw attention to the importance of the *oikos* ("estate," "household," or "family") as an economic entity.[1] The earliest written evidence from the Greek world indicates that *oikoi,* both royal and common, were the basis of the Greek economy: they were the most common units of production and consumption.[2] The polis was a community of *oikoi* rather than of individual citizens. In Athens and elsewhere public legislation and private custom concurred to perpetuate the *oikoi,* which were expected to remain in continuous operation, enduring longer than the life span of any individual member, in order to bear the economic and social burdens imposed by the state.

Neither Marxist nor classical economic theory has thus far taken the entire household into account. Economic historians of the Greek world have virtually ignored the domestic economy, except its agrarian aspect, and have preferred to discuss industries, banking, and trade routes. Neither M. I. Rostovzeff in *The Social and Economic History of the Hellenistic World* nor H. Michell in *The Economics of Ancient Greece* treated domestic labor and its products. In *Le Travail dans la Grèce ancienne* Gustave Glotz presented a brief discussion of the family economy only in his opening chapters on the Homeric period, in which he considered domestic production as part of a primitive world predating the formation of the polis. These discussions impose some distinctions between public and private that are artificial in the context of classical Greek history; furthermore, they distort our view of the Greek economy and other precapitalist economies to make them fit categories appropriate to the analysis of bourgeois capitalism of the nineteenth and twentieth centuries.

The late M. I. Finley, whose work dominated the study of the Greek economy in the mid-twentieth century among Marxist and non-Marxist ancient historians alike, asserted that the Greeks were ignorant of economic theory.[3] Finley grafted onto his study of the Greek economy the modern definitions of E. B. Schumpeter, who described economic analysis as "the intellectual efforts that men have made in order to understand economic phenomena."[4] Therefore, Finley deduced that in Xenophon "there is not one sentence that expresses an economic principle or offers an economic analysis, nothing on efficiency of production [or] rational choice."[5] Finley criticized Xenophon for being "interested in specialization of crafts rather than in division of labour."[6] Thus, he proceeded to reject the work of the earliest Greek economist.

Though Finley does not mention Marx, he refers to the same passage in *Cyropaedia*, 8.2.5—a description of the development of *technai* (arts, crafts, or occupations) in large cities—that Marx used to argue that Xenophon displayed a characteristic bourgeois instinct in his discussion of the division of labor in the workshop. Marx, however, had a better opinion of Xenophon than Finley did: in *Das Kapital* he comments that Xenophon stressed the supreme importance of use-value.[7] Georges Sorel later summarized Marx's comment and added that Xenophon, unlike Plato, shows an understanding of the importance of production.[8]

Finley's anachronistic view of economic theory eliminated by definition much of what the Greeks themselves regarded as the economy: he declared that "what we call the economy was exclusively the business of outsiders."[9] In particular, Finley failed to give full recognition to the private sphere and the contributions of women, both slave and free, to the economy. Beyond admitting that bakers and textile workers were productive, Finley paid little attention to the work of domestic female slaves,[10] although it is likely—as A. W. Gomme has suggested—that they outnumbered male slaves in Athens.[11] Unlike Finley, G. E. M. de Ste. Croix did attempt to integrate women into his explanation of economy and society in *The Class Struggle*. Ste. Croix, a Marxist scholar, stated that all Greek wives should be regarded as a distinct economic class because their role in human reproduction led to political, economic, and social subjugation to men. Despite this awareness, Ste. Croix devoted a mere 12 of 732 pages to the class and status of women; he confessed that "this needs a great deal of further thought."[12]

In societies characterized by strict sexual division of labor—in which most women are excluded from the labor market, cash economy, and ownership of the means of production—the categories that have been applied by economic historians are relevant almost exclusively to men. Because the *Oeconomicus*, with its focus on the domestic economy, does not fit readily into ancient historians' previous conceptual frameworks, it is questionable whether any existing approach has sufficiently illuminated the economy of ancient Greece. Despite their attention to the division of labor and their acknowledgment that Xenophon understood the division of labor among men in workshops, Marx, Sorel, and Finley all failed to realize that Xenophon discusses the sexual division of labor that was fundamental to Greek society.[13] Xenophon was, in fact, the first Greek author to give full recognition to the use value of women's work and to understand that domestic labor has economic value even if it lacks exchange value. This idea was radical in the formal literature of classical Greece and has yet to gain acceptance in modern times.

My recently completed commentary on Xenophon's *Oeconomicus* has led me to reevaluate the contribution of women's domestic labor to the Greek economy. In doing so, I reviewed the activities of both free women and slaves. Endeavoring to avoid the bias of any single genre or type of evidence, I exploited both written texts and archaeological evidence, including studies of Greek houses, artifacts connected with textile manufacture, and Greek vases that depicted women working. In 1988, when I was teaching in Kalymnos in the Sporades, I personally observed the ways in which some women still contribute to the economy through embroidery, weaving, and working with leather. I read many anthropological reports about the work of women in traditional Greek societies. This study contributed to my understanding of the ways in which Greek men conceal the work that women in their families perform at home, so that only men appear to be earning cash; the men then publicly disburse the revenue acquired from women's labor as though they had produced it. This supplementary evidence, important in understanding the *Oeconomicus,* also corroborated much of Xenophon's text and helped me to distinguish among realia, idealization, and image.

In a 1986 essay titled "Ten Years after Pomeroy: Studies of the Image and Reality of Women in Antiquity" Phyllis Culham cautioned against blurring image with reality in the study of ancient women. Culham recommended that, in the search for women's lived experience, male-authored texts be toppled from their privileged position and material artifacts and historical context be examined. I do not go as far as Culham in her antipathy to literary studies, for I believe that images do affect women's lived reality, but I join her in recommending that scholars of women in antiquity have a clear idea of what they are trying to do and what the sources they choose to use will permit them to do.

Culham's strictures continue to go unheeded, and problems persist. This points to one category of work greatly in need of review—that in which theories of literary criticism were applied wholesale by scholars who did not distinguish the description and analysis of ancient male authors' ideas and images of women from the study of women in ancient history. The mere bulk of publications of this type has contributed to an unfounded sense of complacency about our knowledge of women in antiquity. In *Greek Virginity* (translated from *Le Corps virginal*), for example, Giulia Sissa states as her subject: "Did the hymen exist according to the Greek perception of anatomy (among laymen as well as physicans)?" (1); her sources are all male authored, and she presents them from the male viewpoint. The "physicians" and the "laymen" are all men. Sissa does not discuss how their views might have influenced the lives of actual women, and she ignores authors such as Sappho (LP 105a, 105c, 107, 114) and Archilochus (*P. Colon.* 7511), who do provide additional perspectives on how the loss of virginity affected women. The unsuspecting nonclassicist, for whom the translation was probably intended, will probably trust the Harvard imprint and have no idea of how distorted a view of virginity Sissa's book offers.

As Culham also observed, the development of women's studies in classics has been further inhibited by some would-be-historians who do attempt to distinguish the study of women's lives from the study of men's ideas about women. Many of these scholars, trained in literary rather than in historical methodology, may fail to realize that the social history they pursue is often the most difficult of all ancient histories; the sources are mute, sparse, or anecdotal, and the subfields were only recently established. A properly trained historian pays attention not only to gender but also to distinctions of class, age, ethnicity, regional specificity, historical period, and diachronic change.

Preparing an overview of the criticism for the *American Journal of Philology,* I consulted other scholars who shared my interest in women in antiquity. Highest on their list of desiderata was more work on the realia of women's lives; they indicated a need for, among other things, an examination of the public and private spaces in which women habitually moved, of the work they performed, and of the people with whom they interacted daily. The study that follows is a step in that direction. I will analyze the *Oeconomicus* primarily from the perspective of women—the same perspective that Xenophon himself emphasizes in chapters III and VII to X.[14] My project will largely redefine our understanding of the productivity of the Greek household and of its members. I have defined work as productive activity for household use or for exchange.[15] Patriarchy literally means "the rule of fathers." I will explain how patriarchy functions as an economic system in which, first, the male who heads the *oikos* appropriates the labor of his family and slaves in private and, second, the citizen body of men benefit publicly from women's work. Finally, I will show that, in his discussions of marriage and work in the *Oeconomicus,* Xenophon expresses economic principles that are appropriate to the analysis of the Greek economy.

Xenophon's extensive discussion of married life appears in two passages. The first (I–III) records a conversation between Socrates and Critobulus, a member of the liturgical (i.e., wealthiest) class. Critobulus asks Socrates for advice in managing his affairs, for he finds it difficult to meet his personal and public financial obligations. Socrates points out that some men reap profit and others loss from the same assets and that some marriages, through the joint efforts of husband and wife, turn out to be productive, while the treatment other men accord their wives leads to disaster. Moreover, the wife who handles household affairs competently as her husband's partner is his peer in contributing to the financial success of the *oikos*. In a subsequent section (VII–X) Socrates tells Critobulus about a discussion on marriage that he once had with Ischomachus. Like Critobulus, Ischomachus is a member of the wealthiest class, but Ischomachus enjoys a reputation for managing his household profitably so that he is able to contribute to the public weal eagerly and generously.

Ischomachus begins his exposition with a description of the early days of his marriage when his bride (as was usual in classical Athens) was not yet fifteen. According to Ischomachus, his wife knew little when she married him except how to control her appetite, how to weave, and how to assign spinning to the slaves. These accomplishments were not negligible. Inasmuch as women were in charge of the kitchen and gluttony was portrayed in misogynistic and humorous texts as a vice to which females were prone, appetite control merited mention. In order to prevent theft, the mistress of the house needed to know how to weigh out wool for spinning. Furthermore, Ischomachus' wife knew how to read and write; her literacy would have been a decided advantage in keeping track of the household possessions and financial records (VII.36).

The *Oeconomicus* presents a view of marriage as an economic partnership whose goal is the increase of property. Marriage constituted the economic basis of the *oikos*. The wife's dowry consisted of cash and movables; the husband furnished the land and the house with most of its contents. Together they provided the foundation of the *oikos* at the start of a marriage. Some anthropologists have postulated that the dowry is usually found in societies in which women are considered economic liabilities.[16] As Medea stated brutally, a woman needed a dowry to buy a husband (Eur., *Med*. 232–34). Ischomachus, however, does not regard his wife's dowry as simply a sort of trust fund to be used for the support of a person who is nothing but a parasite. In a conversation with his new wife, which Ischomachus relates to Socrates, he stresses the importance of her productive role as chronological precedent to her reproductive role:[17]

> 10) I questioned her more or less as follows: "Tell me, wife, have you ever thought about why I married you and why your parents gave you to me? 11) It must be quite obvious to you, I am sure, that there was no shortage of partners with whom we might sleep. I, on my part, and your parents, on your behalf, considered who was the best partner we could choose for managing an estate and for children that we could find. And I chose you, and your parents, apparently, chose me out of those who were eligible. 12) Now if

some day the god[18] grants us children, then we will consider how to train them in the best way possible. For this will be a blessing to us both, to obtain the best allies and support in old age."

Although his own payments into the household accounts are tangible and continual, Ischomachus values not only his wife's dowry but also her future contributions. He points out that an industrious woman will be honored for her work, even in old age, when other women are despised, presumably because their childbearing years are past and they are considered useless (VII.42). Ischomachus acknowledges that his wife's contribution to the household can exceed his own (VII.13–14): if she is a prudent manager, she can be responsible for more than half the income of an *oikos* in the wealthiest class.

Household productivity depends on a sexual division of labor that is sanctioned by both gods and nature, for it is the result of biological differences between male and female (VII.15). Ischomachus explains at length to his new wife:

13) But at present we two share this estate. I go on paying everything I have into the common fund; and you deposited into it everything you brought with you. There is no need to calculate precisely which of us has contributed more, but to be well aware of this: that the better partner is the one who makes the more valuable contribution.

14) In reply to this, Socrates, my wife answered, "What would I be able to do to help you? What ability do I have? Everything depends on you. My mother told me that my duty is to practise self-control."

15) "By Zeus, wife," I said, "my father said the same to me. But self-control for both man and woman means behaving so that their property will be in the very best condition and that the greatest possible increase will be made to it by just and honorable means." . . .

17) . . . "Wife, the gods seem to have shown much discernment in yoking together female and male, as we call them, so that the couple might constitute a partnership that is most beneficial to each of them."

Obviously, Xenophon's language stresses the natural, divine, and legal division of labor. Ischomachus goes on to cast the various productive tasks necessary for the maintenance of the *oikos* in this same light:

19) First of all, so that the various species of living creatures may not become extinct, this pair sleeps together for the purpose of procreation. Then this pairing provides offspring to support the partners in their old age, at least in the case of human beings. And finally, human beings do not live outdoors like cattle, but obviously have need of shelter.

20) Those who intend to obtain produce to bring into the shelter need someone to work at the outdoor jobs. For plowing, sowing, planting, and herding is all work that is performed outdoors, and it is from these that our essential provisions are obtained. 21) As soon as these are brought into the shelter, then someone else is needed to look after them and to perform the work that requires shelters. The nursing of newborn children requires shelters, and so does the preparation of bread from grain, and likewise, making clothing out of wool. 22) Because both the indoor and the outdoor tasks require work and concern, he said, I think the god, from the very beginning, designed the nature of woman for the indoor work and concerns and the nature of man for the outdoor work. . . . And because the god was aware that he had both created in the woman and assigned to her the duty of nourishing newborn children, he had measured out to her a greater share of affection for newborn babies than he gave to the man. 25) And because the god had also assigned to the woman the duty of guarding what had been brought into the house, realizing that a tendency to be afraid is not at all disadvantageous for guarding things, he measured out a greater portion of fear to the woman than to the man. And knowing that the person responsible for the outdoor work would have to serve as defender against any wrong-doer, he measured out to him a greater share of courage.

26) Because it is necessary for both of them to give and to take, he gave both of them equal powers of memory and concern. So, you would not be able to distinguish whether the female or male sex has the larger share of these. 27) And he gave them both equally the ability to practise self-control also, when it is needed. And the god granted the privilege to whichever one is superior in this to gain a larger share of the benefit accruing from it—whether man or woman. 28) So, because each of them is not equally well-endowed with all the same natural aptitudes, they are consequently more in need of each other, and the bond is more beneficial to the couple, since one is capable where the other is deficient.

After establishing so thoroughly the specific divisions and equalities in labor as a dictate of the gods and nature, Ischomachus stresses that "the law encourages this, for it yokes together husband and wife, and just as the god made them partners in children, so the law has appointed them partners in the estate" (29). Transgression of the law will, of course, incur punishment: "If someone behaves in a way contrary to the nature the god has given him, perhaps his disobedience will not escape the notice of the gods, and he will pay a penalty for neglecting his proper business or for performing his wife's work" (31).

Ischomachus explains his wife's duties to her through the metaphor of the queen bee. This particular image achieves two tasks at once: it naturalizes the wife's economic role in gender as well as in class terms, stressing her authority over the household slaves:

> She asked, "How does the work of the queen bee resemble that which I must perform?"
>
> 33) I replied, "She remains in the hive and does not allow the bees to be idle, but those who ought to work outside she dispatches to their job, and she notes and receives what each brings in, and keeps it until it is necessary to use it. And when the time comes to use it, she distributes a fair share to each. 34) She supervises the construction of the combs inside the hive, so that they are woven beautifully and quickly, and she is concerned that the offspring shall be reared to maturity. When the little ones have been reared and are capable of working, she sends them out to found a colony with someone to lead the new generation."

The analogy between the good housekeeper and the bee can be traced as far back as the sixth century B.C.E. in the poetry of Semonides.[19] The poet makes a direct connection between the virtuous wife, domestic economy, and prosperity. But, while Semonides merely compliments the good wife, Xenophon goes much further. After this exchange Ischomachus reveals this list of responsibilities directly as his wife's future duties, following very closely the language he used in the previous passage.

The wife's labor in the house becomes the basis of her autonomy, of her status as queen bee, and of the possibility that she will rule over her husband if she proves to be a better manager than he is:

> 38) Ischomachus went on: "I was delighted with her response and said, 'wife, because of such thoughtful actions on the part of the queen bee, isn't the relationship of the bees to her, too, of such a kind that when she deserts the hive, not one of the bees considers staying behind, but all follow her?'
>
> 39) "My wife replied, 'it would surprise me,' she said, 'if the leader's activities did not apply more to you rather than to me. For, if you were not concerned that supplies were brought in from outside, surely my guarding the things indoors and my budgeting would seem pretty ridiculous.'"

In fact, Ischomachus' wife eventually sits in judgment of her husband, sentencing him to endure punishments and to pay fines (XI.25).

The *Oeconomicus* is also largely about women's education. In the fourth century B.C.E. education was responsible for the entrance of women into the liberal arts and professions; women began to appear as artists, physicians, and philosophers.[20] Ischomachus had stated that the intellectual powers of men and women were the same (VII.26, quoted earlier); from this premise it is an easy leap to elevate the role of housewife to the status of a profession with important social and economic consequences:

> 41) But, wife, your other special concerns turn out to be pleasant: whenever you take a slave who has no knowledge of spinning, and teach her that skill so that you double her value to you: and whenever you take one who does not know how to manage a house or serve, and turn her into one who is a skilled and faithful servant and make her invaluable; and whenever it is in your power to reward the helpful and reasonable members of your household and to punish any of them who appears to be vicious. 42) But the sweetest experience of all will be this: if you prove to be better than I am and make me your servant. Then you will have no need to fear that as your years increase you will be less honored in the household; but you may be confident that when you become older, the better partner you have been to me, and the better guardian of the estate for the children, the greater the respect you will enjoy in the household.

Owing to her husband's instruction, Ischomachus' wife not only increased her own contribution to the household, but she became capable of teaching others, in turn. The interest on an investment in education is not simple. Ischomachus tells his wife that she can make her slaves twice as valuable by teaching them to be productive, and she protects the investment in human capital by nursing the slaves who are ill (VII.37, 41):

> 37) "However," I said, "one of your proper concerns, perhaps, may seem to you rather thankless: you will certainly have to be concerned about nursing any of the slaves who becomes ill."
>
> "Oh, no," exclaimed my wife, "it will be most gratifying if those who are well cared for will prove to be thankful and more loyal than before."

The sources of ongoing income for an *oikos* based on an agricultural economy were numerous. The *Oeconomicus* mentions income from the sale of horses (II.11, III.9). Slaves, sheep, cash, and other items are also potential sources of income (I.9; II.11; III.17; V.3, 6, 18, 20; VII.41; XVI.1; XX.23). All the human members of an *oikos* can contribute to its successful operation or can produce losses. The husband and the wife can increase the estate (III.10, VII.13–14). The housekeeper (IX.12) and the bailiff, by producing a surplus, can create a profit (XV.1, XXI.10). Even ordinary female slaves can increase the worth of the estate by doubling their own value when they learn to spin (VII.41). Thus, their work will contribute directly to the capital of the *oikos*. Textile manufacture was women's sole productive activity that the Greeks traditionally recognized as making an economic contribution. For example, the Law Code of Gortyn in Crete (published in the fifth century B.C.E., but including earlier laws) directs that in a case of divorce a woman might take with her half of what she had woven.[21]

Historians have followed the ancient sources in not giving textile manufacture the attention it deserves. Among skilled workers listed on linear B tablets from Cnossus and Pylos, large numbers of female and male textile workers are recorded.[22] The females are more than twice as numerous as the males. That these women received the same food rations as the men suggests that their work was considered equally laborious and valuable. The picture painted by the Homeric epics is consistent with the evidence of the tablets. In the *Iliad* and the *Odyssey* female slaves were valued for their handiwork.[23] Their products were a significant commodity in the gift exchange system. For example, the ransom of Hector included twelve each of robes, mantles, blankets, cloaks, and tunics (*Il.* 24.229–31), and Odysseus tells Laertes that he was once given twelve each of cloaks, blankets, robes, and tunics (*Od.* 24.273–79). When we consider the amount of labor that must have been required to produce these textiles, we must reject Finley's view that female slaves were useful primarily for sexual purposes and that domestic slavery and products manufactured by women were important only for household consumption.[24]

Even after the introduction of a moneyed economy, textiles continued to function as liquid wealth, for they could readily be converted to cash. Textiles are recorded in temple inventories like that of Artemis Brauronia (*IG* II^2 1514–29). Articles of clothing are inventoried individually on the Attic *stelae* listing confiscated property (*IG* I^3 421.212–49). Demosthenes (27.10) includes clothing as part of his inheritance and mentions that clothing and bedding served as security for a loan (49.22). In manumission inscriptions from classical Athens spinners constitute the largest group by far of manumitted workers whose special job is recorded. It should be assumed that they purchased their freedom and were able to pay the hundred drachmas required for the dedication of a cup to Athena as a result of their work.[25] That female slaves were considered as productive as males is suggested by the fact that the average price of females and males listed in the Attic *stelae* was the same.[26] Doubtless, those slave women whose primary job was not wool working were also expected to spin if they had any spare time. Xenophon may be referring to such activities when he mentions doubling a slave's value by teaching her to spin (VII.41).

Aeschines (1.97) enumerates the skilled slaves inherited by the defendant Timarchus. Among these he makes specific and detailed mention of a woman who was expert in working flax and who produced sheer textiles for the market. The scholion comments that these goods were very valuable. According to the metaphor employed by Ischomachus in speaking to his wife, female slaves function as the worker bees who weave combs and produce honey—a valuable commodity that can be sold.[27] They change raw materials into textiles. Ischomachus displays the stores of textiles belonging to his *oikos:* some are valuable enough to be locked in the master bedroom (IX.3, 6). This hoard is a portion of the wealth of the *oikos.*

An anthropological study of Sicily supplies information about how such textiles might have functioned as wealth in many spheres of exchange.[28] Until the middle of the twentieth century brides brought to marriages substantial quantities of textiles that they had made and embroidered. These trousseaux were not designated solely for personal use; a portion was kept in reserve and regarded as capital to be exchanged for food or cash in hard times. Of course, such sales were probably surreptitious since the vendors would be reluctant to advertise their economic problems.

In *Frogs* 1346–51 Aristophanes refers to what must have been a common situation: a poor woman in the agora selling what she had woven. As Aristotle states in *Politics* 1322b–23a, poor men were obliged to use their wives and children as slaves. Such a situation was fraught with the potential for dishonor. Women who worked outside the home ran the risk of being considered licentious, foreign, or slaves; as a result, their children's citizenship might be challenged. The Athenian ideal was to keep a wife in seclusion, but a man could seclude his wife and daughters only if he could afford a slave to perform essential chores outdoors, such as fetching water, that were delegated to women.[29] Poor women who needed to work outside the home could not be secluded; consequently, seclusion was a luxury indicative of social and economic status.

Upper-class women furnished with wool could contribute to their own support by weaving—weaving is the only work of respectable women depicted on classical vases—but, if a man were obliged to market the fruits of the domestic labor of the women in his family, he would have tried to conceal this. In *Memorabilia* 2.7.2–12 a large number of upper-class women are forced to move in with their relative Aristarchus, who cannot afford to maintain them. But he hesitates to put them to work weaving and to sell their products, because, as he explains, they are his relatives, not slaves. Weaving was so much a woman's job that, ultimately, Aristarchus is the only member of his household who continues to be idle.

When he persuades Aristarchus to put his relatives to work for profit, Socrates reminds him that most of the Megarians make their living from the sale of textiles.[30] According to Xenophon (*Mem.* 2.7.6), the Megarians bought foreign slaves and harbored slaves who had run away from Athens. Thucydides[31] mentions the runaway slaves but does not specify their sex. Aristophanes (*Ach.* 524), supplies the information that the slaves were female (though we do not have to believe his allegation that they were prostitutes who had belonged to Aspasia).[32] In Megara slaves manufactured inexpensive woolen clothing for export. With the proceeds the Megarians were able to purchase the grain that was essential for their survival. The Athenian embargo against importing Megarian textiles and other products was a significant cause of the Peloponnesian War.[33] In other words, the economy of an important Greek city was largely supported by the work of female slaves.

Finley and earlier economic historians imposed a veil of silence over women's work. To some extent they were probably influenced by the ancient sources, which do not draw attention to the work of respectable women. Weaving, however, was (and still is) work that women could perform indoors, in seclusion. The men in their families could exchange women's products for cash, while the women themselves retained their respectability. Xenophon's *Oeconomicus* provides valuable information about the contribution of women to the economy of the *oikos* and polis. For this reason, in recent years I have been recommending that it be included in the classical canon and read in Great Books and other humanities courses.[34]

NOTES

More detailed versions of some of the material covered in this essay appear in "The Study of Women in Antiquity: Past, Present, and Future"; and in *Xenophon's Oeconomicus: A Social and Historical Commentary* (with a new English translation). With a few obvious exceptions, journal titles are abbreviated according to the form in *L'Année Philologique*. Accepted abbreviations will be used for standard works. Lists of such abbreviations may be found in reference books such as the *Oxford Classical Dictionary*, 2d ed., and in the major Greek and Latin dictionaries. All references in Roman numerals are to chapters of Xenophon, *Oeconomicus*. The additional references to Arabic numerals preceding quotations of translated passages are to paragraphs of chapters.

1. Although in some aspects of the position of the wife, the treatment of slaves, the importance accorded to education, and its wealth and size, the *oikos* described at length in the *Oeconomicus* is well above the average, other historical sources indicate that it is typical of classical Athens in many respects. Furthermore, no other historical source gives such a wide range of detailed practical information on an *oikos*. Therefore, it is reasonable to attempt to glean some information about the economic structure of the normal *oikos* from the *Oeconomicus*.

2. Jon-Christian Billigmeier, "Studies on the Family in the Aegean Bronze Age and in Homer," 14, points out that in linear B kinship terminology is not used to designate the extended family but, instead, is restricted to members of the immediate family. Of course, the fact that the sources are limited to government tallies may have produced this result.

3. "Aristotle and Economic Analysis," 13 n. 44. See the rebuttal by Scott Meikle, "Aristotle and the Political Economy of the Polis," 57–73.

4. *History of Economic Analysis,* 54.

5. *The Ancient Economy,* 19.

6. "Aristotle and Economic Analysis," 4. This criticism might more justly be leveled at Plato, for example, in his description of the nascent city in Rep. 2.369D–E.

7. *Das Kapital,* 1, Karl Marx, Friedrich Engels, *Werke,* 23:388 n. 81. Adam Smith had also seen a connection between the division of labor and the market. See also Ronald L. Meek and Andrew S. Skinner, "The Development of Adam Smith's Ideas on the Division of Labour," 1100.

8. *Réflexions sur la violence,* 366 n. 2.

9. "Aristotle and Economic Analysis," 25. Finley alludes to the mercantile activities of resident aliens and foreigners. P. Herfst, *Le Travail de la femme dans la Grèce ancienne,* 9, also states that the *Oeconomicus* fails to treat what we call the economy.

10. This blindness about women mars Finley's analysis of ancient slavery, inasmuch as his distinction between slave and free—that no slave held public office or sat on the deliberative and judicial bodies (in "Was Greek Civilization Based on Slave Labour?" 145–64; republished in *Slavery in Classical Antiquity,* ed. M. I. Finley, 55)—cannot be used to differentiate women's statuses.

11. A. W. Gomme, *The Population of Athens in the Fifth and Fourth Centuries B.C.,* 21 n. 3. On the population of Athens, see, more recently, Mogens Herman Hansen, *Demography and Democracy: The Number of Citizens in Fourth Century Athens.*

12. G. E. M. de Ste. Croix, *The Class Struggle in the Ancient Greek World,* 101.

13. On the division of labor as the principal incentive for human marriage, see Claude Lévi-Strauss (e.g., *Les Structures élementaires de la parenté,* 2d ed., translated as *The Elementary Structures of Kinship,* 40).

14. The male characters in the *Oeconomicus,* including Socrates, Critobulus, and Ischomachus, are all known from other primary sources, and the wife of Ischomachus may be identical with a woman named Chrysilla in a fourth-century lawsuit. We have relatively abundant information about each persona's wealth and family relationships. When Xenophon's readers were young they probably knew, or had heard quite a bit about, the characters in the *Oeconomicus,* for each was colorful or even notorious. Thus, even if the conversations attributed to them in the *Oeconomicus* did not actually occur as related, they must be representative of the sort of thing that they would have said, or Xenophon's text would scarcely have been credible to his readers. For this reason, I feel that the *Oeconomicus* offers the historian of women enough direct access to the past to warrant a closer examination.

15. For this terminology, see Louise A. Tilly and Joan W. Scott, *Women, Work, and Family,* 3. On the domestic labor debate, see also, for example, Annette Kuhn and Ann Marie Wolpe, *Feminism and Materialism: Women and Modes of Production.*

16. For a review of the anthropological and historical literature, see Diane Owen Hughes, "From Brideprice to Dowry in Mediterranean Europe."

17. Owing to the seclusion of respectable women, Xenophon cannot represent the

speech of Ischomachus' wife directly. She could not have spoken with Socrates as he did; instead, the husband must quote his wife's part in the dialogue.

18. References to a god or gods, here and in the following passages, are conventional and interchangeable. Monotheism is not implied.

19. Fr. 7: M. L. West, *Iambi et Elegi Graeci* 2 (1970):99–104.

20. Pomeroy, "Technikai kai Mousikai."

21. *Inscr. Creticae* 4.72, col. 2.48–52, col. 3.17–24. On women and weaving, see also Sarah B. Pomeroy, *Goddesses,* 9, 30, 40, 149, 199–200.

22. For detailed discussion, see John T. Killen, "The Wool Industry of Crete in the Late Bronze Age"; and "The Textile Industries at Pylos and Knossos." For some titles of specialized jobs, see Pierre Carlier, "La Femme dans la société mycénienne d'après les archives en linéaire B," 29 n. 53. According to Aristotle, *HA* 5.19, and Pliny, *NH* 11.76, a Greek woman invented the weaving of silk.

23. For example, Agamemnon's expectation that Chryseis will both weave and serve as a sexual partner (*Il.* 1.31). In Homer female slaves were frequently freeborn women who had been enslaved by acts of violence such as war and kidnapping.

24. *Slavery in Classical Antiquity,* 58: "domestic slaves, often an unproductive element."

25. *IG* II² 1553–58, in the new edition by D. M. Lewis, "Attic Manumissions" and "Dedications of Phialai at Athens"; and Helen McClees, *A Study of Women in Attic Inscriptions,* 31.

26. See W. Kendrick Pritchett, "The Attic Stelai. Part II."

27. Pliny, *NH* 11.10.22, uses the words *textum* (woven fabric) and *tela* (web) in describing the building of the hive. Though Greek philosophers were uncertain about the sex of the leader of the bees, there was general agreement that the workers were female.

28. Jane Schneider, "Trousseau as Treasure: Some Contradictions of Late Nineteenth-Century Change in Sicily."

29. See discussions in Roger Just, *Women in Athenian Law and Life;* and David Cohen, "Seclusion, Separation, and the Status of Women in Classical Athens." See also Ernestine Friedl, "The Position of Women: Appearance and Reality."

30. The Megarians had no fertile land or harbors or mines (Isoc. 8.117). On the textile industry, see also Ronald P. Legon, *Megara,* 280–82.

31. 1.139.2, 7.27: *andrapodon* and *cheirotechnai.*

32. Aspasia was often pilloried in comedy. Even if Aspasia ran a brothel, how many slaves could she have owned? Ste. Croix, *The Class Struggle,* 506, assumes that the *cheirotechnai* were "*skilled* [itals. his] men." A. W. Gomme, *A Historical Commentary on Thucydides,* 1, ad loc., includes women, for he mentions the female flax worker in Andocides 1.93.

33. For the decree see Thuc., 1.42.2, 67.4, 139.1, Ephorus F 196 (= Diod. 12.38.4), Plut., *Per.,* 29–30. For references to textiles in the Megarian decrees, see, for example, Aristoph., *Ach.* 519, *Peace* 1002 (reading "'k Megaron" in 1000).

34. Thus, for example, in 1991 the *Oeconomicus* was added to the syllabus of the survey of classical literature at the University of Michigan.

WORKS CITED

Billigmeier, Jon-Christian. 1985. "Studies on the Family in the Aegean Bronze Age and in Homer." *Trends in History* 3, nos. 3–4:9–18.

Carlier, Pierre. 1983. "La Femme dans la société mycénienne d'après les archives en linéaire B." In *La Femme dans les sociétés antiques. Actes des colloques de Strasbourg* (May 1980 and March 1981), ed. E. Lévy, 9–32. Strasburg: b AECR.

Cohen, David. 1989. "Seclusion, Separation, and the Status of Women in Classical Athens." *G and R* 36:3–15.

Culham, Phyllis. 1986. "Ten Years after Pomeroy: Studies of the Image and Reality of Women in Antiquity." *Rescuing Creusa: New Methodological Approaches to Women in Antiquity. Helios* 13:9–30.

Finley, M. I. 1985. *The Ancient Economy*. 2d ed. London: Hogarth Press.

———. 1970. "Aristotle and Economic Analysis." *Past and Present* 47:3–25.

———. 1960. *Slavery in Classical Antiquity*, ed. M. I. Finley, 33–72. Cambridge: W. Heffer.

Friedl, Ernestine. 1967. "The Position of Women: Appearance and Reality." *Anthropological Quarterly* 40:97–108.

Glotz, Gustave. 1920. *Le Travail dans la Grèce ancienne*. Paris: F. Alcan. Trans. M. R. Dobie, 1926, as *Ancient Greece at Work*. New York: A. A. Knopf.

Gomme, A. W. 1933. *The Population of Athens in the Fifth and Fourth Centuries B.C.* Oxford: B. Blackwell.

Gomme, A. W., A. Andrewes, and K. J. Dover. 1945–81. *A Historical Commentary on Thucydides*. Oxford: Clarendon.

Hansen, Mogens Herman. 1985. *Demography and Democracy: The Number of Athenian Citizens in the Fourth Century B.C.* Herning: Systim.

Herfst, P. 1922. *Le Travail de la femme dans la Grèce ancienne*. Utrecht: Oosthoek.

Hughes, Diane Owen. 1985. "From Brideprice to Dowry in Mediterranean Europe." *Journal of Family History* 3 (1978). Reprinted in *The Marriage Bargain: Women and Dowries in European History. Women and History* 10:13–58.

Just, Roger. 1989. *Women in Athenian Law and Life*. London and New York: Routledge.

Killen, John T. 1984. "The Textile Industries at Pylos and Knossos." In *Pylos Comes Alive: Industry and Administration in a Mycenaean Palace*, ed. C. W. Shelmerdine and T. G. Palaima, 49–63. New York: Archaeological Institute of America.

———. 1964. "The Wool Industry of Crete in the Late Bronze Age." *ABSA* 59:1–15.

Kuhn, Annette, and Ann Marie Wolpe. 1981. *Feminism and Materialism: Women and Modes of Production*. London: Routledge and Paul.

Legon, Ronald P. 1981. *Megara*. Ithaca, N.Y.: Cornell University Press.

Lévi-Strauss, Claude. 1967. *Les Structures élementaires de la parenté*, 2d ed. La Haye: Mouton. Trans. J. H. Bell, 1969, as *The Elementary Structures of Kinship*. Boston: Beacon Press.

Lewis, D. M. 1968. "Dedications of Phialai at Athens." *Hesperia* 37:368–80.

———. 1959. "Attic Manumissions." *Hesperia* 28:208–38.

McClees, Helen. 1920. *A Study of Women in Attic Inscriptions.* New York: Columbia University Press.

Marx, Karl. 1867. *Das Kapital* 1. Reprinted in Karl Marx and Friedrich Engels, 1969, *Werke,* 23. Berlin (GDR): Dietz.

Meek, Ronald L., and Andrew S. Skinner. 1973. "The Development of Adam Smith's Ideas on the Division of Labour." *Economic Journal* 83:1094–116.

Meikle, Scott. 1979. "Aristotle and the Political Economy of the Polis." *JHS* 99:57–73.

Pomeroy, Sarah B., ed. 1994. *Xenophon's Oeconomicus: A Social and Historical Commentary,* with a new English translation. Oxford: Oxford University Press.

———. 1994. *Women in the Classical World.* 1994. Jointly authored with E. Fantham, H. P. Foley, N. Kampen, and H. A. Shapiro. New York: Oxford University Press.

———. 1991. "The Study of Women in Antiquity: Past, Present, and Future." *AJP* 112:263–68.

———. 1991. *Women's History and Ancient History,* ed. with preface by Sarah B. Pomeroy. Chapel Hill: University of North Carolina Press.

———. 1977. "Technikai kai Mousikai: The Education of Women in the Fourth Century and in the Hellenistic Period." *AJAH* 2:51–68.

———. 1975. *Goddesses, Whores, Wives, and Slaves.* New York: Schocken Books.

Pritchett, W. Kendrick. 1956. "The Attic Stelai. Part II." *Hesperia* 25:178–317.

Rostovzeff, M. I. 1941. *The Social and Economic History of the Hellenistic World.* Oxford: Oxford University Press.

Ste. Croix, G. E. M. de. 1981. *The Class Struggle in the Ancient Greek World: From the Archaic Age to the Arab Conquests.* London: Duckworth.

Schneider, Jane. 1985. "Trousseau as Treasure: Some Contradictions of Late Nineteenth-Century Change in Sicily." In *Beyond the Myths of Culture,* ed. Eric Ross. Orlando, 1980. Reprinted in *The Marriage Bargain: Women and Dowries in European History. Women and History* 10:81–119.

Schumpeter, J. A. 1954. *History of Economic Analysis.* New York: Oxford University Press.

Sealey, Raphael. 1990. *Women and Law in Classical Greece.* Chapel Hill: University of North Carolina Press.

Sissa, Giulia. 1990. *Greek Virginity.* Translated from *Le Corps virginal* (1987), by Arthur Goldhammer. Cambridge, Mass.: Harvard University Press.

Sorel, Georges. 1936. *Réflexions sur la violence.* 8th ed. Paris: M. Rivière.

Tilly, Louise A., and Joan W. Scott. 1978. *Women, Work, and Family.* New York: Holt, Rinehart and Winston.

West, M. L. 1970. *Iambi et Elegi Graeci* 2:99–104.

PART 3

Feminism and the Politics of Intellectual Inquiry

Chapter 8

Archaeology and the Goddess: Exploring the Contours of Feminist Archaeology

Margaret W. Conkey and Ruth E. Tringham

INTRODUCTION

Explicit inquiries into gender and feminist-inspired research have come late to anthropological archaeology, although they are now emerging.[1] Admittedly, this would not be the first time that anthropological archaeology has been accused of "paradigm lag" (Leone 1972). While sociocultural anthropology (and related fields) stepped boldly into the feminist arena, archaeology, for the most part, allowed popular culture (e.g., Morgan 1972) to take up many issues that are within the framework of archaeology and that have long been tangled up with feminist concerns: questions about origins, human evolution, the development of the state, and culture change.[2] Many of the evolutionary models that were promoted by popular culture we would now classify as "feminist essentialism." At first these were given some attention by feminist anthropologists (e.g., Bamberger 1974), with more (e.g., Webster 1975) or less (e.g., S. R. Binford 1979) sympathy. There was an eerie silence from archaeology, especially in the 1970s. In retrospect, we suggest that there are certain legacies from the role played by popular culture that still need to be confronted by feminist inquiries in archaeology.[3]

One highly elaborated and varied set of social movements and belief systems that illustrate this phenomenon involve what we will reductively label "The Goddess Movement." Various aspects and versions (e.g., Stone 1976) of the Goddess Movement have employed archaeological data and interpretations of certain archaeologists (e.g., Gimbutas 1981, 1989a, 1991). Since the movement claims to be a feminist approach to the past, we have begun to investigate its uses of archaeology. Our analysis reveals, however, that there are some deeply problematic issues and implications for feminist archaeology in the movement. Indeed, the themes around which debate and critique of the Goddess Movement must center are central to the practice, method, and theory of contemporary archaeology.

Because proponents of the Goddess Movement make inferences about social and symbolic aspects of the past, because they use material culture (especially "images of females") to anchor their interpretations about past gender roles and relations, and because they invoke "origins" narratives and appeal to feminist archaeologies, the movement provides an important terrain on which to illustrate and probe the parameters of feminist perspectives in anthropological archaeology.

In this essay, we explore some of the history and current state of gender research and feminist inquiry in anthropological archaeology and observations on it. Then we discuss certain features of the so-called Goddess Movement; from there we consider what seem to us to be among the most problematic and provocative aspects of its uses of archaeology. Just as an inquiry into the revival of Goddess religion provides important new perspectives on some crucial feminist concerns, an inquiry into the revival of the goddess religions provides important perspectives on archaeological concerns. We have come to see that our inquiry is just as much about key issues in contemporary archaeological interpretation as seen through the topic of the Goddess as it is about how the Goddess Movement uses archaeology.

Last, we consider the implications of our analysis for the shape of feminist archaeology. Despite the seemingly feminist archaeological accounts of Goddess-centered prehistoric life presented by such archaeologists as Marija Gimbutas and her followers (e.g., Eisler 1987; Gadon 1989), we take issue with the "feminist essentialisms" and with the way in which archaeological data are deployed, invoked, and interpreted. We come to this project as practicing feminist archaeologists whose long-term research has primarily been about the Upper Paleolithic (Conkey) and Neolithic (Tringham) societies of Europe: precisely the past societies and contexts that have been most frequently drawn upon in many Goddess accounts that reclaim a female-centered, eco-harmonious world that "once existed" in prehistoric Europe.

ARCHAEOLOGY, GENDER, AND FEMINISM

Although archaeological accounts have always been "saturated" with gender and gendered implications (after diLeonardo 1991, 8), anthropological archaeologists did not, for the most part, participate in the debates on gender bias, roles, statuses, or inequalities, nor did they engage in discussions on gender theory that occurred in anthropology during the 1970s. Instead, under the influence of the so-called New (or processual) Archaeology, archaeologists investigated "processes" such as the intensification of production, sedentarization, and social stratification at a macroscale and at the expense of "people," although many of these processes actually cried out for theorizing and problematizing gender and other social variables (Brumfiel 1992). Consequently, the 1970s can be described as a decade of missed opportunities to probe into gender dynamics and their integral role in many of the wider processes of cultural action and change on which archaeologists were focused.

The archaeology of the 1970s was primarily uncritical and unreflexive, yielding accounts of the human past that perpetuated androcentrism (see Conkey and Spector 1984; Gero 1983, 1988). Specific illustrations of these androcentrisms have necessarily characterized subsequent literature (e.g., Dobres 1988; Marshall 1985; McCafferty and McCafferty 1988; Nelson 1990; Russell 1987; Watson and Kennedy 1991). Androcentrism exists not merely in claiming for men all of the great inventions and activities of the past but also in the very categories of analysis and objects of knowledge, including both the devaluation of certain data because of its assumed association with females, such as "the domestic" or even plant remains (c.f. Tringham 1991a and Hastorf 1991a, respectively), and presumed "causes" for past cultural activities (e.g., Conkey with Williams 1991, 122–123):

Archaeology has consistently been told to us from a male perspective that adopts "male" as the norm and proceeds from the male experience. In the received view, art is male, with females sometimes as subjects/objects; males take over agriculture because agriculture is the more critical activity. Tools, their production and use, are male concerns and are intimately involved with the evolution of "man." Empires are made by men, and the underlying labor and energy directly attributable to women lies hidden. (Conkey and Gero 1991:18)

The processual archaeology of the 1970s was primarily a solidification of a particular research paradigm that emphasized a cultural systems and cultural process approach, with a decidedly ecological and environmental causality, at the expense of theorizing or investigating the social and especially the symbolic—two domains in which gender is expectedly "at work." Despite its initial optimism about what we could know about the past, many archaeologists became increasingly less confident about making inferences from archaeological data, given the recognition of ever more complex phenomena and processes that effected archaeological sites and materials (such as postdepositional redistributions of artifacts in a site). Many scholars retreated into positivist and empiricist, if not outright skeptical, positions about what we can "know" about the past. Such trends mitigated against taking up both gender and the explicitly self-reflexive issues in critical theory that are required in confronting biases such as androcentrism (Wylie 1991).

At the same time, during the 1970s, some feminist scholars were engaged with issues that impinge directly on, and even derive from and depend upon, *archaeological* data and interpretations and the central concerns of archaeological inquiry, such as human evolution and cultural change. For example, the well-known debate over "Man-the-Hunter versus Woman-the-Gatherer" was one of the first and most widespread issues of feminist anthropology (e.g., Slocum 1975, originally 1970). While archaeological data were invoked, no practicing archaeologists seriously took up the challenges that were implied, such as problematizing an essentialist and timeless view of the sexual division of labor.[4]

Other 1970s feminist scholars focused on the troubling question of the origins of gender inequality and of gender hierarchy, paying close attention to the so-called early state societies of Mesopotamia, Mexico, and elsewhere that archaeology regularly considers a primary research arena. Although the "origin of the state" is a demonstrably "big question" that has made many archaeological reputations (McGuire 1985; Conkey with Williams 1991), there were no archaeologists' voices among the feminist probings (e.g., Gailey 1976; Nash 1978; Rapp 1977).[5] As well, there were other inquiries into gender inequalities and gender hierarchies among so-called egalitarian societies (e.g., Cucchiari 1981; Leacock 1983) or the prestate agricultural societies that laid the basis for state developments (e.g., Barstow 1978). These inquiries should also have attracted archaeological attention either because they offered a source for archaeological theorizing (e.g., Leacock 1977) or because their unquestioned use of archaeological interpretations (e.g., Rohrlich-Leavitt 1977) should have jolted archaeologists into seeing the internal biases and problematic gender assertions of our own practitioners.

Thus the question raised by Wylie (1991) is compelling: "Why is there (only now) an archaeology of gender?" As she suggests, some "space" for raising questions about gender (and, more important, for feminist thinking) opened up through the larger challenges to processual archaeology by the so-called post-processualists that emerged in the early 1980s (e.g., Hodder 1982, 1985, 1986) and that were differentially elaborated throughout the decade (e.g., Leone 1982; Shanks and Tilley 1987a, b; 1989). This space was opened through explicit appeals by most post-processualists to robust *social* theory outside of archaeology; there was, as well, a general demand for understanding past human lives in terms that went beyond the ecological to the symbolic. It is clear however that, after a decade of postprocessualism, many of its advocates have yet to understand much less enable a gender-sensitive archaeology.[6] Despite the challenges raised by post-processualisms, the continued preferences for positivism and empiricism within archaeology may have contributed to inhibiting the engagement with feminist thinking, which, as Stacey and Thorne (1985) suggest, was more readily taken up by fields that are more interpretive than positivist.

The first review article that explicitly took up these issues in and for archaeology was Conkey and Spector's "Archaeology and the Study of Gender" (1984). Although many of the issues raised in the article began to be considered in the later 1980s, the activity level ever since has been pronounced if not explosive (Wylie 1992a). In 1988 a small conference, organized by Gero and Conkey,[7] laid the groundwork for the first edited volume (Gero and Conkey 1991) that explicitly takes up gender and feminist inquiry in North American anthropological archaeology. Influenced by what they heard about this conference (Hanen and Kelley 1992:198; Kelley 1991), the graduate student organizers of the annual Chacmool conference at Calgary University announced the theme for 1989 as Archaeology and Gender; this produced 103 abstracts by contributors from all over the globe.[8]

The papers from this conference (Walde and Willows 1991) and from subsequent ones in the United States (e.g., Claassen 1992) and elsewhere (e.g., in South Africa [1991] and in Australia [duCros and Smith 1993]), as well as a special issue of the journal of the Society for Historical Archaeology (Seifert 1991) and an annotated bibliography (Bacus et al. 1993), all attest to the marked appearance of research, writing, and concern with gender within anthropological archaeology. Other international roots would include the early works of the Norwegian scholars (e.g., Bertelsen et al. 1987 [1977]) and some parallel publications in Great Britain (e.g., Arnold et al. 1988; selections in Baker and Thomas 1990; Ehrenberg 1989).

As with other disciplines, feminist archaeologies will probably manifest a developmental sequence from critique to theory building. Particularly useful and inspirational are studies that have one foot in ethnographic, ethnohistoric, or historic contexts in which gender visibility is less contested or studies that deal directly with the kinds of data or contexts with which archaeologists regularly engage. Such "case studies" with theoretical implications include Moore's (1986) as yet unparalleled study of gendered local village and household space among the Marakwet of Kenya; Braithwaite's (1982) observations on the role of decorated ceramics in the negotiation of gender relations among the Azande of Sudan; the McCaffertys' insights (1988, 1991) about female symbolism and gender ideologies surrounding women, weaving, and spindle whorls in Aztec society; and Arsenault's provocative inquiries (1991) into the representation of women in Moche art and their positions at different times within the sacred systems. There are also essays that grapple with wider issues, such as social power (e.g., Wylie 1992b), or with the possibilities of an evolutionary approach to changes in gender meanings (e.g., Gero 1992). These provide theoretical lenses and ways of thinking and theorizing about gender that are specifically oriented toward archaeological data, problems, and contexts.

The issues raised by taking gender seriously are extraordinarily varied and

have significant ramifications that were never anticipated by conference organizers and participants. As in many other fields, one can envision a full spectrum
of ways to engage with gender in archaeological research and interpretation. At
one end of the spectrum there are those who might agree that it could be
relevant to take "gender" as another variable like "status" or "class," which
have long been part of the archaeological vocabulary, but that to do so does not
mean that there would necessarily be any substantive implications for archaeological theory or practice. This would be the "add gender and stir" approach
(to paraphrase Lerner), or, as Hanen and Kelley point out (1992:200) in their
assessment of the abstracts of *The Archaeology of Gender* papers (Walde and
Willows 1991), a method in which gender concerns are often merely "grafted"
onto extant approaches.

The success of considering such a new variable, some would argue, rests with
the ability of archaeologists to make gender visible, most likely by linking
specific artifacts or household areas or grave goods with males or females, so as
to make inferences directly from these about what men and women did. These
approaches rest on a "gender attribution" that is certainly always useful but is
not necessarily the only or requisite way to proceed (Gero and Conkey 1991:
11–14). This last claim itself would be a point of contention for most mainstream archaeologists who believe that the only way to proceed with gender
attribution is to experience some methodological breakthroughs that will render
gender "visible." However, many analyses that take gender as just another
variable are likely to produce what Friedan (1963) called the "functionalist
freeze": a static, normative, and functional description of what men and women
"did." Furthermore, these approaches do not necessarily question the assumptions underlying the gender attributions and the gender roles that are derived
from them, nor do they consider the rich theoretical resources on the conception
of gender as agency, process, dynamic, and historical; for the most part, such
analyses would not move away from the essentializing and normativizing that
has always—and, for feminists, problematically—gone on.

These limitations raise a set of significant questions for us: Can we simply
incorporate gender—just "add gender and stir"—into existing frameworks of
inquiry that themselves have been derived from intellectual traditions and practices that are either insensitive to gender or are androcentric if not outright sexist?
Is there a fundamental difference in epistemology (and all that it entails) for
archaeologists when they engage with the wider resources of feminist theory or
when they consider gender as a category of analysis?[9] Are we not, in fact, facing
(after Roberts 1993) at least two separate but interwoven tasks: first to demonstrate that gender is archaeologically "visible," that is, to construct an archaeology of gender, and/or second to challenge disciplinary paradigms, structures of
knowledge and bias, that is, to develop an engendered archaeology, a theorized,
self-reflexive archaeology that takes gender and difference as crucial?

Thus, at the other end of the spectrum are those of us who claim that, if feminist implications are taken to their logical extensions, the practice and theoretical framework of the discipline would be radically altered, if not transformed. Ultimately, archaeologists will have to come to terms with the gendered basis of every aspect of archaeology including fieldwork "strategies" (Gero n.d.); artifact and feature drawings (Tringham 1991b); workplace practices (Gero 1985; Kramer and Stark 1988; Sweeley 1992); preferred causalities about how and why past cultures changed (Brumfiel 1992; Conkey with Williams 1992); and, just as important, how we "write" archaeology (Spector 1991, 1993; Tringham 1991a); how we "display" it (e.g., Gero and Root 1990; Gifford-Gonzalez 1993; Handsman 1991); how we define "periods" of the past (after Kelley-Gadol 1976); and what are criteria for the data and acceptable evidence and what we assume about them (e.g., for "stones," see Gero 1991; for "bones," see Gifford-Gonzalez 1992). All these are crucial in the production of archaeological interpretation and archaeological knowledge, and they do lead to certain kinds of accounts of the human past.

The insertion of gender concerns and feminist perspectives into archaeological discourse and debate has fueled the discussions about critical theory and reflexivity stimulated by post-processual archaeology and about such issues as "practice," "relativism," "realism," "subjectivity," "experience," and "multivocality." In other words, raising gender concerns and drawing on feminist critiques have made yet another stab at the "soft" underside of the still relatively rigid archaeological methodologies.[10] Many archaeologists have now been forced to question how we can know *anything* about gender roles and ideologies in past societies (e.g., Hayden 1992)—a question that never seemed to have occurred to them before, even when explicitly dealing with "man the toolmaker," Big Men, or "men the empire builders"!

GETTING INVOLVED WITH GODDESSES: CRITIQUES, CONCERNS, AND IMPLICATIONS

We have found that some of the implications of these developments in archaeology as it grapples with gender and feminism are thrown into relief by examining the ways in which the Goddess Movement, a seemingly feminist social movement within popular culture, conflicts with many of the goals and hopes of both an archaeology of gender and an explicitly feminist, engendered archaeology. For us, the Goddess literature crystallizes some of the central issues of contemporary archaeology and contemporary sociopolitics: it forces us to investigate how material culture is meaningfully constituted and mobilized in particular sociohistorical contexts, including our own. The historic and archaeological evidence that can, and cannot, be found to support the Goddess religion has raised important questions about historical evidence and verifiability about written texts, androcentric symbols, language, and discourse. These questions are fundamental to feminism and they ought to be in any archaeology. Consequently, we are engaged in collaborative research that takes "Archaeology and the Goddess" as its point of departure. Our interest in this larger project emerged from our own participation in developing feminist archaeologies and because we both believe strongly in the role of imagination and speculation in archaeological interpretation. As our longer analysis will show, what is very much at issue in, for example, all of Gimbutas's accounts of the Goddess, is the problematic line between speculation or assertion and "fact" (Tringham 1993).

In the past fifteen years, a suite of ideas about prehistoric matriarchies, female power and empowerment, harmonious gender relations, spiritual redefinitions, ecological consciousness, and the politics of spirituality have been mobilized by reference to and through imagery of "the Goddess" (e.g., Stone 1976; Eisler 1987; Gadon 1989). Many of these ideas are not new: Bachofen's *Das Mutterecht* (1861); E. O. James's *The Cult of the Mother Goddess* (1959); Robert Graves's *The White Goddess* (1966); and Mary Daly's *The Church and the Second Sex* (1968) are but some historical predecessors. And yet various constellations and reconfigurations of these ideas have led to the formation of new and robust social phenomena, such as ecofeminism (e.g., Reuther 1992; Warren 1987, 1991; but cf., Lewis 1992, 33–36 for a critique); neopaganism (e.g., Adler 1979; Starhawk 1979, 1987); religious feminism (e.g., Christ and Plaskow 1979; Culpepper 1987); covens, witches, healing groups—many with their own bookstores, paraphernalia, lectures, retreats, inspirations for dance and other visual arts (in Gadon 1989), and an explosive literature (e.g., Dexter 1990) ranging from text and trade books to magazine and newspaper articles. In a December 1992 issue, the Phoenix *Republic* reported that, according to Megatrends, more than 500,000 people (mostly, but not exclusively, women) "identify" with various aspects of these ideas and issues.

These many social movements and belief systems have been inspired, influenced and organized around a "Goddess hypothesis" or a set of beliefs about the existence and meanings of goddesses in past human societies, especially in prehistory.[11] In its most basic form, the hypothesis (or conviction, to some) is as follows: there were past societies in Europe and the Near East, especially prior to the so-called invasion of Indo-Europeans circa five thousand years ago that were Goddess-worshiping, female-centered, in harmony with their environments, and more balanced in male-female relationships,[12] in which the status of women was high and respected. For many this has religious implications, including the idea that Goddess worship brought a female balance to the forces of the creation of the world and ensured a feminine balance in the human psyche (e.g., Baring and Cashford 1991) and that contemporary religion needs to revive the Goddess religions in the various challenges to contemporary, especially Judeo-Christian, religious traditions (e.g., Stone 1976; Goldenberg 1979).

The "facts" about past societies that the Goddess movement cites are based on the existence of artifacts (such as female statuettes) and interpretations of certain decorative motifs (e.g., spirals) as female. Certain architectural features such as "altars," "shrines," or "temples" (Gimbutas 1980) are then viewed as sacred or religious, as are their associated female characteristics or attributes. These are the archaeological manifestations of the Goddess or of goddesses. In many versions all the diverse goddesses from various circum-Mediterranean locales and varying time periods and "cultures" are brought together and co-alesced into one—the Goddess—as the basis for a goddess religion with its own organized set of beliefs and associated rituals, practices, traditions, and iconography (e.g., Olson 1983). Yet, as Hackett (1989) points out in her critique of the portrayals of the goddesses of the ancient Near East, all too often the values or attributes of the coalesced goddesses are subsumed under some form of "fertility" or other biological function, perpetuating an equation of women with nature.

There are some new features to the contemporary Goddess hypothesis. First, whereas Bachofen and his nineteenth-century followers argued for an original female-centered matriarchy that became a patriarchy in the course of the (unilinear) evolutionary progress of human culture, the contemporary Goddess notions reinterpret the so-called progressive shift to a patriarchal world as "disastrous" (Hepokoski 1992a), not merely for the status of women but also for gender relations (the "dominator" type comes in) and for human relationships with the earth, now dominated and overexploited by men. Second, as Hepokoski points out (1992a: 4), the "goddesses [now] have the status within the human psyche and within prehistoric cultures that is comparable to the status ascribed to male deities in western culture." But isn't this essentially turning the androcentric story into a gynocentric one?

In the case of the ancient Near East, Hackett points out that what appears to be an inspirational reversal of the androcentric version of spirituality, in which the fertility religion of the Goddesses is embraced while the Yahweh and male-centered religion of Israel is supposedly rejected, does not actually represent a celebration of the Goddess-and-nature half of the dichotomy. Upon closer inspection of the historical and contextual information and interpretive complexities surrounding certain of the so-called goddesses of the ancient Near East, the secondary sources—those on which many Goddess advocates and scholars draw—portray a so-called fertility religion, that is really just a "euphemism for ritual sex, for ritual prosecution" (Hackett 1989, 68). Thus, to embrace this fertility religion is to "approve of ritual prostitution, of selling women's (and more rarely, homosexual men's) bodies to feed the treasury of some fertility deity's temple" (74). Even what appears to be a new and gynocentric vision may be more complicated and problematic than followers realize.

There are other problems with the Goddess hypothesis and its use. First, the unilineal evolutionary schemes of the sort proposed by Bachofen and reinterpreted—but not per se problematized or challenged—by Goddess advocates have long been critiqued and discredited in most of the social sciences (e.g., Harris 1968, 180–216). There is no one single evolutionary scheme for all of human history, whether marked by "progressions," as Bachofen and his contemporaries would have had it, or by "devolutions," as the Goddess Movement would see for the period of patriarchy. Second, from the very beginning of inquiries about goddesses, gender roles, and ideologies in prehistory, people (e.g., Stone 1976) projected backward in time from (certain) interpretations of artifacts, texts, and ideas about life in the ancient Near East—a treacherous interpretative method (cf. Ucko 1968). Feminist religious scholars and writers have critiqued both this method and the predilection to lump all the local so-called evidences for goddesses into the single Goddess religion (cf. Ocschorn 1981; Hackett 1989). Above all, as Hepokoski has so astutely recognized, there are serious problems with the underlying assumptions of the Goddess proponents about some fundamental but prickly and complex phenomena and processes, namely, "about gender, symbol, and social practice" (Hepokoski 1992a: 15).

In almost all of its variants, the Goddess Movement appeals to and uses archaeological materials, especially those that it claims to be images of females: female figurines or statuettes and female motifs on ceramics or other media (e.g., in Gimbutas 1989a). Above all, images from the European Paleolithic and Neolithic periods (ca. 30,000 to 5,000 years ago) are claimed to represent fertility and other positively-valued attributes[13] and thus are often taken as material and symbolic evidence for the existence of a world in which females, as a generic category, were valued positively. This literature appeals to these archaeological materials for validation (e.g., for the existence of a female-centered, harmonious world). There is also an appeal to the (impugned) authority of archaeologists for their authentication of the imagery and the societies that produced it. In one form or another some archaeologists have provided this authentication, intentionally or unintentionally (e.g., Mellaart 1967, 1972; Gimbutas 1982, 1989a, 1991; Marshack 1986, 1991).

A thorough discussion of the use of archaeology in these contemporary social movements is a major undertaking that falls outside the scope of the present essay. But our initial investigations of the Goddess Movement have opened our eyes to the rich literature, the complexity of the issues, and the variety of participants and views.[14] We stepped into new debates for us: debates over the patriarchal nature of Judeo-Christian religion(s): the practices, vocabularies, governance, and organization. On one side, there are the revolutionaries, such as Mary Daly, who argued for a separatist way that included explicit references to past matriarchies and goddesses ("Goddess Religion") as crucial to a revolutionary consciousness (*Gyn/Ecology* 1978). On another side, there are reformists, such as Rosemary Reuther, a more moderate critic who nevertheless links theological change with ecology and with a nonbiblical religion that focuses on the Goddesses (Reuther 1987, 1992; Reuther and McLaughlin 1979). If this debate[15] seems familiar to feminists, it is because it raises a very familiar question to feminist thinkers: in order to change, does one have to work outside or can change be generated inside a tradition?

ARCHAEOLOGY, FEMINISM, AND POPULAR CULTURE

In the diverse literature that is part of the Goddess "consciousness" archaeological evidence and prehistory have played a mobilizing role. In discussing the work of theologian Mary Daly (1968, 1978, 1992) and art historian and sculptor Merlin Stone (1976), Mary Jo Weaver writes: "Whereas Mary Daly had engineered the exodus event when she led women out of the Harvard Divinity School Chapel in 1972 (consciously using the exodus story as her theme), Merlin Stone led them to the promised land, encouraging them to experience God as a woman and, later, to connect the experience with . . . Goddess and heroine lore from around the world" (1989:52). Merlin Stone was roundly criticized from the very beginning for her use of Near Eastern archaeology and has now said that it does not matter if there was a "real" Goddess. Both Goldenberg (1979:89) and Christ (1979: 276–78) have also argued that "the historical data on goddesses should be ignored if they do not present an image that is healthful for modern feminists seeking an alternative spirituality" (Hackett 1989: 67, note 6). This indifference to—and rejection of—historical specificity has come to be a central criticism by many feminists (e.g., Rosaldo 1983; Elshtain 1986; Handsman 1991): "The dichotomizing, essentializing threads in 1970s feminist evolutionary models weigh, to paraphrase Marx, like a nightmare on the brains of living feminists" (di Leonardo 1991:26).

Women and men in prehistoric societies are not identical and interchangeable. The end point of rethinking our gendered accounts is not merely to reclaim inventions and origins for women, such as the so-called origins of agriculture, although this may be a central part of the process, as Watson and Kennedy (1991) have shown. The recent emergence of archaeologies of gender confirms why we should inquire into what were surely variable, dynamic, and historically specific gender roles, relations, ideologies, and identities. But the emergence of this kind of gender research in archaeology runs up against an authoritative and totalizing account of "the past" that is widely held in popular cultural views of the Goddess. Although admitting variations, the Goddess Movement's account of life in "Old Europe," with direct continuities out of the Paleolithic, is "matrifocal, sedentary, peaceful, art-loving, earth-and-sea bound" (Gimbutas 1989b: 63). Furthermore, this Eurocentric story is universalized, and gender roles are homogenized, ignoring the agency of prehistoric men and women, as well as their variable roles, identities, and practices. No gender questions are asked: the role and symbolic place of men and women are set and fixed.

The emergent archaeologies of gender that are probing the varied and dynamic aspects of social relations in past societies are perilously constrained by the widespread demand for unambiguous "facts." This demand is fed as well by continuing androcentric or monolithic views, especially in the media, including journals such as *National Geographic, U.S. News and World Report,* and *Discover; The World of Science.* These views are often explicitly endorsed or are carried out with the complicity of archaeologists (Gero and Root 1990; Lutz and Collins 1991, 1993). The September 1991 *U.S. News and World Report,* for example, had a cover story on the new research and debates on the origins of anatomically modern humans. Although artists' reconstructions are now more conscious of the race and color of these (male) ancestors, they are as yet oblivious to females, except for the photograph of one of the so-called Venus female figurines that is presented as evidence of a "probable fertility cult." Thus, men are active—as hunters, tool-makers, and innovators—whereas females are art objects representing the very biological and not cultural essentials of fertility and reproduction.[16]

The centrality of archaeological evidence in the Goddess literature is widespread as a source of inspiration and legitimation. This has recently been heightened by Marija Gimbutas's *The Language of the Goddess* (1989a) and *The Civilization of the Goddess* (1991), which provide a version of (pre)historical data that obviously fits the notion of what is desired and "healthful." The media and her followers have deemed Gimbutas "the archaeological authority" (Tringham 1993), and it is because of her status that we take her work to be emblematic of the problems of the Goddess Movement for both feminism and archaeology.[17] Tringham is particularly "close" to the archaeological work of Gimbutas because she too has been excavating Neolithic sites, houses, and even figurines in southeast Europe for more than twenty years (Tringham 1971; Tringham and Krstic 1990; Tringham et al. 1985, 1992). Drawing on materials from the same region and time period, Gimbutas has "authenticated" a story about the positive place of women in human societies from the Upper Paleolithic of Europe through the Neolithic period, until what Gimbutas calls "Old Europe" was overthrown around 3500 B.C. by a "patrifocal, mobile, warlike, ideologically sky oriented" society that was "indifferent to art" (Gimbutas 1989b: 63).

To be sure, some might ask, how can we object to a view of the past that features a golden age of harmonious gender relations and peace in which women are valued positively? How can we object to the mobilization of this version of European prehistory in and by popular culture in the name of global peace, empowered (rather than overpowered) females, and a "partnership" ideology? Even if we can see the Goddess narratives about Paleo-Neolithic life as narratives of resistance (to contemporary conditions) and narratives of emancipation—and indeed these are their real and important functions in the contemporary world—they appeal to a number of deeply problematic issues that have long plagued feminist theory, and that must be resisted in the emergent archaeologies of gender. These issues have to do with origins, with the relation between sex and gender, with representation, with a focus on gender *roles,* and once again with gender, symbol, and social practice, as evidenced in Gimbutas's problematic treatments of these issues.

The Goddess movement's use of archaeology has produced totalizing and teleological accounts of the origins of gender asymmetry. One present gender asymmetry—that of patriarchy, which itself is not a uniform phenomenon—is invoked, its origins are sought, and then these origins are used to explain the present (cf. Solomon 1989, referring to Delphy 1984). The Goddess narratives locate this "origin" of gender asymmetry in one particular historical context, the coming of the Indo-Europeans circa 3500 B.C., and this particular phenomenon is generalized to account for the entire replacement of another unified and quite homogeneous system—a balanced and matrifocal system—by patriarchy; as in most origins stories, specific historical contexts are quickly lost.[18]

"Gender asymmetry" is thus taken as an essentialized normative phenomenon, conceptualized only in terms of a male/female bipolarity that forecloses on the possibilities for any other possible genders or gender systems. The origins of this male/female sex/gender asymmetry and the origins of patriarchy become a "narrative of closure" (Elshtain 1986), which shuts down our imaginative powers about the many ways in which people could have lived, related to each other, or, in this particular case, responded to the Indo-European presence, itself a contested historical account (see Renfrew 1987).

The "pull" for a universalizing account has led Gimbutas and others to some glaring inconsistencies. On the one hand, Gimbutas (and derivative authors) focus on the Neolithic period—on the sedentary, agricultural communities—yet they invoke a continuity in the symbolic repertoire that "goes back" into the Paleolithic, of twenty-five thousand years ago. On the other hand, their account of the onset of agriculture involves great social change; humans, no longer gatherer-hunters, now came to "control nature." There is, however, no satisfactory account of why the basic symbolic matrix—matrifocal and female, as powerful and fertile, as earth and water—remained essentially intact. Although archaeologists can hardly presume a one-to-one correlation between social change and symbolic change or between social and symbolic continuity, such phenomena must be questioned and problematized, not assumed.

CRITIQUES: THINKING ABOUT FIGURINES

Paleolithic and Neolithic figurines are at the heart of the debate over origins in the Goddess Movement and in Gimbutas's work. They constitute the main database on the religion of Old Europe that Gimbutas (1989a, 1991) has reconstructed. They are thus of prime importance in her conception of Old European life, culture, and history, since according to Gimbutas religion and the spiritual realities directly reflected the social structure (1991). Figurines, however, do not speak for themselves. They have to be interpreted to have meaning in any century. Since figurines have been and can be interpreted in many different ways, each interpretation is a clear indicator of where a writer stands both on the past and on feminism.

As Ucko (1968) has noted, the antiquity of the female figurines dating to the Upper Paleolithic period secured for many interpreters of the later Neolithic period the notion that the Neolithic figurines were indeed "Mother Goddesses" and that this was a symbol of considerable antiquity. Thus, for some time, the interpretations of the female statuettes of the two periods have been linked without question. Female figurines have been found in archaeological sites of the Upper Paleolithic from southwestern Europe (France) eastward into Siberia (fig. 1), especially from sites dating to 26,000–10,000 years ago, and of the Neolithic of the circum-Mediterranean and of central and eastern Europe. The geographic distributions for the two periods are not, however, isomorphic—a fact that has never been adequately considered by the Goddess Movement interpretations. The ways in which these figurines have consistently been described by a wide range of academic scholars and others reflect the primacy of the notion of "Woman" as both an erotic and aesthetic ideal and of contemporary pornographic views of the female body as sexual object (Dobres 1992a, b).

Late-nineteenth- and early-twentieth-century authors claimed that the female figurines—especially those of the Upper Paleolithic—with large stomachs and so-called pendulous breasts (see fig. 1) depicted pregnancy and/or lactation and therefore signified fertility and the magical desires for successful births in order to maintain the viability of the (supposedly precarious) population. Most traditional authors assume that the depiction of biological and essential female traits

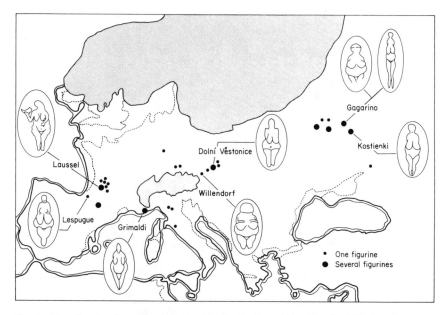

Fig. 1. Map showing the general geographic distribution of certain Paleolithic female figures. Note that the images selected for depiction are exclusively those images that conform to the stereotyped idea that the figurines depict some attention to those body parts assumed to be important in reproduction, fertility or—for some authors—in lovemaking (from Champion et al. 1986, 85, fig. 3.19).

meant that females in the Upper Paleolithic were the objects not just of image-making but of social control and male desire; that their place and functions in Paleolithic society were biologically determined and determinative; and that women's status was therefore less cultural and less central to the highly valued arenas of artistic production, political control, and other domains of social and ritual power. In contrast, most Goddess authors view the fertility interpretation for both Paleolithic and Neolithic figurines as a positive attribution that highlights the cultural importance and centrality of female qualities and biological powers.

Neither approach, however, problematizes the notion of "fertility." That large breasts or large stomachs are agreed-upon conventions of imagery signifying lactation and the more inclusive concept of fertility has never been demonstrated or considered critically. Some authors take the images quite literally, as if they were "specimens" of twentieth-century medical practice (Duhard 1989a, b). Rice (1981) has argued that many of the Paleolithic figurines are more likely to refer to the concept of "womanhood" than to "motherhood," although what motherhood might have meant some twenty thousand years ago in these partic-

Fig. 2. The so-called Venus of Willendorf (Austria), which is no more than four inches in size, despite the frequent illustrations (such as this one) that tend to exaggerate its size and not indicate scale. This is one of relatively few female statuettes from Paleolithic contexts that bear a triangular incision clearly marking the vulva (from Conkey 1989, 38, where the publishers added this illustration without consulting the author of the article).

ular societies is itself problematic; motherhood is hardly a uniform phenomenon (Bolen 1992).

Few considerations of the symbolic possibilities ever take into account the striking *diversity* of female images that are all too readily collapsed under the rubric of fertility images.[19] The Paleolithic statuettes have often been read as sexually charged because the ones that are usually depicted in texts—a non-representative sample to begin with—have large buttocks, breasts, and/or hips. This does not necessarily and immediately signify fertility but reveals a very contemporary (and partial) notion of sexuality. For example, in "The Origins of Art" Onians describes the statuette from Willendorf (fig. 2):

Those areas of her body which are shown in all their rounded perfection are precisely those which would be most important in the preliminary phases of love-making, that is, the belly, thighs, breasts and shoulders, while the lower legs, lower arms, feet and hands are withered to nothing. (Collins and Onians 1978, 12–13)

As Rainer Mack has argued convincingly this citation presents "a list of erotically-charged body parts that are—without legs and feet—made immobile; passive and available for possession" (1989; 1990). Mack shows that scholarly discourse about these Paleolithic female images relies upon—and effects—a hierarchical and gendered subject-object relationship: that is, the appropriation of a female body by a masculine subject (1990; 1992, 235).

In much of the more popularized literature—which includes the uncritical inclusion of Venus figurine interpretations in introductory archaeology texts—twentieth-century sexist notions of gender and sexuality are all read into the cultural traces of "our ancestors": the male-female sex and gender bipolarity, the primary association of the female with reproduction and fertility, the conflation of anatomical sex with gender, and the assumption that these images are unambiguously about femaleness of a limited nature. For the most part, andro-centric and gynocentric views differ *only* in the high status that the gynocentric view would hold for the images within a different system of gender ideology. For both, the authority residing in origins then further legitimizes and natural-izes these notions.

That the female statuettes of both the Paleolithic and Neolithic periods are not all the same in form or context and that females are not the only sex/gender depicted is hardly ever discussed much less documented (but cf. Nelson 1990; Dobres 1992a). For example, quantitative analyses of Upper Paleolithic imagery make it clear that there are also images of males and that, by and large, most of the Paleolithic imagery of humans-humanoids cannot readily be identified as male *or* female (Ucko and Rosenfeld 1972; Delporte 1979); in fact, no source can affirm that more than 50 percent of the imagery is recognizably female. Most images can be called anthropomorphic, at best. With a particularly rich corpus of Upper Paleolithic figurines from Moravia (Czech Republic), Soffer (1993) shows that most of the figurines are animals and that the few human figurines are strikingly diverse and cannot be readily accommodated under a single interpretive rubric such as "Mother Goddess."

Insofar as there is imagery of females, there is no evidence about the sex/gen-der of the makers or of the audience for whom the images were intended. Moreover, few archaeologists have tried to explain why images of females, in the varieties that exist, would have been meaningful to some of the Upper Paleolithic peoples. While Gamble, for example, has suggested that a certain chronological cluster of female images (ca. 26,000–23,000 years ago) may have "functioned" as part of a symbolic system of material culture aimed at establish-

ing and maintaining social alliances across a broad geographic range, at a time
when more open resource zones were needed for successful hunting-gathering,
he avoids asking why images of females would have been meaningful in such a
context (1982, 1991).

For most Upper Paleolithic images of females, there is very little traditional
contextual information, such as associated stone tools, climatic information, or
associated fauna that might indicate how a site was used, how long people were
there, or what the group size or composition might have been. Many statuettes
were found early on and/or by chance (see Delporte 1979), although others
continue to be discovered (e.g., Delporte 1990). The contexts on the statuettes
from sites in the Russian Plain, such as Gagarino or Avdeevo (Gvozdover n.d.),
are more hopeful and promising (Dobres 1992a), as are the large sample sizes,
which allowed one Russian archaeologist (Gvozdover 1989a, b) to document
varying conventions in the making of the statuettes. Conroy (1992, 1993) has
proposed that these conventions may be taken as one indication that gender, as
a concept, was emergent in these societies but not necessarily that it was a
gendered world like ours.

Gimbutas's interpretation of the Neolithic period figurines and associated
architecture of Old Europe raises at least four major concerns that need to be
examined and critiqued. First, any archaeological reader of Gimbutas's narratives would be struck immediately by a style of "argument by assertion," instead
of an explicit linking of specific data to the inferential narratives, as in standard
archaeological style of interpretation. The narrative is presented in an authoritarian way in which the process of inference from artifact to interpretation is
mystified and ambiguities of the archaeological record are hidden. For example,
she writes:

> During the Neolithic there was a renewed flowering of artistic expression.
> The invention of ceramics, c. 6500 B.C. marked the appearance of thousands
> of figurines and vases, temples and their miniature models, wall paintings,
> reliefs, and countless ritual articles. The number of religious symbols multi-
> plied a hundredfold, providing abundant data for deciphering the Goddess's
> iconography. Moreover, the symbolism of Old Europe, 6500–3500 B.C.
> provides an essential key to understanding Paleolithic religion, since many of
> the images are continuous . . .
>
> The figurines *represent* various images of the Goddess, portrayed articu-
> lately with details of attire and headdress, or reduced to bare outlines. The
> latter, *very likely, were ex votos,* or amulets in her image. Figurines have been
> recovered in *temples* on altars, on oven platforms, in specially prepared
> offering places, and in caves and graves. They have frequently been found in
> caches stored in vases, or as miniature tableaux *representing certain religious*
> activities. *Obviously,* groups of figurines were used for the re-enactment of

rituals. The incessant production of figurines witnesses an energetic process shared by all participants. (1991, 222, emphasis added)

Few of the artifacts that Gimbutas refers to—and her book is indeed, as one reviewer has noted, a veritable "art book"—are presented in their archaeological contexts, and few justifications are provided much less developed for the interpretations of certain attributes or forms. Often, for example, Gimbutas suggests that the female imagery all shows a certain "cohesion," but this is not explained. And yet other leading figures in the Goddess literature accept these ideas unquestioningly, reproduce them, and widen their distribution as facts about the past (Eisler 1987; Gadon 1989; even Lerner 1986).

Second, Gimbutas treats the whole of European prehistory as a homogenous unit from the point of view of religion and social organization. The rich variation of European prehistoric material culture is normativized so that the figurine and clay-rich archaeological record of Neolithic Southeast Europe, for example, "stands for" the continent as a whole. But the figurines do not occur in equal quantities (or forms) everywhere in Europe from the Paleolithic to the Neolithic, and any one area cannot, in fact, stand for the whole continent. The differences in distributions need to be investigated and explained rather than normativized or minimized.

Third, an entire body, or "class," of material culture—clay figurines—is given a single interpretation: representation of the Goddess. Their formal variety (fig. 3) is interpreted as "Her" variable manifestations, while the basic interpretation as deity representation remains intact. The very concept of representation is not defined, defended, or explored. Fourth, as the previous points imply, Gimbutas uses modern categories and terms to interpret the past without considering the intentional action and thoughts of the past actors nor the presentism of her labels. For example, she uncritically and problematically uses terms such as *religion, temples, shrines, rituals* that imply, among other things, the clear separation of sacred from profane that is characteristic of modern Western belief systems. These terms should not be used so casually for prehistoric situations without explicit consideration of what such terms imply, both as cultural phenomena and for prehistoric social lives. Some of these terms evoke important and contested issues in anthropological and other studies of religion, ritual, and society: the nature of belief systems, belief and explanation of the world, and the institutionalization of belief; the relationship of the natural, the supernatural, and the liminal in prehistoric cognitive systems; the relationship of ritual activity to the construction and maintenance of ideologies; and the meaningfulness of material culture. These are all highly varied and complex but rarely, if ever, considered by Gimbutas.

What, for example, goes on in a so-called prehistoric temple? Why is it a separate building or space? How do the rituals performed there relate to other

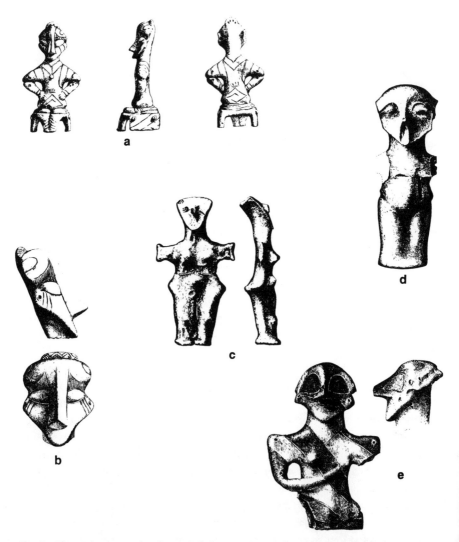

Fig. 3. Clay anthropomorphic figurines from various Neolithic settlements attributed to the Vinca culture of Yugoslavia a: Bariljevo (scale 1:4); b: Predionica (scale 1:4); c: Vinca (scale 1:2); d: Vinca (scale 1:4); e: Vinca (scale 1:2). These show variation even within a single supposed "culture" of southeastern Europe (from Garasanin 1979, vol. 2: Plates 30, 32, and 33).

social action? Who performs them, when, and why? These questions need to be thought through, and possible answers posed, even as hypotheses. To name a building foundation a "temple" or "shrine" (e.g., as at Sabatinovka in Gimbutas 1991, 260–61) because it is empty except for figurines, a clay platform, or a group of clay objects on its floor is to make unwarranted assumptions about function and form (fig. 4). While the use of terms such as *temple, altar, spiritual,* and even *goddess* does more to attract the interest and engagement of contemporary readers than would the more neutral *structure, mound, mundane,* and *figurine,* the terms nevertheless obscure the dynamics of and possibilities for differential human social experience. Furthermore, they preclude alternative interpretations and predetermine function, if not also meaning and meaningfulness.

ALTERNATIVES: RETHINKING FIGURINES

The substantive issue at hand here is not so much the continuing critique or deconstruction of the narrative assertions that dominate the Goddess literature. Rather, the question is how would a feminist archaeological treatment of the prehistory of Europe or, more specifically, of the clay figurines proceed? The value of feminist theory for archaeology is not so much in stimulating matrifocal meanings or a female-centered interpretation for (selected portions of) the archaeological record. This has, however, been the focus of much of the Goddess literature. In our opinion, the new directions and dimensions that feminist theory brings to archaeology lie first in a change in the practice of archaeology itself and in the way(s) the past is constructed and presented: the authoritative optimistically worded "facts" about the past need to be demystified. Second, change lies in the kind of prehistories that are evisaged. In contrast to the essentialized prehistory of Old Europe as written by Gimbutas (and most other traditional prehistorians), an engendered prehistory envisages women as thinking and acting people who affect the course of prehistory. In doing this we think of men as well as women, young and old, and we think of children. We also think about the action and perceptions of these people in their personal histories, both every day and during the course of their lives (Tringham 1991b). Housework and household tensions of dominance and resistance become important objects of study rather than taken-for-granteds (Tringham 1991a).

The process by which the archaeological record—in this case, figurines and spatial contexts—is interpreted and reconstructed by archaeologists and by which it is given meanings that modern readers can relate to is a complex series of inferential steps. In practice each step is fraught with its own challenge of ambiguity and problems of validation. To ignore the ambiguity and to work within the illusion of "proven facts" is to claim that one's interpretation *is* knowledge rather than a "mode of transmitting knowledge" (Bourdier 1989; Tringham 1991b). Feminist theory encourages a celebration and discussion of this ambiguity rather than its mystification. An understanding of the historical context of interpretation is central, which is why we have placed the interpretation

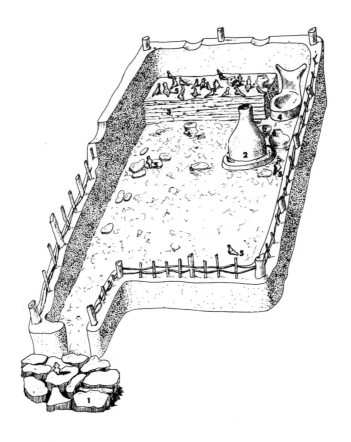

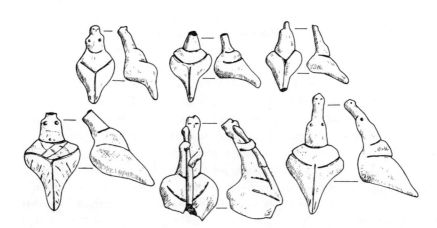

Fig. 4. Reconstruction of a building excavated in the Neolithic settlement of Sabatinovka, Moldavia. An oven, grindstones, a clay seat, and figurines were found on the floor and have been interpreted as a temple or shrine by both its excavator and Gimbutas. The "shrine" occupies seventy square meters. Gimbutas gives no scale for the figurines illustrated here (from Gimbutas 1982, 72–73, figs. 25–26).

of the Paleolithic and Neolithic data as presented in the Goddess literature in the context of its wider cultural and historical positionings. We suggest, for example, that their interpretation should be presented *in relation to,* not in exclusion of, alternative interpretive narratives. Far from being a constant from the Upper Paleolithic through the early and later Neolithic time (over more than some twenty thousand years!), the meaning of the figurines—especially their meaningfulness—is more likely to have been varied and varying, more ambiguous than fixed, and differentially experienced, even at any one point in time (Hodder 1990). We outline below just a few possible paths by which some of these alternative interpretations may be reached.

In a provocatively different view of the Paleolithic figurines, McCoid and McDermott (1992) have suggested that the angle of view from which many statuettes seem to have been formed would be that of a female looking downward at herself, which they call "autogenous." McDermott (1985) has extended this idea to argue that certain Upper Paleolithic images of females were made by women and as part of "processes of physical concern to women" (McCoid and McDermott 1992, 9). Kehoe (1991) has pointed out that some of the so-called female images had to have been suspended in a certain way (given the location of the suspension hole), in which case what are usually taken as female breasts on the top of a straight ivory rod are more "readable," when reversed, as the male scrotum. Some figurines bear incisions and nicks on the back that could easily be accommodated within the Paleolithic calendrics hypothesis (Marshack 1972) as "markings" related to female menstrual cycles. While we could present numerous other alternative visions, the interpretive possibilities for the figurines are not endless because there are at least the constraints of form, media, and contexts. But once the figurines are no longer limited to being either objects of male desire *or* "the" Mother Goddess, there are contextual, stylistic, and interpretive possibilities that both of these inclusive accounts foreclose. This does not mean, however, that both of these accounts could not be part of some of the "readings."

For the Neolithic period, there is a rich literature with highly varied scenarios and hypotheses about what "life was like"—in other words, what might have been the sociocultural context of the figurines—even for the restricted region of Southeast Europe (Tringham 1990; Tringham 1991a, 113–15). There are some points of agreement among numerous archaeologists, including Gimbutas, about the material parameters of the figurines, architecture, and spatial distributions of artifacts on the floors (cf. Chapman 1981; Gimbutas 1982, 1991; Sherratt 1984; Tringham 1990), but there are also multiple interpretations of these phenomena by archaeologists that Gimbutas fails to take into account. There are other points of agreement concerning the general conditions and contexts of life in certain archaeologically documented villages during the Neolithic, such as the intensification of production, the increasing degree of permanence of settlements, and the symbolic elaboration of the archaeological record, including the manufacture of three-dimensional anthropomorphic and zoomorphic figurines (Chapman 1981; Tringham 1990).

Despite consensus about the basic data, there are necessarily many possible interpretations by different archaeologists. These are based on multiple interpretations of the function, the meaning and the meaningfulness of the archaeological data—including figurines—and on varying visions of their context in terms of the nature of the prehistoric people and their lives. Whereas Gimbutas (1991) envisions an egalitarian matrifocal society based on peaceful coexistence, other archaeologists envision villages in which social differentiation and inequality, due to the differing demographic cycles of households rather than a permanent social ranking, were essential elements of social and economic action (Chapman 1990b; Tringham 1990, 1991a; Tringham et al. 1992).

Such differences among interpretations of the sociocultural context of the figurines obviously leads to very different interpretations of their meaningfulness. For example, the vision of an egalitarian context leads Gimbutas to conclude that the figurines represent a deity—mother, earth, fertility—who impersonally embraces all on an equal footing. She also asserts that the increase in the number of figurines in a certain period means that belief in the deity is stronger. On the other hand, an envisioned context of a dynamic and ever-shifting inequality between households has led other archaeologists, including one of us, to relate the increase of figurines in the Neolithic of Southeast Europe to the increased autonomy of households in a village and the need to express such autonomy symbolically (Chapman 1981; Sherratt 1984; Tringham 1990). According to Gimbutas, the high degree of variability in the figurines within a standardized iconography represents different manifestations of the Goddess, whereas others interpret such variation as being related to the variability between individual households (Bailey 1990, 1991).

All of these interpretations contain the implication that rituals involving figurines in any context have the same effect as such rituals and materials in a modern Christian church: that they confirm the legitimacy of the status quo, encourage conformity, and discourage resistance. Gimbutas's scenario of egalitarian peaceful coexistence places a positive value on such conformity and lack of challenge to the authority of the Goddess. However, the alternative models, many of which are grounded in Marxist and neo-Marxist social theory, explicitly discuss such rituals and their material manifestations as strategies by which, in the context of household-based social differentiation, one group—a household, senior members, or senior males—dominates and even exploits another group. In this kind of interpretation, the figurines are overt symbols that help create and maintain ideologies by which it seems "natural" or acceptable that some people have power over the labor, actions, relations, and property of others or have more access to resources and wealth than others.

The story that has been presented by the Goddess literature, following the authority of Gimbutas, is neither the only story nor "the" story, despite its power and seduction for those who actively seek to reimagine the past and to create a "usable" past for contemporary contexts. Nor are any of the alternative interpretations mentioned earlier the "true" one. Many of them, including that of Gimbutas, can be considered plausible within the constraints of the material evidence. These "material constraints" are rooted in the consensus amongst archaeologists as to what they call the "archaeological context." In the case of both Neolithic and Paleolithic figurines, however, little has been made of the varying and yet potentially informing contexts within which figurines were deposited in archaeological sites. For example, some Neolithic figurines have been found complete on the floors of structures, often—but not always—in proximity to corners or ovens (fig. 5). Is this a meaningful spatial association in situ, or is it the result of some post-depositional action, such as trash deposition or modern plowing? There has been strikingly little concern (but cf. Talalay 1987) with what we might call the "use-life" of a given Neolithic figurine: how, for example, might it have been altered, modified, broken, used, reused, re-paired, redecorated, or disposed of? In fact, most figurines have been found in trash pits in a broken state. But exactly how many are found and where (fig. 6)? What do we know about other objects with which they are associated, as well as their depositional histories? How do we differentiate between accidental or deliberate breakage? What materials were the figurines made of, are their tempers and pastes all the same and the same as those used for ceramics and other clay artifacts? How were they formed? At what temperatures were they fired?

These are questions that are regularly asked of all archaeological materials and lead to the material parameters that, although not "facts sealed in stone," form a body of consensus and provide the basis of "higher-level" interpretations and inferences. These are the kinds of questions that are crucial clues to the meanings and meaningfulness of material culture. Why have figurines and other imagery only rarely been subjected to this same level of analysis (see in Tring-ham and Krstic 1990, 397–436)? It is only through such inquiry that we can begin to interpret the possible functions of and for the figurines; from this, we might speculate and pursue the interpretations: were they toys, educational "aids," personal ornaments, markers of special spaces, markers of special people or status (Bailey 1991), furniture of special places or markers of special events, markers of economic or social relations (Talalay 1987, 1993), and/or creators of ideology (Ucko 1968)? In each function listed here among many possible ones that are not mutually exclusive, the term *special* could mean *sacred*, but this term must be defined and explicated (fig. 7).

Fig. 5. Clay anthropomorphic figurine found with a small alabaster figurine and perforated shells on the floor of a house at the Neolithic settlement of Selevac, Yugoslavia (from Tringham and Krstic 1990, pl. 11.1).

Through questions like these, furthermore, we may begin to address the fact that there are certain to have been multiple perceptions and interpretations of the figurines by the prehistoric social actors themselves. The idea that spaces and materials are likely to have different meanings and to be perceived differently by different members—even within the same household, according to their gender, age, social status, etc.—is part of a growing archaeological concern with gender

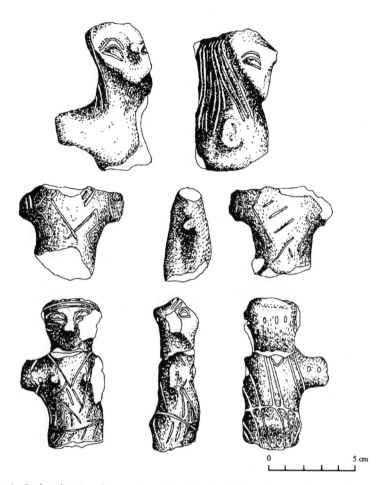

Fig. 6. Broken figurines from various pits at the Neolithic settlement of Selevac, Yugoslavia (from Tringham and Krstic 1990, fig. 11.6).

ideologies within the dominance relations of prehistoric societies (Donley 1982; Moore 1986; Tringham 1991a, 1994). How materials—including figurines— act as media in the construction, enactment, and transformation of such ideologies and the negotiations of power relations is not discussed in the work of Gimbutas or the secondary Goddess literature, but it is an important question among feminist and post-processualist archaeologists alike.

Who or what do the figurines represent: supernatural beings such as deities, dead people, or ancestors? What is the significance of the (frequent) miniaturization of the human form (or of other subjects, such as a Neolithic house)? Is it to

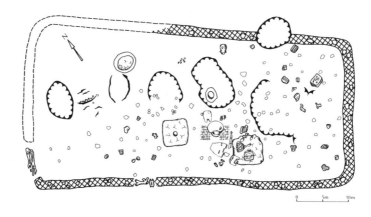

Fig. 7. Groundplan and reconstruction of a building excavated at the Neolithic settlement of Vészto-Magor, Hungary (from Hegedus and Makkay 1987, 87, figs. 3–4). Remains of ceramics and other elaborated clay artifacts, including a figurine were found on its floor. These were interpreted by its excavator as a "cult assemblage" (Hegedus and Makkay 1987) and by Gimbutas (1991, fig. 3.26) as a "ceremonial assemblage."

grasp or control or transcend the reality of a person or a place? Are overt symbols a material text that can be read? Is there an entire subtext that archaeologists are missing in terms of covert symbols? These are all questions that cannot be answered by deploying authoritative "facts," but they must be explicitly addressed as we attempt to interpret the figurines and the archaeological record in our constructions of the past.

It may seem more satisfying to be given the "facts" of temples, shrines, and reverence for a deity, but as feminists we are sure that longer-term interpretive satisfaction is more complicated than that. While we have been suggesting throughout that the Goddess literature does not come to theoretical or methodological grips with the crucial issues of gender, symbol, or social practice, we would also argue that, when it comes to dealing with the figurines themselves, the Goddess literature also sidesteps rigorous engagement with function, meaning, and meaningfulness; that is, with the variability of function, with the mutability of meaning, and with the "referential contexts of social action" (Hodder 1982) within which figurines are meaningful. Thus, the basic questions of archaeological context that have not been taken up by the Goddess literature could shed important and provocative light onto the development and the transformations of symbolic significance and could help to highlight the expected variations in what figurine-making and figurine-using was about. There is a greater role—not a lesser one—for archaeology to play in the interpretation of these materials.

The times when certain imagery stops being created need investigation as well. Why are female statuettes made at different time periods within the Upper Paleolithic, and why would cave paintings have no longer been made at the end of the Upper Paleolithic? Why would figurines no longer be made by the times of Late Copper Age Europe? Gimbutas and other archaeologists agree on some dramatic changes in the archaeological record at the end of the Copper Age in Southeast Europe, one of which is the virtual disappearance of clay anthropomorphic figurines. At this same time, large villages were abandoned and settlements as a whole became almost invisible, but burials under mounds (named *kurgans*) became a visible part of the landscape. What are archaeologists to make of these changes? Are these times of social "collapse" as they are so often depicted? Why would figurines no longer be made? Why would villages be abandoned? Gimbutas attributes the changes, which she calls "the end of Old Europe," to the invasion of patriarchal Indo-European-speaking pastoralists from the north Black Sea steppes (1991, 352–401). The lack of settlement debris as well as the presence of domesticated horses prompt Gimbutas to think of pastoralists, which in turn leads her to conclude that this is a male-dominated society, based on the modern myth that all societies whose subsistence is based on animal keeping are patriarchal and warlike. Moreover, Gimbutas interprets the lack of female figurines as a decrease in the worship of the Goddess deity, as well as a decrease in respect given to women. Is this an unproblematic and obvious "conclusion"? This is by no means an incontrovertible fact.

Since the processes of urbanization that are so often associated with marked renegotiations of gender, including the restriction of women's social action and the marginalization of women's labor and household production, are not part of European life until Romanization (late first millenium B.C.), an equally compelling argument can be made that the supposed devaluation and disempowerment of women did not occur until several thousands of years *after* the Goddess Movement's postulated end of Old Europe. The "patriarchal revolution" that Gimbutas proclaims, on the basis of a decline or disappearance of figurines and "female" symbols, might actually be the product of intensive agricultural urbanism rather than of Kurgan pastoralism.

Thus, we could write a very different prehistory of Europe than the one suggested by Gimbutas, especially since there is no firm evidence for the proclaimed Kurgan invasions of Old Europe bringing to an end both figurines and matrifocal harmony. The observed changes in the archaeological record at 3500 B.C. may alternatively and plausibly be interpreted, for example, as the result of economic and technological changes, including exchange networks (Sherratt 1983, 1984; Chapman 1990a) in combination (or not) with social and settlement changes, such as decentralization of settlement, fission of households, and even a growth in the power of males to control joint action of the scattered villages (Hodder 1990; Tringham 1990).

The disappearance of the figurines is no less ambiguous than the meanings of their representations (Anthony 1991). If figurines were not always—or only—a mere reflection of gender ideologies, then the discontinuity of their manufacture and use could be linked more to varied and changing social, economic, and ideological histories. If the prehistory of women in Europe is viewed nonessentially, a more complex view of prehistory emerges: one of the networks of regional, local, and personal historical trajectories within which certain general trends, including household production and productivity, have varying significance. We can then see how the figurines would have had importance in certain, but not all, historical contexts. We can strive to construct the specific contexts in which figurines would have been meaningful (or not). A belief in a female deity may well have been one significant feature, but this must be made the problem, not the assertion. Thus, a disappearance of figurines may reflect a change in the rituals associated with belief in the Goddess. But it could also reflect a new social context in which the de-aggregation of socially differentiated households negates the need for figurines as a media in the negotiation and the legitimization of power in villages (Tringham 1990), or it could reflect a transformation in the system of rituals and their symbols that characterized the traditions of the large Neolithic/Eneolithic villages of Old Europe. It will take many lines of converging and compelling evidence to address each interpretation. But that is how all archaeology—especially the archaeology of symbols and ideas, of ideologies and social life—must proceed.

An analysis of the Goddess that Gimbutas's work presents reveals how complex, multifaceted, polysemic, and ambiguous any archaeological interpretation of this notion necessarily is.[20] Her monolithic account of "Goddess-oriented Old Europe" forecloses the goals of feminist—and even of traditional—archaeology: to probe and understand how and why humans use material culture and to probe the various symbolic and social complexities of past human lives. And yet Gimbutas and the Goddess Movement provoke compelling questions for both archaeology and feminist theory:

1. How do archaeologists interpret material culture and, in particular, make inferences about symbolic meanings, spiritual phenomena, and social contexts? This is precisely what Gimbutas and others (e.g., Gadon 1989) depend upon to establish the symbolic and spiritual lifeways they reconstruct for the past.

2. What theories of representation exist or need to be developed to address the complex question of what—and how—images "mean," especially images of females and images of women?

3. What do we really know about the current facts and interpretations of the European Paleolithic and Neolithic, so that we might best evaluate the use of archaeological reports and data and the consequent interpretations by writers for the Goddess Movement?

4. How and why are archaeological "facts"—and, by extension, a sense of prehistorical legitimacy—central or necessary to the construction of belief systems? To what extent are origins questions—such as pinpointing the origins of patriarchy—crucial to the reformulation of cultural myths and cultural logics?

5. What are belief systems? Why are particular kinds of belief systems being elaborated at this particular historical moment and especially in certain locales? Why do more than 500,000 people now identify with some parts of various feminist spiritualities, ecologies, and histories?

6. What do we know about the archaeologies of gender and how do we know about them?

7. What kinds of pasts involving gender do we want to construct? What are the relationships among speculations about the past, scholarship, and feminism? In what different ways can we visualize human pasts? What visions take into serious consideration the many levels and the multiplicities of human social action?[21]

THE IMPLICATIONS FOR FEMINIST ARCHAEOLOGIES

The students in our recent classes on archaeology and the Goddess have debated long and hard whether the Goddess literature is or is not feminist: there is a challenge to authority yet a reliance upon authority; there is a challenge to a totalizing patriarchy as inevitable, yet the alternative is another totalizing account. But in assessing if these Goddess narratives are efficacious as feminist narratives of resistance that are desperately needed now, we come back to feminism and archaeology. What does a feminist archaeology look like, and is a tension between those views and the Goddess Movement necessary but informative?

We believe archaeology must be engaged with feminist thinking, and for many reasons: because feminism is about gender and simultaneously about the entire fabric of social life, including the social practice of science; because feminist insights make "what once seemed apparent cry out for explanation" (Yanagisako and Collier 1987, 14); because feminisms invite and provide spaces for pluralisms—but not runaway relativisms; because feminist theory is about the dialogics of interpretation; and because feminist theory provides a wealth of ideas and information about gender and social lives that can be drawn upon, not merely borrowed and "applied," by archaeologists. If archaeologists are the ones to say something about long-term and historically situated processes such as class structure, state formation, and social change, and if we want to say something about the mobilization of material culture in a variety of kinds of human societies, we cannot do so without a recognition of the deep—but not necessarily exclusive—importance of gender. We have everything to gain by approaching the past "as if gender really mattered" (di Leonardo 1991, 8).

Feminist thinking implies that the past is relevant not because it explains or even helps us to understand the present but because it challenges the present. To a certain extent, the Goddess literature does this, but it does so through a "functionalist freeze" (Friedan 1963) that emphasizes normativized, monolithic sex roles. Engaging with feminist thinking and feminist critiques of science as a way to *challenge* the present demands that we take up critical perspectives on the scientistic (not scientific) reconstructions of "the past" that say "This is the way it really was." Even if such reconstructions are feminist inspired and have had a powerful emancipatory impact on many people, these interpretations make for a short-term solution at best. The valorization of what came before "the subordination of women" historically (or before racist hierarchies, the over-exploitation of resources, technological "progress," and violence in all forms) still presents the conditions of a homogenized, totalizing past as inevitable, which has the problematic effect of making people accept the present. Feminist thinking and writing, however, can offer archaeology the power that comes from re-imagining the past and thus imagining a different past. The archaeologist must then use what evidences are needed and available to support these alternatives. How might we better visualize and contextualize "meaningfulness" (of figurines) from the available evidence? What alternative ways are there to understand the variability that we *can* document?

Lerner (1993) has recently argued that the pasts that history has constructed have been "usable" for men, but not by and for women; she urges that this be remedied. While this notion of a usable past is indeed suggestive, it raises an immediate question as to what is usable to whom, and in whose terms. While the Goddess Movement may be popular, in part, because it has created a usable past that appears to help "solve" some contemporary problems, its "narrative of closure" fails to challenge the present, to redefine the relation between the present and the past, or to force reconsiderations of the dominant epistemologies of inequality and difference (Reiff 1993). The role of feminist archaeologists is not confined to nor necessarily predicated upon providing the evidence for a golden age of female status or for when a patriarchy came to be.

A definitive interpretation, even if it is alternative and gynocentric, does not provide the empowerment and liberation from the controlling narratives and practices of androcentric scholarship and cultural logics. What is empowering, in our view, is the recognition and acceptance of ambiguity, which admits the role of constructedness and the possibilities for reconfiguring and renegotiating meanings, including what constitutes evidence. How can we open up, not shut down, the interpretive possibilities? How can we visualize alternative practices of image-making by past peoples when it has been so easy and so professionally rewarding to visualize and to promote a monolithic past and monolithic homogeneous experiences? This recognition of ambiguity mandates necessary dialogues: between the alternative accounts and the empirical evidences and among the interpreter, the interpretation, and the audiences. The contemporary reader and the contemporary subject must participate in and confront the entanglement of ambiguity, history, and the production of knowledge.

Archaeology can contribute to the feminist enterprise of scrutinizing critically the processes whereby knowledge is produced and of developing a body of theory that is explicitly a guide to political practice. Indeed, feminist inquiry has argued that certain categories and descriptions that once made sense "must be reformulated if we are to grasp the shape and meanings of both men's and women's lives" (Rosaldo 1983, 76). But this is a difficult task, since we are "heirs to the very traditions of political and social argument" in which we are trying to intervene and since we have more or less "stayed prisoners to certain categories and preconceptions deeply rooted in traditional sociology" (77). We need to ask consistently: Are we, as feminists, still embedded in scientific traditions of discourse and argument that are patriarchal, dominating and exclusionary? The kind of social knowledge we are after is an "open, contingent and humanly-compelling" social knowledge that stands in explicit contrast to and rejection of social knowledge that is "closed, categorical and human-controlling" (Westkott 1979, 430). Although the Goddess literature has attempted to provide "an open future [that] rests on a new past" (Haraway 1978:50), the "open future" needs far more than what the Goddess literature has created. The task for feminist-motivated archaeologies in the coming years rests on a needed reconceptualization of our practice and of the production and uses of knowledge. Through our initial investigation into the uses of archaeology by the Goddess Movement, we feel we have begun to define the edges of the issues that are integral to an emergent feminist archaeology: gender, symbol, and social practice; function, meaning, and meaningfulness; and history, ambiguity, and the production of knowledge.

Notes

One of us (Conkey) would like to thank the Department of Anthropology and the Women's Studies Program at the University of Michigan for the invitation to visit the campus in March 1992 as part of the Women's Studies colloquia, "Thinking through the Disciplines." Particular thanks go to Dick Ford, Abby Stewart, and Gracia Clark for all their hospitalities and attention to detail that made that visit so rewarding, and a special thank you goes to the archaeology graduate students, who were enthusiastic about the visit and yet appropriately questioned some of the issues we discussed. Both authors extend particular thanks to the many students in our two courses on Archaeology and the Goddess (Spring and Fall 1991) at the University of California, Berkeley. We are especially grateful to Carol Hepokoski, who kept us readily provided with crucial bibliographic references and with insights into how other disciplines and participants view the Goddess, and to Marcia-Anne Dobres, whose help on the essay's bibliography and logic was invaluable. Finally, we both thank the editors of this volume for their infinite patience and continued encouragement, along with their sharp editing, and we thank the University of California, Berkeley Humanities Research program for a grant to one of us (Conkey) that made the larger research project possible during 1992–93.

1. In this essay, we consider the development of feminist and gender research in anthropological archaeology, which has historically and organizationally been differentiated from a variety of other kinds of archaeology in North America, such as from classical archaeology. Most anthropological archaeologists are trained and/or practice within Anthropology, which is more generally considered to be a social or human science (for a recent history see Trigger 1989; or Willey and Sabloff 1993). It is only now that there exists a reasonably sized collection of syllabi for graduate or undergraduate courses in anthropological archaeology that take gender and archaeology—which is, of course, not necessarily the same as feminist archaeology—as their main subject. Some of these are published (e.g., Spector and Whelan 1989; Claassen 1992:137 ff).

2. Other examples of how 1970s popular culture rather than archaeology took up questions of human origins and cultural development from a female vantage point include Davis 1971, Diner 1973, Reed 1975, and Stone 1976.

3. In the last decade or more there has been an increasing gap between feminist anthropology and popular feminist culture. Di Leonardo attributes this to "both increasing specialization in feminist scholarship and the institutionalization of radical or cultural feminism as a counter-culture" (1991: 8).

4. Other important discussions of this debate include Fedigan 1986, Gross and Averill 1983, Longino and Doell 1983, Tanner 1981, Tanner and Zihlman 1976, Zihlman 1978, 1981. For a summary from an archaeological perspective, see Conkey and Spector 1984.

5. Additional probings by feminist scholars, but not archaeologists, into issues surrounding the origins of the state include Gailey 1985, 1987a, b; Muller 1977; Ortner 1978; Reiter 1978; Sacks 1976; and see Silverblatt 1988 for a review.

6. There is important debate as to precisely how the emergence of feminist archaeologies and even gender concerns is related to the wider theoretical and methodological debates among the so-called processual and post-processual archaeologies (e.g., Hanen and Kelley 1992). These debates substantiate that much of the latter has been equally but differently "cool" to feminist perspectives and inquiry (Baker, Taylor, and Thomas 1990; and especially Engelstad 1991, 1992).

7. Funding support for the conference "Women and Production in Prehistory" was generously provided by the National Science Foundation and the Wenner-Gren Foundation for Anthropological Research. Logistical support was provided by the University of South Carolina, Department of Anthropology (see Gero and Conkey 1991, xi–xiii).

8. Wylie has begun an analysis, based on extensive questionnaires to participants in both conferences, to investigate the sources and motivations for all of this heretofore obscured or only nascent interest in gender (see footnotes in Wylie 1992a).

9. For an important critique of gender as a "category" for analysis in archaeology, see Roberts (1993), in which she develops the distinction between the "archaeology of gender" and an "engendered archaeology," and which we find to be a most accurate and provocative characterization of the major leanings within the archaeological approach to gender at this time.

10. Kohl (1985) did not address the influence of feminist thinking but introduced this metaphor of the "soft underside" of a rigid archaeology in reference to the introduction of explicitly symbolic approaches to archaeology.

11. We use the term *prehistory,* although we are uncomfortable with the implications that the peoples of "prehistory"—that is, those without writing systems and our kinds of historical record keeping and texts—therefore had no history/histories. Further, it is clear that to most, but not all (cf. Gadon 1989 on India), authors of the Goddess Movement, human prehistory is synonymous with European-Mediterranean prehistory; this is where the bulk of the Goddess narratives are set, and it is from archaeological contexts in this region that the primary evidence is marshalled. We are also uncomfortable about treating this so-called prehistory as a somehow homogeneous block of time and, by extension, of human culture.

12. Eisler (1987) has coined a term for the more balanced male-female relationships or partnerships; she calls this situation "gylany." She posits these relationships as being in contrast to the contemporary and asymmetrical male-female relationships of the "dominator" type.

13. We are quite skeptical about endorsing these "positive" values, since they are clearly entangled with many current debates about the state of "family values" in contemporary North America. These debates, in turn, are obviously situated within the political maneuverings of conservative and right-wing politics that are very much at odds with

many of the goals of feminist politics. As di Leonardo succinctly notes: "Both feminist essentialists and conservative anti-feminists have continued to draw on the 19th century storehouse of moral motherhood symbolism, stressing women's innate identity with and nurturance of children and nature" (1991: 26).

14. When we decided that we had to get involved in this topic, we scheduled ourselves to team-teach a graduate seminar (spring 1991) and then an undergraduate upper-division course (fall 1991). We have now had in our classes Unitarian Universalist ministers who have neopaganist congregations; we have had witches; goddess artists; healers; religious studies majors; all sorts of anthropologists and archaeologists; and Elinor Gadon, author of *The Once and Future Goddess*, gave an excellent guest lecture. We have read in journals new to us, such as the *Journal of Feminist Studies in Religion*, and found rich materials in special issues on ecofeminism and ecology in *Hypatia* and in edited volumes, such as *Gender and Religion: On the Complexity of Symbols* (Bynum, Harrell, and Richman 1986). We have had to go back to Bachofen (1861), to Elizabeth Cady Stanton's *The Woman's Bible* (1898) and Matilda Joslyn Gage's *Woman, Church and State* (1893). These last two texts "both try to break the link between male authority and God's will, whether that divine mandate is located in a written word (the Bible) or in an institution (the Church)" (Weaver 1989: fn.1). When Mary Jo Weaver wrote her article "Who Is the Goddess and Where Does She Get Us?" (1989), she raised a question we had to engage with as well: "Where did we get HER?"

15. This debate within feminist religious studies was crystallized by Carol Christ (1977) using Sheila Collins's original (1974) distinction between revolutionaries and reformists.

16. An equally egregious example of the combination of sexist archaeological complicity with uncritical journalism is the presentation in the February 1992 issue of *Discover* of the ideas of Lewis Binford concerning the social lives and sexual relationships of the Neanderthals. Binford has been one of the recognized intellectual leaders of archaeology since the late 1960s, which makes his commentary all the more troubling. In this article he draws on a problematic data set from only one archaeological site to present an unqualified interpretation of the social and sexual lives of very controversial ancient humans, who are not fully accepted as being within the range of modern human behavior. While correctly rejecting the unquestioning application of a modern and Western nuclear family model to these prehistoric hominids, Binford sees only one alternative, which he claims necessarily derives from animal behavior studies. This alternative model is that of a sex-segregated society in which males come into contact with females "like visiting firemen" (and he is reported in the article to have said this "while laughing"). Binford seems sure that the archaeological evidence supports differential diets for males and females, yet there is only an unrepresentative sample of bone from this one site (which he did not excavate himself) and no human bone for bone chemistry diet studies. In the same article Binford is sure that women "made smaller simpler tools," and yet he has consistently rejected in his other writings the notion that these kinds of "ethnographic" facts are knowable at all in archaeology (e.g., in Wylie 1991). It is striking that "Lew (Binford) knows" such sex/gender attributions, whereas when other scholars (including female/feminist ones) propose that women might have made stone tools, a peer reviewer

at the National Science Foundation roundly criticizes the very possibility (see Gero 1991: 163).

17. Gerda Lerner's book *The Creation of Patriarchy* (1986) is fascinating in regard to the uses of historical data, for, as a very scholarly historian, she clearly knows how to use and be judicious with historical documents and texts. Nevertheless, she slips into a number of problematic issues once she confronts the archaeological (nontextual) data and interpretations. In particular, it appears difficult for her to question the archaeological materials and interpretations. We presume that this is as much a problem of the authority with which archaeology is usually presented. That is, Lerner draws from (and we critique Gimbutas for) a markedly authoritative voice that is in line with the prevalent mode of discourse among both traditional and New (processualist) Archaeologists who all

offer authoritative optimistically-worded statements about what they have found. They interpret (the archaeological record) according to a very specific [read limited] set of questions which are deemed relevant and answerable, and based on a number of very specific premises (usually unexpressed) about how people behave and behaved in the past. It is these mainstream studies that provide statements on the archaeological "facts," which then become reiterated and reconfirmed in secondary studies that incorporate . . . all the archaeologists' limitations into their own works . . . (Tringham 1994, 189)

Despite the existence of an authoritative discourse within archaeology, Gimbutas diverges from archaeological practice with her arguments by assertions that have increasingly lacked even the minimal "linking arguments" between archaeological materials and the interpretations that are made of them.

18. Many scholars have discussed some of the problems surrounding origins research, especially for feminist thinking, and we will not rehearse the debate here (e.g., Conkey with Williams 1991; Elshtain 1986; Handsman 1991; Moore n.d.; Rapp 1977; and Rosaldo 1983).

19. Even the "identification" of imagery is debated. For example, among the earliest Upper Paleolithic imagery in southwest France, dating to some thirty-two thousand years ago, there are stone blocks with geometric ovaloid forms, among other images. Since the 1910s these forms have unquestionably been taken to represent female vulvas, although no arguments have been developed to make the case (contra Marshack 1991). Very few of the female statuettes have a so-called vulva on them, although there are certainly exceptions, such as one of the major icons of the Upper Paleolithic figurine repertoire, the so-called Venus of Willendorf (Austria) (see fig. 2). This doesn't mean that some of them might not be representations of vulvas, especially since there is considerable variation of shapes lumped under the category of "vulvas" (see Mack 1992, 241, fig. 4). But only assertions have been offered, and these have become entrenched (cf. the critique by Bahn 1986). Not only has the existence of females-as-representational-subjects gone unquestioned, it is often the significance of this practice that has not been subjected to critical assessment.

20. For other critiques of the Gimbutas archaeology and Goddess interpretations, see Anthony 1991, Fagan 1992, and Hepokoski 1992b.

21. Many of these questions lie at the heart of current debates about the nature and potentials of archaeological interpretation (e.g., Baker and Thomas 1990; Binford 1962, 1983, 1986a, b; Hayden 1992; Hodder 1982, 1986, 1990; Leone 1982; Nelson and Kehoe 1990; Shanks and Tilley 1987a, b; Watson and Fotiadis 1990; and Wylie 1991, 1992c).

REFERENCES

Adler, M. [1979] 1986. *Drawing Down the Moon.* Boston: Beacon Press.

Anthony, D. 1991. "Nazi and Eco-Feminist Prehistories: Counterpoints in Indo-European Archaeology." Presented at the American Anthropological Association annual meeting, Chicago.

Arnold, K., R. Gilchrist, P. G. Graves, and S. Taylor, eds. 1988. "Women and Archaeology." *Archaeological Review from Cambridge* 7, no. 1.

Arsenault, D. 1991. "The Representation of Women in Moche Iconography." In *The Archaeology of Gender,* edited by D. Walde and N. Willows, 313–26. Calgary: The Archaeological Association, University of Calgary.

Bachofen, J. 1861. *Das Mutterrecht.* Basel: Benno Schwabe.

Bacus, E., et al., eds. 1993. *A Gendered Past: A Critical Bibliography of Gender in Archaeology.* University of Michigan Museum of Anthropology, Technical report no. 25, Ann Arbor.

Bahn, P. 1986. "No Sex, Please, We're Aurignacians." *Rock Art Research* 3, no. 2:99–120.

Bailey, D. 1990. "The Living House: Signifying Continuity." In *The Social Archaeology of Houses,* edited by R. Samson, 19–48. Edinburgh: University of Edinburgh.

———. 1991. *The Social Reality of Figurines from the Chalcolithic of Northeastern Bulgaria: The Example of Ovcharovo.* Ph.D. diss., University of Cambridge.

Baker, F., S. Taylor, and J. Thomas. 1990. "Writing the Past in the Present: An Introductory Dialogue." In *Writing the Past in the Present,* edited by F. Baker and J. Thomas, 1–12. Lampeter, Wales: St. David's University College.

Baker, F., and J. Thomas, eds. 1990. *Writing the Past in the Present.* Lampeter, Wales: St. David's University College.

Bamberger, J. 1974. "The Myth of Matriarchy: Why Men Rule in Primitive Society." In *Women, Culture, and Society,* edited by M. Rosaldo and L. Lamphere, 263–80. Stanford, Calif.: Stanford University Press.

Baring, A., and J. Cashing. 1991. *The Myth of the Goddess.* New York and London: Viking Press.

Barstow, A. 1978. "The Uses of Archaeology for Women's History." *Feminist Studies* 4, no. 3:7–18.

Bertelsen, R., A. Lillehammer, and J. Naess, eds. 1977. *Were They All Men? An Examination of Sex Roles in Prehistoric Society.* Stavanger, Norway: Arkeologist musem i Stavanger.

Binford, L. 1962. "Archaeology as Anthropology." *American Antiquity* 28, no. 2:217–25.

———. 1983. *In Pursuit of the Past: Decoding the Archaeological Record*. New York: Academic Press.

———. 1986a. "Data, Relativism, and Archaeological Science." *Man* 22:391–404.

———. 1986b. "In Pursuit of the Future." In *American Archaeology Past and Future*, edited by D. Meltzer, D. D. Fowler, and J. A. Sabloff, 459–79. Washington, D.C.: Smithsonian Institution Press.

Binford, S. R. 1979. "Myths and Matriarchies." *Human Behavior* (May): 63–66.

Bolen, K. 1992. "Prehistoric Construction of Mothering." In *Exploring Gender through Archaeology*, edited by C. Claassen, 49–62. Monographs in World Archaeology no. 11. Madison, Wis.: Prehistory Press.

Bourdier, J.-P. 1989. "Reading Tradition." In *Dwellings, Settlements and Traditions: Cross-Cultural Perspectives*, edited by J.-P. Bourdier and N. AlSayyad, 33–51. Lanham, Md.: University Press of America.

Braithwaite, M. 1982. "Decoration as Ritual Symbol: A Theoretical Proposal and an Ethnographic Study in Southern Sudan." In *Symbolic and Structural Archaeology*, edited by I. Hodder, 80–88. Cambridge: Cambridge University Press.

Brumfiel, E. 1992. "Breaking and Entering the Ecosystem: Gender, Class, and Faction Steal the Show." *American Anthropologist* 94, no. 3.

Bynum, C. W., S. Harrell, and P. Richman, eds. 1986. *Gender and Religion: On the Complexity of Symbols*. Boston: Beacon Press.

Champion, T., C. Gamble, S. Shennan, and A. Whittle. 1986. *Prehistoric Europe*. New York: Academic Press.

Chapman, J. 1981. *The Vinca Culture*. Oxford: British Archaeological Reports IA117.

———. 1990a. "Regional Study of the North Sumadija Region." In *Selevac: A Neolithic Village in Yugoslavia*, edited by R. Tringham and D. Krstic, 13–44. Los Angeles: UCLA Institute of Archaeology Press.

———. 1990b. "Social Inequality on Bulgarian Tells and the Varna Problem." In *The Social Archaeology of Houses*, edited by R. Samson, 49–92. Edinburgh: Edinburgh University Press.

Christ, C. 1977. "The Feminist Theology: A Review of the Literature." *Religious Studies Review* 3 (October): 203–12.

———. 1979. "Why Women Need the Goddess: Phenomenological, Psychological, and Political Reflections." In *Womanspirit Rising: A Feminist Reader in Religion*, edited by C. Christ and J. Plaskow, 273–87. New York: Harper and Row.

Christ, C., and J. Plaskow, eds. 1979. *Womanspirit Rising: A Feminist Reader in Religion*. New York: Harper and Row.

Claassen, C., ed. 1992. *Exploring Gender through Archaeology*. Monographs in World Archaeology no. 11. Madison, Wis.: Prehistory Press.

Collins, D., and J. Onians. 1978. "The Origins of Art." *Art History* 1, no. 1:1–25.

Collins, S. 1974. *A Different Heaven and Earth*. Valley Forge, Pa.: Judson Press.

Conkey, M. 1989. "Peopling the Globe: A Report from the Year 2050." *Archaeology* 42, no. 1:35–39, 81.

———. 1991. "Does It Make a Difference? Feminist Thinking and Archaeologies of Gender." In *The Archaeology of Gender*, edited by D. Walde and N. Willows, 24–33. Calgary: The Archaeological Association, University of Calgary.

Conkey, M., and J. Gero. 1991. "Tension, Pluralities, and Engendering Archaeology: An Introduction." In *Engendering Archaeology: Women and Prehistory*, edited by J. Gero and M. Conkey, 3–30. Oxford: Blackwell.

Conkey, M., and J. Spector. 1984. "Archaeology and the Study of Gender." *Advances in Archaeological Method and Theory* 7:1–38.

Conkey, M., with S. Williams. 1991. "Original Narratives: The Political Economy of Gender in Archaeology." In *Gender at the Crossroads of Knowledge: Feminist Anthropology in the Post-Modern Era*, edited by M. di Leonardo, 102–39. Berkeley: University of California Press.

Conroy, L. 1992. "Upper Paleolithic Figurines and the Emergence of Gender." Annual meeting, College Art Association, Chicago.

———. 1993. "Upper Paleolithic Figurines and the Emergence of Gender." In *Women in Archaeology: A Feminist Critique*, edited by H. du Cros and L. Smith, Department of Prehistory, Occasional Monographs no. 22, 153–60. Australian National University, Canberra.

Cucchiari, S. 1981. "The Gender Revolution and the Transition from the Bisexual Horde to Patrilocal Band: The Origins of Gender Hierarchy." In *Sexual Meanings: Cultural Constructions of Gender and Sexuality*, edited by S. Ortner and H. Whitehead, 31–79. Cambridge: Cambridge University Press.

Culpepper, E. 1987. "Contemporary Goddess Theology: A Sympathetic Critique." In *Shaping New Vision: Gender and Values in American Culture*, edited by C. Atkinson, C. Buchanan, and M. Miles, 51–71. Ann Arbor: UMI Research Press.

Daly, M. 1968. *The Church and the Second Sex*. Boston: Beacon Press.

———. 1978. *Gyn/Ecology*. Boston: Beacon Press.

———. 1992. *Outercourse: The Be-Dazzling Voyage. Containing Recollections from My Logbook of a Radical Feminist Philosopher (Being an Account of My Time/Space Travels and Ideas—Then, Again, Now and How)*. San Francisco: Harper.

Davis, E. 1971. *The First Sex*. Baltimore, Md.: Penguin Books.

Delphy, C. 1984. *Close To Home: A Materialist Analysis of Women's Oppression*. Translated by D. Leonard. Amherst: University of Massachusetts.

Delporte, H. [1979] 1993. *L'Image de la femme dans l'art préhistorique*. Paris: Picard.

———. 1990. "La Venus Dansante de Galgenberg." *La Recherche* 21, no. 222:772–73.

Dexter, M. R. 1990. *Whence the Goddesses: A Source Book*. New York: Teacher's College Press.

di Leonardo, M. 1991. "Introduction: Gender, Culture and Political Economy: Feminist Anthropology in Historical Perspective." In *Gender at the Crossroads of Knowledge: Feminist Anthropology in the Post-modern Era*, edited by M. di Leonardo, 1–48. Berkeley and Los Angeles: University of California Press.

Diner, H. [1965] 1973. *Mothers and Amazons: The First Feminine History of Culture*. New York: Doubleday.

Dobres, M-A. 1988. "Feminist Archaeology and Inquiries into Gender Relations: Some

Thoughts on Universals, Origin Stories, and Alternative Paradigms." *Archaeological Review from Cambridge* 7, no. 1:30–44.

———. 1992a. "Reconsidering Venus Figurines: A Feminist Inspired Re-Analysis." In *Ancient Images, Ancient Thought: The Archaeology of Ideology,* ed. A. Sean Goldsmith, Sandra Garvie, David Selin, and Jeannette Smith, 245–62. Calgary: The Archaeological Association, University of Calgary.

———. 1992b. "Re-presentations of Paleolithic Visual Imagery: Simulacra and Their Alternatives." *Kroeber Anthropological Society Papers,* nos. 73–74:1–25. University of California, Department of Anthropology, Berkeley.

Donley, L. 1982. "House Power: Swahili Space and Symbolic Markers." In *Symbolic and Structural Archaeology,* edited by I. Hodder, 63–73. Cambridge: Cambridge University Press.

du Cros, H., and L. Smith, eds. 1993. *Women in Archaeology: A Feminist Critique.* Occasional Paper no. 22. Department of Prehistory, Australian National University, Canberra.

Duhard, J. P. 1989a. *Le Réalisme physiologique des figurations féminines sculptées du Paléolithique Supérieur en France.* Thèse de Doctorat en Anthropologie-Prehistoire, Bordeaux I.

———. 1989b. "Les Figurations de parturientes dans l'art mobilier et pariétal du Paléolithique Supérieur en France." *Bullétin de la Societé de l'Anthropologie Sud-Ouest* 24, no. 4:329–52.

Ehrenberg, M. 1989. *Women in Prehistory.* Oklahoma City: University of Oklahoma Press.

Eisler, R. 1987. *The Chalice and the Blade.* San Francisco: Harper and Row.

Elshtain, J. B. 1986. "The New Feminist Scholarship." *Salamagundi* 70–71:3–26.

Engelstad, E. 1991. "Feminist Theory and Post-Processual Archaeology." In *The Archaeology of Gender,* edited by D. Walde and N. Willows, 116–20. Calgary: The Archaeological Association, University of Calgary.

———. 1992. "Images of Power and Contradiction: Feminist Theory and Post-Processual Archaeology." *Antiquity* 65, no. 248:502–14.

Fagan, B. 1992. "A Sexist View of Prehistory." Review of *The Civilization of the Goddess,* by M. Gimbutas. *Archaeology* 45, no. 2:14–15, 18, 66.

Fedigan, L. M. 1986. "The Changing Role of Women in Models of Human Evolution." *Annual Review of Anthropology* 15:25–66.

Friedan, B. 1963. *The Feminine Mystique.* New York: Norton.

Gadon, E. 1989. *The Once and Future Goddess.* San Francisco: Harper and Row.

Gage, M. J. [1893] 1980. *Woman, Church and State.* Watertown, Mass.: Persephone Press.

Gailey, C. 1976. "The Origin of the State in Tonga: Gender Hierarchy and Class Formation." Presented at the American Anthropological Association Annual Meeting, Washington, D.C.

———. 1985. "The State of the State in Anthropology." *Dialectical Anthropology* 9, no. 1–4:65–91.

———. 1987a. "Evolutionary Perspectives on Gender Hierarchy." In *Analyzing Gender,* edited by B. Hess and M. Ferrea, 32–67. Beverly Hills, Calif.: Sage Press.

———. 1987b. *From Kinship to Kingship: Gender Hierarchy and State Formation in the Tongan Islands.* Austin: University of Texas Press.

Gamble, C. 1982. "Interaction and Alliance in Paleolithic Society." *Man* n.s. 17, no. 1:92–107.

———. 1991. "The Social Context for European Paleolithic Art." *Proceedings of the Prehistoric Society* 57, no. 1:3–15.

Garasanin, M. 1979. *Praistorija Jugoslovenskih Zemalja,* vol. 2: *Neolithic.* Sarajevo: Akademiija Nauka i Umjetnosti Bosne i Hercegovine.

Gero, J. 1983. "Gender Bias in Archaeology: A Cross-Cultural Perspective." In *The Socio-Politics of Archaeology,* edited by J. Gero, D. Lacey, and M. Blakey, 51–57. Research Report no. 23, University of Massachusetts, Amherst.

———. 1985. "Socio-Politics and the Woman-at-Home Ideology." *American Antiquity* 50:342–50.

———. 1988. "Gender Bias in Archaeology: Here, Then, and Now." In *Resistance of the Science and Health-Care Professions to Feminism,* edited by S. Rosser, 33–43. New York: Pergamon Press.

———. 1991. "Genderlithics: Women's Roles in Stone Tool Production." In *Engendering Archaeology: Women and Prehistory,* edited by J. Gero and M. Conkey, 163–93. Oxford: Basil Blackwell.

———. 1992. "Feasts and Females: Political Meals in the Andes." *Norwegian Archaeological Review* 25, no. 1:15–30.

———. N.d. "Constructing Paleo-Man: Engendered Field Practice." Paper presented to Department of Anthropology, Tulane University.

Gero, J., and M. Conkey, eds. 1991. *Engendering Archaeology: Women and Prehistory.* Oxford: Basil Blackwell.

Gero, J., and D. Root. 1990. "Public Presentations Are Private Concerns: Archaeology in the Pages of National Geographic." In *Politics of the Past,* edited by P. Gathercole and D. Lowenthal, 19–37. London: Unwin.

Gifford-Gonzalez, D. 1992. "Gaps in Zooarchaeological Analyses of Butchery: Is Gender an Issue?" In *Bones to Behavior,* edited by J. Hudson, 181–99. Carbondale: Southern Illinois University Center for Archaeological Investigations.

———. 1993. "You Can Hide, but You Can't Run: Representation of Women's Work in Illustrations of Paleolithic Life." *Visual Anthropology Review* 9, no. 1:3–21.

Gimbutas, M. 1980. "The Temples of Old Europe." *Archaeology* 38:41–50.

———. 1981. "The Image of Woman in Prehistoric Art." *ORA* 2, no. 4.

———. 1982. *The Goddesses and Gods of Old Europe.* Berkeley: University of California Press.

———. 1989a. *The Language of the Goddess.* San Francisco: Harper and Row.

———. 1989b. "Women and Culture in Goddess-Oriented Old Europe." In *Weaving the Visions: New Patterns in Feminist Spirituality,* edited by J. Plaskow and C. Christ, 63–71. San Francisco: Harper and Row.

———. 1991. *The Civilization of the Goddess.* San Francisco: Harper and Row.

Goldenberg, N. 1979. *The Changing of the Gods: Feminism and the End of Traditional Religions.* Boston: Beacon Press.

Graves, R. 1966. *The White Goddess: A Historical Grammar of a Poetic Myth.* New York: Farrar, Straus, and Giroux.

Gross, M., and M. B. Averill. 1983. "Evolution and Patriarchal Myths of Scarcity and Competition." In *Discovering Reality: Feminist Perspectives in Epistemology, Metaphysics, Methodology, and Philosophy of Science,* edited by S. Harding and M. B. Hintikka, 71–95. Dordrecht: D. Reidel.

Gvozdover, M. 1989a. "Ornamental Decoration on Artifacts of the Kostenki Culture." *Soviet Anthropology and Archaeology,* special issue: *Female Imagery in the Paleolithic: An Introduction to the work of M. D. Gvozdover* 27, no. 4:8–31.

———. 1989b. "The Typology of Female Figurines of the Kostenki Paleolithic Culture." *Soviet Anthropology and Archaeology,* special issue: *Female Imagery in the Paleolithic: An Introduction to the Work of M. D. Gvozdover* 27, no. 4:32–94.

———. N.d. *The Excavations at Avdeevo.* MS.

Hackett, J. 1989. "Can a Sexist Model Liberate Us?" *Journal of Feminist Studies in Religion* 5:65–76.

Handsman, R. 1991. "Whose Art Was Found at Lepenski Vir? Gender Relations and Power in Archaeology." In *Engendering Archaeology: Women and Prehistory,* edited by J. Gero and M. Conkey, 329–65. Oxford: Basil Blackwell.

Hanen, M., and J. Kelley. 1992. "Gender and Archaeological Knowledge." In *Metaarchaeology,* edited by L. Embree, 195–225. Dordrecht: Kluwer Academic Publishers.

Haraway, D. 1978. "Animal Sociology and a Natural Economy of the Body Politic, Part II: The Past Is the Contested Zone: Human Nature and Theories of Production and Reproduction in Primate Behavior Studies." *Signs: Journal of Women in Culture and Society* 4:37–60.

Harris, M. 1968. *The Rise of Anthropological Theory.* New York: Thomas Y. Crowell.

Hastorf, C. 1991. "Gender, Space, and Food in Prehistory." In *Engendering Archaeology: Women and Prehistory,* edited by J. Gero and M. Conkey, 132–59. Oxford: Basil Blackwell.

Hayden, B. 1992. "Observing Prehistoric Women." In *Exploring Gender through Archaeology.* Monographs in World Archaeology no. 11, edited by C. Claassen, 33–48. Madison, Wis.: Prehistory Press.

Hegedus, K., and J. Makkay. 1987. "Vészto-Magor." In *The Late Neolithic of the Tisza Region,* edited by P. Raczky, 85–103. Budapest-Szolnok: Directorate of Szolnok County Museums.

Hepokoski, C. 1992a. "Beyond the Goddess: A Feminist Critique of the Goddess Hypothesis." Berkeley: Starr King School for the Ministry, Graduate Theological Union.

———. 1992b. "Was There a Goddess Civilization? A Review of *The Myth of the Goddess: Evolution of an Image* by Anne Baring and Jules Cashford, and of *The Civilization of the Goddess: The World of Old Europe* by Marija Gimbutas." *Gnosis Magazine,* no. 25:64–65.

Hodder, I. 1982. "Theoretical Archaeology: A Reactionary View." In *Symbolic and Structural Archaeology,* edited by I. Hodder, 1–16. Cambridge: Cambridge University Press.

———. 1985. "Postprocessual Archaeology." *Advances in Archaeological Method and Theory* 8:1–23.

———. 1986. *Reading the Past.* Cambridge: Cambridge University Press.

———. 1990. *The Domestication of Europe.* Oxford: Basil Blackwell.

James, E. O. 1959. *The Cult of the Mother Goddess: An Archaeological and Documentary Study.* New York: Praeger.

Kehoe, A. 1991. "The Weaver's Wraith." In *The Archaeology of Gender,* edited by D. Walde and N. Willows, 430–35. Calgary: The Archaeological Association, University of Calgary.

Kelley, J. 1991. "Introduction to the Plenary Session: The Archaeology of Gender." In *The Archaeology of Gender,* edited by D. Walde and N. Willows, 2–3. Calgary: The Archaeological Association, University of Calgary.

Kelly-Gadol, J. 1976. "The Social Relations of the Sexes: Methodological Implications of Women's History." *Signs: Journal of Women in Culture and Society* 1:809–24.

Kohl, P. 1985. "Symbolic Cognitive Archaeology: A New Loss of Innocence." *Dialectical Anthropology* 9:105–17.

Kramer, C., and M. Stark. 1988. "The Status of Women in Archaeology." *Anthropology Newsletter* (American Anthropological Association) 29, no. 9:1, 11–12.

Leacock, E. 1977. "Women in Egalitarian Societies." In *Becoming Visible: Women in European History,* edited by R. Bridenthal and C. Koonz, 11–35. Boston: Houghton Mifflin.

———. 1983. "Interpreting the Origins of Gender Inequality: Conceptual and Historical Problems." *Dialectical Anthropology* 7:253–83.

Leone, M. 1972. "Issues in Contemporary Archaeology." In *Contemporary Archaeology,* edited by M. Leone, 14–27. Carbondale: Southern Illinois University Press.

———. 1982. "Some Opinions about Recovering Mind." *American Antiquity* 47:742–60.

Lerner, G. 1986. *The Creation of Patriarchy.* New York: Oxford University Press.

———. 1993. *The Creation of Feminist Consciousness: From the Middle Ages to Eighteen-Seventy.* New York: Oxford University Press.

Lewis, M. 1992. *Green Delusions: An Environmentalist Critique of Radical Environmentalism.* Durham, N.C., and London: Duke University Press.

Longino, H., and R. Doell. 1983. "Body, Bias, and Behavior: A Comparative Analysis of Reasoning in Two Areas of Biological Science." *Signs: Journal of Women in Culture and Society* 9, no. 2:206–27.

Lutz, C., and J. Collins. 1991. "The Photograph as an Intersection of Gazes: The Example of National Geographic." *Visual Anthropology Review* 7, no. 1:134–49.

———. 1993. *Reading National Geographic.* Chicago: University of Chicago Press.

Mack, R. 1989. "The Representation of Prehistory: Archaeology and the Female Body." Seminar paper, Department of Anthropology, University of California, Berkeley.

———. 1990. "Reading the Archaeology of the Female Body." *Qui Parle* 4, no. 1:79–97.

———. 1992. "Gendered Site: Archaeology, Representation, and the Female Body." In *Ancient Images, Ancient Thought: The Archaeology of Ideology,* ed. A. Sean

Goldsmith, Sandra Garvie, David Selin, and Jeannette Smith, 235–44. Calgary: The Archaeological Association, University of Calgary.

Marshack, A. 1972. *The Roots of Civilization: The Cognitive Beginnings of Man's First Art, Symbols, and Notation.* New York: McGraw-Hill.

———. 1986. "The Eye Is Not as Clever as It Thinks It Is (Reply to P. G. Bahn, "No Sex, Please, We're Aurignacians")." *Rock Art Research* 3, no. 2:111–20.

———. 1991. "The Female Image: A 'Time-Factored' Symbol: A Study in Style and Aspects of Image Use in the Upper Paleolithic." *Proceedings of the Prehistoric Society* 57, no. 1:17–31.

Marshall, Y. 1985. "Who Made the Lapita Pots?" *Journal of the Polynesian Society* 94:205–33.

McCafferty, G., and S. McCafferty. 1988. "Powerful Women and the Myth of Male Dominance in Aztec Society." *Archaeological Review from Cambridge* 7:45–59.

McCafferty, S. D., and G. G. McCafferty. 1991. "Spinning and Weaving as Female Gender Identity in Post-Classic Mexico." In *Textile Traditions in Mesoamerica and the Andes,* vol. 2, edited by M. Schevill, J. C. Berlo, and N. Dwyer, 19–44. Hamden, Conn.: Garland Press.

McCoid, C., and L. McDermott. 1992. "Towards Decolonizing Gender: Female Vision in the Upper Paleolithic." Presented at the American Anthropological Association, annual meeting, San Francisco.

McDermott, L. D. 1985. *Self-Generated Information and Representation of the Human Figure during the European Upper Paleolithic.* Ph.D. diss., University of Kansas, Special Studies.

McGuire, R. 1985. "Conceptualizing the State in a Post-Processual Archaeology." Presented at the American Anthropological Association, annual meeting, Washington, D.C.

Mellaart, J. 1967. *Çatal Hüyük. A Neolithic Town in Anatolia.* London: Thames and Hudson.

———. 1972. "A Neolithic City in Turkey." In *Old World Archaeology,* edited by C. C. Lamberg-Karlovsky, 120–31. San Francisco: W. H. Freeman.

Moore, H. 1986. *Space, Text, and Gender: An Anthropological Study of the Marakwet of Kenya.* Cambridge: Cambridge University Press.

———. N.d. "The Problem of Origins: Post-structuralism and Beyond." Interpretive Archaeologies Conference, Cambridge University.

Morgan, E. 1972. *The Descent of Woman.* New York: Stein and Day.

Muller, V. 1977. "The Formation of the State and the Oppression of Women: A Case Study in England and Wales." *Radical Review of Political Economy* 9:7–21.

Nash, J. 1978. "The Aztecs and the Ideology of Male Dominance." *Signs: Journal of Women in Culture and Society* 4, no. 2:349–62.

Nelson, S. 1990. "Diversity of the Upper Paleolithic 'Venus' Figurines and Archaeological Mythology." In *Powers of Observation: Alternative Views in Archaeology,* edited by S. Nelson and A. Kehoe, 11–22. Washington, D.C.: American Anthropological Association.

Nelson, S., and A. Kehoe, eds. *Powers of Observation: Alternative Views in Archaeology.* Washington, D.C.: American Anthropological Association.

Ocschorn, J. 1981. *The Female Experience and the Nature of the Divine.* Bloomington: Indiana University Press.

Olson, C., ed. 1983. *The Book of the Goddess, Past and Present: An Introduction to Her Religion.* New York: Crossroad.

Ortner, S. 1978. "The Virgin and the State." *Feminist Studies* 4:19–36.

Rapp, R. 1977. "Gender and Class: An Archaeological Consideration of Knowledge Concerning the Origins of the State." *Dialectical Anthropology* 2:309–16.

Reed, E. 1975. *Women's Evolution: From Matriarchal Clan to Patriarchal Family.* New York: Pathfinder Press.

Reiter, R. R. 1978. "The Search for Origins: Unravelling the Threads of Gender Hierarchy." *Critique of Anthropology* 3, no. 9–10:5–24.

Renfrew, C. 1987. *Archaeology and Language: The Puzzle of Indo-European Origins.* New York: Cambridge University Press.

Reuther, R. 1987. "Female Symbols, Values, and Context." *Christianity and Crisis* 47 (January): 460–64.

———. 1992. *Gaia and God: An Ecofeminist Theology of Earth Healing.* San Francisco: Harper.

Reuther, R., and E. McLaughlin, eds. 1979. *Women of Spirit.* New York: Simon and Schuster.

Rice, P. 1981. "Prehistoric Venuses: Symbols of Motherhood or Womanhood?" *Journal of Anthropological Archaeology* 37, no. 4:402–14.

Rieff, D. 1993. "Designer Gods." *Transitions* 59:20–31.

Roberts, C. 1993. "A Critical Approach to Gender as a Category of Analysis in Archaeology." In *Women in Archaeology: A Feminist Critique,* edited by H. du Cros and L. Smith. Department of Prehistory, Occasional Paper no. 22, 16–21. Australian National University, Canberra.

Rohrlich-Leavitt, R. 1977. "Women in Transition: Crete and Sumer." In *Becoming Visible: Women in European History,* edited by R. Bridenthal and C. Koonz, 36–59. Boston: Houghton Mifflin.

Rosaldo, M. 1983. "Moral/Analytical Dilemmas Posed by the Intersection of Feminism and Social Science." In *Social Science as Moral Inquiry,* edited by N. Haan, R. Bellah, P. Rabinow, and W. Sullivan, 76–95. New York: Columbia University Press.

Russell, P. 1987. "Women in Upper Paleolithic Europe." Master's thesis, Department of Anthropology, University of Auckland, N.Z.

Sacks, K. 1976. "State Bias and Women's Status." *American Anthropologist* 78, no. 3:565–69.

Shanks, M., and C. Tilley. 1987a. *Re-constructing Archaeology.* Cambridge: Cambridge University Press.

———. 1987b. *Social Theory and Archaeology.* Albuquerque: University of New Mexico Press.

———. 1989. "Archaeology into the 1990s: Comments and Questions Rather than

Answers: Reply to Comments on Archaeology into the 1990s." *Norwegian Archaeological Review* 22, no. 1:1–54.

Sherratt, A. 1983. "The Secondary Exploitation of Animals in the Old World." *World Archaeology* 15:287–316.

———. 1984. "Social Evolution: Europe in the Later Neolithic and Copper Ages." In *European Social Evolution*, edited by J. Bintliff, 123–34. Bradford, Eng.: University of Bradford.

Siefert, D., ed. 1991. *Gender in Historical Archaeology*. Special issue of *Historical Archaeology* 25, no. 4.

Silverblatt, I. 1988. "Women in States." *Annual Review of Anthropology* 17:427–60.

Slocum, S. 1975. "Woman the Gatherer: Male Bias in Anthropology." In *Toward an Anthropology of Women*, edited by R. Rapp Reiter, 36–50. New York: Monthly Review Press.

Soffer, O. 1993. "The Mutability of Upper Paleolithic 'Art' in Central and Eastern Europe: Patterning and Significance." Presented at the Society for American Archaeology, annual meeting, St. Louis.

Solomon, A. C. 1989. *Division of the Earth: Gender, Symbolism and the Archaeology of the Southern San*. Master's thesis, Department of Archaeology, University of Capetown.

Spector, J. 1991. "What This Awl Means: Toward a Feminist Archaeology." In *Engendering Archaeology: Women and Prehistory*, edited by J. Gero and M. Conkey, 388–406. Oxford: Basil Blackwell.

———. 1993. *What This Awl Means: Feminist Archaeology at a Dakota Village*. Minneapolis: Minnesota Historical Society.

Spector, J., and M. Whelan. 1989. "Incorporating Gender in Archaeology Courses." In *Gender and Anthropology: Critical Reviews for Reading and Teaching*, edited by S. Morgen, 69–94. Washington, D.C.: American Anthropological Association Press.

Stacey, J., and B. Thorne. 1985. "The Missing Feminist Revolution in Sociology." *Social Problems* 32, no. 4:301–16.

Stanton, E. C. [1898] 1974. *The Woman's Bible*. Seattle: Coalition Task Force on Women and Religion.

Starhawk. 1979. *The Spiral Dance: A Rebirth of the Ancient Religion of the Great Goddess*. San Francisco: Harper and Row.

———. 1987. *Truth or Dare*. New York: Harper and Row.

Stone, M. 1976. *When God Was a Woman*. New York: Dial Press.

Sweely, T. 1992. "Male Hunting Camp or Female Processing Station? An Evolution of a Discipline." Paper presented at the 1992 Boone Conference, Boone, N.C.

Talalay, L. 1987. "Rethinking the Function of Clay Legs from Neolithic Greece: An Argument by Analogy." *American Journal of Archaeology* 91, no. 2:161–69.

———. 1993. *Deities, Dolls, and Devices: Prehistoric Figurines from Franchthi Cave, Greece*. Bloomington: Indiana University Press.

Tanner, N. 1981. *On Becoming Human*. Cambridge: Cambridge University Press.

Tanner, N., and A. Zihlman. 1976. "Women in Evolution, Part I: Innovation and Selection in Human Origins." *Signs: Journal of Women in Culture and Society* 1, no. 3:104–19.

Trigger, B. 1989. *A History of Archaeological Thought.* Cambridge: Cambridge University Press.

Tringham, R. 1971. *Hunters, Fishers and Farmers of Eastern Europe, 6000–3000* B.C. London: Hutchinson University Press.

———. 1990. "Conclusion: Selevac in the Wider Context of European Prehistory." In *Selevac: A Neolithic Village in Yugoslavia,* edited by R. Tringham and D. Krstic, 567–616. Los Angeles: UCLA Institute of Archaeology Press.

———. 1991a. "Households with Faces: The Challenge of Gender in Prehistoric Architectural Remains." In *Engendering Archaeology: Women and Prehistory,* edited by J. Gero and M. Conkey, 93–131. Oxford: Basil Blackwell.

———. 1991b. "Men and Women in Prehistoric Architecture." *Traditional Dwellings and Settlements Review* 3, no. 1: 9–28.

———. 1992. "Visual Images of Archaeological Architecture: Gender in Space." Presented at the Annual meeting, American Anthropological Association, San Francisco.

———. 1993. "Review of M. Gimbutas, *Civilization of the Goddess.*" *American Anthropologist* 95, no. 1:196–97.

———. 1994. "Engendered Places in Prehistory." *Gender, Place and Culture* 1, no. 2:169–203.

Tringham, R., B. Brukner, T. Kaiser, K. Borojevic, N. Russell, P. Steli, M. Stevanovic, and B. Voytek. 1992. "The Opovo Project: A Study of Socioeconomic Change in the Balkan Neolithic. Second Preliminary Report." *Journal of Field Archaeology* 19, no. 3:351–86.

Tringham, R., B. Brukner, and B. Voytek. 1985. "The Opovo Project: A Study of Socioeconomic Change in the Balkan Neolithic." *Journal of Field Archaeology* 12, no. 4:425–44.

Tringham, R., and D. Krstic, eds. 1990. *Selevac: A Neolithic Village in Yugoslavia.* Los Angeles: UCLA Institute of Archaeology Press.

Ucko, P. 1968. *Anthropomorphic Figurines of Predynastic Crete and Egypt.* No. 24. London: Royal Anthropological Institute.

Ucko, P., and A. Rosenfeld. 1972. "Anthropomorphic Representations in Palaeolithic Art." *Santander Symposium: Actes del Symposium Internacional del Arte Prehistórico,* 149–211. Santander, Spain.

Walde, D., and N. Willows, eds. 1991. *The Archaeology of Gender.* Calgary: The Archaeological Association, University of Calgary.

Warren, K. 1987. "Feminism and Ecology: Making Connections." *Environmental Ethics* 9:3–20.

———. 1991. *Ecological Feminism: A Special Issue of Hypatia* 6, no. 1.

Watson, P. J., and M. Fotiadis. 1990. "The Razor's Edge: Symbolic-Structuralist Archaeology and the Expansion of Archaeological Inference." *American Anthropologist* 92, no. 3:630–46.

Watson, P. J., and M. Kennedy. 1991. "The Development of Horticulture in the Eastern

Woodlands of North America: Women's Role." In *Engendering Archaeology: Women and Prehistory*, edited by J. Gero and M. Conkey, 255–75. Oxford: Basil Blackwell.

Weaver, M. 1989. "Who Is the Goddess and Where Does She Get Us?" *Journal of Feminist Studies in Religion* 5:49–64.

Webster, P. 1975. "Matriarchy: A Vision of Power." In *Toward an Anthropology of Women*, edited by R. Rapp Reiter, 141–56. New York: Monthly Review Press.

Westkott, M. 1979. "Feminist Criticism of the Social Sciences." *Harvard Educational Review* 49:422–30.

Willey, G., and J. Sabloff. 1993. *A History of American Archaeology*, 3d ed. New York: Freeman.

Wylie, A. 1991. "Gender Theory and the Archaeological Record: Why Is There No Archaeology of Gender?" In *Engendering Archaeology: Women and Prehistory*, edited by J. Gero and M. Conkey, 31–56. Oxford: Basil Blackwell.

———. 1992a. "The Interplay of Evidential Constraints and Political Interests: Recent Archaeological Research on Gender." *American Antiquity* 57, no. 1:15–35.

———. 1992b. "Feminist Theories of Social Power: Some Implications for a Processual Archaeology." *Norwegian Archaeological Review* 25, no. 1:51–67.

———. 1992c. "On Heavily Decomposing Red Herrings: Scientific Method in Archaeology and the Ladening of Evidence with Theory." In *Meta-Archaeology*, edited by L. Embree, 269–88. Dordrecht: Kluwer Academic Publishers.

Yanagisako, S., and J. Collier. 1987. "Toward A Unified Analysis of Gender and Kinship." In *Gender and Kinship: Essays Toward a Unified Analysis*, edited by J. Collier and S. Yanagisako, 14–52. Stanford, Calif.: Stanford University Press.

Zihlman, A. 1978. "Women in Evolution, Part II: Subsistence and Social Organization in Early Hominids." *Signs: Journal of Women in Culture and Society* 4, no. 1:4–20.

———. 1981. "Women as Shapers of the Human Adaptation." In *Woman the Gatherer*, edited by F. Dahlberg, 75–120. New Haven, Conn.: Yale University Press.

Chapter 9

Unfolding Feminism: Spanish-American Women's Writing, 1970–1990

Asunción Lavrin

The last two decades have brought about significant changes in the status and social roles of Spanish-American women, the result of both historical developments and of a growing acceptance among women of the need to question their gender roles and to accept the challenges posed by contemporary feminism. The inauguration of the Decade on Women in Mexico City in 1975 forced women of the so-called Third World to reexamine the meaning of feminism as it was then debated by North American and northern European women and to develop a "position" that would reflect what they perceived to be their distinct cultural traditions and socioeconomic situation.

The political circumstances of several countries put women and men in new situations that required a redefinition of gender roles. In Central America the growing struggle against the Somoza regime in the mid-1970s was critical in bringing about the reexamination of the role women would play in the future society that the Sandinistas hoped to create. The collapse of democratic regimes in Argentina, Chile, Uruguay, and Brazil marked a watershed: questioning the authoritarianism of those regimes laid the groundwork for questioning accepted truths about all power relationships in society, including those between men and women. In countries such as Venezuela and Costa Rica, in which the idea of constitutionality seemed to have taken roots, efforts to achieve effective political democracy created opportunities to involve women in the process of reform. And in a country such as Peru, emerging from a technocratic military regime into an electoral system in the mid-1970s, the enormous economic and social problems facing the nation acted as catalyst for women in search of economic and gender equality and greater participation in rebuilding the country. Because dictatorships in several key South American countries restrained the freedom of women to define their agenda, Peru, like Mexico, became the focus of study from the mid-1970s through the mid-1980s.

Redemocratization and revolution helped to extend the concept of political democracy to personal gender relations. Democracy in the nation and at home became a universal aspiration in the 1980s, openly expressed in some South American countries as movements of resistance to military regimes began to consolidate with the full support of women. The call for democracy in gender relations was also heard in countries committed to socialist revolutions and bound to stress class over gender issues.

And yet there was no common political conjunction that forged feminism in Spanish America in the 1970s. The basis of feminist thinking and writing was a set of unresolved social, legal, and economic problems that kept women behind and under men, relegated to forms of behavior increasingly at odds with their perception of their own worth. In the mid-1970s small groups of middle-class urban women began to read North American and European feminist works, seeking ways to break traditional gender relations and to redefine women's roles in society. Sharing the ideas of feminist writers in North America and Europe helped to clarify issues, but it did not mean an unquestioned acceptance of their strategies and objectives. Spanish America is situated between the intellectual world of the West, which has extended its influence for five hundred years, and its own indigenous traditions. It has experienced colonialism as well as capitalism, and it has been profoundly marked by Marxist analysis. The women who read American and European feminist works were inspired by Marxist feminism and shared with the Left the objective of changing social structures and bringing about a more egalitarian society. Feminist expressions in Spanish America have sought to grapple with the area's complex reality: its class and landownership structure, its economic and demographic problems, its ethnic diversity, and its cultural and intellectual traditions.

Chief among the contextual factors affecting the specificity of writings on women and gender have been the concepts of *machismo* and its counterpart, *marianismo,* a dyad closely connected to the public and private spheres of influence and authority, the private as the site of the home, the public the site of all other social intercourse (Stevens 1973). *Machismo,* the superevaluation of male qualities, was said to invite and to support the physical and cultural domination of female by male and to color all acts of men outside the home. *Machos* have "balls" (*huevos* in Spanish) and must prove their masculinity under all circumstances, in their sexual relations as well as in politics, business, or work. Accepting their subordination to men in the public sphere, women are assumed to exercise power and authority in the private sphere, even though men are still recognized as the head of the family unit.[1] Moreover, women must display the feminine behavior that counterbalances the masculinity of men.

Marianismo, a term rich in religious symbolism, bases the power of women in the home on their association to the Virgin Mary and mother of God. Roman Catholicism, commonly accepted as the prevailing religion in the area, defines Mary (*María, ergo marianismo*) as a loving, forgiving, virgin mother who has the capacity for great suffering. A model for real women, Mary is the all-loving and all-sacrificing exemplar of motherhood, whose reward is constant praise and a measure of authority in the family and society. Since the 1970s social psychologists have been trying to understand the syncretic blending of the Christian model of the Virgin Mary with maternal roles in the indigenous religions to explain the sacralization of women's suffering and resignation (Montecino 1988). The model of the "self-immolating" (*sacrificada*) mother has emerged as an important theoretical basis for understanding female subordination to the male throughout time.

The traditional idea that *machismo* and *marianismo* balance each other in a dialectical manner and operate in separate spheres of power has been subjected to further critique in recent years. Analysts have shown that *marianismo* and *machismo* are constantly pitted against each other and that *marianismo* is never free to operate outside the influence of *machismo*. *Machismo* is powerful enough to invade areas of the private sphere, exert pressure over female behavior, and mold gender relations. *Marianismo* can also transcend the home and project itself into politics or public affairs by casting women as *supermadres* (Chaney 1979). A *supermadre* uses or assumes the maternal role to transform the moral authority of motherhood into power outside the home. Playing that role, women can compete with men without losing the prescribed attributes of their gender; indeed, the magnification of those attributes enhances their power.

The functional permeability of *machismo* and *marianismo* forced analysts to explore other interpretive paths, notably patriarchy as a theoretical model involving a complex system of male control over the female. Held to be more flexible and comprehensive than *marianismo* and *machismo* for explaining historical developments (Oliveira 1989; Mallon 1986), patriarchy has superseded earlier interpretations based on the public and private spheres. The patriarchal system in Spanish America operates through the political and the ecclesiastical hierarchies, which exercise their power to codify gender relations, draft and execute legislation affecting women, and uphold social values that weigh heavily over all people's lives. The notion of patriarchy in gender relations has offered an alternative to narrow Marxist interpretations that relied too heavily on economics without taking into consideration a wealth of cultural factors. Patriarchy has thus been added to the concepts of class, capitalism, and dependence to produce the particular interpretations of female subordination that pervade most contemporary feminist analysis and thought in Spanish America.

The panorama of Spanish-American feminism is too vast to be synthesized in any single essay. In the pages that follow I attempt to outline the unfolding of a feminist sensibility between 1970 and 1990. While not all women have been actors in this intellectual and social evolution, its results have affected most of them. As a historian, I seek here the testimony of all those women who have written to analyze their society, to criticize the political system, or to reflect on their own condition, but I use the term *writings* in a very broad and diverse sense.[2] Most of my sources are essays published in books, magazines, and newspapers; some are photocopies of working papers presented in informal women's studies groups; others are lectures given in national and international political and academic conferences. Whether it is journalism or academic writing in disciplines such as sociology, history, or anthropology, these writings share one common denominator: the attempt to develop a sensitivity to the experiences of women in others of the same or the opposite sex.

It is a matter of debate, however, whether this analysis of female gender can, or should, be called feminist. Writing as a feminist implies an intellectual and political commitment to a concept of feminism. Was there a stated, clearly understood concept of feminism among women in Spanish America in the 1970s and the 1980s? Are there special cultural or social factors that give Spanish-American feminists particular characteristics? The answers to these questions reflect the ambivalence and discomfort that Spanish-American women have felt toward "feminism" while attempting to determine its meaning. This situation can only be understood in the context of the history of feminism itself in Spanish America.

As feminist ideas began to be discussed in the late 1910s, a conservative backlash identified feminism as an ideology responsible for fostering antagonism between the genders while robbing women of their special "feminine" nature and masculinizing them. Feminism was regarded as a foreign influence, antithetical to traditional Spanish-American values. Thus, feminists of the first generation spilled much ink trying to demonstrate that feminism and femininity could be compatible and that feminists were not man-haters or virilized women but, rather, women who could fulfill their natural and biological roles as mothers and wives (Asize 1985; Gaviola 1986; Hahner 1990; Lavrin 1985, 1988; Little 1975, 1977; Macías 1982; Miller 1991; Paz Covarrubias 1978; and Urrutia 1990).

By the late 1910s, under pressure to gain legal equality for women in civil and family law and the recognition of women's intellectual capacity to share civic responsibilities with men in public life, feminism was interpreted as legal equality of the genders by most women and men.[3] Nevertheless, from this early period Spanish-American feminism inherited a double—and potentially contradictory—aim both to achieve legal equality with men and to preserve special protection to women as biological and social reproducers. This duality resulted from combining mid-nineteenth-century liberal feminist and socialist feminist ideas. Feminists thus demanded state intervention in the enactment of equality and protection, a position consonant with the centralized political systems of most Spanish-American nations, but they also rejected the violent pursuit of demands, "selfish" personal liberation, and radical antagonism between the genders as alien to Spanish-American culture.

Feminists of the 1970s and the 1980s had to redefine their understanding of feminism against this historical background. Ideological disputes mitigated against the construction of a universal feminist model applicable to all nations and all women concerned with gender issues. Class and ethnicity were important factors in the definition of dominant paradigms. As in the past, political allegiance to ideologies of the Left had a great deal of influence in the positions adopted at any given moment. Because Marxist analysis dominated approaches to structural and functional problems, gender was often subordinated to economic issues in many studies of women before and after 1970, though this did not preclude the study of cultural factors in the determination of gender roles in the family and the community. Indeed, the issue of whether gender ideology is rooted in a historical and cultural experience that may or may not be changed by economic factors was, and continues to be, a topic of great concern to sociologists and anthropologists.

Although the lingering reluctance to accept the term *feminism* compounded the problem of elaborating generalized feminist concepts, several key issues converged in the late 1970s that helped to redefine feminist objectives, whether the women involved called themselves feminists or not. The completion of the reform of the civil codes, a reconsideration of the political value of women's work within and outside of political parties, especially in building grass roots organizations for community projects, a reexamination of gender relations in the family, and a discussion of female sexuality as both a personal and a social issue—all these were crucial to shaping a new feminist agenda. Whether openly labeled feminist or regarded as "women's concerns" by closet feminists, those issues defined the text of Spanish-American feminism in the 1980s.

To be sure, in many instances the civil codes outlining the rights and duties of men and women in Spanish-American nations retained features inconsistent with the legal equality proffered by the laws of the nation. For example, the rights exercised by mothers and fathers over children (*patria potestad*) were undermined by clauses giving men special privileges in some legal situations. Civil divorce remained legally unaccepted in several countries, and the penal codes of others sanctioned double standards of moral behavior and of punishment for men and women. Exposure and discussion of such cases of double standard helped to achieve greater civil equality in Venezuela, Argentina, and Colombia, where legal impediments have been officially removed in the last fifteen years. Still pending is the reform of clauses in the penal code that criminalize abortion—a problem that feminist groups exposed in the 1980s.

The search for a social and political recognition of women's work became a feminist concern in the 1970s. The desire that the financial significance of women's work at the familial and national level be acknowledged, and thus that women gain a role in national policy planning, was a response to the increase of economic pressures in Spanish America. This goal had only been partially achieved by the close of the 1980s, but it helped women to appreciate the economic and political value of their labor, paid or unpaid. Equally important in gaining self-assurance and public recognition has been the increasing participation of women in movements of political resistance to dictatorial regimes, in revolutionary regimes, and in community causes, such as the rights of urban squatters to receive municipal services or in the organizing of centers to provide cheap meals. Women have become more visible, more vocal, and more personally conscious of their needs and their abilities to fulfill them.

THE ACTIVISM OF WOMEN'S ORGANIZATIONS

More than any other factor, the development of women's organizations accounts for the specificity of feminism in Spanish America. The small groups of Marxist-feminists who were influenced by North American and European works had an ephemeral life in the 1970s due to internal dissension or to a lack of financial resources. Their collapse is now attributed to the separation of women into two camps: those seeking to involve working women in developing pragmatic social objectives and those seeking to elucidate the problems of gender subordination first before striving to attract women of all classes to the women's movement (Urrutia 1984; Mariátegui 1975; and Partido Izquierda Unida 1975).[4]

The feminist groups that survived the early 1980s underwent a profound process of introspection and self-analysis. These were the years of "the second growth," when feminists learned that the initial assumption that they knew what was good for all women reproduced patterns of domination of middle-class over lower-class women (Vargas 1984). Pluralism and democracy remain a difficult goal to achieve in all feminist organizations, demanding as it does flexibility and constant self-examination. Although the struggle has taken many casualties and seen many groups perish, new organizations still come to life and give continuity to the presence of feminism in the major urban centers. The key to the success of the organizations that survived the 1980s has been an ability to redefine their goals to meet new political situations, broaden their activities, become more inclusive, and accommodate the preoccupations of women of different classes. They have acknowledged that factors such as ethnicity, social class, education, and age have to be taken into consideration to understand women's subordination and to achieve a better link between reality and the ideals of feminism (Brandel 1985; Campos Carr 1990; Saporta 1992; and Sojo 1985, 69–104.

Activist writers have recognized the efforts of slum dwellers and poor women to organize services for their communities and their families, and they have understood that, in helping such women to achieve their goals, they are also helping them to become conscious of the problems created by gender (Lora et al. 1985; Montaño Virreina 1992; *Presencia de la mujer* 1980). These activists differ from those in the early 1970s who identified the specific needs of women and were anxious to promote a change in gender relations but were reluctant to call themselves feminists. As early as 1969, women such as the Mexican Sociologist Ifigenia Navarrete emphasized the value of daily life as a training ground for confronting larger social issues. Women "can and should engage in a daily and creative activity from within the home, the school room, or the work place"; they must "confer to each and every one of their daily actions a conscious social meaning, so that . . . their preoccupations and decisions, especially those affecting the family, are not theirs alone, but part of a general social framework" (Navarrete 1969, 90–92; Elú de Leñero 1969).[5] Navarette and others, however, did not encourage women to achieve those objectives through any type of feminism.

The feminism that began to take shape in the 1980s depended on self-knowledge and knowledge of the "otherness" of women of a different class or lesser education. This was accomplished by learning about, and with, such women and by allowing them to learn by, about, and for themselves (*10 años* 1988; Acevedo et al. 1988; *La imagen de la mujer* 1981; Lau Jaiven 1987; Pérez Alemán and Díaz 1987). Associations of working and/or poor women rarely begin by defining themselves as feminist, but feminist activists claim that such groups gain a consciousness of the uniqueness of women's problems. Although this assumption is not unanimous and the results have been uneven, most Spanish-American feminist writers believe in the possibility of achieving personal and social change through women's associations at all socioeconomic levels that encourage the discussion of specific women's issues, such as the provision of services to the family, reproduction, and sexuality. Through their organizational activity women will grow confident in their ability to express themselves politically at home and in the community. The many housewives' committees organized in the poor neighborhoods of several capital cities, for example, help to solve immediate problems of inflation and survival in circumstances of poverty. At a higher level of development such organizations help to create a memory of women's lives, a space that women feel is theirs, and, eventually, to redefine social rules of behavior and accommodate "women's values" in the larger society. Several *Casas de la Mujer* (Women's Homes) have been founded in capital and provincial cities to develop a feminist agenda and to foster both knowledge of the law and self-confidence among women of all social classes (*La lucha* 1990; *Mujeres maltratadas* 1990).[6]

Yet some feminists harbor doubts about the effectiveness of such popular centers. In their opinion poor women still lack the gender, and sometimes the ethnic solidarity, to redress the problems of personal and legal female subordination (Ardaya 1986; Bargin 1987; Filippini 1987; Gogna 1987). In Bolivia, for example, the rural—mostly Indian—National Federation of Peasant Women Bartolina Sisa is a powerful organization, but, according to Gloria Ardaya, it cannot reverse female subordination without a strong gender consciousness. Yet even those who are skeptical about the impact of small female groups see that they encourage the discussion of topics of vital interest to women and the sharing of personal experiences without intermediaries—a situation viewed as a prerequisite to the eventual acceptance of feminism by women of all social classes (Lora et al. 1985; Martínez 1989).

Whether or not a significant understanding of feminism is achieved through women's organizations in poor or middle-class neighborhoods, there has been a vigorous multiplication of women's associations in all Spanish-American capitals. Made up of nonhierarchical, democratic groups developing their own interests, this fragmentation is regarded as a healthy development by some. Others consider it problematic, the symptom of a lack of unity and direction, an obstacle to the implementation of objectives that weakens the participatory process. Analyzing this fragmentation and the diversity of women's groupings throughout Spanish America, Mexican scholar Lourdes Arizpe claims that a feminist perspective is obvious even in those women who deny being feminists. Women's interest in incorporating the "personal" into the political space that men have defined in their own image represents a truly revolutionary concept, for Arizpe, whether or not women acknowledge their adherence to a feminist ideology. All these associations make genuine social demands and take the only channel open to them, since traditional male-dominated parties either resist or are unable to incorporate women's concerns (Arizpe 1988, 1989).[7]

The experience of feminist groups who have actively supported revolutionary or radical movements of the Left has not been satisfying, and their reflections on this experience have helped them to define more clearly their objectives as feminists. Gloria Ardaya, a Bolivian supporter of the *Movimiento de Izquierda Revolucionaria* (MIR), a party in which men maintained a traditional gender division of activities and responsibilities (Ardaya Salinas 1986a, b; Vargas 1986, 45–66), recalled the efforts of its Women's Front (*Frente de Mujeres*) to deny any connection with feminism. Eventually, she and other *miristas* concluded that they were feminists and geared their efforts toward understanding the interconnection of sexism, the patriarchal nature of their society, and capitalism.

The case of Bolivia is not atypical. The relationship between the Left and feminism has had an uneven history in the region as a whole. Male leaders have sought female support, but they have adhered to the traditional assumption of the primacy of class over gender in the struggle to change social structures. In addressing the role of women either within their ranks or in society at large, they have upheld the view of women as mothers and nurturers, casting any deviation from traditional notions as foreign or capitalistic. Only in the last several years have male leftists changed their sexist language and attitudes (Barbieri 1987; Puyeski 1987).

The Nicaraguan revolution helps to illustrate the process of conjoining leftist and feminist concepts. Whereas revolutionary Nicaraguan ideas contained only a schematic call for women's rights and equality in the mid-1970s, Sandinista leaders tried to address the needs of women in the revolution upon taking power and created a female association, Asociación de Mujeres Nicaraguenses Luisa Amanda Espinosa (AMNLAE), to channel women's energies. AMNLAE was a mass organization for disseminating propaganda and educating the "common woman" that capitalized on the image of willing revolutionary mothers— cheerfully offering their children to the cause or suffering for the sake of the revolution—and that emphasized the protection and welfare that the state would eventually give working women. The middle-of-the-road line adopted by the organization recognized the existence of specific female demands but assumed that women's needs would be met by the revolutionary achievements; like the government, the AMNLAE adopted a cautious policy on women's reproductive rights and sexuality (Maier 1985, 89; Molyneux 1985, 89; 1988; Murguialday 1990; Pérez 1990, 121; Rodríguez 1991).[8] More openly, the 1987 statement that AMNLAE "rejected tendencies claiming that women's emancipation would result from struggles against men or that it was an exclusive female preserve" (Molyneux 1988, 121–22) reflected a long-held prejudice against feminism as alienating both men and women.

Recent analyses by Nicaraguan feminists on the role of the AMNLAE in the 1980s suggest that it did not succeed in formulating a feminist agenda, because it was torn by internal conflicts and the competing demands of the social revolution. A more genuine feminist discourse was developed in *Barricada,* the revolutionary newspaper that served as a forum for the ideological debates of a small group of feminists who began to object to AMNLAE's bland definitions of women's emancipation, especially after 1985. Women of upper- and middle-class background who supported the revolution examined the contradictions between the Sandinista government's statements and its policies. The result was the formulation of truly feminist reforms in the open debates that preceded the writing of a new Constitution of the nation. From 1987 onward female subordination within the family, male abandonment, physical and moral violence, abortion, sexual education, and women's reproductive rights gained space in discussions of the Sandinista program. The integration of feminism into the revolutionary agenda was achieved from within by women who openly called them-

selves feminists after 1985 and who argued that there was no contradiction between revolution and feminism. As one feminist supporter put it succinctly, "To
be a feminist is the exigency of being a revolutionary" (Murguialday 1990, 242).[9]

Increasing economic obstacles, a civil war, and international pressure made it
impossible to realize many of the objectives outlined by the new feminist leadership in Nicaragua. One of the most important achievements, however, was the
recognition of a nonnegotiable agenda specific to women that differed from
traditional Marxist definitions of emancipation. The inclusion of peasant and
poor urban women in the popular meetings led to the identification of gender-
based subordination as a key point in the feminist agenda. This was surprising
and gratifying for middle-class feminists and suggested the feasibility of bridging
the chasm between gender and class in a leftist context. Unfortunately, the
official rejection of *machista* attitudes and of the hegemony of men in society
was adopted too late—just before the electoral defeat of *sandinismo* in 1990.
Whether or not the intellectual challenge of formulating this agenda remains is a
question for the future.

Critiquing the Left has not been as difficult as critiquing the authoritarian
regimes of the Right, given the repressive means at their disposal. The case of the
Southern Cone nations is emblematic of the means used by women, often the
victims of repression, to become a part of organized resistance to dictatorship
(Alvarez 1990; Jaquette 1985; and Valenzuela 1987).[10] While relatively little is
known in the United States about feminist groups in those countries since the
early 1980s, the Madres de la Plaza de Mayo became newsworthy. They began
as groups of mothers who gathered weekly in the central park of Buenos Aires in
1976 to demand information on "the disappeared"—relatives imprisoned or
executed by the military in what was known as "the dirty war." The military
could not get rid of these women, who drew world attention and helped to
discredit the regime's pretension of stability and to reveal its internal brutality.

The Madres have generated much discussion among feminists. Since the
group's members did not identify themselves as feminists, could these grieving
mothers be regarded as furthering the feminist cause and creating a political
space for women? Or did they use the traditional stereotypes and resort to
strategies that would strengthen traditional gender relations in the long run?
Wearing white head scarves, which transformed them into images of Mary as
Mater dolorosa, they appeared to exploit the emotional appeal of a religious
stereotype. The *marianismo* iconography of sacrifice and suffering merged with
the power conferred to the mother who sought redress and successfully challenged a military regime. Some have denied the Madres any role in the construction of feminism because of the weight of these traditional elements; others have
argued that, without being feminists, they expanded the boundaries of traditional politics and succeeded in making their personal problem a political issue

that eventually helped to weaken the male superstructure. Furthermore, the Madres broke with social expectations and gained an identity precisely because they defended their "right" to be mothers (Agosín 1990; Bousquet 1983; Brandel 1985, 15; and Oria 1987).[11] Over and beyond different views about their achievements, the Madres reaffirmed the value of seeking alternative uses for symbols of motherhood in Spanish America. At the same time, and as the ideological debate in Nicaragua indicates, the use of motherhood to postpone or mask the lack of change is increasingly becoming unacceptable to most mobilized women.

Spanish-American feminists are aware that revolutionary and socialist experiences have not given women equal participation in high-level political posts. They are using their political experience to understand gender relations and using feminism to analyze politics. In the late 1980s the concept of democracy itself was debated, not only as a political system but also as a means of questioning the internal structures of feminist groups, the hierarchical relationship of men and women in the home, and men's interpretation of equal responsibilities and rights for the two sexes (Birgin 1987; Casas 1987). For Spanish-American feminists politics involves more than the aspiration to power in the public arena; it is also "the struggle to recover all the opportunities for self-determination denied women" (Brandel 1985, 3). In the hothouse of the repressive politics of the late 1970s and early 1980s, feminism began to question all expressions of authoritarianism and to stand for a broad understanding of human rights. Feminism in Spanish America differed from its expression in North America or western Europe, where women lived under political systems that allowed free expression and did not threaten their lives.

WOMEN'S VOICES, WOMEN'S WRITING

The reality of political dictatorship in her country and Michel Foucault's theory of knowledge were the foundations upon which the Chilean writer Julieta Kirkwood built what is perhaps the most powerful of feminist voices in South America. Her untimely death in 1985 did not prevent her from making a marked impact on the shape of present-day feminist writings. Kirkwood argued that, whenever the contradictions between Western ideals of equality and the realities of female oppression become obvious, women express their defiance in one way or another, a real and deeply felt defiance, not a "neurotic" desire for alternative political activities (Kirkwood 1980, 1981, 1983, and 1986; see also Chuchryk 1983, 323, 330–36). Although she leaned toward the political Left, Kirkwood reproached leftist ideologies and governments for seeing feminism merely as a set of claims emanating from the private sphere. Because the Left had failed to accommodate the demands of women, the Right had succeeded in manipulating them for their own ends, Kirkwood argued. She understood that political repression creates the appropriate climate for the study of its roots and its manifestations—and the search for its cure. Kirkwood worked within the Círculo de Estudios de la Mujer (CEM), founded in 1979; it was superseded by the Center for the Study of Women (also CEM) in 1984. This and other organizations aimed to build an alternative form of democracy that would put an end to authoritarianism in all forms, especially that of man over woman (Hola 1987).[12] Several research centers have been established since then, which have published perceptive analyses of the role of militarism and patriarchalism in the development of a culture of gender domination (Valenzuela 1987). Similar situations of political oppression have produced groups of active feminists in Uruguay, Paraguay, and Central America (Corvalán 1986; Filgueira 1985; García y Gomáriz 1989; and Prates y Rodríguez 1985).

The writings of Julieta Kirkwood in the mid-1980s also strengthened the testimonial movement known as *protagonismo*. Hope for a change in the female condition, she argued, depended on a redefinition of oppression from within— that is, from women's daily experience of discrimination. Women would translate their experiences into collective political consciousness and political participation. Testimonial studies would be the means for women to recognize themselves and to reach other women, for identifying and revising the objectives of female organizations, and for measuring the state's response to the needs of women in the formulation of policies.

This movement of testimonial writing was based on one of the binding assumptions of Spanish-American feminism since the beginning of the twentieth century: that women must speak to define their own agenda. The spoken word has accompanied the printed word in the unfolding of feminism and has helped to make it a living reality for women. Getting women to use their voices to express their own understanding of womanhood and their experiences as workers, wives, and daughters was a preferred form of feminist initiation in the 1970s. Esther Andrade and Ana María Portugal, two Peruvian journalists, gained notoriety in their country with *Ser mujer en el Perú* (1978), a series of interviews recorded as monologues on achieving self-consciousness as a woman. Whereas this empathetic proximity to female subjects had previously been possible only through literature, now each "portrait" aimed to express the way in which each woman's experience was constructed by her social, ethnic, and economic circumstances. Openly feminist, *Ser mujer en el Perú* challenged stereotypes about women and avoided the limitations of "cold" sociological analysis—an excellent example of the use of journalism in Spanish America to help women value their personal experiences (Andrade and Portugal 1978; Elú de Leñero 1971).[13]

Testimonial texts, such as *Ser mujer en el Perú*, transpose the words of women who have been assumed to lack political views or to understand organization and mobilization. They are nonelitist texts that give voice to those who would have never left a trace in history (Alvarado 1987; Arenal 1986; Barros de Chungara 1978; Burgos Debray 1984; Delpino 1990; Gálvez and Todaro 1985; Montecino 1986; Randall 1972, 1980; and Sejourné 1980). These works have become a new kind of political text, involving the domestic, communal, and national levels. They also symbolize the continued effort of contemporary Spanish-American feminists to give women the opportunity to be protagonists of their own lives, to become conscious of their own destiny, and to be in full command of their actions. *Protagonismo* represents the first-person, singular and plural (*yo* and *nosotras*), an act of female self-advocacy emblematic of the task of mobilization assumed by those who record and publish their own activities and those of other women.

Protagonismo has encouraged women to develop knowledge in areas that are both personal and political, such as sexuality. In the last twenty years the discussion of sexually related topics demanded great courage from feminists, who strove to overcome the sexual oppression of the male and the stereotype of the suffering madonna, to expose the double standard of morality, to question health policies, and to promote discussion of contraceptives, family planning, and abortion. Feminists have spoken for a silent majority in some instances, and in others they have discussed topics and changes that most men and women regard as too radical or premature for consideration in their countries. Physical violence at home, a topic hardly discussed at the beginning of the 1980s, suddenly came into the open, following the feminist exposé of the misogynist system of values encoded in the legal system and in the culture of violence that allowed the political dysfunction experienced in countries such as Colombia, Uruguay, Chile, and Argentina (Vaín 1988; Giberti and Fernández 1988; Sánchez y Egas 1988; *La violencia* 1992; *Mujer/Fempress* 1992, 1–4). The discussion of personal violence has helped to unveil the feelings of women and to underscore the many types of violence that can be committed against women: violence in the cultural realm (sexism in the media and in politics); the psychological domain (fear within the family); in the social milieu (violence in the streets, sexism in the workplace, and political repression); in the sexual sphere (rape and sterilization); and in the actions of some institutional structures (the laws and the church). The debate on violence has become politically charged precisely because it involves both genders and cannot be dismissed as a "women's issue" (Chanduvi Pasto 1985; Eherenfeld Lickewics 1987; *El marco social* 1988; Hiriart and Ortega 1985; Portugal 1989; Silva 1988; Tocón Armas and Mendiburu 1987; and Torrado 1987).[14]

These themes have been taken up in gender-marked writing and become visible due to the growing presence and influence of female writers. Women writers have discussed the meaning that feminism and social struggle hold for them, translating their ideas into socially committed works that reflect the concerns of activists and academics. Writers of the last twenty years, such as Elena Poniatowska, Rosario Ferré, María Luisa Valenzuela, Gioconda Belli, Angeles Mastretta, Ana Lydia Vega, Isabel Allende, Cristina Peri-Rossi, and others, do not examine women exclusively but also the set of values that defines gender relations and political systems in their respective countries (Bassnett 1990; Castedo-Ellerman 1978; Castro-Klarén, Molly, and Sarlo 1991; Fernández Olmos 1991; Ferré 1990; Franco 1989; González and Ortega 1985; Meyer and Fernández Olmos 1983; Picón Garfield 1988).

As this suggests, Spanish-American feminists are not primarily concerned with theory,[15] yet their fieldwork and their writings indicate a significant knowledge of the theories currently under discussion in North America and Europe and a sustained effort to apply those that seem relevant to the realities of their societies. The Mexican anthropologist Marcela Lagarde recently published an incisive analysis of the concept of power among men and women and its expression among Latin Americans, which promises to broaden the field of feminist theory in the area (Lagarde 1990; Sojo 1985). Moreover, the process of writing a history of women has begun, as female historians realize the gender void in the national memory and in the construction of nationality. Unfortunately, scholars lack the financial resources required to engage in sustained academic discussions on feminist theory and methodology. Nevertheless, they do emerge in a variety of ways—in workshops organized by perennially underfinanced centers for the study of women, in the analysis and criticism of the political behavior of the still mostly male national leadership, and in rubbing shoulders with women living in poor neighborhoods.

Academic writing by Spanish-American feminists is primarily exemplified by studies in the social sciences—notably, economics and sociology. Research in those disciplines stimulated the discussion of women's economic role more intensely than any other topic in the 1970s and 1980s. In an effort to develop a national consciousness of women's worth and to force a political and economic reevaluation that would help to undermine male politico-economic domination in the family and the community, female economists and sociologists began to focus on women's massive incorporation into the labor market, especially the informal sector of the economy, which policymakers had neglected (Bonilla 1985; León 1985; León and Deere 1986; and Wienerman 1981, 1987). These studies analyzed the role of urban and rural women in the national and regional economies and the economic structure of poor families in urban and rural settings.

From Marxist analysis some economists and sociologists took the concepts of women as biological reproducers of the productive agents of society and social reproducers of the patterns of production. With these tools in hand they aimed to examine the positive and negative effects on women of economic change and development plans.[16] While these writers were closer to the Left than to feminism, their work had an undeclared feminist subtext. Similar studies have been prepared by professionals at the centers for the study of the population, by governmental agencies, and, since the mid-1980s, by women's studies centers. The pragmatic nature of this research is not accidental. Sociologists and economists are employed by public or private organizations that seek to formulate developmental objectives. They have factored gender into their analyses, and the information they have generated is relevant to any number of social problems. The most recent research focuses on the informal and the service sectors of labor, in which the female presence is overwhelming: women in the "street economy" sustain the home economy in poorer countries, such as Peru, while domestic employment remains a significant occupation in the service sector (Arizpe 1977; Bourque 1989; Butler Flora 1989; Cooper et al. 1989; Osterling 1982; and Schmink 1982). These writings also underline the effects on the family of macroeconomic factors, such as national debts, internal and external patterns of migration, and the cycles of the world economy. While this type of analysis may not be new to industrialized countries, it has only recently begun in Spanish America (Arteaga 1985; Montecino 1984; Todaro y Gálvez 1987; and Valdés 1988).

Peruvian feminist Ana María Portugal aptly summarized the meaning of socioeconomic research for feminism in the mid-1980s when she wrote that to be a feminist did not only mean a battle against sexism, authoritarianism, domestic violence, and the repression of sexuality; it necessarily involved the material conditions of poverty of the majority of the people—hunger, lack of housing and of public health facilities, low salaries, and unemployment. "The challenge," she declared, "is to find the connection between economic discrimination and machista oppression, between capitalist exploitation and patriarchal exploitation" (Portugal 1986).

Spanish-American feminist analysis of the 1970s and early 1980s has shown a primary interest in the relation between gender, development, and capitalism. The definition of capitalism as the external but ultimate causal factor of female oppression confirms the conjunction of feminist and leftist thought in the 1970s and much of the 1980s, a period when the economic conditions of most Spanish-American countries were critical. Given the lack of flexibility of most Spanish-American economies and the ties of economic dependency created by massive investments of foreign capital for over a century, the stance against capitalism is understandable. Thus, a Peruvian feminist could conclude that "the woman of the popular classes is responsible for the maintenance and reproduction of the labor force, providing clothing and food for her family. . . . This is a key element for understanding the marginalization in which women live in our society. . . . The fact that this labor is not paid allows the capitalist to save and increase his profits" (*Presencia de la mujer* 17–18). The argument may be couched in more sophisticated terms to express what many socialist or Marxist feminists believe, as *Feminismo y política* makes clear, that the specificity of Latin American feminism is not its alignment with popular sectors per se but its hope to understand how, in concrete situations, women suffer both sexual subordination and other types of oppression. To patriarchal logic must be added capitalist logic, which further oppresses women, converting them into a cheap and undervalued source of labor as well as consumers who defend the very system that imprisons them. The anticapitalist theme was also very strong in revolutionary contexts, such as that of Nicaragua. In 1984 Milú Vargas Escobar, Sandinista and feminist, wrote that women wished for "a society in which we can look with our own eyes; touch the world with our own hands; translate our experiences in our own mind; create our own words, and remove our mask of exploitation, illiteracy, discrimination, hunger and misery; a mask not only imposed upon us, but encrusted into our skin throughout centuries of imperialism" (qtd. in Rodríguez 1991, 154).[17]

Capitalism has been perceived as a factor that has retarded women's potential emancipation from traditional gender roles (Lavrin 1989, 1992).[18] Transnational corporations, or *maquiladora* industries, which use large numbers of female workers in border areas and in several capital cities, exploit the cheap labor of third world women to sustain the consumer demands of more developed countries. This example, which shows how there can be change without a real transformation of women's economic status, also has intense nationalistic appeal. The nationalistic theme has helped to draw analogies between the position of women and that of the nation with respect to foreign enterprises, since both are at the mercy of foreign markets and economically developed nations. The use of nationalism in the development of gender consciousness adds another dimension to third world feminism and creates potential sources of conflict with feminists of more developed nations (Gálvez and Todaro 1986, 1988; Grau 1982; Múñoz Dálbora 1988; and Rechini de Lattes 1980).

The study of women's economic status has been a key analytical tool in Spanish-American feminist writings. By assessing the effects on women of the macroeconomic system and of the economic decisions taken by the state, female analysts hope to create new strategies for economic change at the micro- and macroeconomic levels and to mobilize women for political action. In their mobilization women should have a clear idea of their subordination and a plan to end it. This plan should not be defined by researchers but, instead, by working women themselves (León and Deere 1986; Valdés 1987). The emphasis on women of the lower economic levels is emblematic of the conscious efforts of middle-class women to bridge the gap separating them from the objects of their study and to give poor women the means to assess their own worth.

Feminism is at a crossroads in Spanish America today. There is a growing awareness of the political relevance of gender issues as they have been tested against authoritarian, revolutionary, and evolutionary regimes. Even women with little education and minimal exposure to sophisticated theories have identified problems specific to their sex and understood the need to create a more balanced relationship between the genders. The issue at stake is when and how opportunities for learning and for making choices about their lives will be available to them and for how long. In some sectors of revolutionary and evolutionary thought feminism exists only as a subtext. Twenty years of social struggle have brought about significant changes of attitude toward feminist issues, but there is still fear, reservation, and inhibition about calling oneself a feminist.

Feminists of various social and ethnic backgrounds in Spanish America are struggling to find a form of individual and collective action that is not divorced from the pressing social and economic needs of their countries. It would be misleading to think that these women represent a marginal movement that merely reflects models created elsewhere. Feminism can have global appeal: sharing the commonality of gender problems leads to commonalities of perception and expression. The distinctiveness of feminism is created by the economic and cultural heritage of each area or each people and the efforts both to "read" models evolved in other countries and to redefine them for one's own context. Feminists have responded to the specific political and economic situations of their nations and succeeded in giving to feminism in Spanish America its own characteristics, nuances, rhythms, and vision of the future. Of course, there is also diversity among feminists within the continent. The commonalities created by similar situations of sexism or of politics (e.g., military, authoritarian regimes) are counterbalanced by each country's specific economic and political situation, its demographic configuration, and its different stage in the development of a feminist consciousness. Thus, each country offers a spectrum of feminist responses. Understanding the nuances of the various countries of Spanish America, despite their common language, common legal heritage, and common cultural understanding of gender relations, is nothing short of essential. At this exciting moment in its development we need to listen to Spanish-American feminism, read it carefully, and preserve the record of its complex existence for future generations.

NOTES

1. Yet there has been a significant number of female-headed families, dating back several centuries and remaining a reality in many areas and in many countries. Their

existence casts some doubts on the solidity of the patriarchal family though by no means obliterates its reality (Gutiérrez 1991; Kuznesof 1989; Lavrin 1989). The existence of a "countercultural" family unit sustained by the mother has helped to give motherhood an axial quality, whether within the legal family or outside it. Motherhood emerges from historical studies with enhanced significance and explains the heavy spiritual and ethical weight it still carries today.

2. In this essay I survey writings in Spanish by Spanish-American women. I quote titles in English if they have proven to be influential in the elaboration of a feminist ideology in the area. Many feminist theoreticians have been translated into Spanish, and it is through translations that their works have become known in Spanish America.

3. The demand for suffrage, which was not a central issue in the early 1900s, had become an important item in the feminist agenda by the mid-1920s, but most countries did not grant it until after World War II.

4. Ana María Portugal and Virginia Vargas, in an interview with Elena Urrutia. For a leftist position see, *Mariátegui y el movimiento feminino* and the program of Partido Izquierda Unida.

5. An official counselor to the presidency and a university professor, Navarrete urged greater participation of women in public activities, but in her efforts to remain "neutral" she uttered no criticism of the government.

6. One of the most active is *Casa de la Mujer* in Bogotá, Colombia, which publishes simple, didactic self-instruction booklets on family and penal law. In Lima, Peru, *Centro Flora Tristán* also carries out similarly active projects combining social work and feminism.

7. Unfortunately, so far neither barrio groups nor middle-class women's associations have been able to gain much leverage within traditional parties (Lau Jaivén 1987, 146–47; *Mujer y Política*, 93–94).

8. Ironically, before 1985 women who insisted on claiming the logical development of the ideology of equality were called *machista* feminists. The prevalence of sexist attitudes among the peasants' organizations is discussed by Paola Pérez. See Tomás Borge's acknowledgment that gender relations do not spontaneously change with economic development, in Maier 1985, 89.

9. An interview with feminist Sandinistas in October 1986 brought about several short but meaningful definitions of *feminism* by women politically active in the revolutionary government. Their definitions were short and pragmatic, such as: "Feminism means not to accept traditional roles of submission"; "All struggle for the rights of women and for their emancipation is feminism"; "One is a feminist to integrate oneself into society." They agreed that bringing the problems of women into the open and discussing them as politically relevant were the most important achievements of the previous years. See Murguialday 1990, 208–48.

10. Although Portuguese-speaking Brazil is not under review in this essay, the feminist movement there is among the most powerful in South America. A comparison with Spanish America would be fruitful.

11. The Argentinean mothers were not the first to seek power through gender role solidarity. A group of mothers began to meet in Chile in 1973, and another was organized in El Salvador in 1981.

12. *La Morada* is another center of feminist activism in Santiago. Feminists sought the protection of the church during the years of dictatorship, but their ties ended because of growing disagreements on key issues. The church continued its own welfare and episcopal work among poor women.

13. Andrade and Portugal follow Simone de Beauvoir's statement that "one is not born a woman, one becomes a woman." Works that registered women's feelings were published before. For example, the 1971 interview carried out by Elú de Leñero compiled women's views on contraceptive methods.

14. See the issue of the Mexican journal *FEM* dedicated to domestic violence (11 [June 1987]: 54).

15. In Uruguay GRECMU, a center for the research of women, has sponsored the publication of several works on women's history and organizes seminars and conferences on women. In Mexico City the "Seminar for the Study of Women" of Colegio de Mexico encourages the publication of works on women and offers classes on a variety of topics.

16. In 1978 Chilean Carlos Borsotti criticized feminist studies for their narrow concern with legal and ideological discrimination and their neglect of the relation between women and development (Borsotti 1978); in his opinion correcting the myopia of the national planner should be the first task of feminists.

17. These writers seem to be inspired by Zillah Eisenstein's work on the relationship between patriarchy and capitalism. For another reaction to Eisenstein's writings, see Sojo 1985, 50–52.

18. The incisive critique by the Left of the inequalities of wealth distribution was already present in the analysis of the early-twentieth-century feminists, many of whom developed under the umbrella of socialism.

WORKS CITED

10 años de periodismo feminista. 1988. Mexico: Planeta.

Acevedo, Marta, et al. 1988. "Mexico: una bolsita de cal por las que van de arena." In *10 años,* 111–48.

Acosta Belén, Edna, and Christine E. Bose, eds. 1993. *Researching Women in Latin America and the Caribbean.* Boulder: Westview Press.

Agosin, Marjorie. 1990. *The Mothers of Plaza de Mayo.* Trenton: The Red Sea Press.

Alvarado, Elvia. 1987. *Don't Be Afraid, Gringo: A Honduran Woman Speaks from the Heart.* New York: Harper and Row.

Alvarez, Sonia. 1990. *Engendering Democracy in Brazil: Women's Movements in Transition Politics.* Princeton: Princeton University Press.

Andrade, Ester, and Ana María Portugal. 1978. *Ser mujer en el Perú.* Lima: Ediciones Mujer y Autonomía.

Ardaya Salinas, Gloria. 1986a. "The Barzolas and the Housewives Committee." In *Women and Change in Latin America,* ed. June Nash and Helen Safa, 326–43. South Hadley, Mass.: Bergin and Garvey.

———. 1986b. "Política y feminismo." In *Feminismo y política,* 38–43. La Paz: Coordinadora de la Mujer.

Arenal, Sandra. 1986. *Sangre Joven. Las maquiladoras por dentro.* Mexico: Editorial Nuestro Tiempo.

Aresti, Lore, et al. 1984. "La violación, delito contra la libertad." *FEM* 8, no. 32 (February–March): 29–31.

Arizpe, Lourdes. 1977. "Women in the Informal Labor Sector: The Case of Mexico City." *Signs* 3, no. 1 (Autumn): 38–56.

———. 1988. "Democracia para un pequeño planeta bigenérico." In *10 años de periodismo feminista,* 327–35.

———. 1989. *La mujer en el desarrollo de Mexico y la América Latina.* Mexico: UNAM.

Arteaga, Ana María. 1985. *Mujeres populares: 20 años de investigación en Chile.* Santiago: Centro de Estudios de la Mujer.

Asize, Yamila. 1985. *La mujer en la lucha.* Río Piedras, Puerto Rico: Editorial Cultural.

Barbieri, M. Teresita de. 1988. "El feminismo y la Federación de Mujeres Cubanas." In *10 años de periodismo feminista,* 159–69.

Barros de Chungara, Domitila, with Moema Viezzer. 1978. *Let me speak! Testimony of Domitila, A Woman of the Bolivian Mines.* New York: Monthly Review Press.

Bassnett, Susan. 1990. *Knives and Angels: Women Writers in Latin America.* London: Zed.

Birgin, Haydée. 1987. "Mujer Hoy: un espacio de las mujeres en los barrios." In *Participación política de las mujeres del Cono Sur,* 1:241–62.

Bonilla, C. Elsy, comp. 1985. *Mujer y familia en Colombia.* Bogotá: Plaza Janes Editores.

Borsotti, Carlos A. 1978. "Situación de la mujer y desarrollo: Acotaciones." In *Chile: mujer y sociedad,* ed. Paz Covarrubias and Rolando Franco, 753–79. Santiago de Chile: Unicef.

Bourque, Susan C. 1989. "Urban Development." In *Latinas of the Americas: A Source Book,* ed. K. Lynn Stoner, 554–80. New York: Garland.

Bousquet, J. P. 1983. *Las locas de la plaza de Mayo.* Buenos Aires: El Cid Editor.

Brandel, Silvina, et al. 1985. *Feminismo y política. Contribución al debate en el feminismo argentino.* Buenos Aires: n.p.

Burgos-Debray, Elisabeth. 1984. *I, Rigoberta Menchu: An Indian Woman in Guatemala.* London: Verso.

Butler Flora, Cornelia. 1989. "Rural Development." In *Latinas of the Americas: A Source Book,* ed. K. Lynn Stoner, 535–58. New York: Garland.

Campos Carr, Irene. 1990. "Women's Voices Grow Stronger: Politics and Feminism in Latin America." *NWSA Journal* 2, no. 3 (Summer): 405–63.

Casas, Nelly. 1987. "Situación actual de las mujeres en la Argentina y estrategias para el cambio." In *Participación política de la mujer en el Cono Sur: Conferencia Internacional,* 1:43–51.

Castedo-Ellerman, Elena. 1978. "¿Feminismo o Femineidad? Seis escritoras opinan." In *Américas* 30, no. 10 (October): 15–24.

Castro-Klarén, Sara, Sylvia Molloy, and Beatriz Sarlo, eds. 1991. *Women's Writing in Latin America: An Anthology.* Boulder: Westview Press.

Chanduví Pasto, Gloria Alicia. 1985. "Violencia contra la mujer." *Brujas* (Medellín, Col.) 5 (April): 52–60.

Chaney, Elsa. 1979. *Supermadre: Women in Politics in Latin America.* Austin: University of Texas Press.

Chuchryk, Patricia Marie. 1983. "Protest, Politics and Personal Life: The Emergence of Feminism in a Military Dictatorship, Chile, 1974–1983." Ph.D diss., York University.

Corvalán, Graziella. 1986. "La acción colectiva de las mujeres en el Paraguay." In *Los movimientos sociales en el Paraguay,* ed. Rodrigo Rivarola, 91–136. Asunción: Centro Paraguayo de Estudios Sociales.

Covarrubias, Paz. 1978. "El movimiento feminista chileno." In *Chile: Mujer y Sociedad,* comp. Paz Covarrubias and Rolando Franco, 615–48. Santiago de Chile: Unicef.

Crispi, Patricia, ed. 1987. *Tejiendo rebeldías: Escritos feministas de Julieta Kirkwood.* Santiago de Chile: Centro de Estudios de la Mujer and Casa de la Mujer La Morada.

Delpino, Nena. 1990. *Saliendo a flote. La jefa de familia popular.* Lima: Fundación Friedrich Naumann.

Ehrenfeld Lenkewicz, Noemí. 1989. "El ser mujer: Identidad, sexualidad y reproducción." In *Trabajo, poder y sexualidad,* coord. Orlandina de Oliveira, 383–98. Mexico: El Colegio de Mexico.

El marco social de la violencia contra las mujeres en la vida conyugal. 1988. Santurce, P.R.: Centro de Investigaciones Sociales.

Elú de Leñero, María del Carmen. 1969. *¿Hacia donde va la mujer mexicana?* Mexico: Instituto Mexicano de Estudios Sociales.

———. 1971. *Mujeres que hablan.* Mexico: Instituto Mexicano de Estudios Sociales.

Farriera, Graciela B. 1989. *La mujer maltratada. Un estudio sobre las mujeres víctimas de la violencia doméstica.* Buenos Aires: Editorial Suramerica.

Femenia, Nora A. 1987. "Argentina's Mothers of Plaza de Mayo: The Mourning Process from Junta to Democracy." *Feminist Studies* 13, no. 1 (Spring): 9–18.

Feminismo y Política. 1986. La Paz: Coordinadora de la Mujer.

Fernández Olmos, Marguerite. 1993. "Women's Writings in Latin America: Critical Trends and Priorities." In *Researching Women in Latin America and the Caribbean,* ed. Edna Acosta Belén and Christine E. Bose, 135–52. Boulder: Westview Press.

Ferré, Rosario. 1990. *El coloquio de las perras.* San Juan: Editorial Cultural.

Filgueira, Carlos. 1985. "Movimientos sociales en la restauración del orden democrático: Uruguay, 1985." In *Movimientos Sociales en el Uruguay de Hoy,* comp. Carlos Filgueira, 9–49. Montevideo: CLACSO.

———., comp. 1985. *Movimientos sociales en el Uruguay de Hoy.* Montevideo: CLACSO.

Filippini, Mabel. 1987. "Una experiencia de trabajo con mujeres de los sectores populares." In *Participación política de las mujeres del Cono Sur,* 1:53–68. Buenos Aires: Fundacióñ Friedrich Naumann.

Franco, Jean. 1989. *Plotting Women: Gender and Representation in Mexico.* New York: Columbia University Press.

Gálvez, Thelma, and Rosalba Todaro. 1985. *Yo trabajo así . . . en casa particular.* Santiago de Chile: Centro de Estudios de la Mujer.

———. 1988. "La segregación sexual en la industria. In *Mundo de mujer: Continuidad y cambio*, 279–320. Santiago de Chile: Centro de Estudios de la Mujer.

García, Ana Isabel, and Enrique Gomáriz. 1989. *Mujeres Centroamericanas: Efectos del conflicto*. 2 vols. San José: FLACSO.

Gaviola, Edda, et al. 1986. *Queremos votar en las próximas elecciones. Historia del movimiento femenino chileno, 1913–1952*. Santiago de Chile: "La Morada," Fempress, Ilet.

Giberti, Eva, and María Fernández, comps. 1988. *La mujer y la violencia invisible*. Buenos Aires: Editorial Sudamericana.

Gissi, Jorge. 1970. "El machismo en los dos sexos." In *Chile: Mujer y Sociedad*, ed. Paz Covarrubias and Rolando Franco, 549–73. Santiago de Chile: Unicef.

Gogna, Mónica L. 1987. "Mujeres y sindicatos en la Argentina actual." In *Participación política de las mujeres del Cono Sur*, 1:69–86. Buenos Aires: Fundación Friedrich Naumann.

Gonzalbo Aizpuru, Pilar. 1987. *Las mujeres en la Nueva España*. Mexico: El Colegio de Mexico.

González, Patricia Elena, and Eliana Ortega. 1985. *La sartén por el mango*. San Juan: Ediciones Huracán.

Gutiérrez, Ramón. 1991. *When Jesus Came, the Corn Mothers Went Away: Marriage, Sexuality and Power in New Mexico, 1500–1846*. Stanford: Stanford University Press.

Guy, Donna J. 1991. *Sex and Danger in Buenos Aires: Prostitution, Family, and Nation in Argentina*. Lincoln: University of Nebraska Press.

Hahner, June. 1990. *Emancipating the Female Sex: The Struggle for Women's Rights in Brazil, 1850–1940*. Durham: Duke University Press.

Hiriart, Berta, and Adriana Ortega. 1985. "Notas sobre feminismo y sexualidad." *FEM* 8, no. 41 (August–September): 2–5.

Hola, Eugenia. 1987. "La práctica de la investigación feminista en Chile: Una experiencia concreta." In *Participación política de la mujer en el Cono Sur*, 2:25–48. Buenos Aires: Fundación Friedrich Naumann.

Jaquette, Jane, ed. 1989. *The Women's Movement in Latin America: Feminism and the Transition to Democracy*. Boston: Unwyn Hyman.

Kirkwood, Julieta. 1980. "La formación de la conciencia feminista en Chile." Santiago de Chile: FLACSO.

———. 1981. "Chile: La mujer en la formulación política," Santiago de Chile: Documento de Trabajo, FLACSO.

———. 1983. "El feminismo como negación del autoritarismo." Mimeo. Santiago: FLACSO.

———. 1984. "Women and Politics in Chile." *International Social Science Journal* 98:625–38.

———. 1986. *Ser política en Chile: Las feministas y los partidos*. Santiago: Facultad Latinoamericana de Ciencias Sociales.

Knaster, Meri. 1977. *Women in Spanish America: An Annotated Bibliography from Pre-Conquest to Contemporary Times*. Boston: G. K. Hall.

Kuznesof, Elizabeth. 1989. "Household and Family Studies." In *Latinas of the Americas: A Source Book,* ed. K. Lynn Stoner, 305–88. New York: Garland Press.

La imagen de la mujer: Seminario Taller. 1981. Cajamarca, Peru: Peru-Mujer.

La lucha de las mujeres en América Latina y el Caribe. 1990. Cuadernos para la mujer. Mexico: Equipo Mujeres en Acción Solidaria.

Lau Jaiven, Ana. 1987. *La nueva ola del feminismo en Mexico.* Mexico: Planeta.

Laverde Toscano, María Cristina, et al. 1986. *Voces Insurgentes.* Bogotá: Editorial Guadalupe Ltd.

Lavrin, Asunción. 1985. "The Ideology of Feminism in the Southern Cone: 1900–1940." Wilson Center Latin American Program, Working Paper no. 169, Washington, D.C.

———. 1987. "Women, the Family and Social Change in Latin America." *World Affairs* 150, no. 2 (Fall): 109–28.

———. 1988. "Female, Feminine and Feminist: Key Concepts in Understanding Women's History in Twentieth Century Latin America." University of Bristol, Department of Hispanic, Portuguese and Latin American Studies, Occasional Lecture Series no. 4.

———. 1989. "Women, Labor, and the Left: Argentina and Chile, 1890–1925." *Journal of Women's History* 1 (Fall): 88–116. Reprinted in *Expanding the Boundaries of Women's History: Essays on Women in the Third World,* ed. Cheryl Johnson-Odim and Margaret Strobel, 249–77. Bloomington: University of Indiana Press, 1992.

———. 1990. "La mujer en Mexico: Veinte años de estudio, 1968–1988. Ensayo historiográfico." In *Memorias del Simposio de Historiografía Mexicanista,* 545–57. Mexico: UNAM.

———., ed. 1989. *Sexuality and Marriage in Colonial Latin America.* Lincoln: University of Nebraska Press.

León, Magdalena. 1985. "La medición del trabajo femenino en América Latina: Problemas teóricos y metodológicos." In *Mujer y familia en Colombia,* comp. Elsy Bonilla, 205–22. Bogotá: Plaza Janes Editores.

León, Magdalena, and Carmen Diana Deere, eds. 1986. *La mujer y la política agraria en América Latina.* Bogotá: Siglo Veintiuno Editores.

Little, Cynthia J. 1975. "Moral Reform and Feminism." *Journal of Inter-American Studies and World Affairs* 17, no. 4 (November): 386–97.

———. 1977. "Education, Philanthropy and Feminism: Components of Argentina Womanhood, 1860–1926." In *Latin American Women: Historical Perspectives,* ed. Asunción Lavrin, 235–53. Westport, Conn.: Greenwood Press.

Lora, Carmen, et al. 1985. *Mujer: Victima de opresión, portadora de liberación.* Lima: Instituto Bartolomé de Las Casas, Rimac.

Macías, Anna. 1982. *Against All Odds: The Feminist Movement in Mexico to 1940.* Newport, Conn.: Greenwood Press.

Maier, Elizabeth. 1985. *Las sandinistas.* Mexico: Ediciones de Cultura Popular.

Mallon, Florencia. 1986. "Gender and Class in the Transition to Capitalism: Household and Mode of Production in Central Peru." *Latin American Perspectives* 13 (Winter): 147–74.

Mariátegui y el movimiento femenino. 1975. Lima: Editorial Pedagógica "Ascencios."

Medrano, Diana, and Rodrigo Villar. 1988. *Mujer campesina y organización rural en Colombia.* Bogotá: Editorial Cerec.

Meyer, Doris, and Margarite Fernández Olmos, eds. 1983. *Contemporary Women Authors of Latin America.* Brooklyn: Brooklyn College Press.

Miller, Francesca. 1991. *Latin American Women and the Search for Social Justice.* Hanover: University Press of New England.

Molyneux, Maxine. 1985. "Mobilization without Emancipation? Women's Interests, the State and Revolution in Nicaragua." *Feminist Studies* 11, no. 2 (Summer): 227–54.

———. 1986. "No God, No Boss, No Husband: Anarchist Feminism in Nineteenth-Century Argentina." *Latin American Perspectives* 13, no. 1 (Winter): 119–45.

———. 1988. "The Politics of Abortion in Nicaragua: Revolutionary Pragmatism—or Feminism in the Realm of Necessity?" *Feminist Review* 29 (Spring): 114–32.

Montecino, Sonia. 1984. *Mujeres de la tierra.* Santiago: Centro de Estudios de la Mujer.

———. 1986. *Quinchamali. Reino de mujeres.* Santiago de Chile: Centro de Estudios de la Mujer.

Montecino, Sonia, Mariluz Dussuel, and Angelica Wilson. 1988. "Identidad femenina y modelo mariano en Chile." In *Mundo de mujer: Continuidad y cambio,* 500–522. Santiago de Chile: Centro de Estudios de la Mujer.

Mujer/Fempress. Monthly magazine published in Santiago, Chile.

Mujer y política: América Latina y el Caribe. 1989. Santiago de Chile: Naciones Unidas.

Mujeres maltratadas, Casas-refugio y sus alternativas. 1990. Buenos Aires: SENDA.

Mundo de mujer: Continuidad y cambio. 1988. Santiago de Chile: Centro de Estudios de la Mujer.

Muñoz Dálbora, Adriana. 1988. "Fuerza de trabajo femenina: evolución y tendencias." In *Mundo de mujer: Continuidad y cambio,* 185–278. Santiago de Chile: Centro de Estudios de la Mujer.

Murguialday, Clara. 1990. *Nicaragua, revolución y feminismo (1977–89).* Madrid: Editorial Revolución.

Navarrete, Ifigenia M. de. 1969. *La mujer y los derechos sociales.* Mexico: Ediciones Oasis.

Oliveira, Orlandina de., coord. 1989. *Trabajo, poder y sexualidad.* Mexico: El Colegio de Mexico.

Oria, Piera Paola. 1987. *De la casa a la plaza.* Buenos Aires: Editorial Nueva América.

Osterling, Jorge P. 1982. "La mujer en el comercio ambulatorio en Lima metropolitana." *Congreso de Investigación Acerca de la Mujer en la Región Andina.* Lima: Asociación Peru-Mujer.

Paiewonsky, Denise. 1988. *El aborto en la República Dominicana.* Santo Domingo: CIPAF.

Participación política de la mujer en el Cono Sur. 1987. 2 vols. Buenos Aires: Fundación Friedrich Naumann.

Partido Izquierda Unida. 1975. *Programa Nacional de Reconocimiento de la Iqualdad y Dignidad de la Mujer.* Lima: Comisión de la Mujer.

Pérez Alemán, Paola, and Pamela Díaz. 1987. *10 años de investigación sobre la mujer en Nicaragua, 1976–1986.* Managua: Oficina de la Mujer.

Pérez Alemán, Paola. 1990. *Organización, identidad y cambio: las campesinas en Nicaragua.* Managua: Centro de Investigación y Acción para la Promoción de los Derechos de la Mujer.

Pescatello, Ann, ed. 1973. *Female and Male in Latin America.* Pittsburgh: University of Pittsburgh Press.

Picón Garfield, Evelyn. 1988. *Women's Fiction from Latin America.* Detroit: Wayne State University.

Portocarrero, Patricia, et al. 1990. *Mujer en el desarrollo. Balance y propuestas.* Lima: Centro Flora Tristán.

Portugal, Ana María. 1986. "¿Que es ser feminista en América Latina?" *Isis Internacional* 5:9–14.

———., ed. 1989. *Mujer e Iglesia. Sexualidad y aborto en América Latina.* Washington, D.C.: Catholics for Free Choice.

Prates, Suzana, and Silvia Rodriguez Villamil. 1985. "Los movimientos sociales de mujeres en la transición a la democracia." In *Movimientos sociales,* comp. Carlos Filgueira, 155–95. Montevideo: CLACSO.

Presencia de la mujer en las barriadas. 1980. Lima: CIED.

Puyesky, Fanny. 1987. "Ponencia." In *Participación política de la mujer en el Cono Sur,* 2:285–300. Buenos Aires: Fundación Naumann.

Ramos, Carmen, ed. 1987. *Presencia y transparencia: La mujer en la historia de Mexico.* Mexico: El Colegio de Mexico.

Randall, Margaret. 1972. *Mujeres en la revolución.* Mexico: Siglo XXI.

———. 1980. *Todas estamos despiertas: Testimonios de la mujer nicaraguense hoy.* Mexico: Siglo XXI.

Rechini de Lattes, Zulma. 1980. *La participación económica femenina en la argentina desde la segunda posguerra hasta 1970.* Buenos Aires: CENEP.

Rodríguez, Ileana. 1991. *Registradas en la historia: 10 años del quehacer feminista en Nicaragua.* Managua: Centro de Investigación y Acción para los Derechos de la Mujer.

Rodríguez, Villamil Silvia, and Graciela Sapriza. 1984. *Mujer, estado y política en el Uruguay del siglo XX.* Montevideo: Banda Oriental.

Saavedra, Rosario. 1990. "Feminismo y organización femenina popular en Colombia." In *La lucha de las mujeres en América Latina y el Caribe,* 18–23. Mexico: Equipo Mujeres en Acción Solidaria.

Sánchez, Patricia, and Raúl Egas. 1988. *El maltrato a la mujer en la relación doméstica.* Guayaquil.

Saporta Sternbach, Nancy, et al. 1992. "Feminisms in Latin America: From Bogotá to San Bernardo." *Signs* 17, no. 2 (Winter): 393–434.

Sejourné, Laurette. 1980. *La mujer cubana en el quehacer de la historia.* Mexico: Siglo XXI.

Silva, Myrna, Judith Astelarra, and Alicia Herrera. 1985. *Mujer, partidos políticos y feminismo.* Santiago de Chile: Ediciones Documentas.

Silva, Uca. 1988. *Lo demás es silencio. La mujer en la crónica roja.* Quito: n.p.

Sojo, Ana. 1985. *Mujer y política: Ensayo sobre el feminismo y el sujeto popular.* San José, C.R.: Departamento Ecuménico de Investigaciones.

Stevens, Evelyn P. 1973. "Marianismo: The Other Face of Machismo in Latin America." In *Female and Male in Latin America,* ed. Ann Pescatello. 89–101. Pittsburgh: University of Pittsburgh Press.

Stoner, Lynn K. 1991. *From the House to the Streets: The Cuban Woman's Movement for Legal Reform, 1898–1940.* Durham: Duke University Press.

Tarrés, María Luisa. "Mas allá de lo público y lo privado." 1989. In *Trabajo, poder y sexualidad,* coord. Orlandina de Oliveira, 197–218. Mexico: El Colegio de Mexico.

Tocón Armas, Carmen, and Armando Mendiburu M. 1987. *Madres solteras, madres abandonadas.* Chimbote, Peru: Casa de la Mujer.

Todaro, Rosalba, and Thelma Gálvez. 1987. *Trabajo doméstico remunerado: conceptos, hechos, datos.* Santiago de Chile: Centro de Estudios de la Mujer.

Torrado, Susana. 1987. "La libre determinación en materia de procreación." In *Las mujeres y la reforma constitucional,* 49–75. Buenos Aires: Fundación Arturo Illía and Fundación Plural.

Urioste, Diana. 1990. "El feminismo en bolivia." In *La lucha de las mujeres en América Latina y el Caribe,* 9–15. Mexico: Equipo Mujeres en Acción Solidaria.

Urrutia, Elena. 1984. "Encuentro en Lima." *FEM* 8, no. 32 (February–March): 17–18.

Urrutia, Mayra Rosa, and María de Fátima Barceló Miller. 1990. "Temperancia y Sufragismo en el Puerto Rico del Siglo XX." Mimeo. Santurce, P.R.: Centro de Investigaciones Académicas del Sagrado Corazón.

Valdés, Teresa. 1988. *Venid, benditas de mi Padre: Las pobladoras, sus rutinas y sus sueños.* Santiago de Chile: FLACSO.

Valdés, Ximena, et al. 1987. *Sinopsis de una realidad ocultada (Las trabajadoras del campo).* Santiago de Chile: CEM and PENCI.

Valenzuela, María Elena. 1987. *La mujer en el Chile militar.* Santiago: Ediciones Chile y América.

Vargas, F. Rosemary. 1986. "Jornada sobre feminismo y política." In *Feminismo y política,* 45–66. La Paz: Coordinadora de la Mujer.

Vargas, Virginia. 1984. "Movimiento feminista en el Peru: Balance y perspectiva." Mimeo, Lima.

———. 1986. "Vota por tí, mujer." In *Movimiento feminista: balance y perspectivas. Isis Internacional* 5, no. 5 (June): 60–71.

Wainerman, Catalina H. 1981. *La mujer en el banquillo de los acusados.* Mexico: Terra Nova.

———. 1987. "Actividades laborales de la mujer y propuestas de información estadística básica." In *Políticas públicas dirigidas a la mujer,* 45–56. Buenos Aires: Fundación Arturo Illía.

Chapter 10

The Poetical and the Political: The "Feminist" Inquiry in French Studies

Elaine Marks

> I am writing to confirm my telephone invitation to you to be a distinguished speaker in the 1990–1991 effort to integrate feminist scholarship more broadly in the curriculum at the University of Michigan. . . . Your talk should . . . focus on feminist research (theory and criticism) in French, and its impact on what we teach and how we teach it.
>
> —Domna Stanton, Letter to Elaine Marks

> Based on this program [the 1989 program for the annual Modern Language Association (MLA) convention], it is not excessive to conclude that feminism presently has a near monopoly on modern French studies, as literary history once did, or as phenomenology or structuralism recently did.
>
> —Antoine Compagnon, "The Diminishing Canon of French Literature"

PREFACE

In order to give my readers a better idea of the positions I consciously occupied while writing this essay, I must say a few words about my growing dissatisfactions with what I clumsily name "feminist dogmas, purity, pieties." I am trying to name the tendency among some feminist scholars in the humanities and in the social sciences to expect all those who refer to themselves and/or to their work as "feminist" to adhere to or to practice the same discourse, use the same shibboleths, write and speak in a prescribed manner. I refer the readers to four of my essays written between 1982 and 1991 that analyze and document my growing and spreading dissatisfactions with feminist fundamentalism: "Feminisms' Wake," in *Boundary II* (1982); " 'Sapho 1990' Imaginary Renée Viviens and the Rear of the *belle époque*," in *Yale French Studies* (1988); my contribution to "Conference Call," in *differences* (1990); and a talk delivered at a Feminist Forum at the Modern Language Association meetings in December 1991 titled "Revisions and Blindspots: U.S. Feminist Theory, 1970–1990."

But more is involved here than my reactions to the texts, the speech, and the practices of other feminists. Perhaps at a deeper level what I have put into question, and even changed my mind about, is one of the fundamental assumptions that underlies U.S. feminisms and other radical directions inside and out-side the academy: the belief in social change. I understand the belief in social change—reiterated in all the major and minor feminist texts of the past twenty-five years—to be the conviction that a radical change in social structures, the equivalent of the dismantling of patriarchy (and for some of capitalism), is the sine qua non for changing mentalities and ending women's (and other racial and ethnic groups') subordinate and oppressed status.

With the benefits of age (of which there are a few), and of being asked frequently (and obliged) to look back, to analyze, and to map roads taken and untaken, I find myself contemplating the resemblance between an older nineteenth-century belief in progress and a more recent belief in social change. The former has been seriously discredited; perhaps the moment has arrived to investigate the history and the rhetoric of the latter. Although this was not my intention in preparing this essay, it may well have been part of my hidden agenda to displace a fundamentalist, literal, and political feminism by a more heretical, imaginative, and poetical-ontological feminist inquiry.

This essay will explore the complex network of tensions engendered by the intervention of the feminist inquiry—more frequently referred to as feminist scholarship or feminist research—in French Studies within the United States. These tensions include questions of definition and boundaries: What constitutes the feminist inquiry in the United States, and what is its genealogy? what are the differences between the feminist inquiry in the United States and in France? what is the relationship of the feminist inquiry in the United States to cultural studies? to Marxism? to poststructuralism? to other theoretical *isms* and to methodologies? what are the differences between the feminist inquiry in French Studies and in other language and literature groupings in the United States? what is French? and what constitutes French Studies in the United States in the 1990s? There are also questions of inclusions and exclusions: Which French and non-French texts does the feminist inquiry in theory and criticism reread in departments of French? which texts are being read that had not been studied before? Has the ideological insistence, particularly in the United States, on the political aspects of gender and race relations in language, literature, and culture had the effect of diminishing if not eliminating the poetical and ontologi-cal dimension of texts? My analysis and comments will be informed by these questions, but I will not attempt to answer them directly. I will furnish examples from theoretical and critical writings by some men and women in French and in other disciplines in the United States as well as references to those French writers who have functioned as models and mentors, as initiators of the desire for theory that has played an important role in the feminist inquiry in French Studies in the United States. I will also try to show how the denunciation of rhetorical, psychoanalytic, and deconstructive theories by some U.S. feminists as elitist and apolitical may have contributed (through an attempt to make these theories politically acceptable) to the dominance of the political over the poetical and the ontological. In the absence of adequate statistics about programs, syllabi, and doctoral thesis topics throughout the United States, I will rely heavily on my own observations and those of my colleagues in the French section of the Department of French and Italian at the University of Wisconsin–Madison from 1970 to the present. I will play the role of an autobiographer rather than that of a historian.

I will argue that the feminist inquiry entered institutions of higher learning in the United States during the late 1960s and early 1970s, bringing with it, in many disciplines and fields, the social and political discourses of the civil rights movement, of wars of national liberation, and of women's liberation movements naturalized in a United States setting. These discourses have produced multiple effects, particularly in large state universities such as the one in which I work. Effects include the establishment of Women's Studies Programs, multidiscipline organizations encouraging the production of new forms of knowledge, and, most important, allowing for the creation of a community among women scholars from different fields and disciplines, thereby assuring support networks, exchanges among disciplines, and structured venues for negotiation and contestation. Women's Studies Programs have furthered the institutionalization of the feminist inquiry, the development of courses informed by feminist analyses within traditional departments, and, at the same time, have enticed many women scholars who received their doctorates in French in the late 1960s and during the 1970s away from exclusive participation in departments of French. In some cases women's studies as well as departments of French have been a temporary stop on a voyage toward Comparative Literature Programs and/or English Departments, particularly in those colleges and universities in which these units have been at the forefront of rethinking research and pedagogy. Viewed in this light, the term *monopoly* in the epigraph, taken from Antoine Compagnon's essay, is "excessive." French Studies in the United States, as I comprehend the field currently, continues to be receptive to theories and models different from those that have come transformed but nevertheless stamped "Made in France" over the past fifty years. At the same time many scholars and researchers engaged in French Studies tend to remain suspicious of those *isms* and dogmas, whatever their provenance, that they deem inhospitable to the textual and the aesthetic and hostile to the poetical and the ontological. This is also *grosso modo* my position.

It has become increasingly difficult to isolate, "in French," the French scene in France, from all the other scenes to which we—usually women scholars who have or have had ties to the feminist inquiry and who work in French in the

United States—have been exposed and on which we perform by reading, writing, teaching, collaborating. I am thinking in particular of Women's Studies, Gender Studies, Feminist Studies, Gay and Lesbian Studies, African-American Studies, Comparative Literature, English, Ethnic Studies, Jewish Studies, and, more globally, Cultural Studies. Many of us, and this *us* includes those women who continue to be involved in French, are connected to, have joint budgeted appointments with, other departments or programs. What we read, what we write, what we teach, and how we teach it is affected by a variety of texts, methodologies, and audiences. The first and perhaps the most important impact of "feminist research and criticism" on those of us trained in French has been not only an enlarged list of the accepted "masterpieces" of French literary texts to include many more women writers as well as writers of both sexes from nonmetropolitan France who write in French, Francophone writers from Africa, the Caribbean, Canada, Belgium, Switzerland, and Indochina, but also our exposure to and interest in literary texts from languages other than French and to texts other than literary: philosophical texts, historical texts, political science texts, psychoanalytic texts, texts of literary theory and criticism, and texts of popular culture.

For example, my primary appointment at the University of Wisconsin–Madison is in the Department of French and Italian, in which I teach graduate seminars in French on "Autobiographical Writings from Gide to Barthes," "Literature and Ideology," "Feminine Writing and Feminist Discourse," "Committed Literature"; undergraduate courses in French such as "Women of Letters: Christine de Pizan to Colette" and "The Jewish Question from the Dreyfus Case to Auschwitz"; undergraduate courses in translation such as "French Women Writers of Today" cross-listed with Women's Studies, "Masterpieces of Twentieth-Century French Literature," and "French and Italian Jewish Writers of the Twentieth Century" cross-listed with Jewish Studies. I also teach graduate seminars and undergraduate courses that are exclusively in Women's Studies, such as "Research in Women's Studies: Topic Focus Motherhood" or "Topic Focus: Writing Women's Li(v)es"; "French and U.S. Feminisms"; and "Reading and Writing Biographies of Women"; "Lesbian Culture"; and "Jewish Women: Writers, Intellectuals, Activists (Rosa Luxembourg, Hannah Arendt, Simone Weil, Irena Klepfisz)." It is not possible for me, given this variety of readings, topics, scholarly investigation, and pedagogical sites, to limit the transformations that have taken place within the academy over the past twenty years to "feminist research (theory and criticism) in French" (Stanton 1990). And it is inevitable that "in French" will be connected to what we—or, rather, in this instance, what I—have been doing since I received my doctorate in French in 1958.

My own position in relation to the integration of "feminist scholarship" into the curriculum has been contradictory. I have remained true to my old unflagging love for the "masters" of European literature, philosophy, and painting, in whose written and visual texts I came to love languages, literature, and art. I have also remained faithful to my feminist—that is to say, political—convictions about the necessity of analyzing literature as an institution, of studying nonmale and non-European writers and writing traditions, and of locating in all texts nonconscious presuppositions that structure representations and figurations of "othering," whether it be of race, class, gender, ethnicity, or sexuality. Until now I have lived comfortably with these contradictions. Indeed, as a reaction to the either/or position held within the academy on this issue, I became passionately in favor of a "polymorphously perverse" (Freud 1905) humanities curriculum that would incorporate literary studies *and* cultural studies, that would encourage glossophilia (Ozzello 1990) *and* rant against monolingualism (perhaps the most pernicious disease of the U.S. academic establishment), that would focus both on language *and* social critique, on the unconscious *and* the nonconscious of texts, on temporality *and* synchrony, on mortality *and*, in Hannah Arendt's word, "natality," the being born into a community (Arendt 1978). I continue to be passionately in favor of curricular discussions that focus less on *what* we read and more on *how* we read, on the effects and the limitations of our reading practices. I also continue to be passionately in favor of a moratorium on the continued use of such monologic fixed expressions as *Eurocentric* and *Afrocentric,* which have, in 1992, lost their initial critical and empowering force, expressions that erase differences of language and culture among European groupings and among African groupings, and that attribute blame and/or power to one or another badly defined and rigidly identified region. I am equally passionate about the need to read together theoretical texts with historical, fictional, and filmic narratives, for example, to read Martin Heidegger and Paul de Man in conjunction with French African and Caribbean literature and women writers, to read Luce Irigaray and Julia Kristeva with philosophical and theological texts as well as with film scenarios. I would advocate reading at the beginning of courses and seminars on literature, in French and in other languages, Hélène Cixous's 1979 essay "Poésie e(s)t Politique" (Poetry Is/and (the) Political), an essay that proposes and sustains on its own terms a double vision, a double discourse, but that clearly favors the poetical-ontological over the political, that subordinates the question of power to the question of being.

A quotation from Sigmund Freud's critique of religion, *The Future of an Illusion* (1927), prompted me to reflect on an important aspect of the feminist inquiry in French Studies:

How can we expect people who are under the dominance of prohibitions of thought to attain the psychological ideal, the primacy of the intelligence? You know, too, that women in general are said to suffer from "physiological feeble-mindedness" (Moebius, 1903)—that is, from a lesser intelligence than men. The fact itself is disputable and its interpretation doubtful, but one argument in favour of this intellectual atrophy being of a secondary nature is that women labour under the harshness of an early prohibition against turning their thoughts to what would have interested them—namely, the problems of sexual life. So long as a person's early years are influenced not only by a sexual inhibition of thought but also by a religious inhibition and by a loyal inhibition derived from this, we cannot really tell what in fact he [sic] is like. (Freud 1927, 78–79)

One of my simple and I hope not too naive theses is that a desire for theory has been a driving force behind the production of texts, the claiming of center stage, and perhaps even a certain exhibitionism by some women scholars in French in the United States since the mid-1970s. I believe that this desire for theory has had a significant "impact on what we teach and how we teach it." Further, I would suggest that this desire for theory is intimately related to the opening of the sexuality-textuality question (the relationship between sexual desire and language, between the unconscious and writing) by both "theory and criticism in French" and, during the 1980s, of feminist theory and criticism in other modern language and literature departments in the United States. It is as if the kinds of theory being proposed by psychoanalysis and deconstruction, the emphasis in much contemporary theory on sexuality, the fact that it was essential for women to engage with these theories, and that there were, as there have traditionally been, many more women graduate students than men in French departments came together to reinforce Freud's assertion that women have been prevented from "turning their thoughts to what would most have interested them—namely, the problems of sexual life." When women are allowed—or, better still, encouraged—to do so, as shown by the number of active women lay analysts in Europe in the 1920s or the group of women in French since the mid-1970s, the results have been impressive. This desire for theory may be contrasted to Paul de Man's "Resistance to Theory" (1982), which he defined as "a resistance to the use of language about language" (13), "a resistance to reading" (15), "a resistance to the rhetorical or tropological dimension of language" (17). As a result of this desire for theory, some women pedagogues in the classroom are teaching female and male students how to analyze and to play with language, how to inspect the material aspect of words, how to recognize contradictions, how to treat a text as transparent, referential, and opaque.

Some women pedagogues are introducing students to reading practices that are different from commonsense practices. Rather than focusing uniquely on the author's intended meaning, they also focus on the ways in which meanings are produced in the reading of a text. Rather than isolating the text from any but the most obvious contexts, they attempt to juxtapose theoretical and literary texts in unexpected ways, as in Barbara Johnson's essay, "Apostrophe, Animation and Abortion" (1987), in which she reads together Baudelaire's "Moesta et Errabunda," Shelley's "Ode to the West Wind," Gwendolyn Brooks's poem "The Mother," and a passage from Jacques Lacan's *Ecrits*. Women in French or those who, like Barbara Johnson, have been in French, are not only, in Cixous's portmanteau word that brings together sex, text, and sect, showing the *"sextes"* (Cixous 1975) of women writers to their students, they are also showing their own *sextes* as they produce new readings, and they are encouraging female students to show theirs.

As the words *desire* and *sextes* indicate, an important contribution of the French connection into our classrooms has come as a response to psycho-analysis, as a series of reactions (whether for or against) to Jacques Lacan and the return to the reading of Freud's texts. I do not mean to imply that all of the women in French work exclusively or even primarily with psychoanalytic theory. But I do note that Lacan's texts, like his seminars, which so many of the "masters" attended, precede in time Jacques Derrida's or Michel Foucault's or Roland Barthes's or Jean-François Lyotard's in France and Paul de Man's or Michael Riffaterre's or Jeffrey Mehlman's in the United States. Indeed, psycho-analytic texts are a major source of this desire for theory, which includes the desire to master the theory, to consider theories about women's sexuality and writing, to emphasize the relationship between women's liberation movements and the body, *and* to work against a theory that privileges the phallus, language, and the symbolic. I have named several of the leading French and American masters with whom many of the women in French have studied. The women in French working in the United States who have been affected by the desire for theory (whatever their present academic affiliation may be) include (and my list is not exhaustive), in alphabetical order: Verena Conley, Laurie Edson, Sho-shana Felman, Jerry Aline Flieger, Nelly Furman, Jane Gallop, Marianne Hirsch, Alice Jardine, Joan DeJean, Barbara Johnson, Peggy Kamuf, Mary Lydon, Christie McDonald, Christiane Makward, Nancy K. Miller, Toril Moi, Leslie Rabine, Naomi Schor, Domna Stanton, and Susan Suleiman.

In order to elaborate further on my title, my questions, and my theses, I will recall several texts-as-events that have marked, since the late 1960s, "feminist research (theory and criticism) in French." Then I will mention briefly what seem to me, in 1992, to be the central debates that have emerged from and/or that organize these textual events and focus on those directions that are most visible: the move away from literary studies to cultural studies; the question of identity; and the difficulty in maintaining a necessary equilibrium between the poetical and the political. I will illustrate debates and directions with texts by Simone de Beauvoir, Hélène Cixous, and Jerry Aline Flieger.

The texts-as-events produced on both sides of the Atlantic, texts whose importance relates either to their original, innovative qualities or to their power to reach a wide public, to disseminate and to vulgarize, include: *Les guérillères* by Monique Wittig (1969); *Speculum of the Other Woman* by Luce Irigaray (1974); *Revolution in Poetic Language* by Julia Kristeva (1974); "The Laugh of the Medusa" by Hélène Cixous (1976); *The Newly Born Woman* by Hélène Cixous and Catherine Clément (1986); "Textual Politics: Feminist Criticism," the winter 1975 issue of *diacritics;* and *Psychoanalysis and Feminism* by Juliet Mitchell (1975); essays in *Signs* (summer 1978) by Carolyn Burke and Elaine Marks on women and writing in France; *New French Feminisms* edited by Elaine Marks and Isabelle de Courtivron (1980); *The Daughter's Seduction: Feminism and Psychoanalysis* by Jane Gallop (1982); *Gynesis* by Alice Jardine (1985); *Sexual/Textual Politics* by Toril Moi (1985); *Displacements: Women, Tradition, Literature in French* edited by Joan DeJean and Nancy K. Miller (1991); and *Revaluing French Feminism: Critical Essays on Difference, Agency and Culture* edited by Nancy Fraser and Sandra Lee Bartky (1992). My list is obviously selective and tendentious. I have highlighted by my choices a tendency to move away from literary studies informed by psychoanalysis and deconstruction toward political studies informed by concepts of agency, culture, and an extreme constructivism.

In spite of this tendency, the central debates that have emerged from these textual and sometimes public events have not changed significantly since the late 1960s. Perhaps the most visible change is the presence on the stage of these debates of feminist scholars in the United States from a variety of fields other than French or literature, from philosophy, political science, history, linguistics, African-American studies, ethnic studies, and cultural studies generally and, of course, women's studies.

In "Parisian Letters" Nancy K. Miller writes to Peggy Kamuf:

My sense of the development of feminist theory since 1981, and in particular since 1985, is that it has been one of intense dislocation. I pick 1985, which I see as a kind of radical turning point, because of two events, two conferences on feminist theory that took place within months of each other that year; both of which have now become books edited by their organizers: *Feminist Studies/Critical Studies,* by Teresa de Lauretis (1986); and *Coming to Terms: Feminism, Theory, Politics,* by Elizabeth Weed (1989). At both conferences, but most dramatically at the first in Milwaukee, where the effects of

polarization were intense and explicit, the splits and fractures within feminisms, and the violence with which they are lived, especially around issues of
race were painfully in evidence. Since then—though I take this moment as an
archival mark, rather than an originary occasion, because the elements of the
struggle had been in place for at least a decade—feminism has been traversed
by currents of conflict impossible to elude. The blindness of a feminist "we"
to its own exclusions has continued to complicate and deeply trouble the
relations within feminism—manifested by an acute selfconsciousness about
the deployment of pronouns; and tempered, if not transformed, by the
grounding assumptions of feminist theory. (I'm thinking in particular of the
powerful fiction of universal feminist subject.) (Miller 1990, 123–24)

What separated Hélène Cixous and Monique Wittig in 1979, what had
earlier, and not in a French context, separated Adrienne Rich and Susan Sontag
in the pages of *The New York Review of Books* in 1975, what separated and
continues to separate Peggy Kamuf and Nancy K. Miller in the pages of *diacritics* in 1982 and again in *Conflicts in Feminism* (1990), is, I think, similar.
One of the writers in each pair—Cixous, Sontag, Kamuf—questions not only
the definitions, the positions, and the efficacy of the persistent use of the terms
feminism or even *feminisms,* but questions the notion that any *ism* can be used
as a rallying point for political, philosophical, and cultural meanings without
becoming a totalized and totalizing entity, in short a dogma and an orthodoxy.
In Sontag's words: "Like all moral truths, feminism is a bit simpleminded"
(1975, 31). On the other hand, in these debates Monique Wittig, Adrienne Rich,
and Nancy K. Miller are defending, and redefining as they defend, a place and
position (not the same one in each case) for the word *feminism* within the
contemporary theoretical and political configuration that includes Marxism,
psychoanalysis, deconstruction, and semiotics. "I still feel the need to sign,"
concludes Nancy K. Miller in "Parisian Letters," "on the map of inclination,
from the place called feminism" (1990, 133).

While we cannot ignore the charges leveled against feminism, coming both
from disciples of the masters and from other female constituencies (women of
color, lesbian women), I would prefer to look at what has been done and
continues to be done in the name of feminisms within Departments of French by
women recently or still in French whose desire for theory has, as I suggested
earlier, been a spur encouraging the proliferation of publications, conferences,
and curricular transformations.

I discern two major directions, each of which involves a concept of the
"other." On the one hand, the other as defined by Simone de Beauvoir in *The
Second Sex* (1949): "She is defined and differentiated with reference to man and
not he with reference to her; she is the incidental, the inessential as opposed to

the essential. He is the subject, he is the Absolute—she is the Other" (xix). This is the other who is oppressed by patriarchy or colonialism, the other whose authorship does not count, the other who is designated by feminisms's insistence on including race, class, gender, and sexual preference in all analyses because all analyses, at some level, are organized through relations of power and through ideology. This, then, is the other of cultural studies as it is frequently practiced by some neo-Marxists, feminists, and multiculturalists in the United States. This other, dependent on a "self," may also be examined in relation to the analysis of binary oppositions within deconstruction, an analysis that posits the second term, the other of the binary, as indeed inhabiting the first term, but unrecognized and repressed. For example, one could postulate that an unrecognized and repressed "She" inhabits "He."

On the other hand, there are the two other "others" as articulated by Jacques Lacan: the "Other" (capital O) as the domain of law and language, the symbolic father, and the unconscious; the "other" (lower case o), the m/other, nurturer, with whom the child at the time of the mirror stage enters into an imaginary relation. It is interesting to note that Lacan's essay "The Mirror Stage as Formative of the Function of the I as revealed in Psychoanalytic Experience" was delivered at the Sixteenth International Congress of Psychoanalysis in Zurich, on 17 July 1949, the same year as the publication of Beauvoir's *Second Sex*.

Women in French who follow (usually with a difference) the paths proposed by Simone de Beauvoir have tended to work with texts and cultural questions about the role, function, and representation of women as other, investigating how and where in texts and institutions othering and exclusion have taken place, what the effects have been on women outside texts, and how, perhaps, the situation inside and outside texts might be rectified. This is the general direction that has been pursued by academic feminists not in Departments of French—for example, those women who contributed essays to *Revaluing French Feminism* (1992). They are, in general, committed to saving feminism from determinist and nihilistic theories, theories that do not explicitly make room for either female agency or social change.

Women in French who follow (but always with a difference) the paths proposed by Jacques Lacan's others have tended to focus their analyses on the unconscious of texts, the place of the Other, and the play of language. Although their work may overlap with "cultural studies"—as, for example, the more recent work of Jane Gallop in which she reads, critically, the essays and public talks of women in French or Anglo-American feminisms—most of the women in French who use Lacan (e.g., Shoshana Felman, Jerry Aline Flieger, Peggy Kamuf, and Mary Lydon) would be more appropriately placed under the older rubric of "literary studies" (again with a difference) in which language as the repressed other and figuration rather than representation play leading roles.

These women are committed to saving literary texts from being overwhelmed by cultural studies, that is to say, in varying doses, by contextual, political, and historical analyses. They fear neither determinism nor nihilism.

I would like to propose examples of these diverse others and of the distinctions I have suggested between cultural studies and literary studies, using as textual illustrations the second part of Simone de Beauvoir's autobiographical fiction on the death of her mother, *A Very Easy Death*; Hélène Cixous's essay "Poetry Is/and (the) Political"; and Jerry Aline Flieger's recent critical study *Colette and the Fantom Subject of Autobiography* (1992).

It is possible to read Simone de Beauvoir's text as a feminist critique of how one becomes a woman, how social constraints within institutions such as the bourgeois family, the church, and the medical profession conspire, through their discourses, to maim and finally to kill Françoise de Beauvoir's spirit, mind, and body. The metaphor of the corset and the laces, at first imposed by oppressive social forces and then internalized by the victim, are repeated throughout this second part, with the suggestion that, were it not for this institutional and discursive oppression, the quality of Françoise de Beauvoir's life and that of other women of her generation, and of her daughters and theirs, would have been substantially different, substantially better. This is a clear, positive feminist message. But it is neither the only nor is it the most eloquent message in *A Very Easy Death*. If one can, indeed, take off the corset, one cannot avoid death, and the "scandal" of the individual death of Françoise de Beauvoir, her irremediable solitude as well as the impossibility of communication between the dying woman and members of her entourage, dominate thematically, structurally, and theoretically any possibility of social change. Furthermore, the text proposes instances through reported dreams and descriptions of involuntary facial movements of the narrator, Simone de Beauvoir, in which she is invaded by and incorporates, in spite of herself, aspects of her m/other. For all its gestures toward the evil effects of those nonconscious assumptions that sustain the ideological basis and the power of Françoise de Beauvoir's bourgeois milieu, *A Very Easy Death* is ultimately, like all literature, a text about mourning, absence, and death.

Both Hélène Cixous in "Poetry Is/and (the) Political" and Jerry Aline Flieger in *Colette and the Fantom Subject of Autobiography* insist from the beginning of their very different texts on the necessity of maintaining a double vision, a double strategy, acknowledging both the poetic and the political, both literary and cultural studies. "There must be a poetic practice in the political practice— (Without this the political kills: and inversely)" (Cixous 1979, 35). Cixous is not suggesting that we move between Auschwitz and roses or the oppression of Iranian women and poems but that, simultaneously, we attempt to change relations of power and pay close attention to the world, both to beings and objects in the world, allowing the other to be. Cixous, and she is not alone among contemporary French writers—I think of Emmanuel Lévinas and Marguerite Duras, for example—view the extermination camps of World War II as instances of radical othering. In their writing they are concerned with new modes of being without appropriating or possessing but, rather, of slowly approaching.

> How may we best approach this elusive work, which refuses to be classified, and in which the "I" is most concealed precisely where it is most candidly revealed? Finding a balance between a textual and a biographical approach is important for all gender-related theories of reading, but this balance is perhaps even more critical in reading an "autobiographical" writer like Colette. For if the text is read primarily as a documentation of social conditions (in the manner of some feminist criticism), or as a symptom of an author's neuroses (in the manner of some psychobiography), the autobiographical axis will assume more importance than the fictional axis, with a consequent loss of literary pleasure. If on the other hand the text's aesthetic characteristics are foregrounded with little reference to the real writing woman (in the manner of some poststructuralist criticism), we risk losing an understanding of the work, either in the psychoanalytic sense (dream-work, mourning-work, joke-work) or in the social sense, which recognizes that literature is communication and that it has an ideological valence in even the least polemical of texts. (Flieger 1992, 9)

Flieger succeeds, better than most contemporary critics with similar projects, in "finding a balance" and maintaining it throughout her study of Colette's fictional autobiographies. She approaches Colette's writing with the same loving care and attentiveness to the texts' strangeness that Cixous advocates in her essay. Neither Cixous nor Flieger imposes an outcome, although both are equipped with the necessary and the latest theoretical baggage. Neither can be said to represent "a near monopoly on modern French studies" (Compagnon 1991, 113), but both represent, in my view, what is most effective and most important in "feminist research (theory and criticism) in French, and its impact on what we teach and how we teach it" (Stanton 1990).

In conclusion, then, "feminist research (theory and criticism) in French" has, in conjunction with other discourses over the past twenty years, enlarged the scope of French Studies. More texts by women are included in the undergraduate and graduate curriculum; more texts by women are studied and commented on in doctoral dissertations written by women. And Francophone literature has slowly but steadily assumed the status of a field within French Studies. The political and ideological bases of French culture have also become objects of scrutiny. Under the impact of Women's Studies Programs literary texts by French women writers in English translation have been placed in syllabi next to literary and theoretical texts by women (and some men) writing in English or in other languages that have also been translated into English. Once again what appears to be an opening or an inclusion has exclusionary effects. The French language, the connotative and poetic dimension of French texts, is lost in the mass of English-language translations.

Feminist discourses, in concert with other politically tendentious discourses, tend to direct arguments and select theories that will help protect the concepts of social change and female agency. Feminist discourses are legitimately fearful of universalizing language, but these discourses run the risk of ignoring theories that are suspicious of progress and social change, theories that attempt to come to terms with human situations and questions for which there are neither practical solutions nor logical answers. This may be the moment for an intervention of French Studies into the feminist inquiry in the United States.

WORKS CITED

Arendt, Hannah. 1978. "Willing." *The Life of the Mind*, 3–239, esp. 110. New York: Harcourt Brace and Jovanovich.

Beauvoir, Simone de. 1953. *The Second Sex*. Trans. H. M. Parshley. New York: Knopf.

———. 1985. *A Very Easy Death*. Trans. Patrick O'Brian. New York: Pantheon Books.

Cixous, Hélène. 1976. "The Laugh of the Medusa." Trans. Keith and Paula Cohen. *Signs* 1:875–94.

———. 1979. "Poésie e(s)t Politique." *Des Femmes en Mouvements Hebdo* 4 (30 Nov.–7 Dec.): 29–32.

Cixous, Hélène, and Catherine Clément. 1986. *The Newly Born Woman*. Trans. Betsy Wing. Minneapolis: University of Minnesota Press.

Compagnon, Antoine. 1991. "The Diminishing Canon of French Literature." Trans. Jeanine Herman. *Stanford French Review* 15:103–15.

DeJean, Joan, and Nancy K. Miller. 1990. *Displacements: Women, Tradition, Literature in French*. Baltimore: Johns Hopkins University Press.

de Man, Paul. 1982. "The Resistance to Theory." *Yale French Studies*, no. 63:3–20.

diacritics. 1975. "Textual Politics: Feminist Criticism" (Winter).

Flieger, Jerry Aline. 1992. *Colette and the Fantom Subject of Autobiography*. Ithaca: Cornell University Press.

Fraser, Nancy, and Sandra Lee Bartky. 1992. *Revaluing French Feminism*. Bloomington: Indiana University Press.

Freud, Sigmund. 1953–74. *Three Essays on Sexuality*. Trans. James Strachey. *Standard Edition of the Complete Psychological Works of Sigmund Freud*. London: Hogarth Press.

———. 1964. *The Future of an Illusion*. Trans. W. D. Robson-Scott and James Strachey. New York: Anchor Books.

Gallop, Jane. 1982. *The Daughter's Seduction: Feminism and Psychoanalysis.* Ithaca: Cornell University Press.

Irigaray, Luce. 1985. *Speculum of the Other Woman.* Trans. Gillian C. Gill. Ithaca: Cornell University Press.

Jardine, Alice. 1985. *Gynesis.* Ithaca: Cornell University Press.

Johnson, Barbara. 1987. "Apostrophe, Animation and Abortion." *A World of Difference,* 184–99. Baltimore and London: Johns Hopkins University Press.

Kristeva, Julia. 1984. *Revolution in Poetic Language.* Trans. Margaret Waller. Intro. Leon S. Roudiez. New York: Columbia University Press.

Lacan, Jacques. 1977. "The Mirror Stage as Formative of the Function of the I as Revealed in Psychoanalytic Experience." Trans. Alan Sheridan. *Ecrits,* 1–7. New York: W. W. Norton.

Marks, Elaine, and Isabelle de Courtivron. 1981. *New French Feminisms.* New York: Schocken Books.

Miller, Nancy K. 1990. "Parisian Letters." In *Conflicts in Feminism,* ed. Marianne Hirsch and Evelyn Keller, 121–33. New York and London: Routledge.

Mitchell, Juliet. 1975. *Psychoanalysis and Feminism.* New York: Vintage Books.

Moi, Toril. 1985. *Sexual/Textual Politics.* New York: Methuen.

Ozzello, Yvonne. 1990. "Saussure and His Difference." Paper presented at the Modern Language Association meeting, Chicago, December.

Sontag, Susan. 1975. "Feminism and Fascism: An Exchange." *New York Review of Books,* 20 Mar.: 31–32.

Stanton, Domna. 1990. *Letter to Elaine Marks,* 27 July.

Wittig, Monique. 1971. *Les guérillères.* Trans. David LeVay. New York: Viking.

PART 4

Dialogues: Feminist Scholarship and/in the Disciplines

Chapter 11

Feminist Studies and Political Science—and Vice Versa

Virginia Sapiro

Women's studies in political science is now more than a generation old. When the Women's Caucus in Political Science was founded in 1969, women who openly considered focusing any of their research or teaching on women were discouraged and dissuaded by teachers and colleagues convinced that such work had to be "political" rather than "scholarly"; in any case, it was deemed of little interest to the wider concerns of political science. In the early 1990s the Women's Caucus remained large and active. At the same time, and following the institution of "Organized Sections" within the American Political Science Association, membership in the Organized Section on Women and Politics Research grew to 450 out of the nearly 12,000 political scientists. A special journal devoted to this area, *Women and Politics,* has been in publication since 1980, and its contents represent only a fraction of the periodical literature published by political scientists each year.

But how much has really changed for political scientists pursuing women's or feminist studies? The discipline is slightly less gender segregated than it was. In 1972–73 11 percent of faculty were women. In 1990 19 percent of faculty were women, including 16 percent of full-time faculty and 10 percent of those with tenured positions. Clearly, the amount of research and teaching has grown substantially. Feminist work has matured considerably in many areas of the discipline. In the early days most work was of the "add women and stir" or compensatory variety, taking conventional questions in different fields, but especially political behavior and political theory, and asking, "What about the women?"[1] In political behavior this meant trying to find out whether women and men differed in political action or public opinion and searching for the mechanisms of the exclusion of women from political leadership. In political theory this meant asking what the canonical political philosophers such as Aristotle and Plato, Hobbes, Locke, and Rousseau, or Mill and Marx said—or didn't say—about women. This work was and is important, but it was not sufficient.

In the early days defining this field as *women and politics* seemed unproblematic because we were primarily interested in how women fit into politics and what their impact was.[2] Some of us now prefer *gender politics*, explicitly reconceptualizing the field as exploring the relationships between gender and politics more broadly defined. Adequate feminist analysis of government and politics cannot conceivably be limited to focusing on *women* and politics.

Now there is feminist scholarship in almost every branch of political science, and in many areas scholars are formulating their own questions and concepts, often in conjunction with feminist studies colleagues in other disciplines.[3] But, for those of us who define ourselves simultaneously in political science and women's studies, two problems remain troubling. First, despite the size of the gender politics community, and despite the fact that most political science departments now offer at least one course in the area, gender politics has not been fully integrated into political science; its theories, questions, and conclusions have not been "mainstreamed" to any significant degree. Both graduate and undergraduate students still often find that, when they try to pursue gender questions in their courses, they meet with resistance or a considerable amount of simple ignorance. After a twenty-year history of gender politics research in political science, students must often take the lead in introducing this area into their studies, as though it were a new field. Of course, many professors have integrated some of this work into their courses. But some resent even the suggestion to do so, as if it were an affront to their expertise or professional judgment.[4] In general, although there has been improvement over the years, political scientists in most fields show little interest in or even awareness of feminist work, even in their own general areas of teaching and research.

The other problem facing the same feminist scholars in political science is that our work has not been fully integrated into women's studies. The representation of political scientists' work in interdisciplinary women's studies journals is low, although for a variety of reasons political scientists may be less likely than scholars in some other fields to submit their work to these journals. But an interdisciplinary field is not interdisciplinary just because publishing outlets are shared by people in different disciplines; it is also interdisciplinary because participants seek out relevant work where it can be found and borrow and reintegrate concepts, theories, and conclusions for their own purposes. With the exception of a very few areas in the social sciences and history, women's studies shows little interest in or awareness of the work of feminist political scientists.

The remainder of this essay will revolve around these two problems, briefly seeking to explain them and suggest remedies. I will begin with the relation of gender politics to political science, focusing especially on the special issues arising from the nature of the subfield in professional political science. I will then turn to the relation of feminist studies in political science to women's studies, focusing especially on the relative standing of the humanities and social sciences, especially with regard to the "science question," but also consider the politics of politics in women's studies and the implications for political science. Since the birth of women's studies, feminist scholars have repeatedly turned a critical eye toward their disciplines in search of the reasons for their marginality. The same must be done within women's studies.

GENDER POLITICS IN POLITICAL SCIENCE

The past two decades of gender politics work in political science has witnessed the production of many—perhaps too many—critical reviews of the inattention of professional political science to women and gender issues.[5] As elsewhere, the underlying problem can be defined in two different ways. The first is primarily sociological or sociopolitical, emphasizing the low number of women and their subordination within the profession. Women's structural position can be understood as causing both suppression of attention to women as subjects and a relatively unchallenged androcentric scholarly conception of women, gender, and sexuality.

The other type of critique focuses primarily on epistemological and conceptual questions, including professional constructions of the nature of knowing and analysis and the impact of these constructions on understanding gender and sexuality in both feminist and nonfeminist theory and research.[6] As in other disciplines, epistemological and logic of inquiry debate in political science surrounding the "feminism question" is informed by many different approaches, including "standpoint" and materialist theories, postmodern and poststructuralist theories, and different varieties of empiricism.[7]

Although the small number of women in political science surely has an impact on the reception of feminist research and teaching, problems having to do with the theoretical and methodological underpinnings of political science are important to understand. I will outline some of these, emphasizing their impact on the integration of gender politics into political science. Specifically, I will focus on definitions of public, private, and politics; the legacy of positivism in empirical methodology; the legacy of the canon in defining theoretical importance; and the political and gender-based construction of professional norms. These constructions are not "caused" by gender, but they do have a bearing on how the gender basis of political science is changed or maintained.

The Public, Private, and Politics

Ever since the early feminist anthropological work of the 1970s, especially essays appearing in Rosaldo and Lamphere's collection, *Women, Culture, and Society* (1974), feminist scholars across the humanities and social scientists have taken the "public/private split," especially the common if not ubiquitous relegation of women and low status to the "private" sphere and men and high status to the "public" sphere as a central problem of inquiry. Certainly, the public/private split has played a key role in theory and research in anthropology and history as well as philosophy. But it takes on special importance in political science, the one field whose disciplinary boundaries are conventionally defined by the public/private split.

Political science is "about" politics and government; it is "about" public life. A standard opening in introduction to politics courses is to reach back to classical notions of the polis, or community, for a means to define the turf of politics. Certainly, even the most mainstream political scientists know that one might talk about the politics of personal life and that personal life may "have an impact on" politics, but the divide for purposes of defining academic boundaries is not widely questioned, and students are often counseled to leave analysis of the politics of private life to the sociologists and psychologists.

Not surprisingly, among the earliest important works of feminist scholarship in political science are those examining the meaning of the public/private divide within historical political thinking (e.g., Elshtain 1974, 1981).[8] Soon feminist scholars began not just to engage in critical discussion of the political significance of the public/private split but also to criticize conventional definitions of politics or political activity and to incorporate into their research human activities and problems usually left to the side by their colleagues. By its subject matter alone, then, feminist research in political science can appear to the mainstream to be outside the boundaries of the discipline or, at least, at its margins.

The Legacy of Positivism

Political science is one of the social sciences in which the bulk of research is empirical in character; indeed, "scientific method" is widely viewed as the ideal approach to research, and quantitative research is accorded high status in at least some of the major subfields of political science. In the large and dominant area of *behavioral* political science (i.e., research focusing primarily on human behavior and thinking rather than, e.g., institutional structures or law themselves), some of the original practitioners were also advocates of *behaviorism,* a theoretical stance derived from a branch of psychology that allows investigation only of phenomena widely believed to be directly visible. This position has largely been abandoned, although it may be reviving to some degree among those working with the increasingly popular rational choice models.[9]

As feminist theorists of inquiry have often noted, many aspects of positivist stances toward research have been employed to suppress feminist research, but chief among these is the dominant construction of *objectivity* and the value placed on it within the positivist tradition.[10] Briefly stated, "good" social science is supposed to be "value free." Objectivity and freedom from values is accomplished by following agreed-upon procedures that can be replicated by any other scientist. Any scientist following the procedures properly will discover the same accurate or true picture of what is "out there." Without repeating the criticisms and issues raised so often and comprehensively by other feminist theorists, even feminist scholars who follow most of the practices of conventional social science methods tend to accept the central point of the diverse criticisms: no research and no set of research procedures can be value free.[11] Indeed, regardless of feminism, a large proportion of empirical political scientists generally hold considerably altered conceptions of the relationship between values and research.

Research labeled "feminist" is widely ignored or rejected within the discipline because the label taints it with political values, because to do research on women appears especially motivated by political or social values and because the results often do not fit with the personal and professional experience of more conventional researchers and therefore *seem* tainted with "perspective." For all the professional arguments about objectivity and logic, it sometimes seems that it is only the feeling of familiarity and comfort that proves objectivity.

It is crucial to recognize that the conventions of science have had a double-edged effect on feminist research in political science. Whatever may be said about the antagonism between positivist norms and feminism, the subfield of the discipline in which science is most valued as a model of research is also the subfield in which there has been the greatest amount of feminist research and one that has probably received the most widespread reading by scholars who do not themselves do research on women or gender. A very large proportion of feminist research in political science focuses on mass and elite political behavior and orientations, exploring such problems as gender differences in public opinion, perception, and political participation and action; gender-based political socialization; and the gender basis of recruitment to political office and the behavior of women and men once they hold leadership positions.

Arguing that the legacy of positivism both inhibits and promotes the study of women, including feminist research, is not as self-contradictory as it might at first seem. Women could "break into" the field by applying many of its own conventions. If an important test of research is whether it follows conventional procedures, the new research on women could often pass the test.[12] Many of us in that field in its early days made what was *in context* a powerful claim: the statements usually made by political scientists about women's political behavior and orientations were generally based on stereotypes and had not been subjected to empirical tests. At the most basic level statements about dramatic differences in women's and men's attitudes toward politics and political issues—some of which persist in the public mind and, indeed, in feminist theory—were, for the most part, unfounded or starkly nondramatic (Shapiro and Mahajan 1986). The relationships between gender-based familial roles and political attitudes and behavior are both more complicated and less clear than conventional wisdom indicates (Darcy, Welch, and Clark 1987; Sapiro 1983). In the legacy of positivism, no empirical statement may rest immune to testing. "Everyone knows that . . ." is no defense; neither is "self-evidence."[13]

The Legacy of the Canon

The dominance of the legacy of positivism offers a part of the explanation for the difficulty of integrating feminist research into political science, but it cannot be anything like the whole explanation. Indeed, although many of the critiques of the dominance of positivism and behavioralism are penned by political theorists, the subfield of theory has been as bad or worse in integrating feminist work. In the non-"science" subfields and communities of the discipline there are values beside "scientific objectivity" that render feminist research suspect. In theory (as in other fields), for example, the measure of scholarly worth is the probing of "universal," or "perennial," problems. Here women lose not on the measure of objectivity versus subjectivity and "bias" but, rather, on the measure of universalism versus parochialism, or centrality versus marginality.

This problem will be especially familiar to those in the humanities who have been party to the debate over the canon. Political theory and philosophy, like the literary disciplines, is commonly a text- and/or author-based field of inquiry; it is largely structured around a historical parade, or canon, of great authors, great works ranging from Plato and Aristotle through Machiavelli to the central figures of modern political thought such as Hobbes, Locke, and Rousseau and Mill and Marx, with many others in between. The contemporary works are probably more variable but include debates over democratic theory and justice or liberalism, republicanism, and communitarianism and revolve around such theorists as John Rawls, J. G. A. Pocock, Michael Walzer, and Michael Sandel.[14]

In political theory, as in other fields, canonical works are said to be self-evidently ("objectively"?) laden with the universal and important human political problems. Although, ironically, a large proportion of the pre-twentieth-century canonical works and authors dwelt very explicitly on questions about women and gender, in this century the explicit attention to women and gender was likely to be ignored as unimportant or inessential to the work.[15] Issues about women have been relegated to the parochial (rather than universal) except, perhaps, as objects of "our" desire (as texts say, not incidentally, in a male voice). For women to write about women and gender, especially in a manner critical of canon and canonical interpretation, is to degrade political theory by making it parochial and particularistic rather than perennial and universal.

FIRST CONCLUSION

There has been considerable research on women and gender in political science over the last two decades, but, judging by the syllabi and footnotes of non-specialists, it has been integrated into the discipline in only minor ways and sporadically. There are some obvious reasons why this has been the case. Politics remains a distinctly "male" cultural domain, and political science remains a male-dominated field. Just as race is not "a problem" for members of a dominant race in a racially structured society, so gender is not a problem for men in a male-dominated arena. As in many other areas, feminists and others differ over where we see gender in the first place; traditional political scientists can see a legislative body overwhelmingly dominated by people of one sex and not see gender as relevant to the picture. Clearly, feminist scholars cannot.

It is not enough to attribute the difficulty merely to the proportion of women in the discipline or even, in any simple way, to the fact that the subject of this discipline—politics—remains culturally identified as masculine. Rather, as I have tried to indicate, there are also professional norms, values, and practices that become part of the process of obstruction. Further, in order to understand a discipline as intellectually diverse as political science, it is necessary to recognize that it consists of overlapping scholarly communities with different values and practices. Somewhat different problems face feminist scholars in different subfields, an issue rarely noted in critical reviews of the discipline.

SCIENCE AND POLITICS IN WOMEN'S STUDIES

Critiques of intellectual inclusion and exclusion of women's studies typically focus on its marginalization within the traditional disciplines. But many within the community of those who live our scholarly lives in both political science and women's studies also sense a lack of integration of our (collective) work into women's studies. Indeed, feminist social scientists in different disciplines often discuss among themselves a shared perception that the social sciences generally are marginalized within women's studies. This is especially strongly felt where empirical research is concerned but also with regard to feminist theory in the social sciences. As in the case of the exclusion of gender issues from political science, this state of affairs must be regarded as a historical phenomenon shaped by continuing shifts in social relations and larger sets of intellectual issues involved in scholarly work. But, as in the case of understanding the integration—or lack of it—of feminism within the disciplines, it is important to analyze the structure lent to inclusion and exclusion by the currently dominant theories, methods, and assumptions.

The forms, objects, and practices of theory and theorizing are somewhat different in the social sciences and humanities, largely because of the different treatment of empirical statements within theory and the different relationship between theory and empirical research. In some areas of social science the term *theory* implies a hypothetical statement that must be examined against evidence and in which the theorist must make clear the ways the theory could be shown to be wrong. Clearly, such a definition would be foreign to most scholars in the humanities, especially in the more antiempirical areas. Indeed, what social scientists and humanities scholars[16] identify as theory is probably an overlapping but not identical set; standards of what constitutes good theory certainly differ in some respects. Given that the majority of scholars are probably not aware of the differences in the very definition of *theory* between the humanities and social sciences, it is no wonder that some conflicts and misunderstanding have emerged.[17] In any case, in recent years humanities-based theorizing has held a privileged position in the eyes of both humanities and social science scholars within the community of feminist scholars.

A widespread view held among feminists in the humanities states that feminist theory and research in the social sciences is much less developed and sophisticated and even less "feminist" than work in the humanities. Just as we see few references to our work among nonfeminists in our own discipline, we note relatively sparse treatment of social science theory and research in interdisciplinary feminist studies; certainly, the attention of humanities feminists to social science feminists is not equivalent to the attention social science feminists pay to the humanities.[18]

There is a difference between claiming women's studies is a "multidisciplinary" or an "interdisciplinary" effort. It is certainly the former; there are parallel research communities and bodies of literature across all of the humanities and social sciences and some of the natural sciences as well. But many of us also claim it is interdisciplinary, meaning that the community of scholars that thinks, theorizes, and seeks answers together crosses disciplinary boundaries.[19]

Thus, just as it is possible and important to explore the barriers between feminist research and the larger disciplinary communities, so it is possible and important to explore the barriers between discipline-based feminist research and the larger women's studies community. Here I will suggest four aspects of the logic and practice of inquiry that inhibit more reciprocal interdisciplinarity especially with regard to political science, both as a social science and as a distinct discipline. These are: (1) the "science" question in feminist studies; (2) the discovery of politics; (3) the political climate and relation to the concerns of political science; (4) the contrast between text- and non-text-centered disciplines in light of poststructuralism. As before, I will outline each briefly and not attempt complete elaboration.

The "Science Question"

Feminist studies has played a leading role in contemporary criticism of the dominant theoretical underpinnings and practices of science. This attention to theory, method, and philosophies of knowing has helped to maintain a vitality and critical edge in feminist studies that is remarkable. But there is an unfortunate side to such widespread raising of epistemological banners. This literature in its (academically) popularized version tends to caricature and homogenize the sciences and social sciences, rendering research that displays signs of accepting any set of scientific norms in making empirical claims suspicious and possibly nonfeminist.[20] These views gain added resonance from both popular stereotype and the "different voices" literature supporting the notion that women are more intuitive, holistic, and connected, in contrast to scientific and mathematical thinking, which is also defined as "masculine" in character.

Logics and practices of inquiry are undeniably related to gender culture and the gender basis of the social structure of related professions. But there is not "science," there are "sciences" (in the same sense as "feminisms"); there is not computer usage, there are different means and styles of using computers (Perry and Greber 1990; Turkle and Papert 1990). Feminist scholars should not buttress traditional dichotomies by making assumptions about what can and cannot be said or accomplished using scientific and empirical modes of analysis. Feminist social scientists who use quantitative analytical methods are not just "squashing people into little numbers." To suggest they do because of an assumed logic of inquiry without considering their work more carefully is simply to fall prey to a revised but nevertheless dangerous form of math anxiety. Feminist scholars in the social sciences are, in fact, exploring the implications of feminist theory for the practices of empirical social science. This requires studying and understanding research practices as well as probing the theory-based logic of inquiry.

The Discovery of Politics

In the era in which women's studies was founded, politics was "everywhere." Whereas explicit attention to politics and government had earlier been relatively restricted in the liberal arts outside a few fields—for example, political science, history, sociology, and philosophy—scholars influenced by the cultural politics of the student and counterculture movement, feminists influenced by the declaration that "the personal is political," as well as others similarly grounded in the politics of the 1960s increasingly pressed their examination of politics in their substantive studies and in the practices of academia.

For those of us in political science, similarly influenced, but also having chosen a field of study explicitly and consciously about politics, the overwhelming academic attention to politics was exciting and encouraging, but in the long run it has also contributed to a certain degree of isolation of political scientists. The excitement of the discovery of politics led to a proliferation of political theorizing often based loosely on current trends and fashions but ungrounded in the long tradition of political debate, discussion, and research; naive with regard to the complexities of politics and political discourse; and resistant to the idea that empirical research about politics has told us much worth knowing. Political science–based feminist theorists often voice frustration with feminist theory that ignores the knowledge gained from the long-standing debates in political theory, even within the "male-stream."[21]

Even recognizing the fact that political science has been undeniably androcentric and despite the fact that politically involved people who pay close attention to the news know a lot about politics, systematic and scholarly study adds considerably to political understanding, political deliberation, and political action. Of course, any simple statement of what has been achieved and what could be offered by one of the liberal arts disciplines is bound to sound silly. But one of the central missions of political science, for example, is engaging in critical reading of major theoretical debates in politics over the last two thousand years. One could not begin in such a short space to outline the knotty problems that are standard fare for consideration by historical political theorists—the questions about the relationships between human character and political organization, the nature and dynamics of power and authority, the problems of human political action and inaction, resistance, and acquiescence, and considerations of democracy, authoritarianism, justice, community, and how these and the range of other political norms relate to political process and structure. In the more empirical vein the mission of political science includes understanding the dynamics of politics at all levels of analysis from the individual to the international level, including political thinking and activity, organization, and processes, and all of these both in their abstract and generalizable aspects and in their particular, national, cultural, or locally bound contexts. Certainly, the recent emphasis on "globalism" is nothing new to a discipline in which two of the major divisions of the discipline are comparative politics (including area studies) and international politics.

Political Climate

In theory (as it were) one might expect a field as devoted to politics as women's studies to seek scholarly counsel from the discipline most self-consciously devoted to the study of politics, much as scholars might turn to historians to help them learn history, to psychologists to learn psychology, or to literary critics to learn how to read. But feminist studies has not tended to look to political science for political theory or analysis very often, partly because of the political climate in which feminist studies developed and the political ideology dominant within feminist studies.

Most feminist political scientists have criticized their own discipline for focusing too much on conventional and formal definitions of politics and political action (e.g., concentrating so heavily on elections and electoral behavior as compared with other forms) and certainly for ignoring the politics of nongovernmental organizations. But the dominant political ideologies of feminist studies have tended to rest at the other extreme of the political continuum, regarding things governmental and electoral as male dominated, irrelevant, and, almost worst of all, "liberal" and "reformist."[22]

Here there are two related problems. First, while the demand to expand the definition of the political is absolutely correct, the tendency, in the process, to downplay the theoretical importance of the state and government to the point at which they appear only where unavoidable (as in analysis of reproductive "rights") is a mistake. Government and politics play a crucial role in structuring sex/gender systems; it simply will not do to ignore scholarly study of how this works. The current worldwide changes in governance and politics should make it overwhelmingly clear this is the case. The fears on the part of Russian feminists, for example, that even if a new democracy is constructed it will be "minus women," and therefore no democracy at all, bears witness to the primary importance of politics and government (Ashwin 1991). In the short history of contemporary feminist studies the crucial influence of two theoretical traditions has contributed to this problem. In the founding days of women's studies one of the most fruitful sources of theory was theoretical Marxism, which defined government as epiphenomenal with respect to economic organization. From a very different direction cultural theories tend to downplay the importance of the institutional and material arrangements such as government. This is not to say that either theoretical Marxism or cultural theory necessitates stripping the governmental out of feminist political analysis, as the work of Petchesky (1984) and Eisenstein (1988), among others shows. But these two theoretical forces together combined, in their actual usage as opposed to theoretical possibilities, to leave government to the side.

A second issue is of concern as well. For a scholarly field that devotes so much energy to theory, including theories of politics, feminist studies tends to be remarkably inattentive to taking care with political theory. Often, to the eye of theorists trained in political theory, terms such as *liberalism* and *reform* seem to serve as much as symbolic flags as they do analytic concepts. Certainly, it is wrong to say that "a concern" with particular problems, such as representation or specific policy changes is in itself "merely" reformist or even indicative of liberalism. Likewise, merely incorporating class into theoretical analysis does not make it Marxist. A topic is not liberal—or Marxist or sufficient to identify any given theory or ideology—an argument is.

My point is not, as it will be taken by some, to argue that liberalism or reformism are adequate bases for feminist theory or politics. Rather, it is that a substantial portion of feminist discussion of what constitutes liberalism, reformism, democratic theory, and their relation to feminism has been distinctly inadequate, at least until recently, with analyses by scholars such as Carole Pateman (1988, 1989) and Anne Phillips (1991). More often comparisons of liberalism in feminist theory with other forms such as socialist or radical feminism are vague, underspecified, and make less clear and useful distinctions among these different types of theory than is often thought. As many political theorists have pointed out, even if the dominant traditions of political theory and political theory debate are afflicted with profound androcentrism and patriarchalism, intensive study of these traditions nevertheless has a considerable amount to offer feminist theory that is, in any case, affected by these traditions. The same is true of the body of work devoted to empirical study of power, governance, collective decision making, and conflict and conflict resolution on the local, national, and global scale. These, after all, are the central subjects of political science.

In fact, attention in women's studies to these problems is already changing as, perhaps, world events make it impossible to be casual about government. There has been a tremendous growth in feminist political history in the last decade, accompanied by a burgeoning of the feminist law literature and some key contributions by political philosophers such as Nancy Fraser (1989). Interdisciplinary efforts to understand gender and the welfare state (e.g., Gordon 1990) bear impressive witness to the change. My argument is not simply that feminist political scientists have been undervalued in the feminist studies community but, rather, that feminist scholars, who, like political scientists, have been developing theoretical, methodological, and substantive expertise with respect to political institutions and processes, have more to contribute to feminist studies than has been recognized in recent years.

The Impact of Poststructuralism and Postmodernism

Poststructuralism and its relatives have had profound effects on scholarship in the last decade, not just within the humanities but also in the social sciences.[23] Certainly, it is possible to see its effects even beyond the community of scholars who accept the name. But, even so, important differences among disciplines mean the influence, reaction, and use, for the most part, will be different. Here I will briefly suggest two differences. First is the distinction between text- and non-text-centered disciplines, together with the standing of empirical statements, and second is the question of intentionality.

Important disciplinary differences must affect the reception of poststructuralist and postmodernist messages. (Such a modern construction!) The disciplines of literature are text-centered; the social sciences (and some humanities disciplines such as history) are not. The point holds even granting that each of these disciplines relies heavily on written texts and even accepting the view that language is not a medium to separate and distinct "reality." To be pedestrian about it, even among those of us especially interested in gender politics, some of us went into our particular disciplines because we wanted to study written texts and some because we wanted to study those things the texts are talking about. Regardless of theoretical background, literature specialists want to produce or read literature as their main task. For others of us the written text is only a medium for holding a conversation about how to solve problems that must be understood in their material dimensions: war, poverty, apartheid, education, natural resources, violence, and so forth. Despite the problem of values and objectivity within social science discussed earlier, for social scientists, including political scientists, that conversation is supposed to include the public as citizens and policymakers.

Part of the goal of a considerable portion of political science is at least the development of citizenship, if not the shaping of policy and government. Certainly, U.S. social science, from the beginning, has pressed toward acting in the world (Ross 1991). If one's scholarly passion is devoted especially to the literary texts themselves, the products of the creative imaginations of authors—even without Author(ity)—the idea that there is nothing but language (at least for scholarly purposes) does not pose as fundamental a problem as it must to the others of us whose primary scholarly passion is devoted to trying to understand and perhaps affect social conditions and problems. Even in the more theoretical and philosophical communities of this social science, and among those whose method is primarily interpretive rather than empirical, scholars are likely to be more sensitive to the empirical and hypothetical aspects and implications of theory and theorizing than may be true in literary fields.

Even in the most text-centered of the fields of political science, historical political philosophy, the conception of the task nevertheless makes the project more one of holding a conversation about things outside the written text. Although historical political philosophers study written texts of political philosophy, training in political philosophy often emphasizes that these texts are media through which political philosophers hold conversations about politics across time and space.

The problem of communication among writers and readers raises a second fundamental difficulty posed by important premises of poststructuralism: the deconstruction of the authorial voice. Certainly, one of the common foci of dispute with regard to poststructuralism and postmodernism is the "empowering of the reader," as it is sometimes put, or the denial of the author and of intention. The importance of this debate for understanding the position of social science is not as simple as whether there is simple meaning or whether meaning can be transferred from person to person or anything of the sort. It should not be forgotten that some of these points, which form empirical assumptions on the part of some poststructuralists, have long been subjects of empirical questions and investigation on the part of many social scientists, especially in social psychology and the fields influenced by social psychology.[24]

The power issue raised by poststructuralists is an important one. Even were it possible to recover pristine authorial meaning or intention, to require that the only way readers may approach a text is to search for and lock themselves into that pristine text is to require a form of slavery on the part of readers. That slavery is even more dehumanizing when placed in the context of the sociopolitical relations within which texts are produced and read. This is, in part, what arguments about "the canon" are about.[25] Feminist scholars and other marginalized groups have fought to release themselves from that slavery.

But for political scientists the political questions, not just of power but also of responsibility, are likely to be even more compelling. In political science the study of the day-to-day life of politics and government reminds us that denial of voice or intention, and certainly the denial of responsibility to seek to understand others' voices and intentions is a fundamental part of some of the most dangerous and terrifying politics the world has seen. Among the common objects of our study are Berlin, Chernobyl, Soweto, Tiananmen Square, and the Plaza de Mayo. The political theorist who has spent a career focusing on the nature of the political, the governmental, in all its tangible aspects must have trouble forgetting how the denial of voice and intention can become part of the "banality of evil," as Arendt (1964) described the character of the Holocaust.[26] Thus, if the empirical urges of political and other social scientists appear banal to those more enveloped in poststructuralism, it is preferable to the more deadly and profoundly painful banalities of life.

SECOND CONCLUSION

These arguments will no doubt seem cranky to some. But the relations within the community of scholars known as women's studies can be subjected to the same kind of analysis feminists have for so long aimed at the communities of scholars within disciplines. Once upon a time (as they say in fairy tales) women's studies scholars tended to claim to be developing a field, a scholarly community. The intellectual differences between feminist scholars and their home fields seemed more pressing than the intellectual differences among feminist scholars across fields.

This is no longer the case. The bodies of literature and theory among feminist scholars within many fields have grown immensely. Those of us who are old enough can remember when it seemed possible to keep up with scholarly activity in the far corners of the academic world. Many of us are now overwhelmed by our own academic neighborhoods.

What is the nature of the relationship among different feminist communities of scholars? What is their future? The answer cannot be found in the sociological aspects of the problem alone—that is, where feminists are housed and whether they talk to one another. Rather, intellectual and methodological questions are crucial as well.

If, as many of us are inclined to believe, feminist studies is more than the sum of its parts, but not a completely separate discipline undefined by the existent disciplinary boundaries and differences, the interdisciplinary feminist community has considerable work left to do drawing connections and developing methods for this joint project.

NOTES

1. It is not entirely correct to call the early 1970s the "early days" of research on women and politics among political scientists; there was sporadic work reaching back to the first decades of the existence of professional political science, founded in 1909 by discontented members of the American Economics Association. Most notably, excellent research was carried out by women such as Sophinisba Breckinridge, the first woman to earn a Ph.D. degree in political science. She, like most other women in the field, was unable to find an academic job within political science and carried her work out within an applied research setting and, ultimately, an academic social welfare program.

2. Throughout this essay *we* refers to the community of scholars doing women and politics or gender politics research within political science.

3. I discuss the current state of the field in Sapiro 1991.

4. The reaction is most evident in the organization of the National Association of Scholars, which sees changes such as the growing influence of women's studies as an assault on the integrity of scholarship and higher education.

5. See Bourke and Grossholtz 1974; Elshtain 1979; Flax 1983; Goot and Reid 1975; Kelley, Ronan, and Cawley 1987; Keohane 1981; Lovenduski 1981; Morgan 1974; Nelson 1989; and Sapiro 1979, 1987a, 1987b, 1991.

6. These different constructions are, of course, related to one another, and a substantial body of work ties them together, largely now through the train of work spun from Carol Gilligan's very influential thesis *In a Different Voice* (1982); as well as Belenky et al. *Women's Ways of Knowing* (1986); and in the sciences, for example, Evelyn Fox

Keller's writing (e.g., 1985). My point here, however, is to distinguish an argument that focuses primarily on who does the thinking (which itself can be explained) to what is thought. For some lively and contentious treatments of the place of the "different voices" discussion in political science, see Tronto 1987; Steuernagel 1987; and Sapiro 1987a.

7. These different viewpoints are well summarized and discussed (outside of political science) in Harding 1991. For one of the few theorists of feminist empiricism, see Nelson 1990.

8. For one of the more recent and best essays on the public and private in political theory, see Okin 1990.

9. Many of these terms—*empirical, quantitative, scientific, behavioral, behaviorist*— are widely confused and are often caricatured by critics of the related practices who are not themselves involved in the relevant types of research. For present purposes, at least, let it be noted that these are not synonymous terms. Rational choice theories are derived from economic models, in which people are posited as individuals with consistent, stable, and conscious goals based in their self-interest and whose choices are based in rational goal-seeking behavior. Research employing rational actor models is a matter of defining optimal solutions for self-interested goal seekers and determining the situations under which optimality is not reached. Many (if not most) rational choice theorists see no reason to study preferences themselves or the sources of preferences and argue one can only study manifest behavior in any case and infer preferences from that. For a brief and relatively jargon-free introduction, see Monroe 1991.

10. I use the term *legacy of positivism* rather than *positivism* itself to recognize that critics of social science, especially those based outside of social science, often overestimate the degree to which those who practice empirical social science actually adhere to positivism in any classic sense.

11. For more complete discussion of these issues, see Harding 1987, 1991; Nielson, 1989. Sandra Harding's work is probably the most well-known among feminist scholars.

12. On the other hand, when, as a very young scholar, I had presented in a convention paper a cross-national comparison of public opinion on the status of women, a very senior and eminent political scientist serving as discussant dismissed my paper on the grounds that one cannot look at public opinion on the status of women the way one could examine other public issues because, after all, "our views of women have to do with emotions, and libidos, and that part of life. It's just not rational in the way other issues are."

13. Having been one of the people who made this claim in print (Sapiro 1979), I am also painfully aware that these claims in turn became subject to intense criticism by other feminist writers, who interpreted the argument to say that androcentric research was a simple matter of "bad science." I suspect that most people who argue that androcentric and misogynist research is bad science would not also argue it is only that.

14. There are women among the list of contemporary political theorists who must be read by any serious student of political theory according to almost anyone's criteria; among these are Hannah Arendt, Hannah Pitkin, and Judith Shklar.

15. For more discussion, see Sapiro 1992, chap. 9.

16. Although it is common for humanities scholars to be referred to as "humanists,"

nothing essential about the nature of humanities disciplines makes their practitioners any more humanist than are practitioners of social science, especially given the variety within both.

17. The definition and evaluation of feminist theory would be a good topic for a feminist studies conference or other serious interdisciplinary efforts. Indeed, at this point it is difficult to define precisely what the differences are. I have experienced a number of situations in which feminist social science scholars could not see what was "theoretical" about a theoretical discussion offered by a humanities scholar. I would not be surprised if the reverse were also true.

18. The primary exception is the widespread attention in the humanities to Carol Gilligan's book *In a Different Voice,* although its findings and theories are often misinterpreted and certainly exaggerated and the bulk of the empirical research responding to that work (other than Belenky, Clinchy, Goldberger, and Tarule 1986) has been ignored.

One of my favorite examples of the contrast concerns an interdisciplinary graduate research seminar in women's studies at my university, in which professors based in social science and in humanities alternate teaching. The seminar is intended and advertised as broadly interdisciplinary, attempting to foster the development of skills to work in an interdisciplinary field. One year, when it was taught by a social scientist, students in a literature department reported that students there discussed the course and argued with one another that they should wait until a humanities professor taught the course; only one humanities-based student took the course with the social scientist. The following year I witnessed many social science students discussing how valuable it would be to take the course that year *because* it would be taught by a humanities professor and therefore would give them important exposure to a different and highly valuable area.

19. I am impressed with Lynn Hankinson Nelson's argument that "individuals are knowers only in a derivative sense," meaning that "epistemological communities" and not just individuals need to be self-reflective in their science, which I would extend to scholarly inquiry more generally (Nelson 1990, 314). Further, I accept the view that much of the vitality of women's studies comes from grounding in traditional disciplines and its continual traffic with the questions, issues, and methods of those disciplines.

20. Many of us have been charged with not being able to do truly feminist work *because* of using empirical tools of social science such as statistics or surveys, even by members of our own disciplines. See, in my case, Steuernagel 1987. It is interesting to note that in their discussion of a conference on women and computers many women— many feminists—felt similarly excluded by virtue of their participating in this "masculine" field. See Perry and Greber 1990, 90.

21. For a few recent examples admittedly chosen haphazardly, see Elshtain 1987; Tronto 1987; di Stefano 1988; Phelan 1990; and Sapiro 1992. This list should also bear witness to the fact that political science–based feminist theorists have considerable disagreements among themselves as well.

22. I remember all too clearly the number of feminist studies activists who declared before the 1980 presidential election that politics, and especially elections, make no difference, or at least none that goes beyond minor reformist changes. I later saw some of

them at demonstrations protesting the effects of the Supreme Court appointments made in the following decade.

23. Although some use the terms identically, when I use *poststructuralist,* I am referring to one distinct characteristic that distinguishes it from the broader movement, postmodernism, as suggested in Pauline Marie Rosenau's (1992) work on postmodernism and the social sciences: the former is more "uncompromisingly" antiempirical, which is one of the important tendencies at issue here.

24. It is important to be mindful that this antiempirical approach to knowledge is based in part on empirical statements about the state of the world and mind, just as the arguments against theory within postmodernism constitute, themselves, a theory, as Rosenau (1992) has pointed out. Of course, that doesn't make these arguments wrong, simply more complicated and interesting.

25. I suspect that in any case students of political theory have not been asked to lock themselves into specific texts as much as may be true in some areas of literature. While there are certainly many political theorists whose work is devoted to understanding what Rousseau or Plato or especially Marx "really meant," probably more political theorists are devoted, for example, to trying to figure out the potential for political community by reading smart and thoughtful writers like Rousseau, Plato, or Marx. One would read the same texts, but the task is quite different. If my point is correct, this difference in task would also constitute one of the points of misunderstanding between scholars in different fields.

26. Lest anyone believe I am claiming a superiority of social science as compared with literature—which I am not—I also recommend David Hughes's 1984 novel, *The Pork Butcher,* for its comprehension of the banality of the evil of the Holocaust.

REFERENCES

Arendt, Hannah. 1964. *Eichmann in Jerusalem: A Report on the Banality of Evil.* New York: Viking Press.

Ashwin, Sarah. 1991. "Development of Feminism in the *Perestroika* Era." *Report on the USSR* (30 August): n.p.

Belenky, Mary Field, Blythe McVicker Clinchy, Nancy Rule Goldberger, and Jill Mattuck Tarule. 1986. *Women's Ways of Knowing: The Development of Self, Voice, and Mind.* New York: Basic Books.

Bourke, Susan C., and Jean Grossholtz. 1974. "Politics as an Unnatural Practice: Political Science Looks at Female Participation." *Politics and Society* 4:255–66.

Brown, Wendy. 1988. *Manhood and Politics: A Feminist Reading in Political Theory.* Totowa, N.J.: Rowman and Littlefield.

Darcy, R., Susan Welch, and Janet Clark. 1987. *Women, Elections, and Representation.* New York: Longman.

Di Stephano, Christine. 1988. "Dilemmas of Difference: Feminism, Modernity, and Postmodernism." *Women and Politics* 8:1–24.

Eisenstein, Zillah R. 1988. *The Female Body and the Law*. Berkeley: University of California Press.

Elshtain, Jean Bethke. 1974. "Moral Woman and Immoral Man: A Consideration of the Public-Private Split and Its Political Ramifications." *Politics and Society* 4:453–74.

———. 1979. "Methodological Sophistication and Conceptual Confusion: A Critique of Mainstream Political Science." In *The Prism of Sex: Essays in the Sociology of Knowledge*, ed. Julia Sherman and Evelyn Beck, 229–52. Madison: University of Wisconsin Press.

———. 1981. *Public Man, Private Woman: Women in Social and Political Thought*. Princeton: Princeton University Press.

———. 1987. *Women and War*. New York: Basic.

Flax, Jane. 1983. "Political Philosophy and the Patriarchal Unconscious: A Psychoanalytic Perspective on Epistemology and Metaphysics." In *Discovering Reality*, ed. Sandra Harding and Merrill Hintikka, 245–82. Dordrecht: D. Reidel.

Fraser, Nancy. 1989. *Unruly Practices: Power, Discourse, and Gender in Contemporary Social Theory*. Minneapolis: University of Minnesota Press.

Gilligan, Carol. 1987. *In a Different Voice: Psychological Theory and Women's Development*. Cambridge: Harvard University Press.

Gordon, Linda, ed. 1990. *Women, the State, and Welfare*. Madison: University of Wisconsin Press.

Harding, Sandra. 1991. *Whose Science? Whose Knowledge? Thinking from Women's Lives*. Ithaca: Cornell University Press.

———, ed. 1987. *Feminism and Methodology: Social Science Issues*. Bloomington: Indiana University Press.

Hughes, David. 1984. *The Pork Butcher*. Harmondsworth: Penguin.

Keller, Evelyn Fox. 1985. *Reflections on Gender and Science*. New Haven: Yale University Press.

Kelley, Rita Mae, Bernard Ronan, and Margaret E. Cawley. 1987. "Liberal Positivistic Epistemology and Research on Women and Politics." *Women and Politics* 7:11–28.

Keohane, Nannerl O. 1981. "Speaking from Silence: Women and the Silence of Politics." In *A Feminist Perspective in the Academy: The Difference It Makes*, ed. Elizabeth Langland and Walter Gove, 86–100. Chicago: University of Chicago Press.

Lovenduski, Joni. 1981. "Toward the Emasculation of Political Science: The Impact of Feminism." In *Men's Studies Modified: The Impact of Feminism on the Disciplines*, ed. Dale Spender, 83–92. New York: Pergamon.

Monroe, Kirsten Renwick. 1991. "The Theory of Rational Action: What Is It? How Useful Is It for Political Science?" In *Political Science: Looking to the Future*, vol. 1: *The Theory and Practice of Political Science*, ed. William Crotty, 77–98. Evanston, Ill.: Northwestern University Press.

Morgan, Jan. 1974. "Women and Political Socialization: Fact and Fantasy in Easton and Dennis and in Lane." *Politics* 9:50–55.

Nelson, Barbara J. 1989. "Women and Knowledge in Political Science: Texts, Histories, and Epistemologies." *Women and Politics* 9:1–26.

Nelson, Lynn Hankinson. 1990. *Who Knows? From Quine to a Feminist Empiricism.* Philadelphia: Temple University Press.

Nielsen, Joyce McCarl, ed. 1989. *Feminist Research Methods: Readings from the Social Sciences.* Boulder, Colo.: Westview Press.

Okin, Susan Moller. 1990. "Gender, the Public, and the Private." In *Modern Political Theory,* ed. David Held, 67–90. London: Polity Press.

Pateman, Carole. 1988. *The Sexual Contract.* Stanford: Stanford University Press.

———. 1989. *The Disorder of Women.* Stanford: Stanford University Press.

Perry, Ruth, and Lisa Greber. 1990. "Women and Computers: An Introduction." *Signs* 16:74–101.

Petchesky, Rosalind Pollack. 1984. *Abortion and Woman's Choice: The State, Sexuality, and Reproductive Freedom.* New York: Longman.

Phelan, Shane. 1990. "Feminism and Individualism." *Women and Politics* 10:1–18.

Phillips, Anne. 1991. *Engendering Democracy.* University Park: Pennsylvania State University Press.

Rosaldo, Michelle, and Louise Lamphere, eds. 1974. *Women, Culture, and Society.* Stanford: Stanford University Press.

Rosenau, Pauline Marie. 1992. *Post-Modernism and the Social Sciences: Insights, Inroads, and Intrusions.* Princeton: Princeton University Press.

Ross, Dorothy. 1991. *The Origins of American Social Science.* Cambridge: Cambridge University Press.

Sapiro, Virginia. 1979. "Women's Studies and Political Conflict." In *The Prism of Sex: Essays in the Sociology of Knowledge,* ed. Julia Sherman and Evelyn Beck, 318–24. Madison: University of Wisconsin Press.

———. 1983. *The Political Integration of Women: Roles, Socialization, and Politics.* Urbana: University of Illinois Press.

———. 1987a. "Reflections on Reflections: Personal Ruminations." *Women and Politics* 7:21–29.

———. 1987b. "What the Political Socialization of Women Can Tell Us about the Political Socialization of People." In *The Impact of Feminist Research in the Academy,* ed. Christie Farnham, 148–73. Bloomington: Indiana University Press.

———. 1991. "Gender Politics, Gendered Politics: The State of the Field." In *Political Science: Looking to the Future,* vol. 1: *The Theory and Practice of Political Science,* ed. William Crotty, 165–88. Evanston, Ill.: Northwestern University Press.

———. 1992. *A Vindication of Political Virtue: The Political Theory of Mary Wollstonecraft.* Chicago: University of Chicago Press.

Shapiro, Robert Y., and Harpeet Mahajan. 1986. "Gender Differences in Policy Preferences: A Summary of Trends from the 1960s to the 1980s." *Public Opinion Quarterly* 50:42–61.

Steuernagel, Gertrude A. 1987. "Reflections on Women and Political Participation." *Women and Politics* 7:3–14.

Tronto, Joan C. 1987. "Political Science and Caring: Or, the Perils of Balkanized Social Science." *Women and Politics* 7:85–98.

Turkle, Sherry, and Seymour Papert. 1990. "Epistemological Pluralism: Styles and Voices within the Computer Culture." *Signs* 16:128–57.

Chapter 12

Disloyal to the Disciplines: A Feminist Trajectory in the Borderlands

Judith Stacey

It is nearly a decade now since Barrie Thorne and I commenced a set of public discussions about the impact of feminism on sociology that we summarized in an essay with the somewhat reproachful title "The Missing Feminist Revolution in Sociology" (Stacey and Thorne 1985). The initial impetus for that project was my participation in a session at a National Women's Studies Association conference in 1982 that had the more politically specific, and, for its period, unremarkable title, "Socialist-Feminist Perspectives on the Disciplines." Few feminist conferences or lecture series would be likely to adopt such a title today, nor would I be likely, if one did so, to be invited, or to agree, to assess sociology under such an aegis. I remain committed to the ideals of economic and gender justice and to those of political and cultural democracy that once undergirded my earlier socialist-feminist identity, but too much has happened in global geopolitics and in feminist theoretical developments to sustain my earlier comfort with the first political term or with the dual structure of such an identity.

Moreover, I can no longer imagine undertaking an essay that presumed that sociology, or any of the existing disciplines, was the appropriate terrain to excavate for a feminist revolution in knowledge. To anticipate discrete revolutions in discrete scholarly disciplines is to betray a decidedly unrevolutionary conception of the disciplinary constructions of knowledge. Had such a feminist "revolution" occurred in sociology, should it not have challenged the discipline's recognizable borders or "essence?"

Shifts in feminist labeling fashions and in my own disciplinary self-conception index a significant set of transformations within feminist political discourse as well as in feminist relations to the disciplines. I discuss these transformations autobiographically by "reading" the trajectory of my own work as a feminist sociologist as emblematic, perhaps some will think it symptomatic, of shifts that have taken place in theoretical and disciplinary fashions in women's studies and social theory more generally. To take this tack is to enact my current "disciplinary" location as an ambivalently postmodernist, reflexive ethnographer. Or, for those unsympathetic with what some have called "the postmodernist turn in anthropology" (Mascia-Lees, Sharpe, and Cohen 1989), it may confirm the judgment of a hostile reviewer of my ethnography *Brave New Families* (Stacey 1990), who labeled its first-person narrative approach "self-indulgent."

Certainly, my trajectory is unique—indeed, in certain aspects, idiosyncratic—and I do not presume that the evolution of my own theoretical and substantive interests typifies that of feminist sociologists. The core of American sociology, if such a decentered discipline can be said to have a core, remains deeply positivist, while its diverse qualitative, interpretive, and theoretical schools have, in varying degrees, accommodated themselves to feminist inquiry without much evidence of conceptual turmoil. Thus, a great many—perhaps a statistical majority—of feminist sociologists continue to conduct valuable empirical research, often with significant policy implications, unaffected and unfazed by shifts in theoretical climates that I have found so compelling and unsettling.[1]

In fact, I believe that it is the idiosyncratic character of my feminist trajectory that might help to illuminate certain notable recent developments in feminist scholarship. My scholarship has always been centered not in sociology but, rather, on the disciplinary borderlands that have nurtured the intellectual audacity feminists have needed to think our ways radically through the disciplines. But in this regard I have begun to find myself increasingly out of step. A great deal of feminist scholarship today seems more entrenched in and bound by academic disciplinary identities than it did when Barrie Thorne and I recorded our reflections on feminist knowledge transformations.

The increased strength of disciplinarity observable in contemporary feminist scholarship can be read, of course, as a cheering index of our astonishing successes. In most humanities and social science disciplines today feminist inquiry has achieved undisputable legitimacy—in some, a level of acceptability approaching normalcy—and the demographic trends seem irreversible. The Sex and Gender section of the American Sociological Association, for example, has displaced the far-better funded research subspecialty of Medical Sociology as the largest "subfield" represented in the organization. In my own sociology department four-fifths of the entering graduate students in the last few years have identified feminism, gender, or women as one of their central areas of interest, and nationally as well as locally, sociology, like other social sciences and humanities disciplines, is a feminizing field.[2]

Yet I am worried, as well as cheered, by these achievements, for this success also breeds new intellectual and political dangers. Because so many feminists can now enjoy sympathetic collegiality and legitimacy within our disciplinary enclaves, there is less compelling impulse for extradisciplinary migrations. As it becomes increasingly possible for feminists to achieve (what was once unthinkable) a fully respectable and rewarded academic career within a conventional discipline, there is less incentive or demand for feminists to acquire counterdisciplinary language and research questions or to participate in the more transgressive forms of knowledge renovation, which I still consider to be crucial. I worry that this may blunt the critical edge as well as the public intelligibility of our once visionary project. Perhaps this anxiety signals my personal anomalous experience. For, precisely during this period of feminization and of feminist incorporation in my official discipline, I have been experiencing my own work and identity as increasingly marginal to "actually existing sociology." Is it this traveler or her disciplinary itinerary that has provoked this anomaly?

Sketched schematically my trajectory through my discipline travels from socialist-feminist historical sociology to feminist and "postsocialist," ethnographic sociology. I have spent most of my research time since my first year as a graduate sociology student at Brandeis University in 1973 studying family revolutions and always by transgressing disciplinary boundaries. The two major research projects I completed since then were preoccupied with a common set of substantive issues—gender, family, and rapid processes of broad-scale social change. They differ greatly, however, in their geopolitical settings, research methods, and textual products. The first, about peasant families and revolution in modern China, trafficked in historical sociology. The book that resulted was a theoretical analysis of secondary literature, organized chronologically and written in a conventional third-person narrative format (Stacey 1983). My second long-term research focused on family change among white, working people living in postindustrial "Silicon Valley," California. After three years of commuter fieldwork, I wrote an ethnography in a first-person, reflexive mode, which incorporated dialogic elements, organized the book somewhat novelistically, and dusted it with *post-* words (Stacey 1990). In my current research, a collaborative study, with feminist literary critic Judith Newton, of male cultural critics, I am no longer studying family revolutions, but I am still gathering life histories to illuminate and intervene in broader political and intellectual transformations.

What little unity is discernible in my work lies in Left feminist political and theoretical domains rather than in research topic, methodology, or epistemology. For better and worse, I work as a disciplinary dilettante. If the undisciplined character of my academic affiliations is somewhat unusual, it has historic roots in the social movement that generated feminist scholarship. It seems crucial to note that, when I entered the doctoral program in sociology at Brandeis University in 1973, I did so as a feminist who had already participated in establishing a women's studies program elsewhere.[3] Indeed, it was my "conversion" to feminism, my commitment to emergent women's studies, and my desire to study and build feminist theory that led me to abandon a doctoral degree in education that I had been pursuing and to enter a social science discipline instead. Feminism was (and remains) my primary—and sociology a secondary, and, indeed, somewhat of an arbitrary—disciplinary affiliation. In fact, when in the early 1970s I looked for a disciplinary context in which to pursue my/our then new interest in feminist theory, I applied for admission to doctoral programs in anthropology as well as in sociology. Looking back, it seems less surprising to me that I should have migrated from the historical to the anthropological borders of my nominal discipline than that it has taken me so long to do so.

My un-disciplined proclivities met few constraints in the Brandeis sociology department, a decidedly maverick program that foregrounded and enacted the decentered character of the discipline that was depicted in one of the first influential books I read about my new field, Alvin Gouldner's *The Coming Crisis in Western Sociology* (1970). Profoundly affected by the radical pedagogy and self-actualization ideals promoted by political and countercultural movements during the 1960s, the Brandeis faculty had eliminated a shared curriculum, or set of degree requirements. Even more unusual for an American sociology department was its pervasive hostility to positivism. Interpretive sociology and theory were privileged at Brandeis, and the privileged body of theory for my cohort of New Left veterans then was Marxism and its Frankfurt School elaborations. My sister graduate students and I quickly identified as socialist-feminists and steeped ourselves in the emergent Marxist-feminist "discourse," a word we had not yet heard of.

We were trailblazing here. Although there were a couple of feminists on the Brandeis faculty, they were no more advanced in this then nascent endeavor than we. Consequently, my principal graduate school experience involved a form of collective self-education. With and without faculty participation, feminist graduate students formed study groups in which we made up a decidedly transdisciplinary approach to feminist sociology as we went along. I also benefited from an exhilarating extracurricular graduate education. By participating in one of the Northeast coast Marxist-feminist groups that emerged in the early 1970s, by teaching (while learning) "Marxism for Women" at a local grass roots Women's School, and later, and most significantly, by serving for more than a decade on the editorial collective of the interdisciplinary journal *Feminist Studies,* I "interned" in feminist theory and developed my un-disciplined approach to feminist sociology. The startling overrepresentation of Brandeis degree holders among feminist sociologists who have published widely recognized work suggests the creative potential of a highly permissive approach to disciplinary training.[4]

This was the intellectual milieu that enabled the audacity of selecting for my dissertation topic a subject about which I had received no formal schooling: patriarchy and socialist revolution in China. Of course, the political milieu that fostered that decision was equally heady and is hard to recapture. Highly romanticized images of Cultural Revolution in China and wildly inflated (or grossly understated) reports that "Women Hold Up Half the Sky" were being deposited on overly receptive anti–Vietnam War shores by waves swelling in the wake of Nixon's historic thaw with China; these inspired enormous curiosity and enthusiasm among American socialist-feminists. Although twenty-five years had passed since the Chinese revolution, the Chinese Communists did not seem to have followed the disappointing precedent set by the Russian Bolsheviks in their earlier postrevolutionary backlash against family and gender policy in the Soviet Union.[5] I was eager to explore the sources and effects of the seemingly more resilient Maoist family revolution.

"Dual-systems" theory, the dominant socialist-feminist framework of the period, which presumed that gender and social class represent two distinct and interrelated systems of domination, influenced my original conceptualization of my study. Because dual-systems theory asserted the relative autonomy and equal significance of gender, it seemed then to be the most promising strategy for liberating feminism from the subordinate position in its "unhappy marriage" to Marxism.[6] Examining the history of the Chinese revolution through the lens of gender and family dynamics, my analysis pushed feminist claims for the fundamental significance and the relative autonomy of gender about as far as they could go. So far, in fact, that they upturned the dual-systems premise with which I had begun my research. The prerevolutionary agrarian crisis, I argued, was also inseparably a patriarchal peasant family crisis, and the resolution of that crisis through policies that built patriarchal socialism was a central vehicle for the victory of the Chinese Communists. Thus, I concluded, gender and class dynamics were inextricably intertwined in the Chinese revolution, and a fully feminist historical materialism rather than a dual-systems model was needed to comprehend this.

By the time I completed my study of the Chinese family revolution I was dissatisfied not only with dual-systems theory but also with the abstract and secondary character of this research and book and their remoteness from the agency of women to which I was committed theoretically. This fed my determination that my next project would involve the sort of primary, "hands-on," qualitative research, that I, like many feminists by the early 1980s, had come to presume was the privileged method for feminist research.[7] Coinciding with my newly expanded personal family commitments—the birth of my son in 1981— this conviction conspired to place geographic restrictions on my possible research fields. The demands and delights of delayed mothering, also characteristic of my generation of feminists, confined my field research options to locations accessible to my San Francisco Bay Area residence. In fact, it seems plausible to me that the emergence of what anthropologists George Marcus and Michael Fischer (1986) approvingly call "repatriated anthropology" in the United States may have been propelled by changes in the gender and demographic composition of their discipline as much as by a principled response to the politically troubled conditions of postcolonial ethnography. The influx into anthropology of women whose family commitments were less portable or expendable than those typical of their male counterparts would in itself have fostered interest in formulating geographically accessible ethnographic questions.[8] Certainly, my own ethnographic impulses were about to be "disciplined" in this manner.

It was during this personal period of research transition that Barrie Thorne and I wrote "The Missing Feminist Revolution in Sociology" (Stacey and Thorne 1985), in which, in a passing comment, we lamented the dearth of feminist sociologists who had chosen to work within the discipline's own rich, ethnographic tradition of community studies. This aside unwittingly foreshadowed the project I was soon to engage—my accidental ethnography of the families of white, working people in California's Silicon Valley. Once again I began with a vintage socialist-feminist subject—working-class gender relationships under postindustrial conditions. Again, too, I began with a historical sociological orientation. In fact, in the project's initial stages I was collaborating with a historian. Our plan was to integrate a historical overview of occupational and demographic shifts in the region and the nation with my untrained conception of a conventional sociological qualitative research design involving numerous semistructured interviews. The political impetus for this research, however, contrasted sharply with the optimistic and innocent motivations for my China study. It was my mounting concern with the antifeminist "profamily" backlash movement in the United States that had been "credited" by many as the grass roots kindling for the 1980s "Reagan revolution."

Given my geographic constraints, it is fortuitous that I lived within commuter reach of an ideal research site for my project. The Silicon Valley was not only a vanguard region of postindustrialization but also one in which the demographic indices of family change were stark and in which feminist ideology once had been articulate and politically consequential. While I selected this research site for its vanguard features, I chose to study a population that I erroneously presumed to manifest the opposite tendencies. Like most white, middle-class feminists, I regarded white and Latino, working-class people as the most "traditional" in their family convictions and behaviors, and thus the primary appreciative audience for the remarkably successful "profamily" performance of the quite untraditional (and unsuccessful) Reagan family.

My formal research design, to interview a large sample of "Anglo" and

Latino people working in and around the electronics industry, unraveled rap-
idly. As my book describes, two interviews that I conducted immediately after
Reagan's landslide reelection in November 1984 profoundly challenged my own
class and gender prejudices and provoked my surrender to the lures of an open-
ended ethnographic quest. First, "Pam," a woman I had known for four months
and thought to be a feminist, revealed to me her recent conversion to evangelical
Christianity and her participation in Christian marriage counseling. One week
later "Dotty," a survivor of an often abusive, thirty-year-long marriage, surprised me with her feminist convictions. Abandoning my research plans, I spent
the next three years conducting intermittent fieldwork among these women and
their kin.

   This accidental—but, I later came to believe, overdetermined—turn to ethnographic methods shifted my disciplinary cross-dressing impulses to anthropology (the discipline that Barrie Thorne and I had earlier rated comparatively
high in our feminist transformation assessments), just when that discipline was
turning reflexive about the power/knowledge nexus of field research and tex-
tuality.[9] This was also a period when postcolonial consciousness, in addition to
demographic changes, had encouraged increasing numbers of anthropologists
to cross-dress as sociologists studying "others" at home.[10] Here, however, I
enjoyed an advantage as a sociologist. Most practitioners of "repatriated anthropology" in the United States were still struggling for full legitimacy in their
discipline, in part because foreign fieldwork has long been one of that discipline's best-equipped border guards patrolling the research terrain it shares with
sociology.

   Doing urban anthropology (or a postcommunity study) as a Jewish, secular
feminist among born-again Christians and hard-living, crisis-riddled people
more than sated my craving for engaged research. It also propelled me spontaneously to struggle with numerous ethical, political, and textual questions about
representation and to engage with some postmodern feminist debates that, by
the late 1980s, were beginning to migrate from literary criticism and the humanities into anthropology, and to a lesser extent into history, but not yet noticeably
into sociology. I lost my feminist ethnographic innocence in the field, as I
explain in an essay written in the midst of this upheaval, "Can There Be a
Feminist Ethnography?" (Stacey 1988). Only a "partially" feminist one is possible, I concluded, intending both senses of the term and placing myself thereby
in the camp of those who reject as utopian the claim that there is such a thing as
a specifically feminist research methodology or even the view that any one
method is specifically suitable for feminist research.[11]

   The partially feminist ethnography I wrote about Pam and Dotty (and me)
bears the traces of these disciplinary and political transitions. I structured the
book as two documentary novellas and wrote it, against resistance from my

male editor, in a reflexive, first-person, and occasionally dialogic narrative style. The novellas, however, are sandwiched inside a more conventionally authoritative, third-person, interpretive sociological account of the history of family revolutions in the United States. Thus, in its structure and style this book enacts my ambivalent relationship to the postmodernist turn in feminist anthropology and exhibits an un-disciplined feminist research and rhetorical stance.

The same tension besets the book's two central arguments. One is avowedly postmodernist, the other an empirically grounded revision of conventional sociological understandings of family and social transformations. I argued first that "the postmodern family" is a useful conceptual category for analyzing the transformation of gender and kinship that has accompanied and helped to shape postindustrial society. Literary critics in a Humanities Institute seminar in which I participated while struggling for an interpretive vocabulary for my ethnography prodded me to develop a theoretical understanding of the elusive concept of "postmodern." Not surprisingly, therefore, I turned to humanists to explicate what I meant when I used "the postmodern family" to signal the collapse of a hegemonic family system. I found that I could readily apply art historian Clive Dilnot's answers to his own rhetorical question, "What is the post-modern?" in an essay on postmodern culture, to current family conditions in the United States. The postmodern, Dilnot maintains, "is first, an uncertainty, an insecurity, a doubt." Most of the *post-* words provoke uneasiness, because they imply, simultaneously, "both the end, or at least the radical transformation of, a familiar pattern of activity or group of ideas," and the emergence of "new fields of cultural activity whose contours are still unclear and whose meanings and implications . . . cannot yet be fathomed" (Dilnot 1986, 245). The postmodern, moreover, is "characterized by the process of the linking up of areas and the crossing of the boundaries of what are conventionally considered to be disparate realms of practice" (249). Similarly, I argued that contemporary U.S. family arrangements are diverse, fluid, and unresolved and that *the* postmodern family is not a new model of family life equivalent to that of the modern family, not the next stage in an orderly progression of family history but, rather, the stage in that history when the belief in a logical progression of stages breaks down. Donning unmistakable postmodernist drag, I wrote: "Rupturing the teleology of modernization narratives that depict an evolutionary history of the family and incorporating both experimental and nostalgic elements, 'the' postmodern family lurches forward and backward into an uncertain future."

The book's second major argument, however, remained a plainclothes' historical sociological one about family revolutions and vanguard classes. A major shift, I argued, has taken place in the class direction of U.S. family change. Most historians agree that the white middle classes were in the vanguard of the "modern" family revolution, that is, the transformation from a premodern, corporate, patriarchal family economy to the male breadwinner "companion-ate" family that transpired between the late eighteenth and the early twentieth centuries. Although the modern family pattern achieved cultural and statistical dominance, most working-class people attained the male family wage, their economic passport to its practice, very late, if at all. I interpreted this to suggest that by the time, the 1960s, that white working-class people got there, another family revolution was already well under way. Once again middle-class, white families appeared to be in the vanguard; frustrated middle-class homemakers and their more militant daughters subjected modern domesticity to a sustained critique, at times with little sensitivity to the effects our antimodern family ideology might have on women, for whom full-time domesticity had rarely been feasible. Thus, feminist family reform came to be regarded widely as a white, middle-class agenda and white, working-class families its most resistant adver-saries. These, after all, had been the presumptions that led me to focus my study of postindustrial family change on white, working-class people in the first place.

But this time appearances were deceptive. Field research convinced me that white, middle-class families have been less the innovators than the propagan-dists and principal beneficiaries of contemporary family change. Instead, I ar-gued that postindustrial conditions have reversed the trickle-down trajectory of family change once predicted by modernization theorists. By studying a family revolution ethnographically, I upturned many of my preconceptions about gen-der, class, and even about born-again Christianity more profoundly than would have been possible using only the more distant research methods of historical sociology. I discovered on the ground, for example, that evangelical Christians are not monolithically antifeminist, nor are their family relationships uniformly "traditional" or patriarchal. And I observed firsthand some of the ways in which many evangelical women and even antifeminist women have been rein-venting family forms as creatively as have many feminists. Feminists have re-ceived far too much credit and blame for instigating postmodern contests over the meaning of "the family," perhaps because we have done so much to chal-lenge the "essentialist" connotations of the term.

Ethnographic research also brought "home" for me the grounds for perva-sive ambivalence about postmodern family and social crises. Observing the everyday traumas and tragedies caused by the irrationality and injustice of contemporary occupational and social conditions reinforced my feminist and still democratic socialist beliefs that equitable, humane, and democratic gender and family policies could go a long way to alleviate the "surplus" family oppres-sion that most women and many men suffer. But I no longer fantasize (as I did when I concluded my book on China with the claim that the People's Republic of China [PRC] had achieved a family revolution but not a feminist family revolution) that even a feminist family revolution could put an end to family distress. There are human costs to the fruition of a fully voluntary sexual and kinship system that no social policy can fully eradicate. No nostalgic efforts to restore the traditional modern family system, however, can offer a more effective, let alone democratic, resolution to family upheaval. For better and worse, the postmodern family revolution is here to stay.

The last chapter of *Brave New Families* ends on that note—indeed, with that sentence. It acknowledges just cause for widespread ambivalence about postmodern family and social conditions but offers no parallel reflections on my own ambivalence about my current relationship to feminist sociology and postmodernist theories. The book itself does not end there, however. Displaying, perhaps allaying, some of my unresolved ethical-textual-political anxieties, I chose to end the book instead with an epilogue in which Pamela appears to have the provocative last word on my reading of her life: "You could never capture me." This somewhat disingenuous democratic gesture, which masks my asymmetrical control over the dialogic and textual conditions of its production, also signals the straddle position I currently occupy within and among contemporary debates about feminism and ethnography.

While my ethnographic rhetorical strategies in *Brave New Families* were somewhat reflexive, dialogic, and decentered, they produced a book that remained incurably humanist in the same sense that feminism and socialism have been humanist projects, committed to the emancipation of subjects who are comfortable naming themselves in gender and class terms. My humanist feminism sympathizes with the critique made by Francis Mascia-Lees, Colleen Cohen, and Patricia Sharpe (1989) of the premature forfeit of a female subject and of the frequent excesses of textual experimentation for its own sake sometimes found in "the postmodernist turn in anthropology." Nonetheless, I am not willing to polarize feminism and postmodernism in this way, for I believe that feminism has been one of the enabling conditions for, as well as a generative force in, the development of theoretical developments often designated loosely as "postmodern." Gender crises embedded in the kinds of family revolutions I have studied through both historical sociology and ethnography have been among the important sources of the crisis of representation, the critiques of unified subjectivity, and the preoccupation with questions of difference, identity, culture, and authority that galvanize postmodern theories.

Consequently, I have recently turned from the study of family revolutions to a project designed to explore the relationships between feminism and postmodernist cultural criticism by men. Migrating even further "afield" from most sociological projects, and adopting the surprising new feminist fashion here of studying men, I am collaborating with feminist literary critic Judith Newton on a project that combines ethnographic and literary critical approaches to contemporary fashions in cultural critique. I suspect that both my choice of collaborator and the linguistic shift evident in our defining this project as *cultural* rather than *social* criticism reflect and reinforce recent shifts in the primary locus of feminist and other radical theories. First, the historic collapse of "actually existing socialist societies" has deepened a crisis in Marxist social thought. At the same time, and perhaps as a result, a right-wing intellectual backlash in the United States has directed much of its energies to an assault on feminist and multicultural challenges to the classic Western canon. Perhaps this explains why the gravitational center of critical theory seems to have swung from the social sciences to literary criticism and the humanities.[12] I worry about and want to understand this tendency even as I find myself participating in it. Thus, beginning with the "new historicism" in literary studies and with what some have termed "the new ethnography" in anthropology, Judith Newton and I began to study and rewrite the stories of the genesis of these discourses in ways that write feminisms into the narrative of these postmodern "turns," even if primarily as a displaced "other" (Newton and Stacey 1993).[13]

As we navigate our routes through the turbulent waters of postmodern feminist debates on men "in" or "and" feminism,[14] we are pursuing a middle course that we began charting while team-teaching a graduate seminar on feminist theory. With most of our students we found many insights developed by feminist and other postmodern theorists persuasive and useful. Striving for ethnographic and textual reflexivity about the nexus of power and knowledge in cultural research and representation seems crucial to us, as do efforts to historicize the conceptual vocabulary feminists employ in our work. Feminists of color, along with other postcolonial as well as postmodern critics, have taught us to mistrust dominant conceptual categories that falsely universalize the experiences and conditions of dominant subjects.[15] And, like other feminists influenced by Foucault, we understand power to be productive as well as repressive.

At the same time, however, we retain conceptions that some poststructuralist theorists eschew, still finding fruitful notions of agency, experience, resistance, and social referentiality, even if the social world that agents construct, experience, and resist is one in which images dominate and, to a significant extent, constitute social reality. Thus, while I can no longer sustain the socialist-feminist confidence with which I once represented the narrative of family revolution in China, and I now find all metanarratives to be inevitably provisional, I nonetheless find them indispensable vehicles for representing relationships of power and injustice, such as those distributed along old-fashioned axes of gender, class, race, and sexuality. For this reason (and others) I am willing to employ, as Gayatri Spivak advocates, a "strategic" use of essentialism (Spivak 1990, 10). Indeed, I confess that, reminded during the Gulf War of the ubiquity of male associations with militarism and physical violence, I found myself entertaining more than strategic ideas about essentialism. I even dared publicly to interrogate monolithic refusals by most feminists, like myself, to consider the possibility that biology might provide more than a semiotic resource for the more lethal aspects of masculinity.[16]

As my trajectory picks its un-disciplined and anxious way through feminist and other bodies of postmodern social theory, my feminist colleagues in literary criticism report a mounting feminist backlash in their discipline against the hegemony of poststructuralist theories, while some feminist critics of post-modern anthropology appear to be moving beyond critique to creative appro-priations.[17] Meanwhile, ironically enough, my home discipline, sociology, is exhibiting increasing symptoms of postmodern courtship: sessions on post-modern selfhood and society have begun to infuse the annual meetings of the American Sociological Association; a late 1990 issue of *Social Problems,* the official journal of the Society for the Study of Social Problems (SSSP), an organi-zation and publication heretofore more noted for its liberal and Marxist sensi-bilities, featured "Three Papers on Postmodernity and Panic" (one by the 1991– 92 president of the organization), followed by "Two Papers on Feminism, Language and Postmodern" (*Social Problems* [November 1990]); and the theme of the 1992 meetings of the SSSP was explicitly "Postmodernity as a Social Problem: Race, Class, Gender and the *New World Order.*"

Interestingly, perhaps perversely, just as the postmodern theory industry has begun to outsource some of its knowledge production sites from a humanities "core" and an anthropological "semiperiphery" to heretofore peripheral soci-ology, "cultural studies" has migrated from Birmingham, England, to displace postmodern theory, as well as feminist theory, as the favored sign and institu-tional site for left-wing inter-, trans-, and counter-disciplinary intellectual work in the United States. The rise of cultural studies over the past few years has been meteoric, with new centers, institutes, conferences, journals, graduate pro-grams, and even undergraduate majors proliferating, despite the severe, often devastating, impact of the economic crisis on higher education. Moreover, this displacement of postmodern theory by cultural studies seems to be coinciding with a notable transfer of intellectual energies from gender and class—the foun-dational cross-bars of socialist feminism—to race and sexuality as the privileged sites of radical theorizing. What is more, this shift from gender and class to race and sexuality is evident not only in the U.S. version of cultural studies, broadly defined, but even within women's studies and feminist theory. So fully has feminist attention to differences among women and to conceptions of multiple subjectivities displaced unitary formulations of gender differences between women and men that it has become challenging to decide whether one still can identify an intellectual terrain that remains a specifically *feminist* project.

Indeed, what many feminists of color came to label "white feminist theory" has been so successfully "mainstreamed" into most of the humanities and a few of the social sciences that queer theory and multiculturalism are displacing feminism as the primary targets of conservative backlash. New Leftist–turned–neoconservative intellectual entrepreneur David Horowitz makes the vanguard role of queer theory explicit in "Queer Revolution: The Last Stage of Radicalism," a rather loathsome diatribe he presented at a self-consciously backlash session of the 1992 meetings of the American Studies Association. Parodying *The Communist Manifesto*, Horowitz begins: "A specter is haunting the American academy, the last refuge of the political left. It is the specter of queer theory."[18] He proceeds to portray queer theory as the final assault by radical theories of social construction on nature, normalcy, and civilization, thereby transferring to queer revolution the privileged status of pariah once "enjoyed" by feminism. Similarly, the widespread political backlash against affirmative action, both on and off U.S. campuses, seems to be directed more vocally against compensatory remedies for racial than gender imbalances.

The rhetoric and outcomes of the 1992 electoral campaign reflected these shifts, as homophobia and racism proved far more potent than sexism in galvanizing backlash voters. Tangible feminist gains in the "Year of the Woman" coincided with antigay rights victories in Colorado and in Tampa, Florida, and a frighteningly close call for a draconian antigay proposition in Oregon, whose language about perversity and abnormality is echoed in the David Horowitz pamphlet. Likewise, Year of the Woman hoopla helped to mask the Democratic Party's active suppression of its traditional racial equality and antipoverty discourses in favor of universalist appeals to a "forgotten" middle class, not so subtly coded as white.

I have indulged these meditations on recent shifts in politics and theory trends at some length, because they are impinging on my own current work as well. Judith Newton and I initially formulated our project as feminist scrutiny of straight, white, male cultural critics, whose attraction to postmodernist and cultural studies projects we first read as efforts to recenter white male theory by displacing both women's studies and ethnic studies. Gradually, however, our project began to evolve into an exploration of biographical, historical, and institutional conditions that foster in intellectuals the development of multiple "traitorous identities,"[19] that is, identification across axes of privilege—with feminism on the part of men, antiracism on the part of whites, antihomophobia on the part of heterosexuals, and with the poor on the part of the well-heeled. Thus, we have begun to expand our "sample" in multicultural, multisexual, and, though this is more difficult, even in limited multiclass directions. At the same time, in conducting oral histories with male cultural critics, we have found ourselves shifting our political posture from one of rectitude, too frequently indulged in identity politics, to a less self-righteous, more collegial, collaborative mode. Although we worry a bit about the risk of fostering our own "traitorous" gender identities in the process, we believe that more would be lost were we to miss this opportunity to help construct a fully feminist multicultural studies as well as to contribute feminist genealogies about its emergence, through active engagement and critical alliance with men.

From a sociological standpoint it is interesting to note that the standard, and generally male-authored, genealogies of cultural studies locate its roots in the 1970s Birmingham Centre for Cultural Studies, an interdisciplinary project in which sociology, particularly of a critical Marxist cast, played an integral part. Yet sociology failed to survive the late 1980s transatlantic crossing of this intellectual vessel, which disembarked primarily in humanities settlements, perhaps, partly because many of the indigenous roots of cultural studies in the United States can be found in feminism, ethnic studies, and American Studies, projects in which literature and humanities scholars increasingly dominate. From this perspective it was oddly comforting to observe anthropologists at their 1992 meetings organizing plenary sessions to express, and to analyze the sources of, their own widespread feelings of marginalization from the vortex of multicultural and cultural studies discourses, intellectual territory in which many anthropologists presumed proprietary disciplinary interests.[20]

These disciplinary disjunctures provide "disloyal" feminists like myself paradoxical new constraints against and opportunities for interdisciplinary work. On the one hand, the increased disciplinarity, specialization, and sheer magnitude of feminist scholarship makes cross-disciplinary feminist discourse ever more difficult. On the other hand, feminism has become a significant presence in cultural studies, a key site of interdisciplinary theory and politics but one in which sociology is even more marginal than anthropology. Consequently, I find myself engaged in an ethnographic project that self-consciously seeks to intervene in the construction of the very "fields"—of cultural studies, feminism, ethnic studies, and queer studies—that we are trying to map.

I conclude these reflections on my travels in feminist disciplinary borderlands with thoughts provoked by Avery Gordon, a decidedly postmodernist, feminist, disloyal sociologist, in her discussion of disciplinary impediments to writing ethnography and literary fictions as sociology:

> Perhaps the key methodological question is not: what method have you adopted for this research? but what paths have been disavowed, left behind, covered over and remain unseen. In what fields does field work occur? (Gordon 1990)

Looking back over my travels to and from the study of family revolutions, I have no desire to disavow my un-disciplined migrant labors in cross-fertilized feminist fields, least of all those which challenge arbitrary and increasingly atavistic disciplinary divisions of knowledge. Indeed, I worry rather less about the consequences of my personal disloyalty to the disciplines than about the costs to feminism of what strike me as increasingly conducive conditions for disciplinary loyalty now evident in the social sciences and humanities. Certainly, I broach my current work on male theorists and feminism confident that attentiveness to what Gordon labels "structures of exclusion" will prove indispensable. After more than two decades laboring in feminist fields, however, I am equally confident that my current project, like all others, will inevitably commit and conspire to conceal its own exclusions and illusions. Yet I find comfort as well as concern in my conviction that it will thereby provide a fertile "field day" for an emerging generation of feminist cultural studies theorists who must confront the challenge of keeping success from spoiling academic feminism.

NOTES

My thanks to Sarah Fenstermaker, Judith Newton, Domna Stanton, Abby Stewart, Barrie Thorne, and Susan Gerard, for helpful responses to an earlier draft.

1. Even the most cursory, arbitrary list suggests the continued vitality and value of contributions by feminist sociologists whose work thus far displays little interest in postmodern theory disputes, for example: Arlene Kaplan Daniels, Evelyn Nakano Glenn, Rosanna Hertz, Arlie Hochschild, Carole Joffe, Kristin Luker, Ruth Milkman, Marcia Millman, Barbara Reskin, Judith Rollins, Barbara Katz Rothman, Lillian Rubin, Diana Russell, Lenore Weitzman, Candace West, and Maxine Baca Zinn. The *American Sociological Review*—the major, and primarily positivist, journal published by the American Sociological Association—routinely publishes feminist articles on such issues as female employment, fertility, family behaviors, status attainment, political behaviors, deviance, and gender attitudes. Feminist work permeates *Social Problems,* the more qualitative and critical journal published by the less mainstream Society for the Study of Social Problems, and Sociologists for Women in Society publishes its own journal of feminist sociology, *Gender & Society.*

2. The proportion of sociology Ph.D. degrees awarded to females increased from 33 percent in 1977 to 51 percent in 1989 (National Science Foundation, "Science and Engineering Degrees: 1966–1989, A Source Book," NSF 91-314 [Washington, D.C.: USGPO, 1991], table 54). Compare this 50 percent increase and achievement of female numerical dominance with the 20 percent increase of Ph.D. degrees awarded to females in all fields: in 1980, 30 percent of all Ph.D. degrees in the United States were awarded to females, and in 1990 the proportion had risen to 36 percent (National Research Council, "Summary Report 1990: Doctorate Recipients from United States Universities" [Washington, D.C.: National Academy Press, 1991]). These figures for completed doctoral degrees likely understate the feminization trends evident among currently enrolled graduate students in sociology and other fields.

3. In 1971 I joined female faculty and students at what was then called Richmond College of the City University of New York in implementing a Women's Studies Program.

As I was an instructor in education, I developed a course on "Women in Education," which inspired my first feminist publication, an anthology I coedited with Susan Bereaud and Joan Daniels (1974).

4. To name just an arbitrary sample of feminists who received degrees from the Brandeis sociology department: Natalie Allon, Wini Breines, Nancy Chodorow, Patricia Hill Collins, Marjorie Davies, Elizabeth Higginbotham, Lynda Holmstrom, Elizabeth Long, Fatima Mernissi, Marcia Millman, Shulamit Reinharz, Judith Rollins, Nancy Shaw, Barrie Thorne, Gaye Tuchman, and Lise Vogel. Barrie Thorne provides a longer list and an insightful analysis of the conditions at Brandeis that fostered this feminist renaissance in "Feminist Sociology: The Brandeis Connection," a presentation she gave at a symposium in April 1984 honoring the twenty-fifth anniversary of the department's graduate program.

5. Because early Bolshevik efforts to undermine patriarchal sexual and family practices were rescinded after the Soviet regime consolidated its power, most social scientists theorized that revolutionary gender policies were strictly instrumental and short-lived. Reactionary gender and family policies would inevitably follow the consolidation of state power by a formerly revolutionary regime. See, for example, Coser and Coser 1977.

6. Heidi A. Hartmann (1981) wrote the essay that galvanized attention to theoretical relations between feminism and Marxism. An important early anthology of "dual-systems" theory was Zillah Eisenstein's (1979).

7. I discuss some of the feminist literature extolling the virtues of interactive field research in "Can There Be a Feminist Ethnography?" (Stacey 1988).

8. I am grateful to Abby Stewart for initiating a provocative dialogue on this issue with me and others.

9. The collection that canonized the reflexive, experimental turn in anthropology was Clifford and Marcus 1986. It was foreshadowed, however, by numerous earlier essays and ethnographies, most of which are surveyed in Marcus and Fischer 1986. Of course, as Barrie Thorne has properly reminded me, my turn to ethnography in itself need not have propelled me outside sociology, where there is also a rich, honorable tradition of ethnographic work starting with the early-twentieth-century urban studies of the Chicago school and continuing in the community studies tradition to which our earlier essay pointed. Once again the primacy of my feminist, antidisciplinary grounding proved decisive.

10. In addition to the works discussed by Marcus and Fischer, see Moffatt 1989; Ginsburg 1989; Zavella 1987; di Leonardo 1984; and Myerhoff 1978. A recent fine collection of feminist anthropological studies of the United States is Ginsburg and Tsing 1990.

11. For other analyses of the quest for a feminist research methodology, see Bowles and Duelli-Klein 1980; Harding 1987; Gross 1987; Stanley and Wise 1983.

12. Thus, humanists rather than social scientists have taken the initiative in organizing Teachers for a Democratic *Culture* (my emphasis), an organization to defend multicultural and feminist curricular reforms against the pernicious antipolitical correctness campaign of the National Association of Scholars and other reactionary groups; the organizational meeting of TDC was held at the December 1991 meetings of the Modern

Language Association. George Marcus offers a helpful comparison of the significance of texts, and hence textual politics, in diverse disciplines and sheds light on the stakes of literary critics in "worlding" their texts, in "A Broad(er) Side to the Canon," an unpublished conference paper he is expanding for book-length publication.

13. I find it gratifying that other feminists are challenging genealogies of postmodernist theory and cultural studies that marginalize feminist contributions. See, for example, Morris 1988; Bordo 1992; Long 1989; and Schwichtenberg 1989.

14. Much of the academic debate about the proper preposition, conjunction, and character of the two terms was initiated by Jardine and Smith (1987). See also Boone and Cadden 1990.

15. The critical literature on this theme is vast. See, for example, Baca Zinn et al. 1986; Mohanty 1991; hooks 1984; and Anzaldúa 1990.

16. I raised this issue while serving as a commentator at the "Unraveling Masculinities" conference at the University of California, Davis, in February 1991. These have been revised for publication (Stacey, 1993).

17. Four particularly articulate critiques of the critical excesses of the antiessentialist "club," are Christian 1987; Modleski 1991; Bordo 1992b; and Fuss 1989. At the November 1990 meeting of the American Anthropological Association, Francis Mascia-Lees, Patricia Sharpe, and Colleen Cohen, the authors of a widely discussed feminist critique of postmodern anthropology, gave, or rather performed, a paper that was decidedly reflexive about its textual as well as political dimensions. They did so, moreover, at a session on feminism and postmodernism organized by Mascia-Lees.

18. Horowitz 1992.

19. We have borrowed this term from Sandra Harding's essay "Reinventing Ourselves as Other," in Harding 1991.

20. This was the basic premise of an entire panel on "Multiculturalism and the Concept of Culture" and other panels. See, for example, Ortner 1992.

WORKS CITED

Anzaldúa, Gloria, ed. 1990. *Making Face, Making Soul: Haciendo Caras.* San Francisco: aunte lute foundation.

Baca Zinn, Maxine, Lynn Weber Cannon, Elizabeth Higginbotham, and Bonnie Thornton Dill. 1986. "The Costs of Exclusionary Practices in Women's Studies." *Signs* 11, no. 2:290–303.

Boone, Joseph A., and Michael Cadden, eds. 1990. *Engendering Men: The Question of Male Feminist Criticism.* New York: Routledge.

Bordo, Susan. 1990. "Feminism, Postmodernism and Gender Skepticism." In *Feminism/Postmodernism,* ed. Linda J. Nicholson. New York: Routledge.

Bowles, Gloria, and Renate Duelli Klein. 1983. *Theories of Women's Studies.* London: Routledge and Kegan Paul.

Christian, Barbara. 1987. "The Race for Theory." *Cultural Critique* 6:51–63.

Clifford, James, and George Marcus, eds. 1986. *Writing Culture: The Poetics and Politics of Ethnography.* Berkeley: University of California Press.

Coser, Rose L., and Lewis A. Coser. 1972. "The Principles of Legitimacy and Its Patterned Infringement in Social Revolutions." In *Cross-National Family Research*, ed. Marvin B. Sussman and Betty E. Cogswell. Leiden: E. J. Brill.

di Leonardo, Micaela. 1984. *The Varieties of Ethnic Experience: Kinship, Class, and Gender among California Italian-Americans*. Ithaca: Cornell University Press.

Dilnot, Clive. 1986. "What Is the Post-Modern?" *Art History* 9, no. 2 (June): 245–63.

Eisenstein, Zillah R., ed. 1979. *Capitalist Patriarchy and the Case for Socialist-Feminism*. New York: Monthly Review Press.

Fuss, Diane. 1989. *Essentially Speaking: Feminism, Nature, Difference*. New York: Routledge.

Ginsburg, Faye. 1989. *Contested Lives: The Abortion Debate in an American Community*. Berkeley: University of California Press.

Ginsburg, Faye, and Anna Tsing, eds. 1990. *Uncertain Terms: Negotiating Gender in American Culture*. Boston: Beacon Press.

Gordon, Avery. 1990. "Feminism, Writing and Ghosts." *Social Problems* 37, no. 4 (November): 485–500.

Gouldner, Alvin. 1970. *The Coming Crisis in Western Sociology*. New York: Basic Books.

Gross, Elizabeth. 1987. "Conclusion: What Is Feminist Theory?" In *Feminist Challenges: Social and Political Theory*, ed. Carole Pateman and Elizabeth Gross. Boston: Northeastern University Press.

Harding, Sandra. 1991. *Whose Science? Whose Knowledge? Thinking from Women's Lives*. Ithaca: Cornell University Press.

———, ed. 1987. *Feminism and Methodology*. Bloomington: Indiana University Press.

Hartmann, Heidi. 1981. "The Unhappy Marriage of Marxism and Feminism: Towards a More Progressive Union." In *Women and Revolution*, ed. Lydia Sargent. Boston: South End Press.

hooks, bell. 1984. *Feminist Theory: From Margin to Center*. Boston: South End Press.

Horowitz, David. 1992. "Queer Revolution: The Last Stage of Radicalism." Pamphlet, Studio City, Calif.: Center for the Study of Popular Culture.

Jardine, Alice, and Paul Smith, eds. 1987. *Men in Feminism*. New York: Methuen.

Long, Elizabeth. 1989. "Feminism and Cultural Studies." *Critical Studies in Mass Communications* 6, no. 2:427–35.

Marcus, George E., and Michael M. J. Fischer. 1986. *Anthropology as Cultural Critique*. Chicago: University of Chicago Press.

Mascia-Lees, Francis E., Patricia Sharpe, and Colleen Ballerino Cohen. 1989. "The Postmodernist Turn in Anthropology: Cautions from a Feminist Perspective." *Signs* 15, no. 1 (Autumn): 7–33.

Modleski, Tania. 1991. *Feminism without Women: Culture and Criticism in a "Postfeminist" Age*. New York: Routledge.

Moffatt, Michael. 1989. *Coming of Age in New Jersey: College and American Culture*. New Brunswick: Rutgers University Press.

Mohanty, Chandra, Ann Russo, and Lourdes Torres, eds. 1991. *Third World Women and the Politics of Feminism*. Bloomington: Indiana University Press.

Morris, Meaghan. 1988. *The Pirate's Fiance: Feminism, Reading, Postmodernism.* London: Verso.

Myerhoff, Barbara. 1978. *Number Our Days.* New York: Simon and Schuster.

Newton, Judith, and Judith Stacey. 1992–93. "Learning Not to Curse, or, Feminist Predicaments in Cultural Criticism by Men: Our Movie Date with James Clifford and Stephen Greenblatt." *Cultural Critique*, no. 23 (Winter): 51–82.

Ortner, Sherry. 1992. "Anthropology's War of Position: Changing the Face of the Field." Paper presented at American Anthropological Association meeting, San Francisco, December.

Schwichtenberg, Cathy. 1989. "Feminist Cultural Studies." *Critical Studies in Mass Communication* 6, no. 2:202–9.

Spivak, Gayatri. 1990. *The Postcolonial Critic: Interviews, Strategies, Dialogue.* New York: Routledge.

Stacey, Judith. 1983. *Patriarchy and Socialist Revolution in China.* Berkeley: University of California Press.

———. 1988. "Can There Be a Feminist Ethnography?" *Women's Studies International Quarterly* 11, no. 1:21–27.

———. 1990. *Brave New Families: Stories of Domestic Upheaval in Late Twentieth Century America.* New York: Basic Books.

———. 1993. "Toward Kindler, Gentler Uses for Testosterone: Reflections on Bob Connell's Views on Western Masculinities." *Theory and Society* (27):711–21.

Stacey, Judith, Susan Bereaud, and Joan Daniels, eds. 1974. *And Jill Came Tumbling After: Sexism in American Education.* New York: Dell.

Stacey, Judith, and Barrie Thorne. 1985. "The Missing Feminist Revolution in Sociology." *Social Problems* 32, no. 4 (April): 301–16.

Stanley, Liz, and Sue Wise. 1983. *Breaking Out: Feminist Consciousness and Feminist Research.* London: Routledge and Kegan Paul.

Thorne, Barrie. 1984. "Feminist Sociology: The Brandeis Connection." Paper presented at the Twenty-fifth Reunion Symposium of Sociology Department, Brandeis University, April.

Zavella, Patricia. 1987. *Women's Work and Chicano Families.* Ithaca: Cornell University Press.

Chapter 13

The Dialogic Emergence of Difference: Feminist Explorations in Foreign Language Learning and Teaching

Claire Kramsch and Linda von Hoene

The following essay reflects an ongoing discussion between the two authors on the dialogic emergence of voice, difference, and cultures in the foreign language classroom and in feminist theory. In the spirit of "contextualization" that is central to both feminism and a critical pedagogy for second language learning, we would like to open this essay with its own context of development—that is, how it was that we came to write this essay and what that process entailed. In the 1990–91 academic year the authors became acquainted with each other's work and research interests in the areas of applied linguistics and feminist theory, respectively. In our discussions of the book Claire Kramsch was writing at the time, *Context and Culture in Language Teaching* (1993), we began to sense intersections between what Claire was proposing for foreign language teaching and current directions in feminist theory. In her book Claire spoke of "faultlines," the need to confront and explore differences and boundaries in the foreign language classroom, of multiple voices and single- versus double-voiced discourse. Seen from a feminist perspective, this work was challenging teachers to move beyond the current emphasis on problem-solving, goal-oriented, mastery-based teaching practices that indeed seemed to strengthen the patriarchal inscriptions of the subject and of society rather than call them into question. Claire's recommendation to move beyond a dichotomous view of cultures typical of foreign language teaching and to develop a "third space" from which to live critically between cultures resonated with the vision of a new type of critical consciousness posited by such feminists as Gloria Anzaldúa (1987), Donna Haraway (1985), and bell hooks (1989), among others. While these ideas have become common themes in women's studies courses, their application to the context of the foreign language classroom was indeed novel. Feminist theory has traditionally focused little on the foreign language classroom as a locus of feminist praxis, and, conversely, applied linguistics has been only minimally receptive to how feminist theory might transform the foreign language classroom. Envisioning the foreign language classroom as a potential site for the conscious construction of a position from which to challenge both intra- and intersubjective relations of power called to mind Julia Kristeva's subject-in-process (1980) and bell hook's work on coming to voice and self-recovery (1989).

In spite of the many intersections and similarities that we sensed existed between developments in feminism and second language acquisition research, the process of writing this essay made us acutely aware of the multiple and distinctly different voices that we individually bring to this project as a result of our different professional and personal contexts. Indeed, our interaction became a microcosm of what we were proposing for a critical feminist foreign language pedagogy: the dialogic emergence of differences in an attempt to promote a critical social consciousness through self-reflexivity and self-revision. What we present here is the articulation of this dialogue. As such, it is meant to be an initial exploration of the present and potential relationship of feminist theory to the social practice of second language acquisition in the foreign language classroom. The first section, written by Linda von Hoene, speaks to the emergence of difference and voice in feminist theory. For those readers who teach foreign languages but are unfamiliar with recent developments in feminist theory, this section is meant to introduce and suggest potential areas of intersection and dialogue between feminist theory and foreign language teaching practices around the topics of difference and voice. Claire Kramsch's section on the emergence of voice and difference in language learning research was written taking these thoughts into consideration. In the third section we dialogue about the concrete development of a critical feminist pedagogy for the foreign language classroom based on two examples of classroom practice. In a third example we observe teachers in training as they discuss the pedagogy of a literary text and make suggestions for reorienting teacher training practices toward a critical double-voiced pedagogy.

FEMINIST THEORY AND THE EMERGENCE OF VOICE AND DIFFERENCE

> As long as it has not analysed their relation to the instances of power, and has not given up the belief in its own identity, any libertarian movement (including feminism) can be recuperated by that power . . .
>
> —Julia Kristeva, "La Femme" cited in Moi, 164

In spite of its relatively short history, contemporary feminism has been characterized by significant struggles with and revisions to the notions of voice and difference. As many feminists have pointed out (e.g., hooks 1984; Fox-

Genovese 1991), the women's movement of the late 1960s to early 1980s was primarily a white, middle-class phenomenon. Taking as its point of departure the situation of the suburban housewife, Betty Friedan's groundbreaking work, *The Feminine Mystique* (1963), was paradigmatic for this limited definition of "woman" that characterized the early years of contemporary feminism. While the women's liberation movement that developed in the late 1960s was indeed revolutionary in bringing to the fore the suppressed voices of white middle-class women, it failed to be self-reflexive as to its own exclusionary practices. Locked in a modernist, universalized notion of a single-voiced, unified female subject, feminism was defined solely in terms of gender, as the struggle of women against patriarchal oppression. In their assumptions that the struggles of women were cross-culturally similar and linked primarily to gender, feminist theorists attempted to find universal causes for women's oppression and to define how women were "essentially" different from men but similar to one another. Steeped in an essentialism that valorized differences only between men and women while erasing differences and indeed conflicts that exist among women, feminism inadvertently partook in dynamics of exclusion structurally similar to the patriarchal ones against which it was struggling. In its exclusive concern with gender as a category of analysis, early feminism aimed its attack against patriarchy, neatly sidestepping issues of racial and economic differences among women that would have forced more privileged women to question their own complicity in the dynamics of racial and economic oppression.

As bell hooks writes in *Feminist Theory: From Margin to Center* (1984, 12), the racial politics of feminism were often directly experienced by women of color in consciousness-raising groups and women's studies courses of the 1970s and early 1980s. Many women of color who had initially placed hope in the liberatory potential of a women's movement often did not return to consciousness-raising groups because of the exclusionary attitudes they experienced there. Indeed, black women often felt more solidarity with black men than with white women.

While Anglo-American feminism of the 1960s and 1970s was couched in a universalizing modernist definition of women that glossed over differences among women in terms of their specific social and cultural contexts, feminism and feminist theory of the 1980s has been characterized by attempts to problematize, and indeed revise, these universalizing, monologic tendencies of early feminism. This shift has been enabled primarily by the writings of women of color and third world women and by the emphasis on difference and the multi-voiced subject fostered by postmodernism.

The publication in 1981 of *This Bridge Called My Back: Writings by Radical Women of Color* was groundbreaking for several reasons: in addition to bringing to the fore the voices of women of color and their responses to the racism they experienced in feminism, this work emphasized the significance of other aspects of identity beyond gender in defining feminism. Thus, it challenged the abstract monolithic notion of woman, insisting that the situation of women could only be defined by looking at the complex intersection of the multiple contexts to which women belong. Instead of stressing similarities, this work called for the vigilant recognition of differences among women in terms of race, class, sexuality, and age. As the editors state in their introduction, regarding the purpose of the book:

> We want to express to all women—especially to white middle-class women—the experiences which divide us as feminists; we want to examine incidents of intolerance, prejudice and denial of differences within the feminist movement. We intend to explore the causes and sources of, and solutions to these divisions. We want to create a definition that expands what "feminist" means to us. (xxiii; also cited in Alarcón 359)

This Bridge Called My Back and other writings by women of color in the 1980s thus posed a painful yet necessary challenge to feminism by bringing to light the multivoiced female subject and the material contexts in which her identity is constructed. Looking back at the impact of *Bridge*, Norma Alarcón notes that, although *Bridge* "has problematized many a version of Anglo-American feminism . . . the impact among most Anglo-American theorists appears to be more cosmetic than not" (357). According to Alarcón, "*Bridge's* challenge to the Anglo-American subject of feminism has yet to effect a newer discourse" (358). Citing Jane Flax, Alarcón attributes this failure to the continued adherence to the notion of a monologic, autonomous subject. Indeed, increased knowledge *about* different cultures, classes, contexts, does not in and of itself lead to the socially transformative practices desired by feminism, unless that knowledge is coupled with a critical scrutiny and indeed destabilization of one's own subject position and an exploration of the many discursive voices that such a position entails. What this involves might be referred to as a process of "self-othering," or, in a less dichotomized relational manner, as a type of dialogic process of recognizing the other in self and the self from the position of the other as the prerequisite to a transformed relation to difference.

A dialogic process that insists on self-reflexivity and self-revision forms the basis, for example, of Kristeva's notion of the subject-in-process, in which the emphasis is on the vigilant recuperation of the stranger within. In *Strangers to Ourselves* (1991) Kristeva points out the importance of making ourselves alien to ourselves as a necessary position from which to support a nonhierarchical relation to difference: "It is not simply—humanistically—a matter of our being able to accept the other, but of *being in his place,* and this means to imagine and make oneself other for oneself" (13). The evocation of the other within is also central to Gloria Anzaldúa's essay "Speaking in Tongues: A Letter to Third World Women Writers," in which the author calls for the recovery of the other within third world women that has been forced into exile through the denial of voice in American culture:

> The act of writing . . . is the quest for the self, for the center of the self, which we women of color have come to think as "other"—the dark, the feminine. Didn't we start writing to reconcile this other within us? We knew we were different, set apart, exiled from what is considered "normal," white-right. And as we internalized this exile, we came to see the alien within us and too often, as a result, we split apart from ourselves and each other. Forever after we have been in search of that self, that "other" and each other. (169)

The dialogic emergence of difference must also be viewed simultaneously as an intersubjective process. As such, it is central to Maria Lugones's concept of "world-travelling":

> But there are "worlds" that we can travel to lovingly and travelling to them is part of loving at least some of their inhabitants. The reason why I think that travelling to someone's "world" is a way of identifying with them is because by travelling to their "world" we can understand *what it is to be them and what it is to be ourselves in their eyes*. Only when we have travelled to each other's "worlds" are we fully subjects to each other. (401)

While contemporary feminism emerged as the uncovering of the monologic voice of woman, it has, albeit with resistance, proved particularly committed to the process of self-revision and the emergence of marginalized voices within its own discourse. Indeed, feminism as a politics of transformation entails the liberation of all marginalized voices, those within the self and those of others, and a willingness, as Trinh T. Minh-ha describes, "to live fearlessly with and within difference(s)" (84). It is to the feminist practice of the dialogic emergence of difference in the context of the foreign language classroom that we now turn.

LANGUAGE LEARNING RESEARCH AND THE
EMERGENCE OF VOICE IN CONTEXT

In a sense learning the language of another person can be viewed as the ultimate illustration of Lugones's "travel to other worlds." Temporarily leaving one's language at the door of the classroom and being willing to express oneself in the language of others can lead to a unique discovery of self in other and other in self. To be sure, such a discovery requires a new perspective on language and language use.

Acquiring a language different from one's own requires internalizing both a linguistic system of rules and paradigms and using these rules in social contexts of communication. By mouthing linguistic forms different from the ones they are used to, learners make their first—and sometimes unsettling—experience of difference in the foreign language classroom. Mouthing foreign words does not mean, however, that one is automatically the author of those words. Developing a voice of one's own in contexts one has not chosen, to express meanings constrained by rules of grammar and ways of speaking that are not one's own, is among the major challenges of the language learning voyage of discovery.

Historically, the learning of "modern" foreign languages has been heavily influenced by the study of the "classical" languages Latin and Greek and their communities of literate writers and readers (Kramsch and McConnell-Ginet 1992). In the 1950s living languages such as German and French were taught like Latin, disembodied languages related to a community of written texts, not of speakers. Language learners were confronted with a different alphabet, the different shape of words on a page, different syntactic arrangements of sentences. By translating these sentences, they were given access to the world of a distant literate community that was unrelated to their own everyday world. Learners had to adopt the sometimes stilted voice of that community of native writers and were never given the opportunity to develop their own.

By contrast, the 1960s gave language learners access to the everyday world of native *speakers,* first in theoretical linguistics, then in second language acquisition research and practice. They were trained into the standard pronunciation patterns and into the conventionalized ways of speaking of those native speakers. But the voice they were required to adopt was, as Chomsky would have it, a mightily idealized voice, ostensibly unaffected by all the vagaries of race, gender, or class. Seen, however, from a feminist perspective, this voice was in fact, as Mary Louise Pratt (1987) describes it, a "linguistic utopia"; far from being neutral and ideal, it was the voice of the imagined community of citizen-soldiers, the modern nation-state (Anderson 1983). As Pratt argues, "Our modern linguistics of language, code, and competence posits a unified and homogeneous social world in which language exists as a shared patrimony—as a device, precisely, for imagining community. . . . The distance between langue and parole, competence and performance, is the distance between the homogeneity of the imagined community and the fractured reality of linguistic experience in modern stratified societies" (1987, 50–51). The audiolingual dialogues and pattern drills of the 1960s represented standard families passing the salt at the standard breakfast tables and playing standard gender roles, thus ignoring the heterogeneity of actual speakers. By striving to inculcate the speech patterns of those ideal native speakers, the audiolingual method never did give language learners the possibility of finding their own voice in the language class. If learners did come to their own, it was outside of class, by going to the country in which the language was spoken or by making their own the highly particular voice of a poem or a song in the new language.

In the 1970s language learning research turned its attention to the ability of the learner to communicate with authentic native speakers in situated contexts of use. The concept of communicative competence—made a focus of social theory by Habermas (1971) and applied to education by Hymes (1972) and Savignon (1972)—broadened the challenge of the learner to include, beside grammatical competence, also pragmatic and sociocultural competence. More recently, the concept of language as "social semiotic" heralded by the educational linguist Halliday (1983) clearly focused the task of language learners on expressing, interpreting, and negotiating meanings that differ along many socially constructed lines. Communicative approaches to language teaching have offered a unique opportunity to have language learners experience in the classroom cultural and social differences and to communicate across national boundaries. Three factors, however, have prevented learners from developing a critical voice and identity of their own: a reductionist view of the social context of language, a tradition of mastery learning, and a monologic view of communication.

The first factor reflects the conditions under which the communicative approach originated. Immigrants to English-, French-, and German-speaking countries had to be given as quickly as possible the threshold level of competence needed to function in their respective host societies. Thus, the social contexts in which the language is learned and used in the communicative approach have been defined according to a generic taxonomy of predetermined "learners' needs" and situations with predetermined scripts: how to make a telephone call, how to find an apartment, how to order a meal in a restaurant. Applied to general education, this approach still assumes that pragmatic needs and goals are universal. Women and men, French, Germans, and Americans are believed to have essentially common needs and common interests, such as shopping, planning vacations, eating out, traveling, and studying. The negotiation of meaning that takes place in the foreign language is, therefore, only a negotiation of grammatical and lexical forms, or a negotiation of reference to a stable common external reality. It has kept learners unaware of the multiple facets of the target groups' cultural identity. It has left them blind to their own social and cultural diversity and has implicitly assumed a consensus between their world and the other. While the use of universal categories such as eating, working, and shopping, for making sense of the foreign culture, reveals differences among cultures, it does not address the conflicts and paradoxes that ensue from these differences and thus misses an opportunity to develop a critical consciousness in the foreign language classroom.

The second factor, mastery learning, is a hallmark of U.S. educational practice. It has reduced the process of self- and other-discovery in education to a series of step-by-step, linearly sequenced tasks. These tasks lead the learner in the traditional lockstep fashion to incremental assimilation of building blocks of knowledge, predicated on the belief that the final product will be equal to the sum of its parts. By taking language as an object to be "mastered," and by talking about language-learning as a "problem-solving," "task-based," "strategic" kind of process, the communicative approach has adopted a military, male nomenclature based on competitiveness and individual performance, rather than as a form of dialogue that explores difference and questions ways of viewing the world as they are reflected in ways of speaking.

Finally, the communicative approach has never really, in practice, abandoned a view of communication that prizes information sharing over mutual understanding. Teachers, interested mainly in having students talk, have become adept at designing task-based activities that require students to exchange information; they rarely ask the students to reflect on why they chose to convey this piece of information rather than that one, based on their unique experiences as male or female, middle class or working class, Anglo American or Asian American, American or French. Furthermore, the communicative approach never really did recognize the multiple and potentially conflicting voices that coexist in each individual learner, as a member of various minority and majority groups. Because it has adopted a mainly reference-based view of truth and meaning, it has had difficulty dealing with symbolism, irony, and metaphor, verbal games, and double entendre. And yet the social reality of the language classroom is defined precisely by the tension between a multitude of psychological, social, political, moral, and linguistic oppositions in conflict with one another for the construction of meaning. If one takes discourse to mean the process by which people create, relate, organize, and realize meaning, then the communicative approach has been ill prepared to take into account the multiple worlds of discourse that coexist in the language class.

Because it wanted to make foreign languages more relevant to everyday life, language pedagogy has broken the monopoly of the pattern drill. Recognizing that learners had up to now only "reduced personalities" (Harder 1980), it has made great efforts to empower them to *do* things with words and to have others fulfill their pragmatic needs. Its view of the learner, however, is still a monolithic entity, male in his conversational maxims (Grice 1975), and unaffected by self-doubt, or by the multiple and often conflicting voices that are likely to inhabit him. Indeed, the negotiation of meaning advocated by the communicative approach has been a transactional process involving clearly defined meanings; learners have not been encouraged to explore the great diversity of potential meanings in others' or in their own cultural self.

TOWARD A CRITICAL, DOUBLE-VOICED FOREIGN LANGUAGE PEDAGOGY

While sex and gender questions have not historically been central topics in second language learning research, a limited discussion started to emerge in the 1980s under the influence of such feminist linguists as McConnell-Ginet (1980, 1989); Ochs (1992); Poynton (1989); Tannen (1992); and Thorne, Kramarae, and Henley (1983). It has taken three different forms: a concern with gender differences as the object of instruction, a sensitivity to gender differences in classroom interaction, and, more recently, a focus on diversity along many lines in the discourse of the classroom.

Traditionally, concerns with gender differences in the foreign language class have pertained to the *object of instruction* (the way native speakers use the language in target cultural situations). Textbooks show, for instance, how male and female native speakers of the language behave in various authentic contexts or how they portray themselves in everyday conversations. Efforts have been made in recent years to eliminate gender stereotypes from language textbooks (e.g., Graci 1989) and to include women writers in course syllabi. Following research done on social interaction in the classroom and on the psycholinguistic conditions of language acquisition, there has been an increased interest in gender differences in the use of language as the *medium of instruction* (the way the foreign code is used in the classroom to teach foreign language use). Teaching language as medium of instruction focuses on how men and women interact in the classroom in the process of learning a new language: different use of learning strategies by male and female learners (Oxford and Nyikos 1989; and Nyikos 1990), sex differences in group work interaction (Pica et al. 1991; Gass and Varonis 1986; and Soulé Susbielles 1988). Yet these two areas of concern have tended to view gender separately from all the other dimensions of difference present in the classroom. Learners have not been encouraged to reflect consciously on difference and voice, and teachers have not dealt explicitly with the diversity of voices in their classes.

Feminist theory can provide ways to overcome the homogenization of voice in the language classroom by viewing language not only as an object of instruction or the medium of instruction but also as a *style of interaction*, a "way of being in the world" (Becker 1984). Teaching language as a style of interaction offers the possibility of critically reexamining traditional ways of acquiring and using knowledge. What is needed both of the teacher and of the students is a metalinguistic and metadiscursive awareness that can explore the enactment of difference and encourage critical reflection and revision of one's own subject position. The community of discourse practices that emerges in the classroom can then choose consciously to produce, reproduce, or potentially resist existing relationships of power, race, nationality, class, and gender (Kramsch 1993).

The notion of single-voiced and double-voiced discourse taken from Bakhtin (1929), and later echoed by feminist thinkers such as Kristeva (1991) and hooks (1989), could be useful here.[1] It has the advantage of addressing the issue of otherness both as external to the learner—in the form of peers, teacher, native speakers, etc.,—and as internal to the new cross-cultural personality the learner has to develop as he or she grows into another way of naming the world. Single-voiced discourse is a talk style in which the speaker adheres to his or her own viewpoint, without perceiving the need to acknowledge and revise his or her own stance by exploring the possibly conflicting voices within and without. In single-voiced discourse speakers do not attempt to view themselves as others see and hear them. In the foreign language classroom, for example, single-voiced discourse would prevent Americans from seeing themselves as they may be perceived from the perspective of another culture or as others in the classroom may perceive them. When speaking with a single voice, learners stand within their usual way of speaking, even though they speak foreign words; they don't recognize that the interaction with another language and culture might put in question their usual way of expressing the world around them. Double-voiced discourse, on the other hand, is consistent with what bell hooks calls "the social construction of the self in relation," in which the self is seen "not as a signifier of one 'I' but the coming together of many 'I's, the self as embodying collective reality past and present, family and community" (1989, 31). In the words of feminist linguist Sheldon, in double-voiced discourse

> the primary orientation is to the self, to one's own agenda. The other orienta-
> tion is to the members of the group. The orientation to others does not mean
> that the speaker necessarily acts in an altruistic, accommodating, or even self-
> sacrificing manner. It means, rather, that the speaker pays attention to the
> companion's point of view, even while pursuing her own agenda. As a result,
> the voice of the self is enmeshed with and regulated by the voice of the other.
> (1992, 99)

In double-voiced classroom discourse teacher and students develop and revise their own views through dialogic interaction with other members of the group. This does not mean that these intra- and intersubjective voices are always in harmony with one another—quite the contrary. Morson mentions the "cacoph-ony of values" that underlie Bakhtin's "play of voices" (Morson 1981, 4), and he adds: "Language, for [Bakhtin] is open to history and social conflict. Each word is open to conflicting pronunciations, intonations and allusions and so may be an arena of social conflict and a sensitive barometer of social change" (6). Nor does it mean that any one speaker uses exclusively one form of discourse over the other; rather, speakers orient themselves differently according to the topic and the nature of the conversation, the voices of the interlocutors, and their definition of the situation of communication.

Feminist theory, with its emphasis on difference and on the multivoiced subject, can make language teachers sensitive to the way language forms are acquired through the interaction of teachers and learners, native and nonnative speakers, in their multiple incarnations across various voices in and out of the classroom. In the following we instantiate the type of dialogic reflection the teacher could engage in with other native or nonnative speakers of the language in an effort to enrich the language learning experience in the classroom. We base our dialogue on concrete examples of classroom discourse taken from two different languages: a beginning German class and an advanced English as a Second Language (ESL) class.

Example 1

In this second-semester, college-level German class, the teacher is an Anglo-American female, the students consist of fifteen males and females of diverse ethnic backgrounds. The lesson was recorded by another teacher of German, who was herself Chinese born. The class is discussing a reading in the textbook featuring personal ads in German newspapers. The textbook authors have erroneously entitled the passage *"Heiratsanzeigen"* (wedding announcements), when the German term for such ads is in fact *Heiratsannoncen* (personal ads with the intention of marriage) or *Ehewünsche* (marriage wishes). The teacher (T) turns to the students in the class (S1, S2, S3, etc.):

T: Habt ihr diese Anzeigen in Deutschland gesehen?
S1: Ja in der Süddeutschen Zeitung.
S4: Hier auch in San Francisco Chronicle, in Daily Cal.
T: Es gibt viele, viele Heiratsanzeigen in Deutschland. Welche Anzeigen sind stereotypisch?
S2: Die erste.
T: Es ist stereotypisch, weil es normal ist. Steve, lies mal vor.
S: "Immer allein frühstücken ist langweilig. Auch allein verreisen ist doof! Frau, 37 Jahre, klein und schlank, sucht Mann, dem es auch so geht. Er sollte Interesse für Sport, Konzert, Kino, Gemütlichkeit und Natur haben—Lehrer angenehm—zwischen 35 und 45 Jahre alt sein."

T: "Immer allein." Wer schreibt hier, eine Frau oder ein Mann?
S5: Eine Frau.
T: "Klein und schlank," das ist stereotypisch.
S6: Meine Mutter hat eine Freundin. Ihr Mann ist tot. Sie möchte neue Männer getroffen. Sie sagt, sie ist eine nette jüdische Frau.
S7: Sind die Männer ein bißchen verrückt oder kriminell?
S6: Meine Mutter sagt, diese Männer sind kriminell. Aber es gibt auch Minister.
S8: Kostet eine Anzeige viel Geld oder nicht?
T: Nicht viel.

[T: Did you see such ads in Germany? S1: Yes, in the *Süddeutsche Zeitung.*
S4: Here too in the San Francisco Chronicle, in the Daily Cal. T: There are many many personal ads in Germany. Which ads are stereotypical? S2: The first. T: It is stereotypical because it is normal. Steve, can you read? S: "Always alone for breakfast is boring. Traveling alone is silly too. Woman, 37, small and slim, seeks man who feels the same way. He should be interested in sports, concerts, movies, Gemütlichkeit, and nature—teacher would be nice—between 35 and 45." T: "Always alone." Who is writing here, a woman or a man? S5: A woman. T: "Small and slender," that is stereotypical. S6: My mother has a friend. Her husband is dead. She would like to meet new men. She says, she is a nice Jewish woman. S7: Are the men a little crazy or criminal? S6: My mother says the men (who answer these ads) are criminals. But there are also ministers. S8: Does an ad cost a lot of money or not? T: Not much.]

Claire: This exchange is not untypical of what happens in language classes, in which texts often serve as mere opportunities to talk (*Sprechsituationen*), and to use, as S6 does, the newly learned modals and dependent clause constructions. The fact that this text is taken directly from a newspaper and has not been prefabricated for pedagogic purposes means that it has to be placed in its proper social context of production. And yet the teacher remains on the level of vocabulary and of the students' personal likes and dislikes. In this regard she is following the textbook that asks "comprehension questions" like: "What do you think of such ads? Which do you like and why? Which stereotypical roles do you find?" But the students' answers reveal a multiplicity of perspectives that would need to be explored in much greater depth.

Linda: I have always steered clear of teaching personal ads in the language classroom. The ones presented here in this book and those that appear in most mainstream newspapers seem to reinforce the objectification of women and are often extremely sexist and ageist.

C: What's wrong with personal ads? People who put those ads are seriously looking for marriage partners. What I find interesting is that the lexical error in the title, which the teacher reiterates in line 4, had potentially cultural implications. The term *heiraten* (to get married) has a much more individual connotation, familiar to American students, than the term *Ehe,* which denotes the societal, institutional aspect of marriage.

L: Yes, it is precisely the terms *personal ads* and *Ehewünsche* that should first be reflected upon in a foreign language classroom practicing a critical, cross-cultural pedagogy. The fact that the word *Ehe* (institution of marriage) is used in the German terminology and not in the English would point to a major difference in the potential purpose of these ads. Unlike the English term *personal ad,* the German term *Ehewünsche* seems to valorize the institution of marriage without calling into question the manner in which that institution has been complicit in the oppression of women. I would encourage this type of critical discussion in the foreign language class. I would start by having students give their responses to this way of searching for a partner.

C: This is in part what the textbook encourages you to do, and that is what the students did here, but it is not enough simply to "express opinions" if we are aiming for a cross-cultural critical pedagogy. If the students use judgmental terms like *crazy, criminal,* one would need to explore further such judgmental terms. By not investigating the stereotypes contained in the text of the ad, the students retained their own preconceptions about the use of such ads.[2]

L: I must say I have always found these ads to be a sign of desperation. Hearing the responses of the students might have enabled me as a teacher to see other perspectives or to understand why many Americans find advertising for a partner so contrived and indeed odd.

C: I didn't know personal ads had that value in the United States. It has historically been quite different in Germany, where at the end of World War I and World War II there were many war widows and a "surplus" of women after each war suffering from social isolation and looking for partners. And one always looks to better one's social position through such ads; for example, marrying a teacher in Germany ensures one social respectability and financial security. Ads are socially very acceptable, and I know several people who have married that way.

L: Yes, but doesn't that point more to the problem that women historically were often not considered full human beings outside of the institution of marriage and that they were often forced to marry because of their financial dependence on men? It would seem necessary to look critically at why women were "isolated" from society if they were not married and if any residual of that can be found in ads today. For example, the teacher in this class could have picked up and problematized the words *immer allein* (always alone) used by the woman in the ad to question the internalization of the social stigma of being single, especially for women.

C: In my view it would also have been interesting to investigate the students' culturally determined ideas about "romantic love" and the Western belief in the ability of the individual to find the perfect partner on his or her own. It might be the American penchant for autonomy and freedom of choice that makes them respond negatively to a somewhat arranged situation. Inviting German native speakers of various age groups to the class or sending the students to interview them outside of class might facilitate this type of self-critical cultural exploration.

L: Yes, this would be consistent with the type of "world-travelling" suggested by Maria Lugones.

C: In another class I observed, the students chose as a term project to collect personal ads written by men and ads written by women, a kind of ethnographic study. They examined which personal characteristics each group chose to portray itself and which characteristics each one looked for in the other. They then analyzed their findings to see if what was sought matched what was being offered. The differences were enormous. It was clear that each one was giving an idealized portrait of him- or herself, based on conventionalized images taken from the media and popular literature. It was interesting to reflect on the multiple refractions of self and other enclosed in the world of personal ads in German newspapers.

L: In using personal ads, I would also encourage students to question the strictly heterosexual world view that is often reinforced in a discussion of these ads in the foreign language classroom. Conservative newspapers like the *Süddeutsche Zeitung* and, indeed, most foreign language textbooks contribute to the suppression of alternative sexual orientations that could be brought up in a critical discussion of these ads. I would make available to the students less conventional German and U.S. newspapers to compare ads both within Germany and between the United States and Germany. One wonders if there might not be a greater attempt in these less conventional newspapers to break with stereotypes and to stress idiosyncratic differences or if stereotypes about body image and age would be upheld there, too.

C: It is also interesting to analyze how gender intersects with class, ethnicity, and age in these personal ads. For instance, the woman looking for a male partner with a teacher's education, an interest in high culture activities,

344 • Feminisms in the Academy

and engaged in a liberal profession marks herself as belonging or wanting to belong to the German educated middle class.

L: Americans would have to understand that the profession of teaching in Germany carries a level of prestige not found in the United States. How did the Chinese Germanist, as a non-Western observer, react to this classroom dialogue?

C: She felt the teacher could have relativized the concept of what is "normal" (conforming to some norm) as well as the Western stereotype of beauty. The teacher could have elicited from the nine students of non-Anglo-American ancestry their views on arranged marriages and matchmakers, or go-betweens. The means may differ, but the objective of finding someone of comparable economic and social background and similar interests is the same in Western and non-Western cultures. The Chinese-born observer linked the newspaper ad to the mobility and fragmentation of Western industrialized societies that produce this form of marriage search.

L: While U.S. and German worldviews are not identical, they can be "disrupted" in a positive way by a non-Western perspective. The extent to which these opportunities for a double-voiced discourse are recognized and developed in the classroom seems to depend on the ability of both teachers and students to call forth these multiple voices. A great deal of perception and cultural sensitivity would seem to be required of the teacher in this type of classroom.

C: Yes, you're right. Moreover, double-voiced pedagogy is not something that can be prepared in advance. The teacher can anticipate the reactions of American students to the extent that she can reflect ahead of time on the differential value attached to love, marriage, and society in the United States and other parts of the world, as Robert Bellah and his colleagues describe so well in *Habits of the Heart*. But, above all, she has to find a space from which she can reflect on a foreign custom and grasp the deeper meaning of the difference between self and other.

L: Yes, had the teacher been trained to think along those lines, she would have been able to pick up on some of the very specific associations that the students made. For example, using terms like *crazy* or *criminal* may be a way of discarding the unfamiliar rather than dealing with it. The teacher may want to take the students at their words and examine which voices speak through them. It seems that, in an attempt to be nonintrusive and nonauthoritarian, the teacher overlooked the possibility of productive intervention. If she is willing to remain open to revision herself, intervention in a double-voiced pedagogy would not be one of rejecting or imposing ideas but, rather, of inviting students to examine the terms they use to speak of their own culture and that of others.

C: This position between cultures that you mention here seems of utmost importance. In a critical language pedagogy it is not sufficient to remain locked in the comparison of two cultural systems—the German and the American tradition of personal ads—and to build each one on its own terms. One has to question the very concepts they illustrate—for example, here the institution of marriage, and the very wording of the texts that give these concepts their social meaning. Such texts can serve to put existing social practices into question.

Example 2

The teacher in this Advanced ESL class is an Anglo-American female; the students, all male, come from Mexico, the Ivory Coast, Japan, and Venezuela. The class is discussing a video clip from the film *Fatso* to supplement the topic in the textbook: "What is the secret of good health?" The film features the plight of a male overeater, ridiculed by his peers and growing ever more desperate as he tries to fight his social isolation through eating. The teacher has given the students some vocabulary ahead of time to understand the film, for example, *to binge/to go on a binge, eating disorder, anorexia, bulimia, support group.*

T: What problem does the video show?
Ss: (*silence*)
T: What are fatness and overweight due to?
S1 (Ivory Coast): The environment doesn't help.
S2 (Mexico): He is addicted.
S3 (Venezuela): Milk and fried foods are fattening, eggs.
T: Have you gotten fat since you came to America?
S3: I don't feel like in Venezuela.
T: Why did the man in the film binge?
S1: Many reasons. Excessive behavior, former deprivation. Something is missing in his life.
S2: Too many ads on TV. They create the desire to binge.
S4 (Japan): He is not wise. The environment is bad, but it's a psychological illness.
S1: Yes, but TV makes it worse.
T: Eating disorders are an illness. Anorexia and bulimia are seen as psychological illnesses. But there are support groups. What are support groups for?

S4: For vices.

Ss: For alcoholics, cross-dressers, drugs.

T: There are support groups for everything: unmarried mothers with children . . .

L: There are so many voices and associations put forth in this dialogue that could be picked up and explored.

C: Yes, despite the sizable amount of student talk, it seems that this talk is pretty single voiced. The speakers don't really reflect on what they are saying to one another.

L: Or on how their views are socially constructed. The teacher also fails to highlight—and none of the students points this out either—that women suffer far more frequently from eating disorders than men. Given that the film is about a male overeater, one can easily overlook that fact.

C: The vocabulary that the teacher chose to give the students already sets the tone. It is the traditional way in the United States of talking about being overweight, calling it an "eating disorder," a purely personal, clinical phenomenon, rather than a "societal disorder" or a "consumer's disease."

L: The non-American voices of the ESL classroom can provide a critical perspective on the American obsession with health and dietary concerns. The students in this classroom excerpt were much more conscious of the potentially negative influence of the media and commercial practices on the health of Americans than the American teacher was ready to admit. It would have been interesting to find out what the African and Japanese students meant by "the environment" and what solutions each of them would propose for the societal causes of being overweight. And whether being overweight carries the same stigma in societies that don't particularly value slimness and physical fitness.

C: What the teacher was teaching was unexamined dominant discourse, not difference. Many ESL teachers don't feel it is their responsibility to help their students critically assess American discursive practices but, rather, to help them adopt them and use them as an American native speaker would. There is no reason, however, why ESL learners should not become *enlightened* native speakers of American English, able to see the world through the other's eyes without losing their own valuable outsiders' perspective.

L: It seems that an American teacher of ESL might indeed have a great deal to confront her- or himself about American culture through the critical voices of nonnative speakers of English. The American teacher here has the unique opportunity, through the ESL class, to call into question her or his own assumptions about the context of eating disorders. This is what I referred to at the beginning of the essay as a process of self-othering. At the same time, the ESL classroom can provide a space for nonnative speakers who are often marginalized in U.S. society to develop their own voices. The "marginalization" that exists for U.S. students in a foreign language class in a university setting is a consciously chosen, and indeed privileged, space of temporary marginality. While it does offer the opportunity to call into question relations of power and oppression in the interstices of cultures and languages, it cannot be compared to the marginalization and the difficulty of coming to voice of students learning English as a second language in the United States.

C: The only way critical awareness can be raised in language classes is through concrete and precise attention to language. Rather than view language as just a conduit for the transmission of information, it is important to look at the words and combination of words people say, as well as the words they do not say, to express their view of the world. For example, in the preceding excerpt the teacher not only does not pick up on the societal explanations offered by the African and South American students, but she echoes the psychological explanation given by the Japanese student: overeating is a purely individual psychological illness. By not questioning them, she perpetuates mainstream American myths of autonomy and self-reliance.

The pedagogy of difference we have suggested in these examples strives to make teachers aware of the many voices that emerge in the classroom in the course of daily activities. The process of naming the world differently is "[not only] pasting linguistic labels on the semantic furniture of the universe" (McConnell-Ginet 1989, 37) but is also another way of seeing and being in the world. People's way of using language enacts and reproduces the ways of speaking of a certain dominant discourse community; when using the language of another discourse community, language learners may enter into conflict with the ways of speaking of that community. Recognizing and being willing to talk about that conflict is the first step toward double-voiced discourse (Kramsch 1993b).

Example 3

The classroom lesson we have chosen for our next and final example provides both an illustration and a metaphor for the transition from single-voiced to double-voiced discourse in the language classroom. Although we shift here from dialogue to essay, multiple voices are still at play in their infinite layerings: those of the two authors of this article, those of the teachers in training, and those of the students in the classroom and of the author of the text under discussion.

Instructors of a second semester German course are discussing how to teach the short story *"Schlittenfahrt"* ("Sledding"; see app.), by the contemporary German writer Helga Novak. In terms of its content this story is particularly well suited to our present discussion of feminism and second language acquisition, as it thematizes the patriarchal erasure of voice and difference among "minority" groups such as children and women. The story tells of two children, "one who cannot yet talk" and another, "older one" playing in the garden and fighting over the sled. Every time the little one screams a man comes out of the house, shouts "Wer brüllt kommt rein!" (Whoever screams comes in!), and slams the door. This happens five times until the older child screams "Daddy, daddydaddydaddy, daaady! Andreas has fallen into the brook!" The door opens just a crack wide; the man's voice shouts, "How often do I have to say it: Whoever screams comes in!" This last sentence remains without an echo. The steady repetition of this injunction throughout the story reflects the ever-present suppression of authentic dialogue.

The way the story is told is intriguing. It begins with the unusual sentence: "Das Eigenheim steht in einem Garten" (The private home stands in a garden). The use of a specific noun taken from real estate terminology (*das Eigenheim*), rather than the generic word *das Haus,* its place in sentence-initial position, the choice of the definite article (*das*) suggesting that this information is known to the reader, are all textual clues that give prominence to the fact that the man's ownership of the house is an important, incontrovertible fact. This first sentence strikes the reader as rather odd, since the house does not feature prominently in the rest of the story. All the action takes place in the garden, and the man hardly appears on the scene, except to repeat the same depersonalized, monologic injunction, "Wer brüllt, kommt rein." The phrase, being void of any dialogic potential, has lost its meaning and doesn't fit the changing events happening in the yard. The smaller child cannot talk yet, but the narrator gives his screams a variety of flavors: he "cries," he "screams," he "sobs," he "squeals," he "howls," he "whines." The man is always referred to as "the man" instead of in terms of his relationship to the children as "the father." The children, on the other hand, are seen "in relation" to one another as "the bigger" and "the smaller" child, even though this relationship is not without conflict. The impersonal distance kept by the narrator vis-à-vis the characters and their actions enhances the brutality and emptiness of the phrase "Wer brüllt kommt rein!" as counterpoint to the seemingly innocuous title, "Sledding." Andreas, who ends up falling into the ice-cold stream, not only cannot talk, but he isn't even given a name by the narrator; he is not only not spoken to or with but, instead, is only pounded by the societal don't-do-this-don't-do-that. The whole story is a mov-

ing indictment of a patriarchal world, hostile to children, to dialogue, differences, and the emergence of potentially conflicting voices, of a world frozen in
its fossilized stereotypes and routinized talk.

Four instructors, teaching parallel sections of the same course, prepare their
lesson for the next day. One of them, Sylvia, has been talking about how she
understands the text; the others become impatient:

John (*looking at his watch*): Are we going to continue this literary interpretation any longer, because I disagree with your interpretation, but
I don't want to go into it because we don't have any time and
anyway what we're discussing is how to TEACH the story, not how to
give literary interpretations of it.

Peter: Yeah, if I stand up there and tell my students how I interpret the text,
that kills the class forever. The main thing is to get the students to
respond to the story, and if I start analyzing verbs and phrases, they
will just shut up and I will lose the class. Anyway, they might have a
totally different interpretation than mine.

Sylvia: But how can you even know what activities to design to teach that
text, if you don't know what the text is about?

Sue: Well, you ask them content questions so that at least you make sure
they know what the plot is about.

Sylvia: But these questions are too simplistic. You might as well just TELL
them what the plot is: two children are playing in the yard, they fight
over the sled, the father comes out five times and tells them to shut
up or else they will come in, in the end Andreas falls into the brook.
There. That's the plot, but it doesn't MEAN anything as such. The
content is boring because the meaning of the story is in the way it is
told. So how can we have the students discover that?

John: I don't believe we have to have them interpret the style of stories in
German 2. It's too far above their level and they are not interested.

Sue: Yeah, these literary stories have such elusive meanings. I am more for
giving them newspaper articles or detective stories.

Sylvia: That's a good idea. One could contrast this story with a newspaper
story relating a similar accident, to show them the difference in
styles. Or even have them write up a story for the local newspaper
the next day.

After some discussion, the instructors decide on a list of possible ways of
teaching the text. The next day four imaginative and creative activities are used.
The teachers give their reports at the next meeting:

• Sylvia broke the class into small groups and had each group discuss and then tell the story from the perspective of one of the protagonists. They did that well; however, she is dissatisfied with the class. She has not drawn any conclusions and is not sure what the students have gained from the story.

• John decided to summarize the plot orally for the students, intermingling errors of fact that the students had to identify and correct. They loved correcting the teacher and it was great fun, he reported.

• Sue had her students write on the blackboard alternative titles for the story, for example, "Wer brüllt kommt rein," "der böse Vater," etc., and reported that the students did that very well. She did not, however, draw any conclusions from the students' various titles.

• Peter put the father on trial. "Let's imagine that Andreas was killed in the accident. The father is put on trial. The older son as an eye witness. Defense attorney. District attorney. Let's bring in the mother." Peter is enthusiastic: the trial was great, the father defended himself by saying that the mother was sick inside the house and the screams of the children were disturbing her. No, he couldn't run after the kids, he had a wooden leg from the war. The class had been a success, the students had been very active and had talked a lot.

It is clear from the initial dialogue that all four instructors were looking for ways of engaging their students in the story, not merely having them regurgitate the plot through "comprehension questions." All four activities not only offered ways to ensure lively classes, in which students would talk and have fun, but they also opened the possibility of discovering how each student viewed the world of the protagonists in relation to his or her own and in relation to the world of the others in the class. The teachers' fear of imposing any kind of interpretation, however, combined with the fact that they have not been trained to explore their students' frame of reference, or context of understanding, did not lead to the double-voiced discourse we are advocating. As they look back on each of their lessons, the four teachers may wish to reflect on how they could have used the very creative activities they had designed to contextualize somewhat more the student voices they had brought to the fore.

For example, Sylvia could have explicitly contrasted the different perspectives given by each group of students on the event. She could have contrasted the adult world of homeowners, military-sounding injunctions, and social consensus, and the child's world of play and confrontation. The two types of conflict resolution could have been compared. In one of the classes in which this text was taught, male students felt sorry for the way society had transformed the man into an automaton; the women in the class felt distressed at the way the man was socializing his children to fit into this type of society. A critical pedagogy would insist on exploring the origin and construction of such responses.

John's technique of intermingling errors of fact in his rendition of the story could have been followed up by a discussion about why they did or did not "fit," not just whether the students had caught the teacher in error or not.

Sue's alternative titles could have been followed through with a discussion of why the students had given prominence to certain details in the story over others, for example, in what way did the title "Der böse Vater" do justice to the meaning of the story or not? Had the students meant to say "the bad father" or "the angry father," considering that the German word *böse* can mean both?

In Peter's class it is interesting to note that the students invented a *practical* justification for the father's injunction "Wer brüllt kommt rein!" such as the mother being ill. This was an opportunity to point to cross-cultural differences. For a German reader this sentence expresses the numerous do's and don'ts of social behavior (e.g., Spielen verboten; Hunde sind an der Leine zu führen [No playing; Dogs are to be kept on leash]). In German society, in which, unlike the United States, there is traditionally a consensus in matters of appropriate social behavior, such an injunction needs no justification or legitimation. It is precisely this consensus that Helga Novak puts into question.

In the course of discussing these three classroom excerpts we began to reflect on the merits and limitations of our own critical practice. As outsiders looking in on and discussing classes we didn't teach, we might indeed be criticized for presenting a type of prescriptive approach to language teaching that this essay intends to move beyond. It has certainly not been our purpose to pass judgment on the teachers represented here but, rather, to bring to light the untapped potential of foreign language classrooms. Our aim was to use concrete instances of classroom practice to define a new type of pedagogy based on dialogue rather than on the mere transmission of knowledge.[3]

Readers might argue that, by talking about other teachers without their participation, we are silencing the very voices we wish to bring to the fore. Yet, while dialoguing with teachers about their own teaching practices is an essential aspect of the pedagogy we propose, the point here has been first to come to terms ourselves with what such a critical pedagogy might entail, both for classroom teaching and for the training of foreign language instructors.

By suggesting a new pedagogy and new forms of teacher training, we are aware that we are challenging the very definition of language teaching as currently understood in academia. Rather than being just grammar and vocabulary practice, or even conversational practice, the critical pedagogy we advocate requires the linguistic and cultural awareness that usually—but not automatically—comes from advanced studies in literature or linguistics. It also requires a deep familiarity with the social and cultural history of one's own and of the other society. Moreover, our view of language teaching makes no intellectual distinctions between the study and the pedagogy of language, literature and culture—a view that goes against the grain of established academic structures. For example, as students of literature or linguistics, many graduate student teaching assistants are led to believe that language teaching, while financially necessary, and even enjoyable, is intellectually less serious than their graduate studies.

By calling for a different type of pedagogy, we draw on our own graduate training in literature and linguistics and on our long-term experience in language teaching. It is always easier to see in hindsight the links that the traditional compartmentalization of knowledge in academia prevents one from seeing during the course of one's training. The current reshuffling of intellectual boundaries among various disciplines of the humanities makes us hopeful that language learning can assume a new role within undergraduate education.

CONCLUSION

In this essay we have tried to describe a new direction in foreign language teaching that is interested not in producing "talking heads" but, rather, as in the words of bell hooks, in "educating for critical consciousness." As we have argued, central to the development of critical consciousness in the foreign language classroom, as well as in the world at large, is a transformed response to the notion of difference. As Audre Lorde has stated:

> Institutionalized rejection of difference is an absolute necessity in a profit economy which needs outsiders as surplus people. As members of such an economy, we have all been programmed to respond to the human differences between us with fear and loathing. . . . But we have no patterns for relating across our human differences as equals. As a result, those differences have been misnamed and misused in the service of separation and confusion. . . . We do not develop tools for using human difference as a springboard for creative change within our lives. (Lorde 1984, 115)

The foreign language classroom can potentially facilitate a feminist praxis geared to creative change and the construction of solidarity and equality not in spite of but rather because of difference. In the dialogic encounter of two languages and two cultures—each with its own multiple variations according to gender, race, class, etc.—lies the opportunity to reflect critically upon and revise our own individual and cultural practices of human interaction.

In their reflection on the nature of ethnographic fieldwork the anthropological linguists John Attinasi and Paul Friedrich (1994) identify two sorts of dialogic encounters. Of the first type are the "relatively repetitious, formulaic, routine, even banal and vacuous sorts of dialogues that make up the great majority of conversations. . . . These ordinary dialogues serve mainly to maintain a status quo in friendships, families, and neighborhoods" (9). The second type of dialogue is "a catalyst of change between dialoguing imaginations" (10). Dialogues of that type elicit a "fundamental realignment and reevaluation" of psychological values in the minds of the interlocutors. "The meaning of such dialogues is hardly or rarely realized at the time but emerges dynamically as they are ruminated on, reduced, expanded, reactualized, and rerepresented, often with reversal or slowing down of tempo, and otherwise transformed through subsequent imaginings" (28). Attinasi and Friedrich call such dialogues "dialogic breakthroughs."

As teachers reflect upon past teaching experiences, they too can encounter opportunities for realignment and reevaluation of their and their students' perceptions. These insights can help them imagine and anticipate future encounters with the overlapping boundaries between self and other. This type of foreign language pedagogy requires, indeed, a new approach to teacher training, one that focuses on the social construction within language and culture of the many "I's" (hooks 1989, 31) who inhabit each person. For, if we wish to encourage our students to "go so far as to question the foundation of their beings and makings" (Trinh 88), we must engage in that process ourselves.[4]

APPENDIX

SLEDDING

The private home stands in a garden. The garden is big. Through the garden there flows a brook. In the garden are two children. One of the children cannot talk yet. The other child is bigger. They sit on a sled. The smaller child cries. The bigger one says, give me the sled. The smaller one cries. He screams.

A man steps out of the house. He says, he who screams comes in. He goes back into the house. The door closes behind him.

The smaller child screams.

The man appears again in the door. He says, come in. C'mon, hurry up. You come in. None of this. Whoever screams comes in. Come in. The man goes inside. The door slams.

The smaller child holds the rope of the sled tight. He sobs. The man opens the door. He says, you may ride the sled, but not scream. Whoever screams comes in. Yes, yes, yes. That's enough. The bigger child says, Andreas always wants to ride the sled alone.

The man says, whoever screams comes in. Whether he is called Andreas or any other name.

He closes the door.

The bigger child takes the sled away from the smaller one. The smaller child sobs, squeals, howls, whines.

The man steps out of the house. The bigger child gives back the sled to the smaller one. The smaller child sits down on the sled and sleds.

The man looks up at the sky. The sky is blue. The sun is big and red. It is cold.

The man whistles loudly. He goes back into the house. He closes the door behind him.

The bigger child calls, Daddy, Daddy, Daddy, Andreas doesn't want to give back the sled.

The door opens. The man sticks his head through the door. He says, he who screams comes in. The door closes.

The bigger child shouts, Daddy, Daddydaddydaddy, Daaady, now Andreas has fallen into the brook!

The door opens a crack wide. A man's voice shouts, how often do I have to tell you, whoever screams comes in.

NOTES

1. Foreign language teachers are not usually familiar with the concept of "voice" as we are using it here. Those interested in teaching only the forms of the language may see in it an acoustic phenomenon that refers to the sound and prosodic patterns of isolated phonemes, words, or sentences, or they may view it as one grammatical aspect of the conjugated verb, that is, the active or the passive voice. However, those concerned with teaching the uses of language by speakers in a variety of situations define *voice* as the way speakers position themselves vis-à-vis their utterances and vis-à-vis their listeners. The concept of voice as we use it in this essay follows this third definition and refers to the production of speech *in specific contexts of human dialogue*. It is akin to the way Bakhtin and his colleagues view voice, namely as a dialogic unit of meaning: "To express oneself means to make oneself an object for another and for oneself ('the actualizing of consciousness'). This is the first step in objectification. But it is also possible to reflect our attitude toward ourselves as objects (second stage of objectification). In this case, our own discourse becomes an object and acquires a second—its own—voice. . . . Any truly creative voice can only be the *second* voice in the discourse" (Bakhtin 1986, 110). It is through the mirror of our many interlocutors that our discourse can become an object to itself and that we can discover the many "voices that inhabit us" (Morson 1981, 8).

2. The concept of double-voiced discourse can be used even at the beginning levels of language instruction to make learners linguistically more vigilant. It does not call for lengthy philosophical discussions in English. Rather, true to a critical pedagogy of the

foreign language, it questions what is said by questioning the *language* in which it is said: comparisons among synonyms, contrast with English usage, social resonances of words and phrases. In the days when translation was fashionable, such an attention to the choice of words and their cultural connotations was usual practice in language teaching. Now that language pedagogy emphasizes oral communication, many students and teachers think that "anything goes" and that face-to-face interaction solves all communication problems. This essay is a plea to rehabilitate a critical "reading" of spoken and written texts in the course of the language classroom's daily activities. We are aware that, by advocating a greater attention to the use of language in language classes, we open ourselves to misunderstandings. Some might view our plea as an opportunity to return to the purely grammar-based methods of yesteryear; others might see it as advocating separating the teaching of culture and language, leaving the first to be taught more efficiently and thoroughly in English. The feminist pedagogy we have sketched throughout these examples builds on the advances made by the orally based approaches to language teaching but rehabilitates the critical tools that come from a high degree of literacy in the foreign language and an understanding of social and cultural difference.

3. It is clear that the teachers observed had not been trained to view their role as anything but "facilitators," "moderators," and "conversational partners" in their classrooms and that their main concern was to have their students "express themselves" as uninhibitedly as possible in the foreign language. We can hardly expect them to teach in ways for which they have not been trained.

4. We would like to thank Sabrina Soracco, Rosemary Delia, Amy Weisman, and Kay Henschel for many useful comments they made on earlier drafts of this essay.

REFERENCES

Anderson, Benedict. 1983. *Imagined Communities*. London: Verso.

Alarcón, Norma. 1990. "The Theoretical Subject(s) of This Bridge Called My Back and Anglo-American Feminism." In *Making Face, Making Soul: Haciendo Caras*, ed. Gloria Anzaldúa, 356–69. San Francisco: Aunt Lute.

Anzaldúa, Gloria. 1987. *Borderlands / La Frontera: The New Mestiza*. San Francisco: Spinsters/Aunt Lute.

———. 1981. "Speaking in Tongues: A Letter for Third World Women Writers." In *This Bridge Called My Back: Writings by Radical Women of Color*, ed. Cherríe Moraga and Gloria Anzaldúa, 165–74. Watertown, Mass.: Persephone.

Attinasi, John, and Paul Friedrich. 1994. "Dialogic Breakthrough: Catalysis and Synthesis in Life-Changing Dialogue." In *The Dialogic Emergence of Culture*, ed. Bruce Mannheim and Dennis Tedlock. Urbana: University of Illinois Press.

Bakhtin, Mikhail. 1986. *Speech Genres and Other Late Essays*. Ed. C. Emerson and M. Holquist. Trans. V. W. McGee. Austin: Texas University Press.

———. [1929] 1971. "Discourse Typology in Prose." In *Readings in Russian Poetics: Formalist and Structuralist Views*, ed. L. Mateja and K. Pomorska, 176–96. Cambridge: MIT Press.

Becker, A. L. 1984. "Toward a Post-Structuralist View of Language Learning: A Short Essay." In *An Epistemology for the Language Sciences,* ed. A. Guiora, 217–20. Detroit: Wayne State University Press.

Fox-Genovese, Elizabeth. 1991. *Feminism without Illusions.* Chapel Hill: University of North Carolina Press.

Friedan, Betty. 1963. *The Feminine Mystique.* New York: W. W. Norton.

Gass, Susan, and E. Varonis. 1986. "Sex Differences in Nonnative Speaker–Nonnative Speaker Interactions." In *Talking to Learn: Conversation in Second Language Acquisition,* ed. R. R. Day, 327–51. Rowley, Mass.: Newbury House.

Graci, Joseph P. 1989. "Are Foreign Language Textbooks Sexist? An Exploration of Modes of Evaluation." *Foreign Language Annals* 22, no. 5:477–86.

Grice, Paul H. 1975. "Logic and Conversation." In *Syntax and Semantics,* vol. 3: *Speech Acts,* ed. P. Cole and J. Morgan, 41–58. New York: Academic Press.

Habermas, Jürgen. 1971. "Vorbereitende Bemerkungen zu einer Theorie der kommunikativen Kompetenz." In *Theorie der Gesellschaft oder Sozialtechnologie: Was leistet die Systemforschung?* ed. J. Habermas and N. Luhmann, 101–41. Frankfurt: Athenäum.

Halliday, M. A. K. 1983. *Language as Social Semiotic.* London: Edward Arnold.

Haraway, Donna. 1985. "A Manifesto for Cyborgs: Science, Technology, and Socialist Feminism in the 1980s." *Socialist Review* 80:65–108.

Harder, Peter. 1980. "The Reduced Personality of the Foreign Language Learner." *Applied Linguistics* 1, no. 3:262–70.

hooks, bell. 1989. *Talking Back: Thinking Feminist, Thinking Black.* Boston: South End.

———. 1984. *Feminist Theory: From Margin to Center.* Boston: South End.

Hymes, Dell. 1972. "On Communicative Competence." In *Sociolinguistics,* ed. J. B. Pride, and J. Holmes, 269–93. Harmondsworth: Penguin.

Kramsch, Claire. 1993b. "Language Study as Border Study: Experiencing Difference." *European Journal of Education* 28, no. 3:349–58.

———. 1993a. *Context and Culture in Language Teaching.* Oxford: Oxford University Press.

Kramsch, Claire, and S. McConnell-Ginet, eds. 1992. *Text and Context: Cross-Disciplinary Perspectives on Language Study.* Lexington, Mass.: D. C. Heath.

Kristeva, Julia. 1991. *Strangers to Ourselves.* Trans. Leon S. Roudiez. New York: Columbia University Press.

———. 1990–91. "An Interview with Julia Kristeva: Cultural Strangeness and the Subject in Crisis." *Discourse* 13, no. 1:149–80.

———. 1980. *Desire in Language.* New York: Columbia University Press.

Lorde, Audre. 1984. *Sister Outsider.* Freedom, Calif.: Crossing Press.

Lugones, Maria. 1990. "Playfulness, 'World'-Travelling, and Loving Perception." In *Making Face, Making Soul: Haciendo Caras,* ed. Gloria Anzaldúa, 390–402. San Francisco: Aunt Lute.

McConnell-Ginet, Sally. 1989. "The Sexual (Re)Production of Meaning: A Discourse-based Theory." In *Language, Gender, and Professional Writing,* ed. F. W. Frank and P. A. Treichler, 35–50. New York: Modern Language Association of America.

————. 1980. "Difference and Language: A Linguist's Perspective." In *The Future of Difference,* ed. H. Eisenstein, 157–66. Boston: G. K. Hall.

Moi, Toril. 1985. *Sexual/Textual Politics.* London: Methuen.

Moraga, Cherríe, and Gloria Anzaldúa, eds. 1981. *This Bridge Called My Back: Writings by Radical Women of Color.* Watertown, Mass.: Persephone Press.

Morson, Gary S. 1981. "Who Speaks for Bakhtin?" In *Bakhtin, Essays and Dialogues on His Work,* ed. G. S. Morson, 1–19. Chicago: University of Chicago Press.

Novak, Helga. 1980. *Palisaden. Erzählungen.* Darmstadt and Neuwied: Hermann Luchterhand Verlag.

Nyikos, Martha. 1990. "Sex-related Differences in Adult Language Learning: Socialization and Memory Factors." *Modern Language Journal* 74, no. 3:273–86.

Ochs, Elinor. 1992. "Indexing Gender." In *Rethinking Context: Language as an Interactive Phenomenon,* ed. A. Duranti and C. Goodwin, 335–58. Cambridge: Cambridge University Press.

Oxford, Rebecca, and Martha Nyikos. 1989. "Variables Affecting Choice of Language Learning Strategies by University Students." *Modern Language Journal* 73, no. 3:294–99.

Pica, Teresa, L. Holliday, N. Lewis, D. Berducci, and J. Newman. 1991. "Language Learning through Interaction: What Role Does Gender Play?" *Studies in Second Language Acquisition* 13, no. 3:343–76.

Poynton, Cate. 1989. *Language and Gender: Making the Difference.* Oxford: Oxford University Press.

Pratt, Mary Louise. 1987. "Linguistic Utopias." In *The Linguistics of Writing: Arguments between Language and Literature,* ed. N. Fabb, D. Altridge, A. Durant, C. Maccabe, 48–66. New York: Methuen.

Savignon, Sandra. 1972. *Communicative Competence: An Experiment in Foreign Language Teaching.* Philadelphia: Center for Curriculum Development.

Sheldon, Amy. 1992. "Conflict Talk: Sociolinguistic Challenges to Self-Assertion and How Young Girls Meet Them." *Merrill-Palmer Quarterly* 38, no. 1:95–117.

Soulé-Susbielles, Nicole. 1988. "Mais que peuvent-ils donc bien se dire? Exploration du travail de 'paires.'" *Les Langues Modernes* 32, no. 6:24–31.

Tannen, Deborah, ed. 1992. *Gender and Conversational Interaction.* Norwood, N.J.: Ablex.

Thorne, Barrie, Cheris Kramarae, and Nancy Henley, eds. 1983. "Language, Gender, and Society: Opening a Second Decade of Research." In *Language, Gender and Society,* ed. B. Thorne, C. Kramarae, and N. Henley, 7–24. Rowley, Mass.: Newbury House.

Trinh T. Minh-ha. 1989. *Woman, Native, Other: Writing Postcoloniality and Feminism.* Bloomington: Indiana University Press.

Contributors

Margaret W. Conkey is a Professor of Anthropology and Affiliate in Women's Studies at the University of California, Berkeley. In developing the fields of symbolic and social archaeologies, she has published extensively on gender issues including the coedited volume *Engendering Archaeology: Women and Prehistory*. Her current research is focused on the social geographies of "art" and material culture of the late Upper Paleolithic in the French Midi-Pyrénées.

Linda von Hoene, a graduate student in German at the University of California, Berkeley, is completing her dissertation on the representation of female subjectivity in psychoanalytic interpretations of fascism. She has presented papers on the intersection of race, class, and gender in the racial politics of German fascism and has published translations of articles on eighteenth-century women's autobiography and Enlightenment poetics.

Natalie Boymel Kampen is the author of *Image and Status* as well as *Women in Classical Antiquity*, written with Elaine Fantham, Helene Foley, Sarah Pomeroy, and Alan Shapiro. Professor of Women's Studies and Art History at Barnard College, she is currently editing an anthology, *Sexuality in Ancient Art*, and writing a book about gender in Roman art.

Claire Kramsch, Professor of German and Foreign Language Acquisition at the University of California, Berkeley, has published extensively on the application of psycho- and sociolinguistic theory to the teaching of foreign languages in institutional settings. She is the author of *Discourse Analysis and Second Language Teaching, Interaction et discours dans la classe de langue,* and *Context and Culture in Language Teaching*.

Asunción Lavrin is the editor and coauthor of *Latin American Women: Historical Perspectives* and of *Sexuality and Marriage in Colonial Latin America*. She is the author of numerous articles on women in colonial and contemporary Latin America, and her book *Women, Feminism, and Social Change: Chile, Argentina and Uruguay, 1890–1940* is forthcoming in 1995. Professor of History at Arizona State University, Lavrin is at work on a study of nuns in colonial Mexico.

Helen E. Longino, Professor of Philosophy at Rice University, has published many essays in feminist philosophy and the philosophy of science. She is coeditor, with Valerie Miner, of *Competition: A Feminist Taboo?* and author of *Science as Social Knowledge.*

Jeanne Marecek's work concerns the study of gender in psychology, with a special focus on clinical psychology and psychotherapy. Professor of Psychology and a member of the Women's Studies Program at Swarthmore College, Marecek recently spent two years in Sri Lanka, examining constructs of psychological distress and culture-specific healing practices. She has coauthored, with Rachel Hare-Mustin, *Making a Difference: Psychology and the Construction of Gender.*

Elaine Marks is Germaine Brée Professor of French and Women's Studies and currently Chair of the Department of French and Italian at the University of Wisconsin, Madison. She has published books, edited volumes, and written articles mainly on twentieth-century French literature with an emphasis on mortality, sexuality, and women writers. She is completing a book on *The Jewish Presence in French Writing.*

Nellie Y. McKay writes on African-American literature, feminism, and multicultural education. Professor of American and Afro-American literature at the University of Wisconsin, Madison, she is the author of *Jean Toomer, Artist, A Study of His Literary Life and Work,* editor of *Critical Essays on Toni Morrison,* and coeditor of the forthcoming *Norton Anthology of African American Literature.* McKay is working on a study of black American women's autobiographies.

Sarah B. Pomeroy is the author of *Goddesses, Whores, Wives and Slaves: Women in Classical Antiquity, Women in Hellenistic Egypt from Alexander to Cleopatra,* and *Xenophon's Oeconomicus: A Social and Historical Commentary.* Coauthor of *Women's Realities, Women's Choices: An Introduction to Women's Studies,* Pomeroy is now writing a history of the Greek family. She is Professor of Classics, Women's Studies, and History at Hunter College and the Graduate School of the City University of New York.

Mary Poovey is Professor of English at the Johns Hopkins University. Her most recent book is *Uneven Developments: The Ideological Work of Gender in Mid-Victorian England.* She is currently working on *Figures of Arithmetic, Figures of Speech,* a book-length study of the relation between statistics and aesthetics.

Mary Romero, the author of *Maid in the U.S.A.,* is presently working on a book based on the life story of the maid's daughter. Associate Professor of Sociology at the University of Oregon, Romero is the coeditor of two volumes of conference proceedings—*Community Empowerment and Chicano Scholarship* and *Estudios Chicanos and the Politics of Community*—and of two special issues on Latinas in *Frontiers* and *Latino Studies Journal*.

Virginia Sapiro is Professor of Political Science and Women's Studies at the University of Wisconsin, Madison. Her books include *The Political Integration of Women: Roles, Socialization, and Politics, A Vindication of Political Virtue: The Political Theory of Mary Wollstonecraft,* and *Women in American Society: An Introduction to Women's Studies.*

Judith Stacey writes on family change, feminist theory, and critical ethnography. Professor of Sociology and Women's Studies at the University of California, Davis, Stacey is the author of *Patriarchy and Socialist Revolution in China* and *Brave New Families: Stories of Domestic Upheaval in Late Twentieth-Century America.*

Domna C. Stanton, Professor of French and Women's Studies at the University of Michigan, is the author of *The Aristocrat as Art* and *Women Writ, Women Writing: Gender, Discourse and Difference in Seventeenth-Century France.* Her edited volumes include *The Female Autograph, The Defiant Muse,* and *Discourses of Sexuality: From Aristotle to Aids.* Stanton is currently the editor of *PMLA.*

Abigail Stewart has recently published *Theorizing Feminism: Parallel Trends in the Humanities and Social Sciences* (with Anne Herrmann) and *Women Creating Lives: Identities, Resilience, and Resistance* (with Carol Franz). Professor of Psychology and Women's Studies and Director of the Women's Studies Program at the University of Michigan, Stewart is conducting comparative analyses of longitudinal studies of educated women's lives and personalities.

Ruth E. Tringham, Professor of Anthropology at the University of California, Berkeley, has worked extensively on the prehistory of Europe. Her excavation of 6,000-year-old Neolithic and Copper Age villages in Yugoslavia provided the research for her monograph *Selevac: A Neolithic Village in Yugoslavia.* Tringham's recent publications focus on feminist interpretations of architectural remains and juxtapose conventional reporting of the data with interpretational narratives and visual imagery.